THE GEM OF ENGLAND

A Time-Traveller's Guide to Visiting the Matlocks

ROSEMARY THACKER

COUNTRY BOOKS

Published by Country Books/Ashridge Press
Courtyard Cottage, Little Longstone, Bakewell, Derbyshire DE45 1NN
Tel: 01629 640670
e-mail: dickrichardson@country-books.co.uk
www.countrybooks.biz

ISBN 978-1-910489-24-6

Back cover:
Glynn Waite

Printed and bound in England by 4edge Ltd., Hockley, Essex
Tel: 01702 200243

CONTENTS

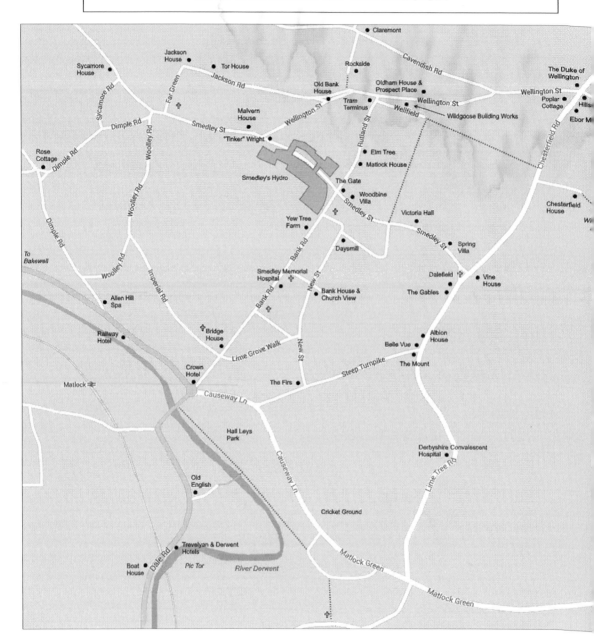

MATLOCK BATH

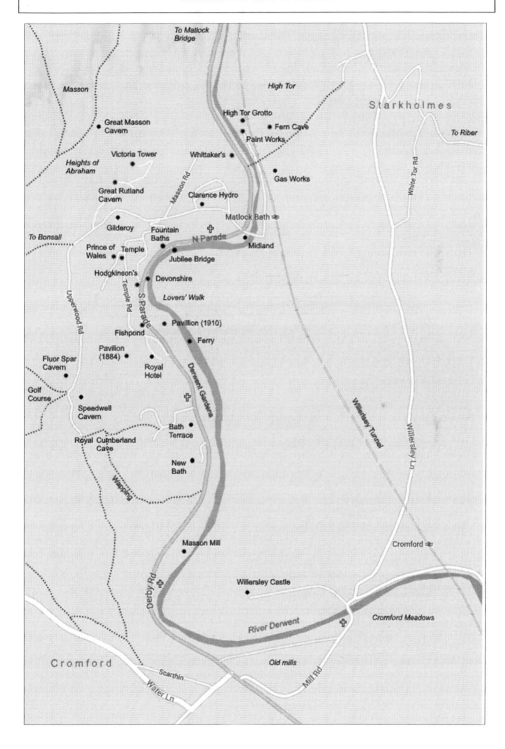

ACKNOWLEDGEMENTS

I should like to thank the staff at Matlock Local Studies Library, the Derbyshire Record Office, Chesterfield Library and the British Library. Thank you to Derbyshire County Council for allowing us to explore "Smedley's Hydro" from bottom to top.

Thank you to the following for their memories, information and illustrations:

Jean Douglas, Doreen Buxton, Jane Williamson, Margaret Oakes, Charles Beresford, Leah Maltby, Justin Barratt, Don Moss (for the diary of Mrs Allen and Miss Round), Jane Middleton-Smith (John Smedley Ltd), Potter & Co, William Twigg Ltd, Wildgoose Construction Ltd, Andy at US-Retro, and the Peak District Lead Mining Museum. I especially want to thank Glynn Waite for being so generous with his photographs.

I am very grateful to my husband and sons for providing unstinting help with producing the illustrations, reading and improving the text, fixing the computer, and accompanying me on many walks round the Matlocks.

Day trippers in Matlock Bath.
[Glynn Waite]

PREFACE

In 1936 my grandfather came to Matlock to receive treatment at Smedley's Hydro. He was a very sick man by then. In 1908, nearly thirty years before, he had come in the prime of life to stay at Malvern House Hydro on Smedley Street. I have often wondered about his impressions of the town. Why did he think Matlock was actually worth visiting? What was his treatment? What did he do to fill his spare time? Who might he have met? What had changed in those three decades between his visits?

Grandpa Gladstone Taylor was a textile engineer from Middleton Junction, a village of cotton mills west of Oldham. The week after his visit to Matlock in August 1908, he proposed to my grandmother; they were married later that year in Barcelona. Gladstone worked in Spain and Portugal until the First World War, selling and installing cotton mill machinery. In the 1920s, he worked mostly in Italy, but he travelled as far east as Budapest and Bucharest. His letters show he was a witty man. He would have been an entertaining dinner companion with plenty of travellers' tales.

By 1936 Gladstone's passport photo showed him to be a shadow of his former self, sick with chronic arthritis and a tired heart. The only time my mother met him, she brought my father with her parents to Matlock to meet her future father-in-law. She remembered driving their tiny Morris 8 up Bank Road, willing it to reach Smedley Street with its full load. Gladstone was waiting for them in the entrance hall at Smedley's Hydro, seated in front of a huge potted palm. A couple of months later he died.

Why did Gladstone and thousands of other Victorian and Edwardian visitors flock to Matlock and neighbouring Matlock Bath? The two settlements developed separately and at different speeds and times. Several books have been written about John Smedley and his introduction of hydropathy to Matlock Bank. There are other histories of Matlock, old and recent, with information in various formats; I do not wish to repeat their contents. I want to look at the Matlocks from another point of view. What was it like to be a visitor here during three different decades: the 1880s, the 1900s and the 1930s?

The entrance hall of Smedley's Hydro.

Gladstone Taylor:
the inspiration for this book.

If you're not well,
come to
Matlock

INTRODUCTION

The first criteria for any holiday resort must surely be the scenery. The hills and valleys around the Matlocks were famed for their dramatic beauty: high limestone cliffs, gritstone crags and fast flowing rivers. Early visitors like Daniel Defoe actually found the countryside rather bleak; but then poets such as Erasmus Darwin and John Ruskin began to see a more romantic landscape. One early hydropathist on Matlock Bank, writing under the pseudonym "The Sherwood Forester," wrote some often-quoted lines in 1863:

> When Nature had completed Switzerland, there was left one beautiful fragment for which she had no further use in that country; so she set it in Derbyshire, amid a framework of romantic hills, and in time it came to be called the Gem of the Peak. That Gem is Matlock.

Many guide books did coin the title "The Switzerland of England". Although, as Moncrieff wrote in 1908, it was:

> ...more loudly admitted in the days when popular excursions did not reach the real Switzerland, yet admissible enough in its way, so long as one be not deluded about it by superlatives.

A local mineralogist called William Adam had written probably the most famous guide to Matlock Bath in 1840 which he called the Gem of the Peak. However, the local newspaper produced for tourists ultimately gave the whole area another title: the assertive "Gem of England".

Paradoxically those very scenic rocks and rivers brought industry. Both types of stone were heavily quarried; the limestone region was further mined for lead, fluorspar and other decorative minerals. The rivers attracted early textile mills, also powered by the water outflows from the mines and known locally as soughs. The geology of the area produced naturally heated mineral-rich waters.

The early tourists probably saw no problem with this mix of beauty and industry, but by the 1930s the public liked its holidays unmarred by signs of commerce. The contemporary fascination with conservation and heritage has seen today's Matlocks become neatly wedged between a National Park and an industrial World Heritage Site.

At the beginning of the 19th century the Matlocks were separate settlements with farmland or woodland between. The largest settlement then was Matlock Bath, which really looked more to Cromford and Wirksworth as its neighbours. It had a history of being visited as a spa town from the late 17th century and still retained several hotels and lodging houses.

The medieval centre of Matlock was the Town, clustered around St Giles' church. With the neighbouring Starkholmes and Riber, it was a very agricultural settlement, but many of the inhabitants worked in various mills and manufacturing trades. As far as visitors were concerned the Town always remained something of a backwater.

Up the Dale from Matlock Bath were Matlock Bridge, Green and Bank. Before John Smedley opened his hydro on the Bank in the early 1850s, agricultural labourers, mill workers and framework knitters were scattered in cottages along country lanes. This was the area that the coming of the hydros transformed.

Matlock Bath was a spa. The water flowing from the hillside was itself thought to have healing properties because of the minerals it contained and the temperature at which it naturally flowed. The water could be drunk or bathed in. It was always acknowledged that important elements of spa treatment were the change of air and scenery, with a certain amount of gaiety and entertainment. The patients needed to keep their spirits up.

The heyday of the fashionable spa exclusively for the upper classes was over, but the new middle classes were able to afford their own luxuries. The arrival of the railway in 1849 brought a new enthusiasm for attracting tourists of every class. A visitor returning now from a hundred and thirty years ago would recognise much of Matlock Bath.

Matlock Bank was a hydropathic resort. Hydropathy was the treatment of disease by water using it as a vehicle to apply different temperatures to sick parts of the body. As long as the water used in the treatments was clean, it did not matter what minerals it contained.

> *Water, in its varied conditions from ice to steam, is the chief agent in Hydropathy, as drugs are of the allopathic school. We consider that, as illness or loss of health is so frequently and readily caused by the excess or deficiency of heat, especially in connection with water or moisture, that Providence would supply mankind with some simple and efficient remedies, which we could procure readily and make use of, without the necessity of searching for them in far distant countries and deep-seated mines, or by resorting to the complicated chemical processes which so many famed medicines are subjected to before being available for the cure of disease.*

This was the introduction to *Hydropathy* by Archibald Hunter in 1883. He ran a hydro at Bridge of Allan in Scotland. His son, Dr William Bell Hunter, became John Smedley's assistant and then successor.

Hydropathy was first practised in Matlock according to the teachings of John Smedley. He trained bathmen who opened their own premises and in turn coached their own families. Smedley set out his ideologies in a manual called *Practical Hydropathy* first published in 1862. He claimed that chemical drugs were at war with the functions of the body, but that hydropathy comforted and worked with the body. By applying water to the surface of the skin, he could set in motion the apparatus for purification, purging away the offensive matter that was causing the sickness through the pores and glands. Good nutrition was also vital in that no disease or injury could be cured without making better blood, and better blood could only be made by a good diet.

But this book is not a history of hydropathy. The treatments are only described from contemporary accounts. Who knows if they worked? The visitors certainly thought they did and that was what mattered. The baths – and patients – were clean, the food was nourishing and simple, alcohol was discouraged, exercise was encouraged, copious amounts of water were drunk, bed times were early – who

Lovers' Walk.

would not feel better after a month under such a regime? The alternative treatments for much of the period described involved patent medicines which contained powerful and dangerous drugs, chancy surgery, blood-letting, unhygienic hospitals, and a medical science still feeling its way into the modern world. Hydros provided a safe environment compared to hospitals before nursing became a profession. The larger hydros employed their own resident doctors or brought in the local GPs as consultants. In this way they retained respectability and reputation. Moreover, once the accommodation and the initial consultation fee had been paid for, these doctors presented no more bills.

Using local newspapers, contemporary accounts, guide books, maps, photographs and brochures, I have tried to describe what the visitor would experience, whether staying for a month or making a day's excursion.

There was a weekly Matlock newspaper expressly produced for the visitors. Initially it was a seasonal publication from May to October, but from 1890 the season extended to the whole year. The first part listed visitors to the main hydros and hotels, but eventually even the smallest boarding house sent in the names of its guests. Gradually the content built up to include descriptions of places to visit, railway timetables, post office hours, church services etc., as well as general news. But, above all, it was a vehicle to advertise the names of the guests who had enjoyed themselves, and perhaps entertained their fellows, by singing, playing a musical instrument, acting or succeeding in a sport. As the hydros became more sophisticated, it was an advertising organ to tell others to what lengths the establishments had gone in supplying non-stop activities and first class entertainments.

This was an era when it mattered enormously who was your fellow guest. Old acquaintances could renew their friendships. Inquisitive ladies could note who was

11

visiting from their locality and gossip about them. They could devise strategies to glimpse well-known visitors and criticise their fashions and behaviour. A mother could plan where to be seen with her unmarried offspring. A businessman could make contacts. This was also the age when new money could mingle with the old aristocracy. Everyone was equal when swathed in towels before breakfast.

The newspaper changed owners and titles: the *Matlock Visitor* or *Register* or the *Visiting List* – but, to simplify matters, it is always referred to here as the *Visiting List*. Another source for research was the associated *High Peak News*. Both papers always had a strong editorial element which spoke out strongly for the progress of the Matlocks as tourist resorts, exhorting the town councils and businesses to do the right thing.

> *From towns and cities of our island home*
> *The Matlock Visitors in numbers come*
> *And often too are much pleased to see*
> *The foreign stranger from beyond the sea.*
> *For Matlock now throughout the world is known*
> *From torrid regions to the Arctic zone.*
> *Some Matlock Visitors may trace their birth*
> *To every country of this bubbling earth.*
> *Our circling hills are oft the rendezvous*
> *Of travelling Gentile and of wandering Jew.*
> *Henceforth within our pages will appear*
> *The names of all such as may tarry here.*
>
> J Buckley, 1868, an early editor of the *Visiting List*.

To avoid having a very lengthy reference section, the reader can assume that short phrases in inverted commas with no other citation came from these newspapers.

High Tor.

MATLOCK BANK
(OR THE CASE FOR HYDROPATHY)

How various are the ways of man devised by him in time of need,
How oft he tries plan after plan could he from fell disease be freed.
Look at him swallow powders, pills. Give him black draughts, he'll take them
    too
Try issues, setons, cure his ills; blister, burn, caustic, drug him blue,
Try him with Holloway's little pills; Morrison's Balls may suit him better.
Perhaps he likes newspaper puffs, perhaps he rather likes being gulled,
Surely he's fond of suchlike stuffs, or does he like his purse strings pulled?
Another box of quackery trash, a bottle more of patent lotion,
Another dose of stomach wash – Ah yes! I'll try of this a portion.
I rather think I want a purge, I don't feel well at all today.
My stomach's rather weak, I'll gorge with these patent nostrums, yea
I'll have some more blue pills and quaff some more black draughts to make
    me well.
Does not the thought nigh make you laugh, and yet tis true the tale I tell.
Tis true 'tis seen in daily life; thousands who do it and we say
With quackery now the country's rife; it seems the order of the day.
What, what! pause ere it is too late, while yet vitality remains;
For He who made both small and great, and on our forms bestowed such
    pains,
Never designed us to abuse such organism grand indeed:
Made us but all things right to use – this is a portion of my creed.
Have you abused this precious gift of health by breaking Nature's laws?
Retrench! Refrain! Your habits shift. Pause on the brink of ruin, pause!
Think, and not only think, but act – act like a man with good intent:
See all your trunks and boxes packed. A Water Cure Establishment
Is where you'll find the pearl you seek; there you the panacea will find.
Fresh vigour, rosy-tinted cheek, new vital force with peace of mind –
Nature is helped there – no force – not drugged to death to cure disease;
You'll find the torturing pain appease.
Perhaps you say where shall we go or look to find this sweet repose?
The spot that I would point you to, a many, many of it knows,
And thinks of it with great delight; people of every grade and rank
Have found here health – that jewel bright – the place I mean is Matlock
Bank!

A poem sent to *The Matlock Visiting List* by a patient at Rockside Hydro, 1868

THE 1880s

My first is useful to my feet.
My second's to secure my treasure.
My whole's a place where people meet
For pastime and for pleasure.

Old riddle for Matlock

THE VISITORS ARRIVE ...

Most visitors to the Matlocks arrived courtesy of the Midland Railway Company. Their lines from London had reached Rowsley in 1849 and Manchester in 1867. The line ran north-west through Millers Dale[1], where passengers could take a branch line to Buxton. There were five or six trains daily in each direction, at speeds which would compare favourably with today. It was claimed that several visitors came to the Matlocks as part of a continental tour. They could leave Matlock by the 9.00am train, lunch in London, dine in Boulogne and be in Paris by bedtime.

Travellers from London and the Home Counties would appreciate the lush water meadows of the Derwent valley before the hills begin to close in at Whatstandwell, whose station at this time was behind the old Derwent Hotel and very primitive. It was described in the *High Peak News* in 1888: "a more miserable railway depot on a wet, windy night could not exist out of the wild west". Then passengers glimpsed Willersley Castle, the home of the Arkwright family, before the train stopped beside the pretty French-style buildings of Cromford station. Immediately after came Willersley tunnel. Gentlemen would have jumped up to close the windows to prevent the smoke rushing in.

Soon the train drew up alongside the long platforms of Matlock Bath station, designed to take excursion trains on Bank Holidays. Here the brick and timbered buildings were designed to resemble a Swiss chalet. There was a short shelter, then a ladies' and gentlemen's waiting room. The lofty booking hall was at the front, with the booking office to the north. On the platform were a public weighing machine and a drinking fountain. W H Smith's had had a book stall since 1875, which moved into the booking hall in 1887. The line was also crossed by a bridge in 1887, similar to the one which can still be seen at Cromford: fears had been voiced about the danger of people walking across the rails. On the up (London-bound) platform was only a signal box, although waiting rooms were planned in 1888.

As they alighted at Matlock Bath, the visitors' eyes would be drawn to the far slopes, dotted with villas, and the giant hillsides of Masson and High Tor, clothed with many fewer trees than today. Around the station were beautiful displays of flowers. The Midland Railway divided £100 a year between stations which the Company considered worth the effort. Mr Richardson, the stationmaster, often

---

1. The *High Peak News* nicknamed Millers Dale "Patience Junction". At night, dingy oil lamps with "peculiar shades" prevented one reading anything.

received the largest grant – £6 by 1890. With this, he was able to raise over 5000 plants. One year he planted out a thousand geraniums. With the help of Mr Nash from the W H Smith bookstall, he wrote slogans such as "Matlock Bath Switzerland of England", "Good hotels and hydropathic establishments" and "Grand concerts in the Pavilion" in white spar pebbles in the grass. The *High Peak News* suspected he paid for many of the plants himself and exhorted the public to help him with this enormous task. After winning the Midland Railway's first prize for five consecutive years in 1895, Carter's began to send him free seeds.

Cab drivers waiting outside Matlock Bath station and the Midland Hotel.
[Peak District Lead Mining Museum]

Less attractive was the large gas holder which loomed behind the station buildings. Occasionally it emitted smells which the *Visiting List* described as even worse than sewerage. The sulphurous gas could produce "an awful sensation in the head". By the end of the decade the meadows by the station had been defaced by a noisy new quarry near the entrance to Willersley tunnel, and Drabbles sawmill.

A line of horse-drawn cabs met every train. Matlock Bath's cab drivers had an aggressive reputation – they jealously guarded their stands against intruders from the Bridge. The larger hotels sent their own carriages. There were many prosecutions of the Bath's cab drivers for carrying more than their licensed number of passengers; one of Mr Briddon's drivers in 1881 carried seven people in a one horse hackney. His defence was that everybody did it. In spite of a system of licensing, drivers left cabs unattended, failed to display fares and engaged in noisy touting; hours of Local Board meetings were taken up with discussing the recalcitrant cabmen.

Hopefully, it would not be raining. There were many empty promises from the Midland Railway to build better station waiting rooms and a canopy. The *Visiting*

15

List commented that it was a pity the Director of the Company had never suffered from a pile of wet suitcases; a roof would then soon appear. In September 1892 promised improvements were described as "of the poorest description" and "merely the provision of conveniences". A canopy was built in 1895, but covered only 20 yards of the down platform. On the other side was a "draughty shed".

Did anyone descend from the train, and stand with a pile of luggage, who had really meant to go on to Matlock Bridge? Apparently several travellers asking for Matlock at St Pancras booking office were quizzed, "Which station?" "We are going to the baths." "Oh well, then you want Matlock Bath." The Manager at Smedley's Hydro claimed 150 passengers per year went astray.

Hydro guests for Matlock Bridge had to pass through two more tunnels and a rocky cutting, with a glimpse of dusty quarries, before pulling into a larger station with a rather less pretty and peaceful aspect. Matlock Bridge Station, with many wharfs and sidings, was adjacent to stonemasons' cutting and loading yards, with several coal and timber businesses adding to the bustle and noise. In 1890 a travelling crane was installed. A tall chimney on the riverside, visible on many post-cards, belonged to an old rag (or perhaps paint) mill.

The only shelter at the entrance to Matlock Bridge station.
[Glynn Waite]

Passengers arriving from Manchester would be very dismissive of the short tunnels from the south. They had travelled through many longer ones, several of which are now open to cyclists on the Monsal Trail. They had crossed spectacular viaducts at Millers Dale and Monsal Head, they had passed lead workings, enormous quarries, and lime kilns, travelling through what many considered at the time to be a harsh, bleak landscape. They entered the Derwent Valley at the second Rowsley station. The original pretty station building, designed by Joseph Paxton, had become marooned in a goods yard when the line on to Manchester had been diverted to avoid Chatsworth. It is now marooned in Peak Village.

The second Rowsley station with canopies to shelter important guests to Haddon Hall and Chatsworth

The new Rowsley station had beautiful and extensive large glass canopies and even a subway, which must have really annoyed the people of the Matlocks – but the guests of the Dukes of Devonshire and Rutland needed to be kept dry! In January 1881 a lady visitor waiting for a train to Buxton had crossed the line to the waiting room on the up platform. Thinking her train was due, she walked back across into the path of the Manchester express. She was only identified by her belongings. The jury at the inquest recommended that the subway be built.

After Rowsley, passengers would see the chimney and headstocks of Mill Close lead mine on the right where Enthoven's works now stand. The mine had been re-opened in 1859 by Mr Wass of Lea smelting works. Teams of horses could be seen taking the ore twice a day between the two sites. Mill Close still thrived when lead mining in Derbyshire was otherwise in a sharp decline. On the north side of the valley, the hillside was quarried in several places for gritstone: at Fallinge, Stancliffe,

17

and Hall Dale. Local passengers might have also pointed out Stancliffe Hall where the famous engineer Sir Joseph Whitworth was living with his second wife, until his death in 1887. At Darley Dale and Rowsley stations would be seen wagons of timber, coal and stone as well as trees and shrubs from Smith's and other nurseries, grown on the south-facing acid soils of Darley hillside.

On a sunny day, to a passenger looking forward to his holiday, Matlock Bridge Station might have seemed "a scene of great life and gaiety". In comparison with its size it dealt with more passengers and goods than any other on the line. There were many sidings with coal and stone wharves where there is now the bus station, car park and entrance to Sainsbury's. We are lucky that some of the passengers' buildings survive on the up platform, as also does Paxton's station master's house. There were also unattractive waiting rooms on the opposite platform, connected by a very ugly iron footbridge in 1875. In winter the waiting rooms had coal fires.

However, a letter in 1883 described the station's "uninviting aspect". The up waiting room was described as a "dingy hole", the down ones as "diminutive structures". The booking office was very cramped, with a fire which was not always lit when it was cold. Invalids had to be carried about on unsheltered platforms. They had already been lifted down from the trains because the platform was too low until 1904. Visitors had to queue outside in the rain for their transport.

In June 1883 a deputation of 400 local businessmen met the Manager of the Midland Railway at Derby with a petition asking for improvements. The Manager claimed he had not known there were any hotels at the Bridge or indeed many passengers. Again in 1884, a deputation went to Derby. The footbridge, with its steps, was a problem for invalids. They asked for a subway to take bath chairs – in vain. In winter, foot warmers were delivered to Bakewell by the last train from Derby, but there were no means to heat them in the early morning. They were still cold when the first train left for Derby at 7.40am.

In 1886 the Chairman of the Local Board admitted that the Midland Railway officials were very courteous, but said that the station, "is a disgrace to the place". New waiting rooms in 1889 were described as, "distorted erections, cribbed, cabined and confined". Apparently many passengers refused to alight at Matlock thinking it was a stop merely "erected for cattle loading". "We have seen ladies in despair at Rowsley. Their luggage is at Matlock and they are several miles away." The ladies must have been even more confused by the railway sidings at Rowsley which even by 1883 were described as immense.

There were bright notes – in 1888 the Derby to Manchester express was fitted with experimental electric lights under the control of the guard, but they grew rather dim when the train slowed down. In 1889 third class passengers on longer journeys were provided with lavatories, like the first class. This was only on the main express trains: the local ones had no corridors. After a violent incident in an enclosed carriage on the Derby train, the *High Peak News* bemoaned that even "downtrodden Russia" was more advanced in this matter.

Several of the hydros met visitors with their own carriages, the drivers shouting out the name. Licensed cab drivers were supposed to display a table of charges, but there were occasional instances of over-pricing, which was tempting in busy periods. The cabs were inspected each April, after which the drivers were entitled to wear a badge. Every autumn the cabmen were treated to a dinner in the assembly rooms over the Market Hall.

In 1889 a visitor called Miss Winifred LePage took pity on the cabmen waiting in the rain and playing cards in their cabs. With a public subscription she provided them with a shelter at the station, complete with a stove, lamp, towels, maps and newspapers.

In 1884 there were complaints about bad language used by the cabmen waiting on Smedley Street, where the Hydro had built them a shelter in 1877. The Board threatened to move them along to All Saints' Church, out of sight and sound. However, in 1888 a new cabmen's shelter was ready across the road from Smedley's entrance door, so the hall porter could call on them easily in turn. They did not like this, probably because they felt they were being watched. They still roamed about noisily, distressing patients with their uncouth language floating through windows on the lower floors. In 1889 Smedley's claimed they could not use some of the bedrooms near the stand.

The old narrow County Bridge with no refuge for pedestrians.
Note the sharp turns into the railway station.
[Glynn Waite]

The journey to the hydros began by crossing Matlock Bridge itself, then known as the County Bridge because the County Council was responsible for its upkeep. There were long and lengthy queues as it was only a single span wide until 1905. The stone and coal wagons, carrying loads of up to twelve tons, had to manoeuvre round a sharp curve into the station yard. The *Visiting List* noted one drug (wagon) carrying a block of stone being pulled by sixteen horses! The corner was improved in 1894, but the bridge was still a problem. There was only a very narrow space for pedestrians.

19

Once over the bridge, the visitor could see the hillside of Matlock Bank stretching before him. It was still very sparsely settled: large fields remained, especially to the west. The substantial buildings of the hydros in spacious grounds would have stood out quite prominently, often identified by their name written on boards fixed near the roof. The Y and 'S of Smedley's sign has left a shadow on the wall which is still visible when the creeper dies back.

WHERE SHALL WE STAY?

Tourists in the 1880s did not book ahead to the extent that we do now. Or they may have only sent a letter or telegram to announce their arrival, hoping a room would be free. Hotels and guest houses placed advertisements in magazines and news-papers, but I suspect word of mouth was more important. Guide books with advertisements could be purchased, often at W H Smith's. The cabs waiting at the stations would have recommended places, probably for a "fee".

Matlock Bath visitors had a good choice of hotels, from the New Bath, the Royal and the Temple at the posher end, to the public houses such as Hodgkinson's and the Midland. There were other establishments which no longer exist or have changed their use such as the Prince of Wales above the Temple, the Devonshire on the riverside, the Rutland Arms opposite Masson Mill and the Bath Terrace next to the New Bath. There were also many rooms to let above the shops and restaurants and in private houses around Holme Road. The 1887 Directory listed about three

NEW BATH HOTEL, MATLOCK.

dozen addresses taking visitors. They often had (and still have) enticing names such as Alpine Villa, Belle Vue Cottage, Clarence Villas and Rose Cottage.

Matlock Bridge visitors had mostly come for hydropathic treatment, as described later, but there were also public houses and rooms to let. When the hydros were full, many guests slept out and became day-patients. In the early 1880s there were fewer than a dozen private houses advertising rooms, such as Larch Tree Cottage, Tor View, Dale View and Woodlands Cottage, but many public houses.

No longer used as hotels on Dale Road are the old Queen's Head on the corner of Snitterton Road (currently an estate agent and shops) and a Temperance Hotel named from Samuel Brown, its owner in 1876 (now Potter & Co solicitors). He offered limited hydro treatment for ladies only.

The majority of the other licensed inns still exist. On the main roads into the town are still the Boat House, the Railway Hotel, the Duke of Wellington and the Duke William in Starkholmes. The Red Lion remains at Matlock Green, but the Horse Shoe Inn has recently been converted into housing. The Gate on Smedley Street was very important for guests at Smedley's who craved a drink in a teetotal regime.

From the 1850s, the census and trade directories had listed several lodging house keepers who sometimes said they were hydropathists. In most cases it is impossible to identify the actual property. From the 1880s addresses become clearer and mid-decade twenty hydropathic establishments were listed in Matlock, although all through the decade small hydros came and went. Most of these buildings remain in some form, so their location is not usually a problem. However, many of them were extended during their career as hydros and all have been adapted to new uses since. One needs to look at postcards and advertisements of the time to see their original appearance.

The larger establishments were Smedley's, Rockside, Chesterfield House, Matlock House, Jackson House, Bridge House, Poplar Cottage and Belle Vue. The medium sized hydros were Elm Tree, Tor House, Prospect Place, Malvern House, Bank House and Church View, and Sycamore House. The rest were really quite

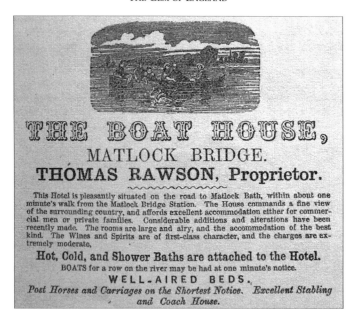

small. They were private houses which offered basic treatment and they have, on the whole, reverted to private houses: Rose Cottage, Woodbine House, Spring Villa, Old Bank House, Fairview House and Vine House.

Visitors to the hydros generally came for long stays of a month or more, to give the treatments a chance to work. They could take advantage of lower tariffs in the winter: at Smedley's it was also 10% cheaper for visits lasting longer than a month. Some of the boarding houses were used by the young children and nursemaids of patients, who were unwelcome in the hydros. Some hydros did allow young children, but they certainly had to bring their own nurse.

The names of all the guests could be found in the *Visiting List* by 1890. At the beginning of the decade the list was not patronised by all the hydros and other places to stay, so visitors were encouraged to sign themselves in with Miss Else at the newsagent on Dale Road.

STAYING IN MATLOCK BATH

The date always given for the origin of Matlock Bath as a spa resort is 1698 when bath houses and lodgings were first built. The oldest of these became the Old Bath Hotel, but its buildings were very run down by the 1860s. The function rooms were used, but it was no longer listed as a place to stay. In 1864 the whole site including the hotel, taproom, stables and pleasure grounds was put up for auction in three lots, but only the stables and taproom sold, which became the Fishpond Inn. (The Old Bath Tap had provided accommodation for stablemen and visitors' servants.) Later that year, the Old Bath Hydropathic and General Hotel Company was formed to buy the remainder. They hoped to raise £25,000 in £10 shares. Contracts to design and build went out in 1865 and were taken up by Manchester firms. The contents and fittings of the original hotel were auctioned off in early 1866. Several black Derbyshire marble mantels were listed in the sale, as well as one hundred and fifty sash windows: are they now in local houses?

TEMPLE HOTEL,

MATLOCK BATH.

After several financial hiccups, the Royal Old Bath Hotel (soon shortened to the Royal) was built on the site at a cost of £40,000. Plans show it was not in the same place as the Old Bath, but to the south on its pleasure grounds next to the vinery. It opened in late 1878 with accommodation for 150 guests in eighty bedrooms which led from a 200 foot long corridor. It was usually described as a noble gothic edifice built of sandstone. The *High Peak News* in 1879 said its natural tepid swimming bath was the largest in Derbyshire. A magnificent conservatory was built to encourage winter guests. On the walls was a collection of oil paintings said to be worth a thousand guineas. The grounds stretched for six acres and included the Royal Well, now the only remaining structure.

A Major Wieland was initially named as the man in charge, but he was a retired army officer and secretary of companies; presumably this was only one of them. The Royal had several owners and managers during the 1880s, until bought by Mr Maximilian Linder, who was the German vice-consul in Birmingham. He leased it to Mr Thomas Tyack in July 1889 at £500 per year. Before him, a manager called Mr Archibald Hinton (late of Castle Mona Hotel, Douglas) had begun its transforma- tion into a hydro with Turkish, Russian, vapour, needle, spray and wave baths in the basement, all approached from within the hotel by a wide corridor with Minton tiling. The local GP Dr Moxon became the consultant and the head bathman was George Doughty, brought from the Palace Hydro, Southport.

Guests in the seventy foot dining room were still sitting at the one long table which had been a tradition at the Old Bath. They moved up to the "top" during their stay. One visitor in 1888 described how guests were given a "ticket" at dinner on which to write requests. He asked for fine weather and tennis balls – both were supplied the next morning!

The original exterior parts of the New Bath Hotel still show a handsome Georgian

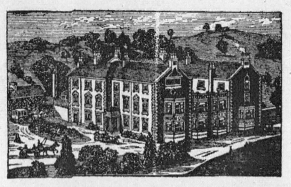

TYACK'S NEW BATH HOTEL.
MATLOCK BATH.

RECENTLY enlarged and newly furnished. A First-class old established Family House, with every modern improvement and convenience. Adjoining the New Pavilion and Public Gardens. The best situation. Twelve acres of the most Beautiful Grounds in Derbyshire, from an adjoining Mansion recently added to the Hotel for the exclusive use of its visitors. A large Swimming Bath in the House. A Dairy Farm kept. Fishing, Lawn Tennis. A large Ball-room; Balls weekly during the season. A first-class Concert at the Pavilion twice daily. Hotel 'Bus meets each Train. Waggorettes to Haddon, Chatsworth, and Dovedale, daily, from Hotel. For terms (which are strictly moderate) apply to T. TYACK, Proprietor.   43m

The plunge pool under the New Bath Hotel,
when the building was for sale in 2013.

building built on an eminence above the Derby turnpike road. It was traditionally called after its owners' names. The Saxtons, father and son, owned it from c1797 to 1855. Then Miss Ivatts with her niece Mrs Emma Jordan, and her daughter, had the lease until the late 1870s. (Emma's cousin William Ivatts was one of managers at the Royal Hotel in the early 1880s.) Thomas Tyack arrived about 1879 to change the name to Tyack's. In the 1861 and 1871 censuses he had been a school-teacher at Clayton Le Moors in Lancashire, but born in Cornwall. I wonder what set him on his very successful second career?

The New Bath catered for the wealthier middle classes and had always been popular with Americans: Mr Tyack was known to be very good at dealing with them. It was said the Vanderbilt family had stayed there more than once. The original building was extended in 1886/7 with an additional "mansion" and the old rooms were refurbished. There were four sitting rooms, dining, smoke, coffee and billiard rooms and bedrooms for over fifty guests. A new ballroom was furnished with the first sprung dance floor in the county, a pleasure for those who enjoyed the "terpsichorean art". (Sprung dance floors were a boon for dancers because they absorbed the impact on the feet and reduced tiredness. Their history is vague, but they may have been introduced from the 1870s.) A concert room was also advertised with a resident musician called Evelyn Timmins. In the basement was (and still is) a sizeable plunge pool fed by natural spa water.

The gardens stretched from the house along the terrace to Walker's Bath Terrace Hotel. A visitor wrote of a "delightful garden of terraces, and, amid yews and larches, elms, mountain ash and stately oaks, artistically planted parterres, glowing with fuchsias, larkspurs, foxgloves, pansies, roses of every hue, the blue iris, deep-tinted geraniums and hundreds of other gay flowers". There was a marble fountain from which visitors could drink the spring water.

The main feature of the twelve acres of grounds was the enormous Monarch lime tree under which tables were set for tea. The central trunk had a circumference of 14 feet, but the branches spread out for fifty feet, supported on poles. It was reputed to have been bred from a tree growing near Napoleon's grave on St Helena. In July 1888 it "housed" a performance of *Midsummer's Night Dream* with limelight and fairy lamps before a fashionable audience. Next to it in the garden was a pool where tame goldfish swam in the warm water. There was another pond near the stables which is still there. The tree was blown down in a gale in 1912.

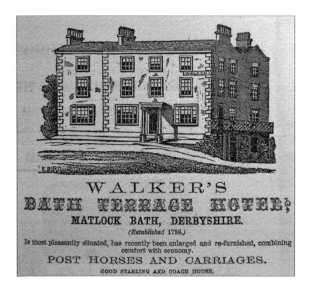

WALKER'S
BATH TERRACE HOTEL,
MATLOCK BATH, DERBYSHIRE.
(Established 1798.)
Is most pleasantly situated, has recently been enlarged and re-furnished, combining comfort with economy.
POST HORSES AND CARRIAGES.
GOOD STABLING AND COACH HOUSE.

Would you ask me the charms of the New Bath Hotel?
There's a linden that grows in the garden so well
That its branches o'vershadow a full rood of ground,
As you may prove truly if you'll only go round;
And its limbs are supported by 49 stakes
Like the banyan that grows by Hindoustan's lakes.

Fresh food was produced on the hotel's own dairy farm. Mr Tyack also bought another fourteen acres of land at the rear of the hotel for the view.

Guests at the New Bath were shown around by Jack the dog, a retriever who died in 1885 aged twenty. He had been bought from a rat catcher many years before. He would join guests on drives or accompany them on walks into the village. In 1882 George Sims, the author of the poem beginning *It is Christmas Day in the Workhouse*, had enjoyed his company.

Once Mr Tyack managed both the Royal and the New Bath hotels, he advertised them together as "Two First Class Family Houses". Mrs Tyack was an accomplished pianist and the pair were very active in the town holding many charity balls and concert evenings. When Mr Tyack's lease ended in 1898, all the contents were sold – hundreds of items from a rare Sheraton sideboard, fifteen hundred yards of Axminster and Brussels carpets, fifty bedroom suites, many decorative vases, and a "costly Drum pattern dinner service of 431 pieces" down to the pea sticks in the garden. Other dishes had a "NBH" monogram and several of the spoons were marked "Tyack". There were indicators of fine dining: oyster and sardine dishes, custard cups, every type of wine and spirit glass, and 165 dozen wines still unused in the cellar. Surely some of the items found their way into local houses and may still be there.

At right angles to the New Bath on the same eminence was Walker's Bath Terrace Hotel, established in 1798, which became Taylor's Bath Terrace by 1887. It had been the site of the first Post Office in the town. The building had recently been enlarged and had an excellent large coffee room, four drinking rooms and twenty bedrooms. On the roadside below were two cottages, a bake house, a lock-up shop and a petrifying well.

The Temple Hotel had been built as a quieter annex to the Old Bath, linked by a promenade. By this time it was reached by a private driveway at the end of Temple Road. It contained a drawing room, a coffee room and four other public rooms, with 20 bedrooms. A refreshment room for large parties was located in the outbuildings, as well as stabling for eleven horses. Terraced gardens stretched below the road.

The buildings on South Parade had been built in the late eighteenth century as "The Great Hotel". This had been broken up in the 1830s, leaving only Job Hodgkinson and his hotel at one end; this had previously been known as the New Inn. Job's niece Annie and William Brooker had since taken the licence to the wine and spirit vaults, which sold alcohol at wholesale prices "straight from the docks". There were "rock-hewn ale and beer cellars" to the side where they kept the barrels cool, which tradition claimed stretched back to lead mines in Bonsall. Next door they owned a shop, with a new plate glass window fitted in the 1890s. Across the road were gardens with steps down to the river. They had a dining salon on this green, where bands performed on Bank Holidays. On the far side of the Devonshire

Hodgkinson's Hotel on South Parade.
Howe's original bookshop was next door.
[Glynn Waite]

Hotel were their six-stalled stables and coach house.

The Devonshire (Arms) Hotel, built in the 1830s, backed on to the river, over which hung balconies. It was just north of the Waterloo Road junction so the road here was dangerously narrow – probably little more than the space now occupied by the parking bay and pavement. Holiday drinkers spilled out onto the road and obstructed the traffic. There are very few photographs of the hotel, but they show a three-storey building with twin bay windows on the first floor. Next door were their own and Hodgkinson's stables.

On the hillside behind the Temple was the Prince of Wales Hotel, which is now a very pretty house. It could be seen from below because they hoisted a flag surmounted with feathers in their tea gardens.

Near the station were the old Midland and the newer County & Station Hotels, which both had good plain accommodation and gardens onto the road. The Midland's guest book proudly displayed the signature of Henry Morton Stanley from 1871, acknowledging "every possible comfort after his roaming life abroad". There was also the George Commercial Hotel, still a building with arched windows and balconies, and the Peveril Temperance Hotel (next to the chapel) on Derwent Parade.

Clarence House Hydro was built in Matlock Bath in 1871 by Joseph Roberts on

Massonside – now at the top of Holme Road. Later in the 1870s it was run as a temperance hotel by William Cartledge from Lime Tree View boarding house on Matlock Bank. A Dr Samuel Armstrong, who may previously have been a GP in Ilkeston, restored the business to a hydro and the Rev. Richard Nicholson from Matlock Bridge House Hydro ran it from 1887. The house could accommodate about forty guests and was popular with minsters and professional men. It boasted a separate bath house when everyone else advertised inside facilities. There were ornamental gardens and a tennis court. The business was sold in 1894 when Nicholson was declared bankrupt.

One might wonder about sanitary arrangements in all the hotels and guest houses. The Local Board sanitary surveyor made a report in 1888, because he wanted to install new drains and tanks. In Matlock Bath's 463 houses and hotels there were only 165 water closets, of which 150 were in the centre of the village. The surveyor wanted two tanks on Orchard Holme for the centre, one tank in Glenorchy Chapel grounds for the 7 water closets at that end (there were none in Scarthin), and one tank for the 11 closets to the north. He wanted to convert the remaining privies into proper earth closets which could be emptied each week. This scheme was not carried out and the subject of better sewerage provision occupied both Local Boards, separately and together, for many more years.

STAYING AT MATLOCK BRIDGE AND BANK

For thousands now are wasting sad and slow
Of dire diseases, who – did they but know –
Could we but tell them, make them understand –
Our Derwent is the Jordan of this land;
That on its banks are rising fast and wide,
Houses of Healing, where sick folk abide,
And very soon their normal health obtain
And lose their growing anguish and their pain.

J Buckley, 1868

SMEDLEY'S HYDRO

Smedley's Hydro before the programme of great building works.

The old dining room at Smedley's Hydro
with communal tables.

Looking straight up Bank Road, Smedley's Hydro dominated the view, even though the building before 1888 presented a more modest edifice than today's Derbyshire County Council offices. John Smedley was a hosiery manufacturer at Lea Bridge who became a convert to hydropathy when traditional medicine failed to cure him of debilitating physical and mental symptoms which lasted for several years. A visit to the hydro at Ben Rhydding near Ilkley in 1851 restored his physical health and was the catalyst for a new spiritual life devoted to the care of his employees and ultimately the wider public. He began treating his millworkers in cottages in Lea and then took private patients into his home, but he soon ran out of space.

One of his trainees had been a framework knitter called Ralph Davis, who took his finished work to Lea Mills. He rented Alexander's Cottage on Matlock Bank to run as a hydro by himself, which he did for eighteen months. John Smedley bought the cottage and two others from a Thomas Bunting in November 1853 for £400 and became Davis's landlord and advisor. After a further eighteen months, Davis moved out, leaving the Smedleys to expand their hydro over the next twenty years into a thriving concern which could treat 2000 patients each year. They bought up the surrounding land and spent a great deal of money in transforming the original cottages into one rambling establishment so that visitors could move from bedroom to reception rooms to bathhouse without going outside. Their patients began to include the wealthy middle classes who could afford lengthy stays in the country. John Smedley died in 1874 and a limited company with a Board of Directors took over from 1875. They appointed a manager and resident doctors. Importantly, they took a long-term view of the venture and secured capital to begin an ambitious programme of expansion. The architect was George E Statham, always described as "of Matlock and Nottingham". Mr John Wildgoose and his sons Lawrence Thomas and John William did all the building work at Smedley's in the years to come.

In a speech in 1894 the then manager, Mr Challand, described how the original and neighbouring cottages had been joined up with wood and glass extensions to

29

*A remaining fireplace in Smedley's
main bedroon block.*

provide public rooms and bath houses. To this "bizarre structure" had been added an eastern wing, then the "oppressively solid mass" of the great castellated west wing which had been designed by Smedley himself as the main bedroom block in 1867. One call still see these bedrooms: the offices which occupy them retain the numbers they were given in the 1870s. A few still even have a fireplace. L du Garde Peach tells us that the new Board substituted more hygienic hair mattresses for the old feather beds:

> One can only hope the change-over was made between patients: a client who went to his room full of blissful anticipation, only to find that his feather bed had been spirited away, would need a lot of cold packs to help him get over it.

Between the two wings Mr Challand described the main public rooms as "gaping at every seam to both wind and rain". A report to the bank in 1880 described the east wing, with its 47 bedrooms, as "chaos" and ripe for demolition. The transformation of the building was managed in four planned stages, without disturbing the guests.

> Taking the area which had to be dealt with, we divided it into four sections. In order to be able to vacate the first of these, we erected a building on the far side of the road. This we connected to the main building by means of a bridge over the road and a culvert beneath it. We proceeded with due precautions to pull down section one and erected upon its site an edifice fit to relieve the section to be dealt with next.

In the early 1880s visitors entered the main hall from the road to find the Superintendent's room where they were registered. The old kitchen, offices and some bathrooms led off from here. Then came the gentlemen's room and library, fitted with sofas and writing tables. The books were of a scientific and religious nature, not light reading! The south side of the long (96 foot) dining room was glazed to make the best of the view. The walls were hung with pictures. Down the centre were

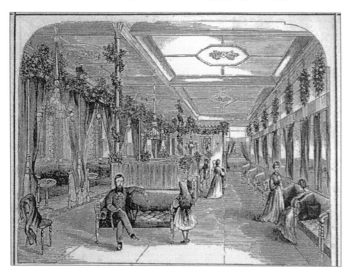

The original drawing room at Smedley's Hydro.
The idea of private alcoves was kept in the new design.

long tables seating up to two hundred guests. Beyond was a 200 foot covered promenade open to the south west.

The old drawing room was like a conservatory with a wooden roof on one side. The huge plate glass windows had crimson and blue stained glass margins which glittered in the sunshine. The back wall had seven recesses with couches and tables and green curtains, so that patients could be private and free from draughts while being able to see what was going on. There was a double row of couches down the centre of the room and more in front of the windows, but the 30 by 60 foot area left plenty of space for promenading.

Steps outside led down to John Smedley's large chapel with a spire, by then leased to the Methodist Free Church. The grounds, with their walks and alcoves, were mostly to the south west at this time. The old bath houses were situated underneath the drawing room. These were each 25 feet wide and 100 feet long, warmed by steam piping. They contained separate "boxes" for private treatment, each supplied with hot and cold water and steam. Opposite each box was a curtained bed for the "packing" treatment.

The first of the four new building phases dealt with the entrance hall and staircase: the new structure was opened in August 1882. Inside were massive arches, walls lined with Walton Lincrusta (heavily embossed wallpaper invented in 1877) and floors paved with encaustic tiles. The grand staircase of oak with a walnut balustrade led up past the colourful stained glass of the John Smedley memorial window. A hydraulic hoist was installed to lift patients to any landing. Electric bells could summon help from all parts.

Across what was then still called Broome Head Lane, they had already built the new block mentioned above. It was linked to the main building by a bridge, as we can see today. There were sixteen staff bedrooms, a servants' hall, and a steam laundry (whose arched windows are still prominent). Visitor's items to be washed

The main staircase at Smedley's Hydro with the John Smedley memorial window.

A remaining water fountain outside the dining room.

could be given to the chambermaid, but the quantity of bed linen, towels and table cloths must have been enormous.

The history of building at Smedley's was always one of adding more bedrooms: supply lagged behind demand. The second phase of expansion therefore began in 1884 by adding fifty new bedrooms. Walnut bedroom furniture was bought at £36 per suite, as well as some marble fireplaces from Norman's of Bakewell. The new dining room – the current Council Chamber – was opened in January 1886 with speeches and songs: *Home Boys Home, The Vicar of Bray* and *Rule Britannia*. Twenty eight Corinthian columns link the walnut panelling. Unusually, the room has no windows except for in the lantern ceiling. The lighting came from six brass chandeliers. Twenty seven tables were purchased which could seat ten or twelve. It was thought to be a good idea that single people were thereby made to mix in. In addition, right up to 1939, everybody sat down to dinner together and stayed

The lounge corridor at Smedley's Hydro.

Smedley's lounge corridor today.

through all the courses, whether they wanted them or not. In a side room the waiters could heat a thousand plates.

From the entrance hall a long, wide corridor led to the far end of the west wing. Unlike the cold appearance this corridor has today, it had carpets, lamps and sofas for visitors to sit on while assembling for meals: in fact it resembled a cluttered Victorian drawing room. There is still one of the water fountains provided throughout the building because patients were encouraged to drink three cups of hot and cold water before meals. There were other small private dining rooms for the delicate patient or their visiting families. A small smoking room was allowed, flaunting one of John Smedley's edicts.

The third phase began in 1886. By 1888 the main front was connected to the west wing by a large tower, which now flies the County Council flag, and a façade in a style described as Renaissance, featuring a massive porch with stone columns. A new corridor led from the entrance hall. Either side of the portico, and on the roof of the drawing room described below, were sitting out areas with deck chairs and couches, over which large shades could be drawn. At the same time were built a private dining room, a gentlemen's cloakroom, the matron's and manager's offices and twenty eight more bedrooms. Fifty five foot brass bedsteads were bought at eight guineas each and all was kept warm with steam pipes.

The main improvement for the visitor was the new drawing room which had replaced the old dining room area. This palatial new room, still largely visible today, was constructed with an iron and concrete roof to form a promenade above. The ceiling was painted cream with gold, terracotta and pale blue mouldings. At one end was a stage flanked by Corinthian columns with ante rooms for the performers.

The walls were hung with Japanese paper below the dado and plain blue above. The carpet, which had been hand-made in Bohemia, came in sections, but weighed a ton overall. The guests described the thick pile as like walking on moss. On one side were six recesses for sitting, one of which had a fireplace. The seats were upholstered in steel blue velvet to match the alcove curtains. All the fittings were in solid carved walnut. The centre settles and ottomans were in various colours, but

Note the portraits of John and Caroline Smedley:
"the founders". The larger alcove on the left had a
fireplace. The central sofas could be turned to make rows
for concerts. Card posted 1911.

blue and gold predominated; they were designed to take apart to form rows during entertainments.

On the south side, six huge windows had stained glass depictions of the Muses in the fanlights. They were made by Shrigley & Hunt of Lancaster who charged 200 guineas for the designs. (They had also designed the John Smedley memorial window on the staircase.) The windows were fitted with both embroidered blinds and velvet curtains. On either side of the doors were hung in 1900 full-length portraits of John and Caroline Smedley,[2] she in a dark blue satin dress. A screen by the door prevented draughts.

William Knowles senior,
the gardener at
Smedley's Hydro.
[Potter & Co]

Walter Evelyn Timmins

The drawing room was opened with a dinner and a concert by the Buxton Pavilion Band, with solos sung by some of the guests. The *High Peak News* questioned why the Pavilion Band consisted of German musicians, led by Herr Hermann Kiel – did we not have English players? However, the conductor was Evelyn Timmins from Derby, already mentioned. John Barnes played for the ball in the evening.

An engine house was built next to the laundry to supply Swan Incandescent electric lighting in the main rooms, corridors and staircases, which would have been a real novelty for most of the guests. In the new drawing room 70 lamps shone from seven electroliers, with Venetian shades. The stage was equipped with twenty foot-lights. In the front portico a great Sunbeam arc light of 600 candle-power shone out. With over two hundred more new lights in all the reception rooms, the building must have looked spectacular from the town below. The gas lamps were retained for

2. These were painted by a Derby artist and photographer called G. P. Bristow. They were presented to Smedley's by Mr. A. S. Marsden-Smedley in 1896 to hang in the dining room, but were moved during a redecoration. They now hang in the boardroom at John Smedley's mill at Lea, but cut down at the knees.

SMEDLEY STREET,
MATLOCK BANK.

W. Knowles & Son,
Dealers in all kinds of
MUSICAL INSTRUMENTS.

PIANOS by MONINGTON & WESTON, which are Perfection in themselves, the Tone is Soft and Sweet, which renders them so good for singing and for standing in tune—there is nothing in the Market to equal them. Prices from **Twenty Guineas** upwards, The above Pianos are Warranted for Ten Years.

ORGANS from **Six Guineas** upwards, by the best English Makers.

HARMONIUMS from **£5** and upwards.

VIOLINS—4/, 5/, 7/6, 8/6, & up to £10 kept in stock. Also FITTINGS of all descriptions. E Violin Strings, wire, 1d. & 1½d each. Gut Strings from 3d. to 6d. each. Violin Fourth Strings from 2d. to 1/- each. Acrabelle Strings, 3d., 4d., and 5d. each.

Melodians from 2/9 upwards.

A LARGE QUANTITY OF PIANOFORTE SOLOS.

4/- copies from 1/ to 1/8 each. 3/- copies from 9d. to 1/3 each.

THOUSANDS OF CHEAP MUSIC

emergencies. An electric lift was installed in 1890.

In 1881 the Directors purchased the land in front of their new building from Job Knowles to start laying out the extensive terraces and pleasure grounds. The shelters, some of which still exist, were roofed with red tiles. The first lawn tennis courts were set out and a path laid round the still uncultivated field. The head gardener was William Knowles who had been there fifty two years when he died in 1914, with his son as his deputy from 1876. William was a nationally-recognised expert on growing calceolarias. He could grow them over three feet high and supplied the seed to other nurseries. He was also a good musician and sold or hired musical instruments from a shop in Smedley Street from c1880. They advertised pianos, autoharps and melodeons (a kind of accordion), from 3/9d to thirty shillings.

There was a covered exercise area, which the County Council later used as the Local Studies Library. Bath chairs could be hired as well as donkeys or a donkey cart for a gentle excursion towards Hackney. However, there were still piggeries in the garden and rats were a problem. From 1887, the water supply came not from wells but a reservoir on Matlock Moor next to the town's source. There was much digging up of roads to lay pipes and the Local Board ordered Smedley's well closed in 1888.

Until 1884 the Managers at Smedley's changed frequently and we know little about them. There was a Mr Head in 1877 and Mr Green or Greer in 1878. After a James Burden resigned in 1881, the Board received ninety applications for the post, but nobody impressed them. A Mr Bee "flew by mutual consent" in September 1883 and he was followed by Mr and Mrs Beblin. However, Alfred Douglas, the son of the cashier at Lea Mills, had joined the staff at the age of seventeen as the Company cashier for a wage of £60 per year. He worked his way up to be Manager by 1884 – the first of only four managers over the next seventy years. He began at a salary of £200 which rose to £325. Henry Challand, his brother-in-law, became bookkeeper at

A sunny day at Smedley's Hydro with shades on the terrace.
[Glynn Waite]

a salary of £80.

Weekly board cost between £2/12/6d and four guineas. A private sitting room cost a further 42/-. A guest could have a fire in their bedroom for 9d at night and 1/- during the daytime. Bills were paid weekly on a Wednesday.

Breakfast was at 8.30am, after the first round of treatments, but one could get tea with bread and butter or cocoa and biscuits from 7am. Dinner was at 2pm and tea at 6.30pm. Once everyone had sat down for dinner, the steward said grace and read out the menu. The food was fairly plain with a great many milk puddings and stewed fruit. A note by the Board in 1883 sanctioned sausages for breakfast one day per week, bacon twice and fish three times. There was a plentiful supply of preserves and marmalade, so requests for a chop as well were frowned upon.

After dinner one was expected to lie down on the terrace or in the drawing room. Two other customs persisted from the Smedley era. Prayers were said twice a day after breakfast and at 9pm. Patients were sent to bed at ten thirty and the gas lights extinguished. Anyone tempted to disobey was gently reminded that it was the staff who would be in trouble. Insomniacs would hear the night watchman doing his rounds and the creaking of the steam pipes providing the central heating.

At half past ten the watchman comes and rings his little bell,
And then to smoke and drawing rooms we all must say farewell;
And should you not feel quite at ease and chance your bell to ring
He'll bring you up some cocoa-nibs, the cure for everything.

J Jacoby, a guest at Smedley's in 1890

Stillroom maids could bring tea and coffee or special drinks to the dining room all day, plus toast and snacks. Visitors who arrived between meals ate in the reception room, where they could also eat *a la carte* at extra cost. Each floor had a housekeeper in charge of the chamber maids who wore plain print dresses in the morning and black dresses with caps after 2pm. There was no maid service after 10pm, but an electric bell would summon the night watchman who was qualified to give simple treatments. It is clear from the censuses that many visitors of private means brought their own nurses and companions who would presumably be at their beck and call day and night. Tipping was strictly forbidden, so that no-one was put under any obligation. The management considered staff wages were high enough.

One key member of staff was the house attendant. His job description is in a notebook of 1882 in the Record Office. He was expected to visit every part of the hydro at least six times per day to check temperatures. There were thermometers in the public rooms, which were to be kept at between 60 and 64 degrees. Using the furnace, ventilators and a system of opening and shutting windows, he had to keep the temperatures constant and the rooms fresh. He worked from 7 to 10.30am and from 6 to 10.30 pm. At night he had to take into account the heat from the gas lamps. He was given the strict instruction that, "no patients be allowed to meddle with the heating and ventilation". He had two secondary tasks: trapping rats, mice and cockroaches and carrying invalids.

THE OTHER HYDROS

Information about the other hydros is very piecemeal for the 1880s and before. Research often results in no more than a list of owners with only tantalising glimpses of what the visitor would have found. Many did call themselves a "home from home" and I believe they were just that: typical large Victorian houses with comfortable and over-furnished public rooms. Their expansion into substantial businesses – or their demise – belongs in the next chapter. There were also very small hydros, which were little more than a private home with a couple of spare rooms, where only the most basic treatment was available.

John Smedley encouraged several of his bathmen and their wives to open their own hydros. In the 1860s demand for treatment began to exceed supply, especially from patients who could not afford long treatments at Smedley's Hydro. Ralph Davis, who had begun the original business on Matlock Bank, had two brothers who also took the opportunity offered. A couple of other hydros were built by satisfied patients who wanted to pass on their good fortune.

Once over the County Bridge, visitors would first come to **Bridge House Hydro**. The original house is still discernible in the centre of the District Council Offices building on Bank Road. A Dr Adams and his son-in-law Dr Josiah Cash from Coventry practised there; the latter stayed until at least 1876. They did not actually say they were hydropathists, but in 1861 Richard Freckingham was their bathman.

The next owner, the Rev. Richard Nicholson from London, was a friend of Caroline Smedley's and was sometimes described as her chaplain. His advertisement in 1881 targeted "Ministers and Christians"; his fellow clergymen were charged lower tariffs. From 1887 he also owned Clarence House Hydro on the road up to the Heights of Abraham in Matlock Bath. However, the Reverend was declared bankrupt in 1894 and both businesses were sold. (He and his wife spent the

Bridge House Hydro,
now part of the District Council Offices.

rest of their lives with their daughter in Liverpool.) Bridge House became Matlock Town Hall; the Local Board's first meeting there was their last before they became an Urban District Council.

Above Smedley's Hydro on Rutland Street was **Matlock House Hydro**, built in 1863. It was originally called Manchester House allegedly because it was built by a

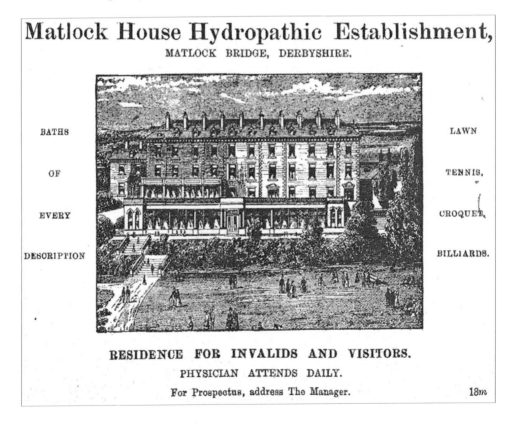

Manchester wine dealer called Lee. It had a very complicated history of owners and managers. One of the first was probably the Rev. James Shore, who eventually established Buxton Hydro. Another source said the first proprietor was a Mr Frost from Lea, whose son was still a bathman at Rockside Hydro in 1928. A new wing built in 1865 brought the accommodation capacity up to one hundred, but a year later the hydro was in the hands of a creditor after another manager, Mr Wilcox, had left.

A sale notice in 1866 used the new name and described a handsome drawing room measuring 48 by 20 feet, a commodious dining room of 80 by 20 feet, a ladies drawing room, a billiard room, eight private sitting rooms, 54 bedrooms, several bathrooms, and a gymnasium, all furnished with elegant furniture. It was bought by Mr Nichols, an architect from London, as an investment. A Matlock Bank Hydropathic Company ran the hydro from 1868, with Dr Edward Haughton as their first manager.

The Rowlands from Rockside Hydro took over the tenancy from about 1869 to the late 1870s, for a time running both establishments between them. In 1881 Edmund Dobson from Ilkley was the proprietor with Dr Moxon as consultant. They specialised in nervous depression and debility. As at Smedley's, it was forbidden to discuss treatments at mealtimes and bed time was 10.30pm, with the gas turned off at the mains at 11pm. A chop ordered for breakfast or tea cost an extra 6d!

In December 1884 the hydro was described as tenantless and forsaken, with only a caretaker in residence. In 1885 a new tenant arrived: Mr Taylor Davis from Yorkshire and the manager in 1887/88 was a James James. In 1889 a syndicate of local businessmen including Dr Moxon and Mr Arkwright bought the business and installed a Miss Eleanor Wise as manager. This seemed to settle matters down.

The house was then described as like entering a nobleman's mansion with a charming collection of art works on the walls. As well as those described above, there were rooms for music and quadrille (a card game). Gentle currents of fresh warm air were blown over guests by "Constantine's patent apparatus". Photographs show two substantial glass conservatories facing south over terraced gardens of two acres at the front and side. The guests apparently included eminent personages from the world of letters. It is still the rather plain substantial building on Rutland Street, which many of us remember as the Tax Office and is now Rutland Court.

Above Matlock House Hydro was the more modest **Elm Tree Hydro** for 25 guests, now 68 Rutland Street. Its foundation is a mystery. The first proprietor I could find was Thomas Curzon from Crich, a bath attendant in 1871. He was at Elm Tree in 1876, but he died in 1881. In the 1881 census George Drury a medical electrician from Bath was in residence.

In 1882 William Bramald, a furniture dealer from Barnsley, was the proprietor. He had been cured at Smedley's after being on crutches for two years. He was a widower by 1891 and one description mentioned an "affable, kind and sympathetic" Mrs Higginbottom managing all the domestic arrangements. Their regime was "maintained by a regular and well-considered set of rules, cheerfully accepted by every person of good sense and politeness". Lights were turned out at 10pm. Mr Bramald superintended all the excursions himself and took refreshments of every description on picnics. Late arrivals at meals incurred one penny fines,

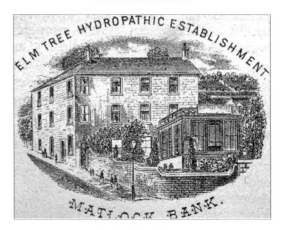

On Rutland Street,
this is now a private house.

which were sent to the Deaf and Dumb Hospital in Derby. The site did not really allow for extensive outdoor sports, but billiards, bagatelle and chess were popular.

High above the junction of Rutland Street and Wellington Street was Rowland's or **Rockside Hydro** built in 1862/3 by Charles Rowland, a retired cabinet maker from Burton upon Trent who had been a patient at Smedley's. He first opened Grafton House Hydro in Coton in the Elms near Burton, where his wife Sarah was born. Buckley's Guide assured readers that at Rockside he devoted his whole time and attention "to the comfort of those who are in tolerable health, as well as to the weak and feeble". There was an entertaining episode in 1866 when he must have put in a manager called Wyles who proved unsatisfactory. Mr Rowland posted a notice in the newspaper saying he still owned the contents of the house, but Mr Wyles did have a kind of stable sale of his own belongings which included two carts and horses, four pigs, a pile of manure and the rhubarb in the garden!

While the Rowlands took over Matlock House, their niece and her husband James Burton managed Rockside for a time, but she died after only two years of marriage in 1875. The manager during the 1880s was also a nephew, William Atkins, with his

Charles Rowland's Rockside building.

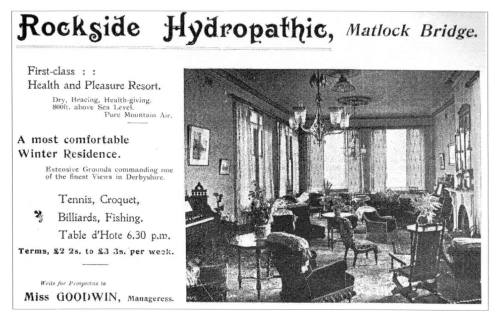

Rockside Hydropathic, Matlock Bridge.

First-class : :
Health and Pleasure Resort.

Dry, Bracing, Health-giving.
800ft. above Sea Level.
Pure Mountain Air.

**A most comfortable
Winter Residence.**

Extensive Grounds commanding one
of the finest Views in Derbyshire.

Tennis, Croquet,

Billiards, Fishing.

Table d'Hote 6.30 p.m.

Terms, £2 2s. to £3 3s. per week.

Write for Prospectus to
Miss GOODWIN, Manageress.

The old drawing room before the Goodwin's rebuilding programme.

wife and sister Ann. Mr Rowland had retired to live in Claremont House on Cavendish Road. In 1889 the Atkins bought The Grove in Darley Dale to open a new hydro; for a few years they managed both.

The original Rockside building remains in the plain block on the left at the back. This had an extensive south-facing glass fronted veranda warmed by water pipes which was large enough to be used as a ballroom. The large drawing room was furnished with a motley collection of chairs and tea tables but had a beautiful carpet and lots of books. There was a piano for guests to play. The billiard room upstairs, and lit from the ceiling, was described as having plenty of elbow and cue space. Five acres of gardens stretched to the side with tennis, croquet and bowls lawns.

To the left down Wellington Street was one of the small hydros called **Old Bank House**. Jonas Brown had come from Mansfield to work at the hat factory at Lea, but he became John Smedley's head steward for twenty years before setting up on his own. The house is now hidden behind a high wall.

Continuing up Wellington Street was the 40 bedroom **Prospect Place Hydro** built by Thomas Davis, Ralph's brother, in 1857/59. Details are scarce for this period: it was sometimes described only as an annex to Poplar Cottage. The land to the east and north across Cavendish Road was marked as a nursery on the map.

Below the corner of Wellington Street and Chesterfield Road was **Poplar Cottage Hydro** which had been opened by Ralph Davis. In 1868 he sold it to Mr Knowles who sold it to Thomas Davis in 1874. He added a four-storey wing in 1885. A bath-house built in 1880 contained 4 shallow, 2 rain, 2 douche and 5 sitz baths as well as vapour baths. The house, still with some gardens, now belongs to Derbyshire County Council and is surrounded by office buildings.

Prospect Place Hydro after its expansion with Oldham House.

Poplar Cottage Hydro in its final condition.

Well away from the main road was **Chesterfield House Hydro**, now the Convent nursing home. In the 1860s Ralph Davis had bought a dairy farm called Flates from Arundel Bowring, a farmer from Hackney, and commenced his own hydro building. After leaving John Smedley, he had been treating patients at Poplar Cottage, **Ebor Mount** (opposite Poplar Cottage) on Chesterfield Road and **South View Hydro** on the Bank. (South View had been run for several years by a Mr and Mrs Hawley, also ex-Smedley employees, but by 1882 this building had become Smedley's Memorial Hospital.)

Continuing down Chesterfield Road was **Belle Vue Hydro** run by Mr and Mrs Matthew Stevenson; he too had been a Smedley bathman. After her husband's death

HYDROPATHIC ESTABLISHMENT,

SOUTH VIEW COTTAGE,

MATLOCK BANK.

(Within a few minutes' walk of Matlock Bridge Station.)

MR. & MRS. RALPH DAVIS,

Original Managers of the present Hydropathic Establishment for Mr. Smedley, beg to return their grateful thanks for the generous support and patronage they have received during the last eight years they have practised the

MILD WATER TREATMENT,

Having had many persons of both sexes under their care, who have been cured of various diseases by their mode of treatment, after every other means had failed, they beg to apprise the Public that they are now carrying on the mild system of WATER CURE with continued success. Also

THE TURKISH BATH,

On an Improved Principle.

The finest Water, the purest Air, and most Romantic Scenery.

BOARD, LODGINGS, AND TREATMENT:

Males, 17s. 6d. per Week. Females, 15s. per Week.

in 1888 Mrs Stevenson married Adam Allsop. There had been a hydro called Stevenson's from 1860 but the exact location remains unclear. This must have been an earlier building than the present block which was described as newly erected in 1871 when it was for sale, presumably unsuccessfully. The thirty or forty patients could enjoy "quoit flinging", croquet and bagatelle. They also advertised free fishing (they gave out tickets for the fishing clubs) and shooting over six hundred

Belle Vue Hydropathic Establishment, Matlock Bridge, Derbyshire.

This hydro at the top of Steep Turnpike
is now private accommodation.
[Glynn Waite]

Belle Vue Hydro today at the top of Steep Turnpike.

acres. Was that on Matlock Moor? The building is now the block of apartments at the left-hand summit of Steep Turnpike.

There were four or five small hydros in this area. A short-lived hydro was run by Mrs Holmes in **Fair View House**. Another was at **Vine House** on School Road. They had both given up by the next decade. A Sarah Martin ran an establishment for ladies only somewhere near Prospect Place. **Spring Villa Hydro** is thought to be the house now called the Old Mill House on Smedley Street East, run by Mr and Mrs John Wheeldon. William Monk at **Albion House** on Chesterfield Road, just above Belle Vue, offered "medical gymnastics" in the 1876 and 1881 directories. He advertised himself as an "electrician, Galvanist with rational hydropathy, and medical manipulator". In 1871 he had been a kinesipathist on Pope Carr Terrace and at Smedley's. This was the treatment of disease with muscle exercises. He later moved to Matlock Bath.

In 1861 a Dr Spencer T Hall opened **Wellfield House** as a hydro and homeopathy centre. He was a famous author and poet from Sutton in Ashfield known as the Sherwood Forester. (He is quoted in the Introduction.) He dabbled in phrenology and claimed to have cured the author and feminist Harriet Martineau with mesmerism. He wrote books on hydropathy and eventually settled in Kendal, but died a pauper in Blackpool in 1885. In 1867 Wellfield was listed as being managed by Mr Joseph Crowder, late bathman at Smedley's. He was still a bath man in 1871, but then returned to his original trade as a plasterer. In 1876 Mrs Neary was listed as running a lodging house in the building along with the abruptly named "Lupton and Neary" hydro.

Woodbine Villa, run by a Mrs Knowles for ladies only, was at the current 60 Smedley Street East; the house then had bay windows and a porch. In the 1860s it had been owned by Mr and Mrs William Crowder but managed by a Mrs Littlewood. In the mid-1890s "Professor" Thomas Alexander practised "electric botany" at Woodbine Hydro and Invalids' Home using herbs which possessed their own magnetic force and natural affinity with different parts of the body. He thought electricity was Nature's greatest healer, so he used magnopathic batteries and belts. He wrote a manual reminiscent of John Smedley's entitled *Chronic Diseases and Remedies for them* in 1894. He sold various cures such as syrup of Stillingia and the compound Buchu: both herbs still in use today. Mrs Alexander dispensed female pills such as Uncum used by Indian squaws. Professor Alexander wrote a *Lecture to Men Only* (6d post free) on the subject of "diseases of error". Rejecting the use of mercury to cure sexually transmitted diseases, he advocated using his patent medicine "Con=Fi=Do". He also wrote some quite sensible advice about family planning.

However, a Thomas Alexander Booth Pemblington gave Woodbine Hydro as his address in the bankruptcy court in 1897. He was also convicted for fraud in Bradford in 1876 and sentenced to twelve months. The ancestry records for his wife Mary suggest strongly that this was the same man. By 1911 Thomas was running a dental practice in Chesterfield, while Mary continued as a herbalist. Two records say he had a damaged hip.

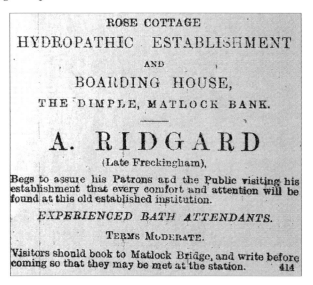

Crossing to the other side of the Bank, **Rose Cottage** was at the fork of Dimple Road and Hurds Hollow. This may have been Rose Cottage Inn, or even the Rose and Crown, run by a cabinet maker called James Croft. Then Richard Freckingham[3] from Smedley's, who had also worked at Bridge House, claimed in 1881 that he had been in business for twelve years: "dropsy successfully treated". He announced he was going abroad, so he sold the business to Aaron Ridgard[4], a grocer and lodging housekeeper in Matlock Bath. Mr Ridgard also owned property in Hope Terrace, as well as buying Nether Green and the Cascades in Bonsall, which led to speculation that he was going to set up hydros there. Rose Cottage is now Rosegarth bed and breakfast.

---

3. Mr. Freckingham actually moved to Haddon House Hydro in Buxton.

4. Mr. Ridgard's two sons were often mentioned in the newspapers as fighting on two fronts: South Africa and North West India. The latter died in Burma in 1906 on his way home.

On Smedley Street West, the tall building of apartments now opposite the alms-houses was **Sycamore House Hydro**, perhaps established c1883 by a bathman from Mansfield called John Dawes. He had been a lodger at William Crowder's in Wellington Street in 1881. Was he trained nearby at Old Bank House by a fellow citizen from Mansfield?

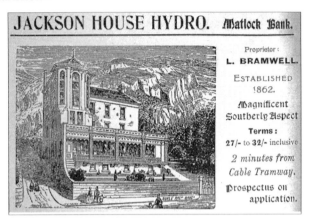

This really was the Switzerland of England!

Returning to All Saints Church, one could look up Far Green and see **Jackson House Hydro** in a prominent position and always boasting of its marvellous views. It had been established in 1862 by George Barton, another of Smedley's bathmen, with accommodation for fifty. By the late 1880s it was leased by Mr and Mrs J L Dean. Mr Barton senior had died in 1875 and his son retired a rich man – although he soon began building anew as will be seen in the next section. It was claimed that "by a novel process, the proprietors are enabled to raise or lower the temperatures of the rooms and corridors".

Next door was the slightly smaller **Tor House Hydro**, built in 1862. It is the only hydro building to have since been entirely demolished. It was opened by another Davis brother, George, who had worked at Smedley's for nine years. He was frequently called back to there to deal with difficult cases. The hydro was quite a simple building, which only ever had two reception rooms, a billiard room, and twenty seven bedrooms, as well as the bathrooms.

Along Smedley Street West, one came to **Malvern House Hydro** for 20 guests, run by Job Smith, a well-known local politician and philanthropist. The house was built by his grandfather, but Job was abroad when it had been advertised for sale in 1866 as being partly fitted out as a hydro. After working a short time at Smedley's as the second cook, Job went travelling to the Americas (1862-1868) with Arrow Smith from the Darley Dale nursery family. The house had a parlour, sitting room, eleven bedrooms, two bathrooms, two water closets and pleasure and kitchen gardens. At some point a great china bath made by Farnley Clay & Iron Co. was installed. It had a roll top which allowed it to be thoroughly cleaned. Job applied for a bar license in 1886, saying he had safely managed a large hotel in Vancouver, but it was refused on Smedley's claim that their dipsomaniacs would be too tempted. Job never married, but his sister Sarah helped him in the business.

DAVIS'S
Tor House Hydro
And Boarding Establishment,
MATLOCK BANK,
—— Derbyshire. ——

Established 1858.

A Splendid Summer and Winter Residence for Visitors and Invalids. South Aspect. Sheltered from North and East Winds.

N.B.—Mr. George Davis is now the only one of the original Davis family practising HYDROPATHY under —— the late Mr. Smedley's system. ——

Terms from 28/- and upwards per week.
Four Minutes from Tram Terminus.
Apply GEORGE DAVIS, Proprietor.

*The only hydro premises
to have totally disappeared*

LEFT: *Mr. Job Smith of Malvern House Hydro.*
RIGHT: *Malvern House Hydro today on Smedley Street West.*

47

Malvern House Hydro.

Bank House and Church View Hydro with room for 60 patients was on the corner of New Street and Oak Road, now the County Record Office. An advertisement for Church View in 1871 said it had just been opened by a Mr Mycock from Smedley's, but Henry Ward soon took over. In 1872 he added Bank House. He had

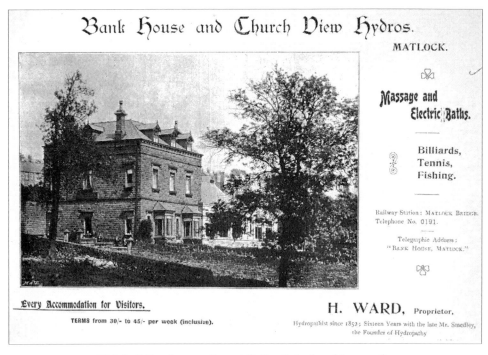

This building became Ernest Bailey School and is now the Derbyshire Record Office.

The old Lime Tree View guesthouse,
converted into the Convalescent Hospital.
[Glynn Waite]

been head bathman with the Smedley's for sixteen years from 1852, but started on his own with several boarders in Pope Carr Road in a hydro called "Ward's". Every year in August, Bank House Hydro gave the old people of Matlock a tea in a tent in the grounds. They then had to listen to homilies from the local vicars, but thankfully ended the day with games, dancing and fireworks.

There was one long-standing guest house which had advertised since c1857. This was Lime Tree View[5] on Lime Tree Lane, now Road. (There was an ancient lime tree nearby.) William Cartledge was the manager in the late 1860s for Mr Parsons, but it

Dale Road and the Old English Hotel before the Red House was built in the early 1900s.
[Jean Douglas]

---

5. Rossetti and Lizzie Siddal, the pre-Raphaelite artist and his model, stayed in 1857.

was for sale in 1872 and Mr Cartledge moved to the Clarence House Hydro in Matlock Bath. The owners were able to claim proximity to the burgeoning hydros, but also offered a pony to take visitors to the public Fountain Baths in Matlock Bath. In 1889 it became the Derby and Derbyshire Convalescent Hospital as described later.

From July 1881 the visitor who did not require hydropathy had a new place to stay. With two frontages and costing £8,000, the Old English Hotel built by the Mattocks family, occupied a prominent corner position on Dale Road, surviving as a hotel until very recently. The 45 up-to-date bedrooms had hot and cold water. The interior was furnished throughout by Maples of London, including an expensive and beautifully carpeted staircase. There were extensive gardens and a river front for boating and fishing. The grounds occupied the triangle of land to the south enclosed in a loop of the river which had been a rifle range. Some of the first guests stayed for Derby Agricultural Show which took place conveniently at the Derby Midland Hotel, easily reached by train. A company soon bought the building and the first manager was a Mr Leman.

A year later tennis courts, a dancing green and a bowling green were opened with a firework display. A 150 candle-power gas lamp allowed dancing to Matlock Prize Band until 11pm. Over the next decades, the pleasure grounds supplied a venue for many Matlock events, notably sports and brass band concerts.

However, there was soon a serious glitch in the hotel's prosperity. In November 1884 a fire started in the tower over the hall door. The Mattocks family, who had recently re-purchased the business, were nearly ruined; the damage was extensive, with the newspapers reporting that only the shell remained.

Fire engines came from Masson Mill and Squire Bateman at Middleton. The Derby fire engine, allowing time for a telegram to be sent, arrived four hours into the conflagration with hoses too short to reach the river.

Several locals were prosecuted for making off with the contents of the bar. One enterprising group floated a ten gallon barrel of whisky down to the Bridge. In the following months Mr Mattocks became the victim of a vicious campaign by the local temperance movement to cancel his liqueur licence, but he did re-open with a less lavish building. The newspapers gave many reports about what they called the "Blue Ribbon Army" of the temperance movement. The Matlocks had several temperance hotels at various times.

Across from the still surviving Railway Hotel was the old Crown Inn, run by Mr Pegler. In 1882 he applied for his licence to be transferred to the new Crown Hotel then being built in its prominent position on the corner of Bank Road. The Reverend Nicholson objected because this was very near his Bridge House Hydro. Presumably his fellow ministers would be too tempted! The old Crown premises went steadily downhill as a lodging house and temperance hotel, but were not demolished until 1906 in a road widening scheme. The new hotel opened in June 1883 boasting first class stabling and a billiard room. It catered mainly for business-men and commercial travellers. Photographs show the building, lately the Co-op Bank, surrounded by a low wall and bushes, with the entrance porch and the stables on Bakewell Road. Residents asked for the shrubs to be removed in 1906 to free the road more for cars.

*   *   *   *   *   *   *

The Crown Hotel, lately the Co-operative Bank.

At night the view of Matlock Bank from the Bridge was one of twinkling lights gleaming from windows and balconies "giving the whole place a very brilliant and fairy-like effect", or even resembling a "hillside of fireflies". Smedley's seen from below was described as floating like a great ship.

If a new visitor to one of the hillside hydros opened his window and leaned out at night, what might he see and hear? After the noise of traffic and quarrying had died down, the night would seem very quiet to a city-dweller. Today one can some-times hear the "hum" of Enthoven's – could one then have heard the thud of the three pumping engines at Mill Close mine? If a night train passed along the valley bottom, he might see steam and the red glow from the fire-box. In the town were gas lamps – although never as many as the public wanted – they would have given a soft glow compared with today's harsh lights. Oil lamps, candles and gas lights in houses would show here and there on the hillsides. When Caroline Smedley died in 1892 it was commented that the town missed the friendly lights from Riber Castle. Fainter still, the observer might have glimpsed the twinkle of lantern light as lead miners from Bonsall and Cromford walked over Masson to their shift at Mill Close Mine.

The new visitor could close his window and retire for the night, feeling rather apprehensive about what was in store for him the next day...

DOWN TO THE TREATMENT ROOMS

One of the main publicity points for the Matlock hydros was that the baths were usually inside the accommodation building, unlike the facilities at Continental spas. Housing, in the winter especially, was more important than climate and a patient need never go outside. The houses were warm, but well-ventilated. The patient was not only spared the fatiguing journey to Europe but Mediterranean winters were damp anyway!

Man's life is as a vapour here below,
Beneath this stone the facts exemplified.
Brown was esteemed wherever he did go,
At Smedley's they steamed him till he died.

Here lieth the body of poor old Fritz
Killed by ye chilli and chillier sitz.

Two entries to an epitaph competition
run at Smedley's Hydro, 1879

The sitz bath.

Hydropathy at its simplest was the use of water to deliver heat and cold to the body to stimulate circulation and relieve pain. Its external application to the skin was considered to be very safe. The whole body or any small part could be cooled or made to sweat with various packs and baths. For local applications poultices were used to draw morbid matter to the surface where it could exit through the pores. Further stimulation and pressure could be applied with various sprays, douches and massages. In due course electrical treatments and mineral baths were added to the range of treatments available, as well as the latest physiotherapies from the Continent.

> *The simple spring waters of Matlock, which have no special or recognisable medicinal properties, but are remarkably pure and soft, are found singularly efficient for hydropathic purposes.*
>
> The Smedleys of Matlock Bank, Henry Steer, 1897

The water did not need to have any mineral content: it was for external use only. The gritstone on the Bank contained several natural springs of clean water which supplied the early hydros adequately via their own wells. Later the water supply came from a reservoir on the summit.

John and Caroline Smedley had been very "hands on" in their hydro. They both wrote manuals of hydropathy which described all the treatments in great detail, listing them by numbers for ease of reference. They saw each patient on arrival and filled out a bath book of treatments, diet and exercise. Ladies could write to Mrs Smedley in advance about delicate "female" complaints and her manual was

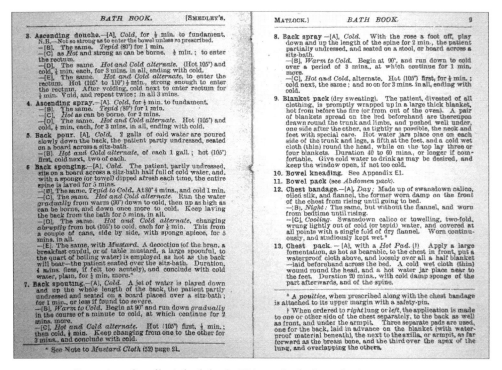

*Pages in a Smedley's bath book. This method of numbering treatments
was used throughout the hydro's existence.*

written specifically for them. In 1872 Dr William Bell Hunter was appointed to help John Smedley. Dr Hunter stayed until his own early death in 1894, partnered by several other doctors, ultimately by Dr W Cecil Sharpe.

In his manual John Smedley seemed to list every ailment known to man, rejecting the failed attempts to cure them by medical doctors. He claimed that his own remedies on the other hand were simple and effective. It was the case that patients to the hydros did often immediately feel better because of the pain relief properties of heat and massage, enforced rest, a nutritious diet and good company. Hydrotherapy must certainly have done less harm than bleeding or taking the harsh and addictive drugs of the Victorian era.

The Smedleys rejected the cold water treatment used in other hydros as being too drastic and harmful to delicate constitutions. They favoured a tepid or mild water cure using a wet pack. A cotton or linen sheet was dipped in tepid water and then wrung out. The patient was wrapped in this sheet and well tucked in. On top was placed a mackintosh and two dry blankets to keep the body warm. After the prescribed treatment time, the patient was rubbed vigorously.

There were sitz baths for sitting in shallow water – ladies did not even need to take their clothes off! Many smaller baths existed for immersing different joints or body parts. Fomentation cans could be filled with hot water and laid on different limbs to draw blood to that area. Treatments continued with a douche or shower; again this could be directed at affected organs with needle sprays. Illustrations often

THE ASCENDING DOUCHE.
"Now Sir, please to take a seat here."

Preparing for the packing.
"Why my nearest and dearest friends'
wouldn't know me. I'm a perfect mummy."

LEFT: [Picture the Past]
CENTRE: *An ascending douche: "of the greatest service in cases of piles. The water need not
be renewed above once a week". John Smedley's Handbook of Hydropathy.*
RIGHT: [Picture the Past]

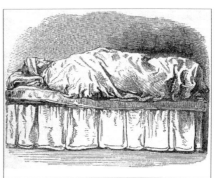

LEFT: *The leg bath – at least the patient has removed his boot.*
CENTRE: *The steam box: steam enters via pipe "D".*
John Smedley's Handbook of Hydropathy.
RIGHT: *The wet pack treatment.*

depicted the ascending douche – patients sat on a wooden box with water shooting
upwards.

Vapour baths were given to open the patient's pores during which a patient sat
in a chair swathed in blankets except for the head. Boiling cans of water containing
bricks were placed under the chair for fifteen minutes while the patient sipped cold
water to replace the lost fluid. There were also steam boxes such as jockeys use now
to lose weight. Hot dry packs were applied when the patient needed to perspire
over one specific area.

Black bran mustard or chilli paste packs were used directly where there was
inflammation, for ailments such as sore throats, earache, deafness, sprains and tic

doloreux – now called trigeminal neuralgia. The paste was a mixture of olive oil, spermaceti (a waxy substance obtained from the head of sperm whales) and chillies or mustard.

> *Do you know George at Jackson House?*
> *A right jolly fellow is he,*
> *With his mustard and water, and jokes without end,*
> *He's as merry a man as needs be.*
>
> *Only make friends with Bathman George*
> *And you'll find him true to the core,*
> *And when the mustard bites so keen and warm,*
> *He'll quickly bring you some more.*
>
> From verses by a patient at Jackson House Hydro

In serious cases a crisis was induced: the patient was wrapped in wet calico which was covered in a mackintosh and bandaged into position. Although the bandages were changed three times a day, the treatment might go on for weeks. The outcome could be precipitated by a bread or linseed poultice. Eventually the skin erupted into a rash and unpleasant-smelling boils, but this was a good sign. The morbid matter was thereby brought to the surface and rendered harmless: the body henceforth was able to heal itself.

In the 1880s other treatments were being introduced. Turkish Baths, which were not really like those in Turkey, were popular in Victorian times for social, hygienic and therapeutic reasons. In hydros they helped patients to relax and could relieve rheumatic pain, bronchitis and gout. There were usually three chambers heated by increasingly hot air. Temperatures of around 120 degrees (50 Celsius) were suitable for the feeble, but the third room was heated to over 200 degrees (93C) – attendants watched out for signs of distress. Afterwards, the patient could take a cold plunge and be massaged; this was termed "shampooing" from a Hindu word which meant pressing. Then followed a period of relaxation.

Russian Baths were steam baths at a temperature of 110 degrees, not unlike a sauna. James Holmes was the Russian and Turkish Bath attendant at Smedley's; he had been there for forty years when he died in 1904 and was estimated to have helped 200,000 patients. T P O'Connor described him having "a great drooping moustache" and "the expression of his blue eyes and his firm mouth is severe. But at half past six in the morning he is already bubbling over with high spirits". He whistled when the patient's two minutes in the Russian Bath was up, and they should move to the Turkish.

Also in the 1880s electric treatments became available, using batteries which could provide continuous or interrupted currents. The electricity was used to heat different parts of the body or to actually send pulses through it to stimulate tired muscles. The bath electrician was advised to test each electrode on himself first. Descriptions were very basic at the time. Faradisation was said to involve the patient sitting with both feet on a metal electrode, covered in a moist flannel, while the other electrode was moved over the body to draw the current through. For Galvanisation treatment, the negative pole was placed on the patient's stomach while the positive pole was moved over the spine for ten minutes. Electric baths could be taken: the water was heated to 90 degrees before the patient was immersed. The current was then sent through the bath for about twenty minutes, or until the patient felt faint. It apparently gave one the sensation of a "full head". Patients could also be given short electric shocks or sparks, or an "electric wind".

The medical regime remained the same throughout Smedley's entire existence. A new patient was seen by the doctor for a single payment of one guinea (free for clergymen and doctors), which was fixed in 1883. The treatment was planned out and entered in each patient's own bath book. Then the head bathman or matron took over. The doctor would see the patients again weekly, or one could ask for an extra consultation via the bathman. There were about forty bathing staff and "rubbers", although in 1888 it was reported that proper massage had been introduced as opposed to ordinary rubbing.

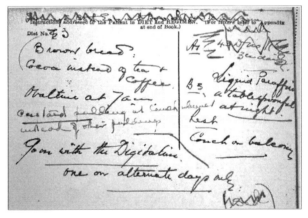

A typical "diet page" in a bath book from Smedley's Hydro.

The bath book contained a kind of code because all the treatments were given numbers. For example in Smedley's time, 1 was a cold dripping sheet, 38 was a wet pack, 51 was a steam bath, 81 a mustard pack and 242 chilli paste. These numbers did change as more complicated and up-to-date treatments were introduced, but the simple idea did not. The prescribed numbers were listed, along with the patient's weekly weight and diet and exercise instructions.

Diet was very important: John Smedley wanted to make "better blood" by helping the stomach to work more efficiently and avoid indigestible food. The meals, except at holiday times, were plain and wholesome (Smedley's was notorious for stewed fruit). But some patients were given quite specific regimes to follow with invalid foods like beef tea. Patent foods such as Revalenta (made from lentils), rusks with milk, or the later Benger's were available from 11am.

> *Now in your little book you'll find detailed what you're to eat,*
> *Revalenta, porridge and but sparingly of meat;*
> *Of Spanish onions, frequently, stewed apples don't forget,*
> *Not quite your taste, well never mind, you'll get to like them yet.*
> J Jacoby, a patient at Smedley's in 1890

The main sessions in the baths took place before breakfast, 6.30 – 8.15am, mid-morning, 10 – 1pm, in the afternoon between 3 and 5pm, and in the evening between 8 and 9.30pm. The Turkish and Russian baths were open in-between times.

The original baths at Smedley's were described as consisting of:

a long range of small comfortable rooms or stalls, each fitted with a seat and toilet requisites, a supply of sheets, blankets etc. and both hot and cold water taps, and what are called sitz baths. These stalls open from a corridor, and opposite to each is a kind of bed, with curtains to each, used for the purpose of "packing" the patients, while at the end is an open space in which the "dripping sheets" are administered, and where shallow and vapour baths are prepared.

> When Matlock I'm asked in great raptures to go,
> With its hills and its dales and its rivers that flow,
> I'm expected to like the kind treatment I get,
> Tho' indoors and out I get nothing but wet.
>
> I'm kept there an hour unable to move,
> My patience, I must think, in order to prove,
> When as warm as a pudding and feeling quite nice,
> I'm plunged in cold water – much colder than ice.
> From verses by a patient at Matlock House Hydro

One much repeated rule at Smedley's was the prohibition of alcohol on medical grounds, instigated by John Smedley and never rescinded. There were many stories of the lengths patients went to get alcohol delivered in medicine bottles from the nearby pharmacy and the Gate Hotel. Smoking was also forbidden in the early days: it was claimed John Smedley's great uncle had died in a burning bed.

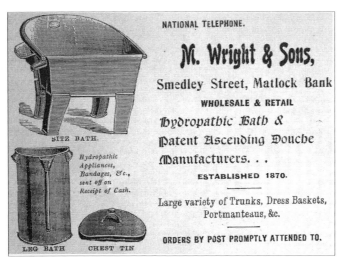

NATIONAL TELEPHONE.

M. Wright & Sons,

Smedley Street, Matlock Bank

WHOLESALE & RETAIL

Hydropathic Bath &
Patent Ascending Douche
Manufacturers. . .

ESTABLISHED 1870.

Large variety of Trunks, Dress Baskets,
Portmanteaus, &c.

ORDERS BY POST PROMPTLY ATTENDED TO.

SITZ BATH.

Hydropathic
Appliances,
Bandages, &c.,
sent off on
Receipt of Cash.

LEG BATH   CHEST TIN

What was his telephone number?

Exercise was important for the treatment, but it was strictly regulated. Fitter visitors could descend every morning but Sunday to the drill room under the billiard room. Here James Montgomery was in charge until his death in 1887. Then for many years an ex-army officer called Sergeant William Cocking presided. He still wore his uniform and carried a silver knobbed cane. His waxed moustache was twisted to points. He practised calisthenics, single stick exercises and the like. (Sergeant Cocking also acted as one of Smedley's hall porters and he was in charge of both of the hydro's fire brigade teams from 1888[6]. In his spare time he drilled the local militia and played the flute.)

Some patients wanted to carry on their treatment at home. They could arm themselves with John or Caroline's manuals – half a crown or "free" by post for 36 postage stamps – and buy the necessary equipment. Smedley's had a saleroom to the left of the front door stocked with baths and bandages. Wright's hardware store on Smedley Street sold more equipment including sitz baths.

STAYING IN

Early mornings in the hydros were taken up with treatments, followed by breakfast and morning prayers in the drawing rooms. The chapel which John Smedley had built in his grounds was leased out and later became a boiler house, but there were plenty of old and newly-built churches for Sunday and weekday services.

The smaller hydros remained homely and simple. A visitor to Jackson House described returning for supper after a walk on his first night, "The saloons were lighted and all the visitors (about 40) were busily occupied with milk and oatmeal porridge. I could never touch it at home, but I became an enthusiast before I left". After supper, family prayers were led by a "president" elected from the visitors, who happened to be a Methodist Minister. Then everyone read before bed and lights out at 10pm.

> Now all who've stayed at Smedley's for any length of time,
> I'm sure will coincide with these remarks of mine,
> And all ye happy mortals to whom the place is new
> Before you've been here 14 days will find they are but true.
>
> Tho' from the point of view of health 'tis hard a fault to find,
> And this 'tis true the management must chiefly bear in mind;
> I'm not the only patient who has shed a silent tear,
> Despairing e'er to solve the point of what one can do here.
>
> In perfect desperation I have seen some ladies knit,
> Whilst others with their work in hand just yawn and idly sit;
> And things have come to such a pass that gentlemen they tell
> In sheer despair have torn their hair and learnt to knit as well!

---

6. Three dozen hand grenade fire extinguishers had been purchased in 1883.

The evenings are enlivened oft with solos and with songs,
While one kind lady told us of poor old woman's wrongs,
Yes, were it not for such things and here and there tableaux,
How we should manage to kill the time, why goodness only knows.

A spelling bee the other night they managed to arrange,
Why even that I heard it said was welcome for a change;
With almost Spartan courage eleven ladies took their seats,
Whilst we prepared ourselves to hear their wondrous spelling feats.

by J Jacoby, a patient at Smedley's in 1890

The larger hydros were beginning to take entertainments quite seriously. The guests elected a committee amongst themselves each month to organise competitions and concerts; this demonstrates the long-term nature of most of the visits. From 1889 at Smedley's they were given a budget of fifty shillings per week. Men and women were elected to the committees, but the Chairmen who presided at balls and Christmas dinners were always gentlemen. Entertainment was still largely home-made. Presumably new arrivals were quizzed as to their musical and acting abilities. Did some take music and instruments in the hope they would be asked? The newspaper reports were unfailingly complimentary, but there must surely have been many disasters.

A tableau vivant posing in Smedley's garden.
Photo taken by John Clark.
[Derbyshire Record Office]

Tableaux vivants and charades became popular and would be fun with all the dressing up involved. A report for Matlock House said furs and ermines were "gladly lent" for an evening of six *tableaux*. One production at Smedley's was described in detail: the execution scene from the life of Mary Queen of Scots was so moving, "a solemn awe fell upon the audience". But then everyone was cheered up by an Eastern Bazaar and Slave Market with an unlimited variety of costume and

TROUBLE AT SMEDLEY'S?

There is a curious hand-written anonymous note book in the Record Office which makes interesting reading in conjunction with a second one which supplemented the Board of Management's minutes. In the latter, it is noticeable that no doctor stayed very long as Dr Hunter's assistant. It has already been noted that before Mr Douglas the managers also came and went rapidly. Between 1880 and Hunter's death in 1894 the junior doctors were Maccall in 1880, Wilson in 1882, Tennant in 1883, Joseph George Garibaldi! Corkhill in 1887, Whitby in 1889, and Sharpe in 1891. They each began at a salary of £100 per year and seemed to "resign" soon after they had asked for a raise. Dr Hunter, on the other hand, was earning £1250 in 1883 and £1500 by 1889. The Hunters at this time were living in the Hydro. In 1877 Mrs Hunter was paying £3-8-6d a week and her daughter £1-14-3d but by 1878 the family was staying free of charge.

Now we come to the other notebook. This noted unreasonable expense claims by Board members and a few complaints. But overwhelmingly it was a diatribe against the Hunters. One Board member called Dr Hunter a "brat". He said his father had been merely a cabinet maker who travelled on a pony giving treatment until settling at Bridge of Allan. Apparently he now refused to visit Matlock because of his son's haughtiness.

Mrs Hunter was rude to the matron Mrs Hesketh who resigned. Once she ordered her to pick up an umbrella she had dropped. She constantly criticised the work of the housekeeper. She snubbed Mrs Wildgoose, the wife of the Chairman. She did not allow the assistant doctor to sit at her table.

Mrs Hunter also used the Hydro's horses and on one occasion broke a horse's knees and then denied she had been out. Another time she ordered the Hydro's coach, and to "get her off", George the coachman, Herbert his assistant, the hall porter, a nurse and a second female were all employed carrying rugs and cushions.

Mrs Hunter had demanded and been allowed free lodging. When one new suite of furniture arrived at the Hydro, she took the mirror and thus spoilt the set. Miss Hunter sent back food to the kitchens and was rude to waiters. She demanded expensive chicken dishes. She played battledore noisily in the corridors. She let her dog roam the Hydro when guests were denied their own pets.

Dr Hunter was undeniably popular with the patients. At Christmas dinners and other functions, and when he died, he was praised to the skies. But in the note book, Mr Crowther of the Board was quoted as saying, "If we are to do the best possible for our shareholders, we must submit to this domineering style, which is most galling. The longer we retain him, the more powerful he becomes and the more arrogant".

Dr. William Bell Hunter, the consultant at Smedley's Hydro.

The Hunters did eventually move into their own home: Hillside (now West Lea) on Chesterfield Road – presumably to everyone's great relief.

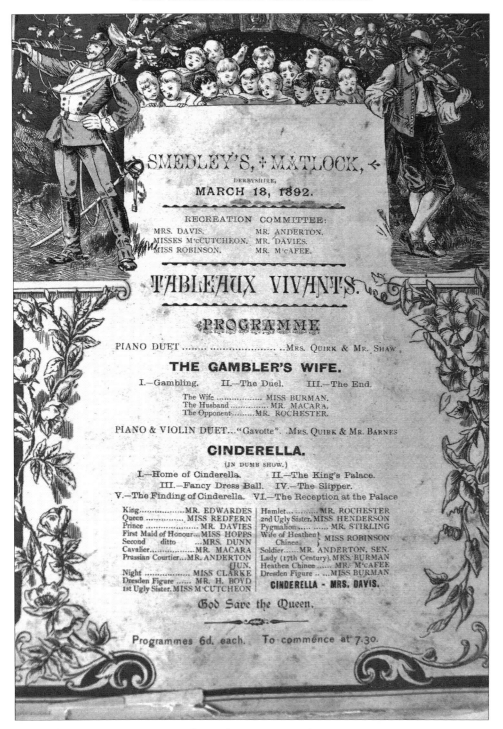

[Derbyshire Record Office]

Cinderella tableau
[Derbyshire Record Office]

Poplar Hydro group
[Glynn Waite]

Bowls at Sycamore House Hydro.

music. The gentlemen especially appreciated the "row of beautiful girls in white drapery with bare arms roped together".

Smoking concerts were enjoyed by the men once tobacco was permitted. A chairman was elected for the evening to keep the conversation going and a few musical items were performed. People could move about and come and go, rather than sit stiffly in chairs. From 1898 a few modern ladies joined in at Smedley's.

Most of the hydros had billiard tables by the end of the decade and both sexes played. Indeed the women often won matches if the men were handicapped. The ladies at Smedley's had asked for a bagatelle table in their drawing room in the 1870s and the game was mentioned at Belle Vue too: this was an early form of bar billiards. When the contents of the New Bath were sold in 1898, they included a mahogany bagatelle table from the sitting room, as well as a full-sized billiard table.

The New Bath sale numbered several mahogany loo tables too, as well as card tables. Loo was a very popular card game earlier in the 19th century, but was making way for whist. Many of the older ladies played cards every evening; these games gradually became more organised with daily prizes. It was fairly easy to set

The grounds of Matlock House Hydro.

up a lawn to play quoits, bowls, battledore and shuttlecock (early badminton), or croquet, even before the hydros constructed their proper sports grounds. Smedley's laid out lawn tennis courts in 1887, but tar-paved them in 1892. Presumably all the hydros had some books and magazines in the drawing room and the newsagents and stationers in the towns set up lending libraries which long-term visitors could join. With the treatments, meal-times, prayers, concerts and games, as well as the outings on offer, which are described later – not to mention an early bed-time – I doubt Mr Jacoby can have really been as bored as he made out.

Dancing eventually became very popular, both at the hydros and down in the town. The Board at Smedley's actually forbade dancing in 1883 except before 10pm at Christmas, but this edict seems to have been relaxed quite quickly. A good public dance started around 9 pm and continued until 3 or even 5 am, with supper around midnight.

In the 1880s were many descriptions of Calico Balls. These were meant to encourage the cotton trade in Lancashire where calico printing had been "brought to perfection". A Calico Ball at the Old English in March 1882 featured a room decorated in the printed cotton, while the ladies wore many new designs; sixty guests danced until five in the morning. In 1884 a Calico Ball for children was held at the Fountain Baths assembly room.

From Recreation Committee Book 3: John Barnes and his orchestra played for dances in Matlock for over forty years.
[Derbyshire Record Office]

The New Bath Hotel built a new wing which included a salon for dancing. It featured a special floor with cross girders supported by spiral springs – a sprung dancing floor which was copied by the hydros some years later. They held the County Ball there in January 1886, graced by the Curzons of Kedleston Hall and other aristocrats, so a superior band was brought in from Leicester. In the 1898 sale catalogue were two semi-grand Broadwood pianos and an American organ.

Rockside Hydro held its annual grand ball on August Bank Holiday. Many other local rooms were used for public dancing: the assembly rooms on Dale Road and the Fountain Baths, the Pavilion and the ballroom at the Royal Hotel.

The dancing was more often than not to Mr J H Barnes's Quadrille Band from Matlock Bath. The Barnes family and their various ensembles featured at nearly every dance in the Matlocks over the next forty-five years. John was a school teacher with three brothers, but their father Samuel was a hosier. He had a shop on Derwent Parade from where they also sold pianos.

Smedley's and Rockside Hydros were beginning to set up the traditions which persisted until the Second World War. They were both famous for their Christmas celebrations. Smedley's at this time had a Christmas lunch at 2pm (six o'clock from 1890) with three long tables of diners. Rockside had a dinner at six o'clock. The decorations were very home-made with paper garlands and lots of mottos and messages such as "Health and Happiness to Dr and Mrs Hunter" written in white wool on scarlet flannel.

Smedley's also had a tradition begun by John Smedley and eventually copied by most of the hydros: a staff supper and ball at the New Year when the servants and their families were waited upon by the guests – no matter how distinguished. In 1882 this took place in the new servants' hall where guests had erected a Christmas tree surrounded by presents for the staff. Mr Doxey, the foreman of the carpenters, proposed a toast to Mr Burden, "their excellent and popular manager" and suggested they engage the same visitors to wait upon them the next year. Eventually the numbers present grew to over five hundred and the event was held in the new dining room. At midnight the whole assembly joined hands to sing *Auld Lang Syne*.

As the decade progressed, the celebrations at Smedley's became more lavish. They introduced a grand Christmas Eve (later Boxing Day) ball in 1886, for which Mr Barnes and his band played for many years. The numbers at the Christmas dinner grew to over 200. With their French chef Francois Lecalvez (from Brittany with a Parisian wife), the menu changed from plain roast beef, mutton and jugged hare to delicacies such as *Supreme de volaille en demi d'oeuil, salmis of grouse a la financiere*, and *Galantine de dinde en belle vue*. The dinner concluded with speeches and toasts interspersed with solos from talented guests.

The decorations became more exciting, especially with electricity. On the dining tables were silver epergnes full of chrysanthemums with electric lights attached. In 1891 Monsieur Lecalvez made a sugar Eiffel Tower. In 1895 he sculpted HMS Majestic, a battleship launched that year, out of ice and sugar.

The balls also became more sophisticated affairs by the end of the decade. On Christmas Eve 1890 the ballroom (still the dining room) was described as looking like fairyland with dainty screens, lofty palms, flowers, flags, banners, huge mirrors, and Japanese lanterns, all illuminated by the "soft but steady and brilliant electric light". Mr Barnes's band played the latest *valses*. The older matrons were mostly dressed in black with costly lace and jet jewellery but the young girls had white and pink gowns. The buffet, in a picturesque cave, was loaded with creams, cakes, custards and fruits.

It may have been a coincidence, but why was the report of Christmas at Smedley's in the newspaper nearly always on the same page as Christmas Day at Bakewell Workhouse?

At Bonfire Night in 1891 there was a very expensive-sounding firework display at Smedley's. The poor patients were deafened by huge shells and rockets. A shell "with lilac and laburnum blossom" was followed by Italian streamers and a mine of "jewel-headed cobras". The hour-long display the following year, watched by a thousand people, included a balloon carrying the fireworks.

> *Kind friends good night, I think I quite told what I had to tell,*
> *And maybe several details which I shouldn't have done as well;*
> *And in future should it happen that you don't know what to do,*
> *Why go and write some nonsense such as I've read out to you.*
>
> J Jacoby

GOING OUT

Since 1865 the Matlocks had been run by separate Local Boards who were responsible for public health and welfare, sanitation and general town improvements. The Medical Officer was always able to make one important boast in his annual report: the Matlocks had a very low death rate. In 1898, this was reported to be 7 per 1000, in 1901 10.5 per 1000: both among the lowest in the United Kingdom, which was then

Howe's Fountain Baths – and a dusty road.

running at an average of twenty.

The main road – now the A6 – was still termed the "turnpike" although the toll bars had been thrown open in the previous decade. The toll cottages remained for many years. At the Derby entrance to Matlock Bath was Warm Wells tollgate cottage at a very narrow bit of road next to the weir just before Wapping. (The gate pillars are now up by the New Bath Hotel.) There was a tollgate at the bottom of Holt Lane, but this had been moved to Artists' Corner. Steep Turnpike toll cottage in Matlock can still be seen. Other toll bars had been opposite the Duke of Wellington on Chesterfield Road, in Darley Dale and towards Tansley. The only "free" entry to the Matlocks had been through Starkholmes.

After the turnpikes were abolished, the 1878 Highways and Locomotives (Amendment) Act required that half the cost of maintaining the "main roads" was made a charge on the County. When County Councils were formed in 1888, they were supposed to pay the full costs, but there were many disputes. Moreover, the care of an increasing number of new residential and commercial roads within towns was a constant drain on local finances.

Care of the roads resulted in the one subject bound to ignite the wrath of visitor and citizen alike – DUST. Dust clouds were a topic in the first *Visiting Lists* in the 1850s and they were still a topic in the 1920s. Many roads in Matlock were still little more than cart tracks with deep ruts. However, the main streets had been asphalted or macadamised, often several times. This did not mean they had been treated with tar. It meant they had been surfaced with about nine inches of graded broken stones,

The macadamised road surface in Matlock Bath. The crushed stones were pressed down by the council's steam roller, only to be churned up again by iron wheels such as seen on the cart.

[Glynn Waite]

67

the top finished with a four inch layer of compressed limestone dust which turned into a concrete surface when wet. Other finishes were constantly tried too. The councils had a water cart to lay the dust in dry weather and they could hire the County Council steam roller to flatten the sharper stones. This was the theory.

The practice was different. The water cart never seemed to appear when needed. It also drenched people's shoes as it went past. The steam roller was a traction engine and therefore forbidden on Matlock's medieval bridge; coming from Derby it had to travel up and down via Starkholmes to reach the town centre. By 1891 even this was no longer an option when Willersley bridge was deemed too fragile. In 1886 Matlock Local Board made enquiries about the cost of buying their own 3½ ton horse roller. Any expense such as that, or buying another water cart, brought complaints from councillors representing Starkholmes and the upper Bank areas. They had poor roads and no lighting – why should they contribute?

A visitor to Jackson House in 1878 had written, "We alighted at Matlock Bridge and found the white dust lying inches thick on the roads". A newspaper correspondent in October 1881 complained, "The howling winds and blinding dust of the desert scarcely bear comparison". When it rained, everybody's shoes were covered in "an adhesive substance akin to mortar". Lady's sweeping skirts were ruined by the lime. The solid wheels of the traffic ruined any newly-asphalted surface in days.

> *Dust to dust is man's sad fate*
> *No matter whether small or great;*
> *But none so dusty can be found*
> *As those who live on Matlock's ground.*
> *Each carriage has a dusty shroud*
> *And followed by a dusty cloud.*
> *There's dust on railings, gardens, door,*
> *Each Matlockite is dusted o'er.*

There was no single asphalting method: a road could receive a covering of limestone, ash, gritstone, granite, tar, cinders (very smelly) or a mixture of any. It depended on the gradient or what was cheap at the time. Limestone for the roads was broken up in the quarries in Dale Road. Tar was made opposite the gas works on Bakewell Road and in the Dale; complaints were made against the tar barrel parading through the town every midday. Tar did not stick to wet limestone and had to be laid in hot weather – more complaints! Matters did not improve until the roads were regularly tar-sprayed or treated with Tarmac in the 1920s. There were several experiments to try to solve the problem, which are described later.

The speed of new housing, especially on Matlock Bank, meant new roads often remained un-adopted for several years, but the Local Boards tried to make the house-owners do repairs. This led to many disputes – the inhabitants of Holme Road were eventually taken to court. They did not see why they should spend money, only to make a road fit for adoption. Adopted roads could be straightened out and widened, kerb stones were fitted and footpaths paved. However, paving stones were constantly cracked by heavy barrows delivering to shops.

The old County Bridge.
Newspapers often mentioned the litter on the river bank.

There were two gas works: one behind Matlock Bath station built in 1852 and one on Bakewell Road, where the new flats now stand by the Sainsbury roundabout. On a map c1879 there was a third gas works nearer Darley Dale, but this was labelled disused by 1898. Both towns had gas lamps in the centre, but there were always complaints about the darker outskirts. New and better lamps were being installed all the time. At Matlock Bridge, the posts were cream on the upper half, with light blue bases and black bands. A substantial and ornamental light on a square pedestal was erected on Matlock Bridge in 1890 to augment the previous single light in Crown Square. Starkholmes was still completely in the dark.

However, having street lamps did not mean they were lit. The first few lamps had been lit in Matlock Bath on 5 November 1854. They stayed on until midnight for the first and last time to celebrate the fall of Inkerman during the Crimean War. The lighting committee of the Local Board decided which months to employ a contract lamplighter who had to reset and wind the timers. In the 1880s the season was from mid-August to April. The lamps were only lit for a few hours, so there were constant complaints that they were being extinguished too early at weekends, certainly before 10pm and more often 9.30pm. In 1895 the Local Board at Matlock Bath had agreed to a month's trial to leave the lights on until 11pm – to make it look as if someone lives here, as the newspaper remarked. Presumably it proved too expensive because a visitor in 1896 described leaving a concert at 10.30pm on a dark August evening. He and his friend had to feel their way. They fell off a kerb and ran into some ladies "much wider than ourselves", then knocked into several men "who did not like it".

The gas quality also varied. In March 1884 it was described as providing a "bilious luminary" and a "wretched vapour". Many households were looking out their candles. Mr Ward at Bank House Hydro complained at a Local Board meeting that his visitors were using candles even when the gas was lit.

Whilst the Matlocks were justly famed for their scenery and the overall landscape was definitely rural, a visitor would not be able to escape scenes of real and thriving industry. They might even visit Smedley's mill at Lea or one of the factories in Lumsdale to see the machinery and buy their products. Charabanc drivers would point out Arkright's eighteenth century cotton spinning buildings at Cromford. The old mill complex had had no textile works since lead mining activity in the early 1830s had diverted the water power supply. Some of the buildings were empty, but there was a brewery and a hosiery goods store. In November 1890 many local people and visitors turned out to witness a spectacular fire in one six-storey building, fanned by a strong breeze. The contents were insured, but not the building, and it was speculated Mr Arkwright had lost about £5000.

However, Masson Mill on the turnpike was still a going concern for the Arkwright family, using the river as a power supply. The tourists would have seen a smaller building compared with today: the five-storey brick building with Venetian windows built in 1783. Next door was a paper mill built by Messrs White and Shore in 1771, which became Simons & Pickards, who also had a factory in Via Gellia. Fifty men and boys made brown and blue writing paper from rags and brown paper from old rope. They worked day and night with a twenty-four hour stoppage each week for maintenance. Was there an unpleasant smell as in modern pulp mills?

Jewitt in the late 1870s described seeing the mill girls at Masson mill – a common enough sight for northern visitors, but perhaps a novelty for others:

> Here at the gate of the mill, the factory girls congregate by scores at meal times, and sit in picturesque groups and rows along the footpath, and under the walls, and woe to the luckless individual who by any eccentricities in dress or personal appearance excites their attention, or subjects himself to a running fire from their voluble tongues.

In certain weather conditions, the clatter of hundreds of spindles was clearly audible from Matlock Bath. In 1888 electric lighting was installed on all the floors, which must have been a wonderful sight at night. They used hydro-electric power from the Derwent, which led to speculation that the town could do the same. In the same year, a steam engine was installed so that production could continue whatever the state of the river. The engine was named Rebecca after Mrs Arkwright. The manager said he employed nearly 400 people making 18,000 miles of thread per week.

But surely the most noticeable industry in the Matlocks must have been the quarries. Many of them are still visible but silent now. Imagine a time when all of them were working. Matlock Bridge Limestone Company called its men in with a loud steam horn which disturbed invalids on the Bank. Every day at least one quarry would be blasting the rock loose. Jewitt described walking out of Matlock Bath, just past the railway station. Men came running out of one of the quarries on the left, now barely visible through the trees. They shouted a warning, then, "the men crouched under the rock or stood up close to the wall and not a word was spoken by any of them". There was a loud explosion and stones were hurled across the road in the tourists' path. A new quarry was opened in Matlock Bath by the Shaw Brothers next to the railway station. They used a baton system to signal whether it was safe for a train to approach after blasting.

Mr Cassels of Megdale Farm, across the valley from the gas works, complained several times to the Local Board about stones from Cawdor Quarry landing in his farmyard, even coming in through his bedroom window. He complained, "Everyone about the farm is in constant danger of being maimed or killed". His farm is long gone, although it was later used as a quarry office. It was on Snitterton Road, where there is now a void behind Sainsbury's.

The Dale had many quarries: three beyond Bruntswood Terrace in Matlock Bath and several before, after and behind the Boat House Inn – the publican must have had a dreadful dust problem.

Those of us living on Matlock Bank know how sounds echo round the valley; often we cannot tell the direction or source. The blasting, grinding, crushing, tapping and chiselling of stone must have been a constant background noise from the quarries and the railway station dressing floors, where millstones were ground for Scandinavian and American pulp mills. Stone sills, columns and capitals were sent ready-carved to building projects around the country. The sound was described in one book as "the musical clink of the quarrymen's tools", but was it really that pleasant? The roads were always blamed for the dust, but surely some of it came from the quarries – it still does, and from much more distant ones.

All around the Matlocks were houses, churches and shops in various stages of build. Then there was the creaking of wood and harness and clopping of hooves as the heavy horse drays delivered the stone, timber and coal around the town. They must have delayed every other vehicle on the steep hills.

There were several fires in the 1880s, such as the one at the Old English described above. In 1889 the Red Lion public house was damaged, followed shortly by an embarrassing conflagration in the Local Board office. Both Local Boards resolved to raise a public subscription for a fire engine, but Matlock Bath failed to deliver any funds. Matlock Bridge and Bank collected £200 on their own, enough to buy Mr Bateman's machine from Middleton and new uniforms. The vehicle was kept initially in a shed at the Boat House, but was later lodged behind the Town Hall. For several weeks the crew toured the area performing demonstrations. Lady Whitworth even invited them to tea. Their first real outing was to Steven's paint works under High Tor when the ochre store caught fire.

MATLOCK BATH

The date of 1698 is always given for the establishment of Matlock Bath as a spa with accommodation and bath houses. The very clean spring water, channelled then to the Old and New Bath Hotels and the Fountain Baths, still flows at a steady temperature of 68 degrees. The village had remained relatively inaccessible, compared with its richer contemporaries, until the road from Derby was blasted through the rocks at Scarthin early in the 19th century, followed by the arrival of the railway in 1849. This meant the development of the spa had been very modest and catered for those wanting a quiet time, although the list of visitors had included Lord Byron, John Ruskin and the young Princess Victoria.

However, Matlock Bath had rather stagnated as a place to stay during the years when the hydros were beginning to transform the Bank. A letter to the *Visiting List* in October 1881 summed up what many were thinking. The writer claimed the residents were deploring the "degeneracy of the place". The "palmy days of yore" when they were able to line their pockets were "relics of the past". The Local Board

*The drinking fountain
at the Fountain Baths.*

was criticised for its lethargy. "What inducement is there for visitors to spend their leisure moments in Matlock Bath? Absolutely none." There were "no gardens, no promenade, no pavilion or music, no public institution of any kind, not even a library". Water was in abundance but could not be properly supplied to the houses.

*The most photographed view of Matlock Bath, with its museums and wells.
Boden's confectioners was the shop with the arched window. Card posted 1904.*

(This was an issue until the 1900s.) Visitors arrived in hope and packed up in despair – to go to Buxton!

Another visitor described Matlock Bath as alright for being "a bit ill" or needing a "bit of recreation". There were "no bath chairs, no lifts up the hills, and a very short boat trip". There were many complaints about the lack of seats to relax upon. The main perennial complaint was that everything on offer involved a payment, even if it was only a penny or two: "If it is in any way worth seeing, it will be subject to an extra charge".

So what was there to do? Thousands of visitors did come on Bank Holidays, as we shall see. They must have had some expectations.

Balconies and window blinds survive in Matlock Bath.

We are lucky that the sweep of shops and restaurants along the river still survives in Matlock Bath. If the cars were removed, the visitor of old would still recognise much of the view: the Museum or South Parade from the 1790s, the Fountain Villas and Derwent (or North) Parade with its Post Office, shops and restaurants from the 1840s. The chapel with the spire was opened in 1867. There were extra buildings on the riverside, as can be seen on many postcards: the Devonshire Hotel, the Royal Museum, shops and cafes, stables and outhouses for the businesses opposite. A few shops retain the mechanism for lowering blinds to prevent glare spoiling the window displays, but in the 1880s nearly every shop had a colourful awning. In June 1882, the Local Board asked for some of the blinds to be raised because top hats were being knocked off.

Much was written about the souvenir shops in Matlock Bath and how they lowered the tone with their cheap ornaments. However, there were spa and marble shops called "Museums," on Museum (South) Parade. Herbert Buxton's Royal Museum, petrifying well and gardens was across the road by the river, entered by gates with lofty obelisks. These businesses had workshops where men worked Blue John and other decorative fluorspars, and marbles – polished limestone such as the

This well was on the riverside opposite South Parade.

famous black Ashford Marble. Seventeen men said they were decorative stone workers in the 1881 census, making urns, vases and statues as well as smaller inkwells, candlesticks and jewellery. In 1890 Alfred Greatorex of Great Masson Cavern won first prize at the Worshipful Company of Turners exhibition and the freedom of the City of London for a Blue John vase, bought by the Lord Mayor for fifteen guineas.

There had been a confusing number of "Royal" museums in different premises at different times in the previous hundred years. Smith's Royal Museum, previously Vallance's, Walker's or the Central Museum, boasted patronage by the Dukes of Devonshire and Rutland, and advertised vases of amesthystine and topazine, Egyptian obelisks and Italian alabaster. Samuel Smith also had a petrifying well and boats. The projecting bay window on Museum Parade had been Mawe's Royal Museum, followed by Adam's. Originally this had been the dining room of the Great Hotel. Mr Dakin of the Fountain Baths had a Museum at the beginning of the decade. Others listed in 1876 were Boden's spar shop near the toll gate, Gregory's in Albert House, Hartle's near Walker's Hotel, King's on Waterloo Road, Pearson's opposite the obelisk, Mrs Smedley's on New Bath Terrace, T Smedley's opposite the church, and W Smedley's near the New Bath.

As well as being skilled craftsmen, the Museums were run by knowledgeable geologists who had collected minerals from all over the world, which they sold with engravings and books. Mr Howe, the stationer at the Fountain Baths, was also described as an antiquarian, geologist and botanist, with a fine collection of Derbyshire minerals. In 1889 he showed the North Staffordshire Field Club his

Visitors left objects to be "turned into stone" – eggs were popular.

collection of fossils, while Mrs Howe supplied refreshments. On the southern end of Museum Parade was also a Literary Institute reading room where lectures and discussions took place.

Some of the items made were far from cheap, but the industry was thought to be stagnating. In 1884 an exhibition was staged to boost the trade and local musicians staged "promenade" concerts to bring people in. Choice items of inlaid marble were brought from the South Kensington Museum (later called the Victoria and Albert) and from Chatsworth and other big houses, but visitors remained disappointingly few.

Associated with the Museums were half a dozen petrifying wells, often in roadside booths of which traces remain. Most of them were between the church and the Fishpond. The items displayed were not really turned to stone, but they were encrusted with a quarter-inch layer of calcium compounds deposited from the spring water which was sprayed over them. The majority of the objects were small such as eggs, tea cups or bottles; bird nests were popular. The Bodens displayed deer antlers from Chatsworth and the Ogdens a human and a lioness skull. The items were regularly moved around so that they did not stick together. They were enclosed so they did not grow algae. Visitors could leave souvenirs to be collected the following year.

Many of the premises on the Parades had shops on the ground floor and dining rooms upstairs, such as Barnes refreshment rooms and the Fountain Baths. The dining rooms would not be needed in the winter; they were only packed out on summer weekends and Bank Holidays, so the ground floors had to have everyday

Thomas Asbury's chemist shop in Matlock Bath.

uses. The shops tried to cater for locals and visitors; they were probably larger establishments than would be usual for a relatively small settlement.

John Boden was one very prominent tradesman on South Parade and in the Crown Buildings at Matlock Bridge. As well as his normal bakery business, he supplied food for functions at the Pavilion and other venues. He could also provide the table linens, plate and cutlery needed for outside catering. Inside his bread and cake shop were marble-topped counters with brass fittings; his dining room across the road could seat 200 people.

Mr Nicholls was a harness maker who could supply leather goods of all kinds from his double fronted showrooms on South Parade; ladies could buy dressing cases and hat boxes. Thomas Asbury had one pharmacy at Matlock Bridge and another on Derwent Parade next to the church. The previous chemist called Platt had advertised a new toilet water called "Matlock Bath Bouquet" at 1/- or 2/6d per bottle. Mr J A Scorer was a draper and dressmaker at 1 Derwent Parade who claimed to have the latest stock from the best London and Berlin fashion houses. William Bryan's men and women's dress shop at Cavendish House on the corner of Holme Road could also cater for the visitor: he advertised artistic millinery, mantles, sunshades and boas.

Since 1784 Samuel Skidmore & Son had been a family of hosiery manufacturers with premises on Derby Road in Matlock Bath and Smedley Street on the Bank. They liked visitors to see them at work using the old frames and hand looms. Their superior products were shaped on the loom, not cut out and seamed. They made

Making hosiery on a hand loom.

underwear and stockings in silk, cashmere, lisle (polished cotton) and wool, specialising in black silk hose "with or without Balbriggan toes and heels". Visitors from overseas could use the mail order service. Samuel Barnes & Sons on Derwent Parade had also made silk underclothes since 1860. Their shop and dining rooms were in the substantial building between Rose Cottage and the Fountain Baths.

Photographic studios were important for the holiday trade. Day trippers might only want a souvenir of their visit; but longer-term visitors needed *cartes-de-visite* to

Advertisement from 1886 for the newly re-built public swimming bath:
the only one not attached to a hydro or hotel.

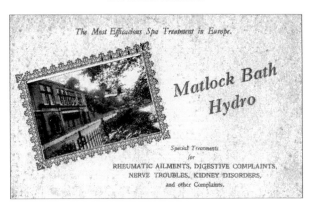

A brochure for the Fountain Baths.
[Peak District Lead Mining Museum]

give out to their new friends. They would have time to pose for quite elaborate portraits, which were also needed by the local worthies who perhaps hoped to get their photograph in the newspapers. The local publishers, such as Howe's, needed photographers to take landscape views for their souvenir and guide books. John Clark on South Parade claimed patronage from the Emperor and Empress of Brazil, as well as the Prince and Princess of Wales: presumably he had been commissioned to take official portraits when they visited. His studio was taken over by John William Hilder mid-decade.

On the way out to Matlock Bridge, Mary Whittaker manufactured lemonade, ginger beer, quinine tonic and aerated waters, orange bitter and champagne cider etc. using pure spring water. The bottling plant, which used steam machinery, was housed in a rather ramshackle range of buildings along the main road. Although the factory has been demolished, the family's three-storey house is still prominent.

Day visitors and locals could use the Fountain Baths which had been built in 1786, but were replaced by a new establishment offering hydropathic treatment in private rooms in 1883. Some sources say Joseph Dakin of the Royal Museum was responsible for the new building, but others say the Howe family. The Howes were certainly in charge by 1887 and his widow continued after William's death in 1890.

The original spring water had been rather cold, but the owners had found warmer water further back in the hillside which filled a spacious swimming pool, whose water at the constant 68 degrees was replenished eighteen times each twenty four hours. The interior was furnished like a conservatory with ferns; outside the building a row of lime trees overhung the road. The pool opened with several demonstrations of swimming feats such as swimming four lengths underwater and smoking under water without the cigarette being extinguished. Bubbles rose to the surface when anyone dived in. Ladies only could swim on Tuesday and Friday mornings. The original roof of the pool has been removed for safety, but the observation platform remains. The pool was used by many swimming clubs, schools and groups over the years, before the goldfish were moved in.

In the hydropathic cubicles, the water could be heated to any temperature from eight o'clock in the morning. Patrons could also drink from a fountain at the top of the stairs to relieve their lumbago, gout, indigestion or kidney complaints. The fountain is still there, but the cubicles have been replaced by tropical fish tanks.

To the front, William Howe, mentioned already as a noted geologist, had an extensive book shop, with music and fine art for sale. He also ran a circulating library and one could even hire a piano. He published souvenir and guide books. On the first floor he managed the Matlock Bath assembly room where many concerts and balls were held, including weekly dances in the winter run by John Barnes. The facilities were described as very comfortable with good acoustics.

The Heights of Abraham was a thirty acre pleasure ground opened in the late eighteenth century in the style of the time: a kind of ordered wilderness. A great variety of trees and shrubs such as rhododendron were planted, with flowers bordering the zig-zag paths. They led past a rustic summer house with tufa walls and a thatched roof. The trees were perhaps getting overgrown by the 1880s, but the paths were in good order. The Victoria Prospect Tower, with its 50 step spiral staircase, was described at this time as dirty and worn. However, nothing could detract from the view from the top. As today, several routes down the hillside or rambles to Bonsall were recommended.

The prominent castle-like building high on the hillside in Matlock Bath was the

On the Heights of Abraham, a business run by the Sprinthall family.
[Glynn Waite]

Upper Tower House of about 1830, usually lived in by the lessee of the Heights. There was a tea garden in the front. The west entrance to the Heights was the crenelated lodge on Upperwood Road. The East Lodge entrance was a cottage orne on Masson Road, built in the 1860s to replace the Round House on Waterloo Road: this many-sided building was built soon after the gardens were opened, probably as the first pay kiosk.

Note the table of minerals on display.

There were several routes up to the Heights of Abraham. The very fit went uphill past Hodgkinson's Hotel, the Temple Hotel grounds and the Prince of Wales Inn. The road was paved with what Lancashire visitors called "petrified kidneys". The climb was slightly less steep going up Holme Road. "Jerusalem ponies" (donkeys), sporting smart saddle cloths, ear caps and rosettes, carried the more infirm up the hill. These donkeys had been a bone of contention with the residents for many years. They and their "rude lads" congregated near the obelisk leading up to the Royal Hotel. (This used to indicate the Royal Old Bath Hotel, not the Temple.) The donkey keepers were supposed to be licensed, but this was not easy to enforce. In 1886 James Rouse and his daughter were licensed for "asses", but he was prosecuted in 1888 for allowing a donkey to stray thirty yards in front of his pack. The police witness said, "the defendant's donkeys are a great nuisance and the man had been cautioned previously". An article in 1871 had remarked on the donkey boys being "lavish with their blows"; but this was because "the equestrians were most un-merciful with their weight".

The guide books always listed caves to visit, although not always the same ones.

Bonsall: a stroll over the hills from Matlock Bath.

Most Matlock caves did not have stalactites or stalagmites. Their beauty came from the minerals and crystals which glistened in the gas light. Visitors also took candles to peer in the nooks and crannies. Some caves had pools of clear water which the visitors were encouraged to drink. Outside were tables of minerals to buy. It was also of course just a thrill to be underground in the dark, unless you agreed with the grumpy American Nathaniel Hawthorne who visited in 1857: "a very dirty, sordid, disagreeable burrow, more like a cellar gone mad than anything else".

On the Heights was the Great Rutland Cavern, the largest in Matlock, which had been the Nestor (or Nestus) lead mine but opened as a show cave c1812. The rock which had been blasted away to make a safe opening now formed a terrace. The guide to the caverns was described as genial but "very deaf". He gave out ancient-looking greasy candles in small sticks, even though the cave was lit by gas. The vast "Roman Hall" was always described as being large enough to shelter 10,000 men, although one wonders about the calculation. The guide pulled a gas chandelier up on a pulley to illuminate the ceiling. There was a pillar with ribs like the trunk of an oak tree and a clear basin called Jacob's well. Visitors dropped coins in the pool from which they were given a glass of water.

Nearby was Great Masson Cavern, opened in 1844, which was "easily traversed" and "the visitor emerges, without retracing his steps, at a height of 700 feet above the river". There were traces of Roman lead workings and huge veins of calcite in the main gas-lit hall. The Greatorex family who owned the cave were also very skilled spar workers.

The Albion refreshment room in Matlock Bath.

There were several other show caves which had usually been old lead mines. The whole hillside of Masson and the meadows behind the railway station were riddled with mine shafts, not safely capped as today. Early guide books write of a few miners and their families still working, providing a quaint glimpse of a disappearing life. One young man from Leicester was lucky to be found alive in 1880 after spending 48 hours without food or drink at the bottom of a hole.

The Royal Cumberland Cave was reached by steps from the top of Clifton Road:

This card was used as an order acknowledgement
by J Greatorex at Harvey Dale quarry.

The entrance to the Fluor Spar Cavern. Card posted 1906.
[Glynn Waite]

there was a wooden pavilion where on could sit and wait for the guide. It was owned by William Smedley who also had a spar shop and ticket office on the turn-pike at the bottom of Clifton Road. Inside the cave were several steps up and down before entering a passage over a hundred yards long with perpendicular sides and a flat roof: "one of the most perfectly marvellous places which can possible be conceived" as it said in Black's 1872 *Tourist's Guide to Derbyshire*. It was the cave which most showed geological movement with huge rocks seemingly tossed about until they balanced their huge weight on small points. The guide lit a magnesium ribbon to make the rocks appear like sleeping giants.

Above the Heights of Jacob was the Fluor Spar Cavern owned by Jacob Raynes, which boasted, "No stooping required". A *Visiting List* in 1872 said the towns-people had sheltered inside the cave in 1745 when Bonnie Prince Charlie's progress to Derby had struck them with terror. Jacob's petrifying well on the Cromford Road had been the one patronised by Princess Victoria on her visit in 1832. She chose a bird's nest to be petrified. Did she ever receive it?

Speedwell Mine was on the bottom corner of what became the Pavilion Gardens and may have still been worked for lead at this time. This cavern did have beautiful white stalactites. Last of all up the hillside was the Devonshire Cavern which was relatively small but did have stalagmites.

The Lovers' Walk, the wooded area over the river with alcoves and rustic seats, had been created in the mid-18th century on land belonging to the Arkwrights and was appreciated for its variety of ferns and wild flowers such as pansies, geraniums and orchids. It was leased to Mrs Walker, whose husband Thomas had been the manager until his death in 1871, but had been in the family since c1758. The Walkers also had boats and a petrifying well across from the ferry. Thomas had taken the Royal Museum from Vallance's, but had no children to inherit the businesses. Mrs Walker was followed by William Ratcliffe and then his mother until her death. Two main zigzag paths had been created up the 200 foot high cliff; one was called Birdcage Walk. The path continued along the top, with viewpoints over Matlock Bath and behind to Starkholmes. One summer house was erected just below "Lover's Leap" at the summit and another one near the river. Where the Willersley Castle grounds were reached was the Cascades: a mossy outfall from a thermal spring. At the beginning of the 1880s, the Walk could only be reached directly by the ferries.

A path led down from the main road behind Briddon's Fishpond stables to the white Ferry House, tea rooms and ticket hut. The ferryman pulled his boat across by a rope (later a wire) strung between trees. The ferry and café were run by another family called Boden, who were grocers and caterers. As well as the ferries, there were several landing stages for pleasure boats. Owners of businesses on the Parades had gardens on the riverside from which they hired a few rowing boats. At this time they also roped off "their" bit of river for 50 or 60 yard stretches, which annoyed the visitors.

A circular ramble to Cromford could be taken which returned via the Lovers' Walk. Until the death of Frederic Arkwright at Willersley Castle in 1923, he was seen as the lord of the manor in Matlock Bath. He owned the Lovers' Walk and High Tor, rights to use the river, and several cottages and farms. His wishes were always respected by the Local Board and the later Urban District Council.

The ferry and Ferry House – note the rope for pulling the boat across. Card posted 1910.

Willersley Castle, the home of the Arkwrights: the grounds were open on certain days.
Card posted 1907.

Mr Arkwight opened the grounds of Willersley Castle to the public on Mondays from May to October: tickets could be obtained in the hotels. A pleasant walk could be taken along the Derby turnpike road, which was perceived then as quite hilly. One walked past the parish church and up towards Walker's Bath Terrace Hotel, and the New Bath, then down to the old Warm Wells toll bar cottage. The road was very narrow here as it passed the Rutland Arms and the old King's Head at the bottom of Wapping. A few of the white-washed cottages still had thatched roofs. Beyond Masson Mill was Glenorchy Chapel and house, before the rock-bound path behind Scarthin Rock to Cromford church and the bridge over the river.

After walking through Willersley Castle grounds, one had to find the gate into the Lovers' Walk. This was kept locked (it can still be clearly seen), so one had to find the gardener, who must have become quite irritated at times. However, if caught in a good mood, he showed visitors the grapes and pineapples in the greenhouses. One visitor described being quite unable to find the gate. He had to disturb the family in their private gardens, from where he was sheepishly escorted back down the private drive by the Arkwight sons. Each November the conservatories were opened so that everyone could admire the chrysanthemums.

On the river below the Castle was a trout hatchery run by Matlock Bath and Cromford Angling Club to supply the local fishing clubs. It was run by a committee with Mr Clark at the Post Office as secretary. Eggs were reared locally or brought from Lathkill Dale and Loch Leven. The fish were fed with minced raw flesh until they reached a length of nine inches, when they were released. Sixteen earthenware and wooden trays were capable of hatching five thousand eggs. Fishing tickets were sold by the Post Office and Hartley's at Matlock Bridge. Belle Vue Hydro gave them out for free.

Matlock Bath and Cromford Angling Club's fish hatchery
in the grounds of Willersley Castle, 1894.

The Darley Dale Fishing Club was founded in 1862 using water between Darley Bridge and Rowsley; this makes it one of the oldest in the country. The Matlock Bath Club was formed in 1884 using the six miles of river down to Whatstandwell. The chairman was Mr Arkwright. In 1887 an article in *The Field* reported that, "the best grayling streams in England are in easy distance of this spa (Matlock Bath)". Members could fish any time, but visitors were restricted to 6am to 9.30pm. The Rutland Arms near Masson Mill advertised fishing from their garden.

Another popular walk took visitors past the railway station and up the path to Starkholmes and Matlock Town where the church could be visited. In 1882 an entrepreneur tried to interest the Local Board in a new road up this path, at his expense, lined with villas and a hydro – this would have spoiled the meadows which still exist between the two settlements.

Starkholmes could also be reached by a steep path from the bottom of Dale Road, after crossing a footbridge near the Boat House Inn. The first wooden footbridge, paid for by public subscription, replaced a ferry in 1872; but this had been washed away by a dreadful flood in February 1881. A replacement iron bridge on stone piers was built by early 1883.

The path led also to the entrance to High Tor grounds. The Tor itself is justly famous for the drama it lends to the scenery between the Matlocks. Many poems have been written and many paintings executed in its praise:

Great wall of adamantine strength!
What time were thou uplifted?
What ages since have run their length?
What generations drifted?

The huge perpendicular limestone face rising from the river is still rated as a hard climb by mountaineers. There were fewer trees then, so the looming rock seemed even more dramatic. Allowing tourists on the summit has always been a risk and there have been casualties. In 1886 Jesse Locke from Dorchester, staying at Matlock House Hydro, fell to her death. The newspaper agreed fences would be unsightly, but wondered about safety ropes.

The cliff top was owned by the Arkwright family who had laid out walks and a carriage drive from Starkholmes to the summit and opened the Fern and Roman caves. Below the cliff top is a path still called Giddy Edge. On the summit was a refreshment room. In 1879 the grounds were leased to the Matlock and High Tor Recreation Company which largely consisted of local business men.

High Tor entrance cost 4d, with the Fern and Roman caves an extra 1d. In poor weather their floors were a "sea of mud, because these were really just fissures left from lead working". Health and safety keeps us out now. When music was played on the Tor summit, for example at Easter, it could be heard all over town.

At the foot was the privately owned High Tor Grotto: "the greatest work of Nature's crystallization in Derbyshire", which stretched 70 yards back into the hill-side. It was reached by a rustic wooden bridge from the 1830s until a flood in 1880, but it was soon replaced. The mineral shop owner specialised in items made from Blue John and prided himself on correctly naming his rock samples. Advertisements mentioned a visit by the ex-Empress Eugenie of the French in 1856, who expressed herself "highly gratified". Visitors in the cave could be startled by the rumble of trains going through the nearby tunnel.

The Albert Hall roller skating rink was built in 1877 for £3,000 on land now occupied by Rockvale Terrace. It advertised "healthy exercise and enjoyment" with

Mr. Leggoe's roller skating rink was off Holme Road, now under Rockvale Terrace and Villas.

facilities for tennis, quoits, skittles, cards and dominoes. (The 1880s was the first boom period for roller skating using equipment manufactured in the USA.) A local councillor called Mr Leggoe bought the business at Christmas 1879. The rink was 122 by 52 feet, a space which could also seat 600 diners, many more than in Mr Boden's restaurant. A modern kitchen was equipped with gas cookers. There were staff bedrooms above, reached by a ladder, and a dancing platform to the side with a canvas roof and a grand view over the railway station.

In 1880 Mr Leggoe applied for a licence to sell beer to his diners, promising to stop dancing and close at 9pm. One opposer had objected to any dancing because of the evils which arise from dance halls, which he condemned as "plague spots". Also, the rink was on the hillside among the houses of gentry. Mr Leggoe then tried to claim the dancing platform was really for Sunday School teas! The licence was refused.

However, dancing classes were soon resumed, and the "gentry" were perhaps disturbed by the occasional brass band. In 1881 the Reverend Nicholson of Bridge House Hydro gave a series of religious services at the rink. He showed "dissolving views" of the Prodigal Son and the miracles using powerful limelight magic

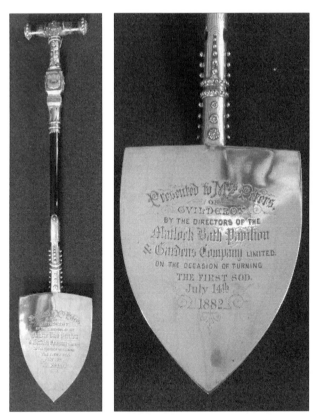

The ebony spade, inlaid with gold and silver, used by Mrs Peters to turn the first sod in Matlock Bath Pavilion grounds, July 1882.

THE
PAVILION

Which is situated in its own

GARDENS

Include the Romantic Rocks, Dungeon Tors,
Terrace, Pagoda, Pulpit Rock, Lakes,
Harbours, Tennis Courts, and many
miles of circuitous Walks.

Open Daily from 9 a.m. to sunset.

From their elevated position a grand view of
Matlock and the surrounding objects
of interest can be obtained.

TENNIS!   CAVERNS!!

VISITORS SHOULD SEE THE

Speedwell Stalactite Cavern,

*Which contains fine specimens of
Crystals, Dog-Tooth, Fluor Spar, Stalactites,
Stalagmites, &c.*

Admission 3d. each.

lanterns.

In October 1881 the Matlock Bath Improvement Association had a meeting with local tradesmen. They decided to launch a company to buy the hillside area called the Romantic Rocks behind the Royal Hotel, which was for sale for £3000. Twelve men guaranteed £1,100 and the rest was to be raised by issuing 12,000 shares at £1 each. Thus was created the Matlock Bath Pavilion and Gardens Company. Mr Charles Peters who lived at Gilderoy was the Chairman.

In July 1882 they held the first ceremony to launch the Pavilion. Mrs Peters turned the first sod with an ebony spade inlaid with gold and silver. She also used a small wheelbarrow to carry the earth a short distance. The next ceremony in May 1883 brought the Mayor of Derby, Sir Abraham Woodiwiss, on a special train with the Mayor of Nottingham in support. Sir Abraham laid the foundation stone with a silver trowel. (He was a shareholder and director of the Company, but sadly he died a few months before the opening.) For the next year, residents and visitors alike could watch the stone and glass edifice rise behind the Royal Hotel – surely as spectacular as any hall in a French or German spa?

The Pavilion was opened on 6 August 1884 by Lord Edward Cavendish MP. They had hoped for the Prince of Wales, so Lord Edward had to keep apologising for not being him. Messages went astray between the party inside and the local militia outside, so the vicar's blessing was drowned by gunshots. The guests lunched in a marquee in the grounds of the New Bath.

The Pavilion grounds covered an area of 16 acres which the gardener, Mr Speed [7]

---

7. Edward Speed came from a family of famous gardeners born in Cambridgeshire. He became the Matlock Bath surveyor until 1890. In the 1891 census he was the licensee at the Old Vine Vaults on Derwent Parade. His brother, Thomas, was the Head Gardener at Chatsworth, but he committed suicide in 1883. Their cousin, Walter, was the Head Gardener at Penrhyn Castle in Wales.

of Cambridge, had transformed in twelve months from a bare hillside on which half a dozen unsightly cottages had been demolished. There were two entrances with turnstiles, one from Clifton Road, with a gravelled carriage drive, and the other from Temple Road. Visitors entered through pillared gates to pay their 6d admission at an Italian-style ticket office. Reserved seats inside the building were 6d extra.

Winding paths (said to be three miles in total) snaked back and forth to the Victoria Cavern and the old Romantic Rocks or Dungeon Tors, transformed with newly planted honeysuckle, roses, ivy, and British ferns. *Bulmer's History & Directory of Derbyshire* in 1895 described the scene:

> *At a considerable height above the Pavilion is the entrance to the Speedwell Cavern, and a little below this the limestone cliff has been rent by some mighty convulsion of nature, and huge fragments of rock stand in an upright position. The space between the detached cliffs and the parent rock is little more than sufficient to permit visitors to pass in single file. The rocks rise to a great height and shroud the narrow passage in so deep a gloom that our forefathers appropriately named them the Dungeon Tors.*

The Victoria Cavern was rich in deposits of fluorspar which sparkled in the gas light. There were seats along the path inside and at the farthest point visitors could hear a subterranean spring. However, this cave did not stay open for long. In other parts of the grounds rustic grottos and summer houses had been constructed, water had been trapped in ornamental lily pools, and two tennis courts were ready for

An advertisement in the Matlock Visiting List, 1884.

play. Everywhere were parterres of bright flowers. On one festive occasion the rocks were lit with five thousand crystal lamps and 700 Japanese lanterns – how many men did it take to light them?

The building itself cost £8,000 and was designed by John Nuttall of Matlock. It aimed to be indispensable to winter visitors as it could shelter up to two thousand people. It contained a concert hall with a lantern roof to seat 800; there were also a reading room, cloakrooms and kitchens. Promenades to the north and south opened on to the three terraces, each 100 yards long with impressive flights of steps up to the main building. The middle terrace had shady alcoves and the top terrace had a stone balustrade from which to admire the view.

The first event was the Matlock Bath Horticultural Society flower show. The Coldstream Guards Band was booked, but they became diverted to a large military funeral; they did turn up at a later date.

The first musical director was a Mr Kent, a gold medallist (they never said for what in these descriptions); but he was soon replaced by the more suitable-sounding Otto Bernhardt, who stayed several years. In the season there were three or four performances a day: perhaps a military band in the afternoon, a piano recital at tea-time, a band in the early evening and an instrumental concert from 7.30pm. Bernhardt's was a twelve-man orchestra and all his musicians were capable of performing solos. Their salaries compared well with the band at Buxton pavilion, which was one reason why the business never made a profit. Local bands also played, but most popular were the famous military bands. People were allowed to dance to the music at no extra charge.

Well-known musicians were patronised by house-parties brought by the Arkwights, but the *Visiting List* often bemoaned the small audiences for a prestigious performer. In September 1885 Charles Halle gave a piano recital, and the Midland Railway obliged with a special train from Derby. By 1889 this had become Sir Charles and Lady Halle's "annual concert". She was a famous violinist called Madame Norman-Neruda. On the last concert of the season in 1885 the orchestra played Haydn's *Farewell Symphony* while the 2000 guests "including gentry" watched rockets and coloured fire light up the gardens. In the 1888 season, Mr Hilton's band took over the residency.

One local musician who performed at the Pavilion was Walter Evelyn Timmins, already noted at the New Bath Hotel and Smedley's Hydro. He was born in Derby in 1868 and went on to teach the violin at Manchester School of Music, as well as conduct orchestras. His descendants have a memo saying he would be paid three guineas for two concerts in Matlock in 1890. A review for a concert at the Pavilion described him being greeted with rounds of applause and praising "his broad tone, graceful bowing and phrasing". He played Sarasate's *Fantasy on Faust* "with great fire and brilliancy".

In January 1889 the Pavilion Company was wound up and bought by a Mr Williams from Birkenhead for £9,000. No dividend had ever been paid, because the cost of the entertainments was never covered by the revenue. At the end of the decade, the entertainment became more varied with pantomimes and variety acts such as Oscar Leroy, King of the Slack Wire, and Joseph Darby, Champion Jumper of the World – he really was! One of his tricks was jumping over a hansom cab. (His memorial statue is in Netherton, Dudley.) The Edison Phonograph was introduced on the stage in 1890 – the first death knell for live music, although then hailed as "the latest wonder of the age".

Refreshments were supplied by John Boden, the confectioner on South Parade. Nobody was allowed to use their ticket for re-entry, so anyone slipping out for a drink had to pay again. Because the building was a fair way from the public houses, the management applied for a beer and wine licence every year; it was always refused, in spite of the claim they averaged 800 visitors a day. This was a shame because the roads down into the village were treacherous: several people rushing down the hill from the Pavilion to bars or to the station injured their ankles.

This Old Bath Hill actually became the subject of a farcical dispute between an absentee land-owner called Mr Sellors and the Local Board. The landowner had erected a large post between the turnpike and Temple Road to prevent carriages using what he claimed was a private path. In December 1887 the town was woken by an enormous explosion and many thought the gas works had blown up. In fact someone had tried to dynamite the post, but unsuccessfully. A few months later, the stump appeared dressed as a man hanging from a tree on South Parade.

> *Never dare to obstruct a road or stand in people's way*
> *For folk will go where they have the right, no matter what you say.*
> *I stood it long to suit my friends – I thought them in the right.*
> *What a fool I was I did not go when they used the dynamite.*

The following March, Mr Sellors employed two men to defy Mr Speed (the Local Board surveyor) by erecting two steel pillars set in deep concrete, while he looked on helpless.

In 1887 the town decided to mark the Queen's Jubilee with a bridge and gardens on the riverside from opposite the Fountain Baths to the Midland Hotel. This meant visitors no longer had to use the ferry to access the Lovers' Walk. On the paths themselves, the trees were thinned out and rocks exposed. The promenade gardens,

The Jubilee Bridge repainted, 2014.

designed by Mr Speed, replaced a very narrow older footpath by the river and some neglected vegetable gardens, with an ugly fence. They transformed what had been an "untidy and slovenly frontage" for a stretch four hundred yards long and 16 feet wide. Turf was laid and flower beds planted. The area was enclosed by a light iron railing on a dwarf ashlar wall and the river side was properly walled off. The improvement also meant visitors had somewhere to sit. There had been many previous complaints about the dearth of public benches.

The bridge was made in the Butterley Iron-works, Ripley. The outer face of the girders was painted a warm stone colour, the inner sides were a bluey grey. The scrollwork was picked out in a deep chocolate brown with golden yellow finials. The girders were bolted on the south side, but free to move on the north side to allow for expansion in hot weather.

Sadly, none of the above was actually ready for the Jubilee in June. The work was paid for by public subscriptions amounting to £500, although the committee in charge ended up paying more than their fair share. In 1888 the gardens and bridge were handed over to the Local Board at a dinner – free of debt. Unfortunately no-one seemed to have expected the high legal fees incurred by the transfer; the Board bad-temperedly agreed to pay them.

Just in time for the twenty-five excursion trains which came on Good Friday 1889, a switchback railway was erected on part of Orchard Holme by a Mr Bratby of Derby, costing him £400. This was in the area now containing the public gardens, and stretching along below the road past the church. The railway was a gravity driven roller-coaster with humps which gradually decreased in height to keep the momentum going. It was built on a wooden framework about 140 yards long. Ten passengers in each car were shoved off, to be caught at the other end, where they were dragged over the last hump and pushed back on a second track. The church goers and local residents must have loved the screaming and rattling. A letter that October called it an abominable eyesore "covered all over with hideous flaring advertisements, rivalling the custom in vogue with our American cousins".

The switchbank's advertisement claimed that a Dr Cullimore advocated the ride for liver sufferers, but half a dozen rides were needed for the full effect. From 1890 the business was run by the Buxton family, who also owned the Royal Museum. It is often said that they carried their takings home in a wheelbarrow on Bank Holidays – perhaps they did need a barrow for the weight of pennies from the turnstile and slot machines. While the Council was embroiled in all their improvement schemes described in the 1900s, the Buxtons quietly developed the rest of the site with landscaped gardens, thermal fishponds, a café and a petrifying well.

Apart from the narrow dusty roads through Matlock Bath, visitors had to contend with smells and noises. Everyone was subjected to an obnoxious smell every four days when the purifiers at the gas works were cleansed. There were many earth closets as described earlier. Although these must have been emptied regularly, there were perhaps whiffs in hot weather. The quarries were a constant source of bangs and scrapings, apart from the rumbling wagons which carted the stone away.

The ferry lands were a rather muddy area, also the site of a disputed lead mine. They led on to Orchard Holme. As well as the land taken up by the switchback railway, part of the site was used by the Local Board as a tip until the late 1890s, although they did not own it – they were criticised in 1885 for not spreading the rubbish out evenly. Guests at the Royal then complained about smells and the Board promised to burn more rubbish, but did this really help? Tips were mainly a

A view down the river from the ferry in Matlock Bath in 1894.

The Ferry dining rooms and grounds in the 1890s, showing the rough area used as a Local Board tip and disputed by lead miners.
[Peak District Lead Mining Museum]

nuisance because they attracted rats. (This was still a problem in the Matlocks until the 1930s.) In 1890 one irate merchant in Bakewell had ordered a hamper by train, but it was left in the station overnight. Rats had "spoilt a cream cheese and half devoured a rabbit", but he received no compensation.

A letter written in praise of the Promenade, and a new garden wall at the Devonshire Hotel, described how the town then became "a compound of stables, workshops and dog kennels". There was indeed a very large stable on the site of the present-day Pavilion, which belonged to the Briddons. It had been the stabling for the Old Bath Hotel. The pond in front was much larger than now and used to water the horses and clean the vehicles. They had a fleet of cabs, but this was chiefly where one hired a carriage for outings. Mr Briddon was in trouble in 1884 for his barking dogs. More livery stables were to be found up Clifton Road at Portland House Mews, owned by a John Wildgoose. He cunningly licensed his wagonettes under the Stage Coach Act to avoid cab licence fees. However, he became bankrupt; Mr Leggoe took the business and he was criticised for leaving manure on the road. Most hotels had their own accommodation for visitors' horses and carriages, as well as their own vehicle to collect guests from the station. Hodgkinson's Hotel's stables across the road by the Devonshire were also a collection point for the town's manure.

Briddon's stables and the horse pond (later fishpond).
Note the large urn in the spar shop window.
[Glynn Waite]

The subject of travel between Matlock Bath and Bridge by "public" transport for those who could not walk or wait for a train could have filled a book by itself, albeit a very boring one. The various cab and omnibus companies vied for licences and vexed the Local Boards and later District Councils with their antics. In 1879 a "Matlock Omnibus Company" advertised horse buses between Matlock Bath station and the Horse Shoe Inn on Matlock Green each way every hour for 2d outside and 3d in, but such companies were started and wound up with regularity. Timetables did not really exist: one just had to wait and hope a vehicle turned up.

The Dale itself, between the Bath and Bridge, contained the little settlement called Artists' Corner, where painters set up their easels to sketch High Tor. It was described in the 1870s as consisting of "picturesque villas and cottages of gentility". There was a tearoom from which visitors could take trays to sit by the river. Between the Corner and Matlock Bath, the house known as Tor Cottage (now the High Tor Hotel) was very prominent on every postcard. It was built in 1829 and was nothing to do with Admiral Collingwood as is often claimed.

In 1889 alarm bells were rung when the land by the river was marked out into building lots by the County Council. Mr Peters of Gilderoy called a public meeting to form a committee and raise a subscription to buy the land, which was ultimately successful. Houses would have ruined any views across the river. The many schemes subsequently put forward to make a promenade between the two Matlocks all came to nothing; Matlock Bath Local Board was even accused of using the land as a rubbish tip. Now we have a car park.

However, in 1897 the Dale was enhanced by the small chapel built on the hillside

The postcard sent by the author's grandfather to his intended fiancée in August 1908.
He has written "Weather gloriously fine".

dedicated to St John the Baptist. (My grandfather sent my grandmother a postcard of it in 1908 at the beginning of his campaign to get married.) The architect was Sir Guy Dawber; he also designed the arts and crafts cottages at the bottom of St John's Road.

The Dale area was never one of unadulterated scenery. There were small quarries, the paint works and Whittaker's soft drinks factory at the Matlock Bath end and large quarries such as Harvey Dale, which are still very visible at the Bridge end. On the roadside near to the bridge to High Tor was a smelly tar-boiling house and a fume-filled lime kiln. Many visitors in the 1870s had remarked on the pleasant resinous odour from a stand of pine trees between Artists' Corner and the Boat House: the tar probably put paid to that!

MATLOCK BRIDGE AND BANK

The 1880s was a decade of great expansion on the Bank, although postcards and maps still showed large areas of fields close to the town centre. Many of our houses were built in this era: solid gritstone homes at a rate of thirty to forty a year. This expansion of the Bank, as opposed to the housing stagnation at the Bath – even a decline in the population – was a matter for envy. Matlock Bridge Local Board was gaining plenty of money from increasing rate revenue.

Before the hydros were built, the few shops were by the bridge or at the hamlets on the Green and up in the Town. A map of 1879 shows very few buildings to the south on Dale Road or east of Crown Square – those shown were old and dis-reputable, such as a smithy at Park Head. A tremendous spurt of building between 1880 and the First World War brought most of the shops we use today along Smedley Street, down Bank Road, around Crown Square and especially down Dale Road. Most were substantial two or three-storey gritstone-faced buildings with living accommodation for the shopkeeper above. Many still have date stones and

A Matlock Bank view when hydros and churches dominated the scene.
[Jean Douglas]

initials, such as the 1889 Crown Building, now Costa Coffee. (The initials "TS" either side of the door remain a mystery.)

The shops were quite diverse because they supplied the local people and the visitor. The visitors wanted gifts, new clothes, toiletries, flowers, photographs, medicines, hairdressing, books, stationery and the necessities to continue treatments at home. Adjacent to Smedley's was the shop of W Handford, a tinman and brazier. As well as manufacturing baths he could supply chili paste and mustard bran. In 1870 Michael Wright opened his shop to sell baths and other hydropathic equipment as well as trunks, hat boxes and portmanteaux. In 1888 he applied for a patent for a combined douche and commode. Many of us remember the shop as Tinker Wright's, but this has now become apartments, called Tinker's Place. One tiled

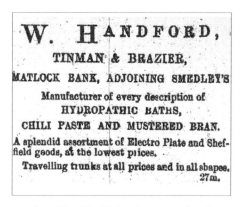

Mr. Handford's business pre-dated
Michael "Tinker" Wright's shop.

doorstep remains with the shop name.

A few framework knitters remained on the Bank who managed to thrive with new custom from the hydros. J W Potter's hosiery works on the Dimple, where there are still industrial units, supplied his shops at Buxton House on Dale Road and in Buxton itself. His advertisements were prominent in the newspapers because the writing always went in the opposite direction to all the other text. William Crowder on Wellington Street specialised in very fine stockings and underwear. He sold straight from the factory where he welcomed visitors to see his old frames working. Guests at the hydros could order an item to be made and delivered during their stay. Smedley's Hydro had a shop just inside the front door where fine woollen goods could be purchased, along with home-hydro equipment.

One of the earliest buildings still prominent on Dale Road (in 2015 Fat Boys and the Conservative Club) was the Market Hall which opened in May 1868, built in "Continental Gothic" style by a company of local investors. Inside were twelve lock-up units with glass fronts and two rows of open bench stalls down the centre. In 1881 they tried to get a kind of farmers' market established here on Thursday after-noons for butter, eggs and poultry. Several of the lock-ups called themselves "bazaars" selling all manner of cheap items.

Above the shops was an assembly room for dancing and concerts which could seat 500 people. In September 1868 a famous music hall performer called Arthur Lloyd came and they managed to cram in an extra one hundred people. The room was also used as the JPs' courtroom and the Local Board's offices were in the building. The enterprise, which included rebuilding the old Queen's Head Hotel, never paid out a dividend; it was sold in 1884 to Alderman Smith of Derby as a going concern for £4350. By 1890 a circulating library with over 1000 books was also established here. At the end of the decade there were complaints that the assembly room was very cold in winter, for example when the famous musical hall artist Harry Liston performed his *"Football Muff"* one February night in 1891. Later the room was used as the drill hall.

Harry Liston.

Next to the Market Hall was the Beehive Stores run by W Surtees Lugg, followed by Mr Treadgold. They advertised hydropathic bathing mustard, scotch oatmeal, and Egyptian split lentils "as used in hydropathy, zordone etc." – what was that? Treatment at a dentist's surgery down Dale Road called Richardson & Glover was free for Smedley's patients every Monday between 1pm and 5pm.

Opposite the Market Hall was Else's stationers, a branch of a chain of grocers called Marsden's, a Bank, and a famous gown and hat shop in Derwent House. This had been owned by Thomas Walters, but it survived into living memory as Henry Marsden's. They had a good stock of fashions, but were best known for their staff of at least twenty seamstresses and milliners who could make anything the visitors and locals desired, including mourning dress. Bolts of cloth were carried up to the hydros for ladies to make their selections. (This rather plain building is now Matlock Antiques Centre.) The room at the back overlooking the river is where the hats were made. The last two shops before the Bridge were Henry Barnwell's, a watchmaker and jeweller, and Asbury's dispensing chemist, used by Dr Hunter who apparently did occasionally resort to drugs. Asbury's windows displayed huge glass jars filled with red, blue and green coloured water. The Post Office was in the building now occupied by Fleur.

Across Matlock Bridge was William Robey a hairdresser and perfumer who claimed to be by appointment to HRH Duchess of Cambridge and HSH Duchess of Teck. His shop was probably taken over by William Phillips who had originally set up in Matlock Bath. In one of the three shops at Park Head, Mr Phillips boasted clean water and new soap for each customer. Hair brushing was done "by

Inside Marsden's drapery, now Matlock Antiques Centre.

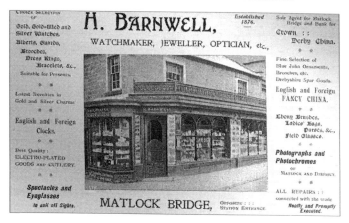

This shop was on the site of the HSBC bank on Dale Road.

machinery". He also sold newspapers and cigars to his gentlemen. He soon opened a hairdressing salon in Smedley's basement where ladies could have *"coiffures a la Romaine"* in 1892. Lady customers to his shop on Crown Square were assured of a large stock of human hair for their extensions. They could then cover these up with a visit to Peter Holmes drapers and milliners across the road in the Crown Buildings.

Next to Phillips hairdressers was another outfitter called Castle and Hurd, then by the bridge was Robert Orme's grocers and wine shop. Behind these shops was

A very rare view of the shops at Park Head: a newspaper office, Phillips the hairdresser, Castle & Hurd drapers and Orme's grocers. To the left are untidy hoardings –
a perennial eyesore in the Matlocks.
[Glynn Waite]

an unsightly smithy which may have been there since the seventeenth century. There was also an ugly advertisement hoarding. Across the road on the river's edge was Kirkham's at "Ye Sign of Ye Luckie Shoe" which sold any footwear from dress shoes to walking boots. They had many shoe lasts stored in the basement so that they could manufacture shoes to order for frequent customers. To their right was yet another drapers called Hilton, but the biggest shop on this row was H G Hartley's which occupied two floors of the large double-fronted premises now housing PeliDeli and Sellors jewellers. Mr Hartley sold everything made of leather, including large trunks and portmanteaux. He also branched out into sporting gear, becoming famous for fishing equipment, tennis rackets and bicycle spares.

Round the corner from Hartley's was William Pride's fish, game and fruit shop, able to cater for the best dinner parties. His suppliers sent fish daily from the ports and rivers: oysters, lobster, turbot and salmon. Pheasants, quail, snipe and partridges, geese and ducks all arrived in their proper season. As well as British fruit, oranges, pineapples and grapes were imported for the dessert courses. He also

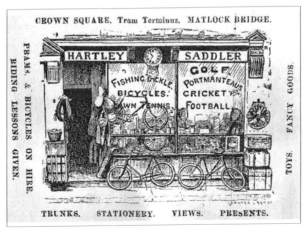

One side of Mr. Hartley's double-fronted shop.

The top of Lumsdale had good footpaths.

had a shop on Smedley Street. After William died in 1921, his wife Harriet carried on with her nephew, who eventually changed the shop's name to Arthur M Tookey. It was said Mrs Pride would "split a raisin" to make the scales balance, so customers looked in to see if a more generous assistant was serving.

When John Smedley joined Ralph Davis on the Bank, Smedley Street was called Broome Head Lane. It was a narrow rutted thoroughfare with grass growing down the middle. It took until the 1890s to straighten the street and provide pavements because of problems with the property owners who had pig-sties and other out-buildings jutting into the roadway. In 1887, for example, the surveyor removed several old cottages on Smedley Street and a barn and urinal by the Crab Tree Inn "which was a great obstruction and nuisance". In 1890 Wellington Street was also being widened to 30 feet.

As Smedley Street West was widened and new shops were built, Job Smith, the owner of Malvern House Hydro and a local councillor, wanted to plant a boulevard of lime trees, but he had to content himself with planting trees here and there on the Bank. (At a later date, he did get his row of limes on Lime Grove Walk.)

In the early days of the 1880s there were still open wells on Smedley Street, Jackson Road (where a child had drowned in 1882) and Rutland Street. People were advised not to drink the water, but they used it to wash clothes.

There had been a previous co-op store where All Saints Church hall now stands; but in May 1891 the Co-operative Society started building their new shops and offices opposite Malvern House, replacing some old thatched cottages. The three shops sold drapery, groceries and shoes, while above was an assembly room which could hold three hundred people. (This building has all been taken over by the County Council.)

The Wishing Stone at the top of Lumsdale.

On the corner of Rutland Street by Smedley's laundry block, a Mr Houseley built the Central Buildings in 1890 with shops below and a social club upstairs. At the far end of Smedley Street East, on the corner with Chesterfield Road, the Cavendish boys' boarding school was built at the same time. The boys put on several concerts for the town over the years. (This building has been incorporated into a block of flats.)

Apart from the hydro buildings, the other large buildings appearing on the Bank in this decade were churches. There was already the Congregational Church on Chesterfield Road whose spire was prominent on many old postcards. It was demolished after a fire in 1969, leaving the Sunday school on the corner of Smedley Street as the place of worship. On Bank Road were the buildings of the old Primitive Methodist Church and Sunday school, built in 1865 and 1878 respectively. Lower down Bank Road in 1883 the Roman Catholic Church opened, and in 1884 Matlock Wesleyan Church was consecrated; this later became the Methodist and United Reform Church. In 1882 the foundation stone was laid for All Saints Church, which took two years to build. The sharp increase in population on the Bank and the needs of hydro visitors had made another Anglican church necessary.

There was very little building between Crown Square and Matlock Green. The cricket pitch was where the football ground is now and football was played on a field which is now part of Hall Leys Park. Causeway Lane was just that – a banked road trying to keep traffic above the frequent floods, with a deep dyke on one side. It was built to bear the weight of stone drugs coming to the station from the quarries in Tansley, but it was dangerous for cabs. The Else family of auctioneers lived at The Firs (now the Library). At the bottom of Steep Turnpike was the toll house with a bricked up window, which can still be seen on Harley House. There was a stand of beech trees on the land now taken up by Iceland and the bottom of Firs Parade.

There were two hospitals on the Bank, catering for the poorer classes and for patients who were actually ill – not always the case at the hydros. Walking up Bank

Road from the Bridge, visitors passed the Smedley Memorial (Hydro) Hospital on the right (later the Youth Hostel and now apartments). (Until 1882 this had been South View Hydro with a James Hawley as manager.) Dr Hunter was the consulting doctor and Mrs Smedley kept an eye on everything. There were 24 bed-rooms for 30 patients. It had been hoped to supply a free service, but annual subscriptions of £1 admitted one patient, and £10 meant they could stay there for life. Each patient then had to find ten shillings a week for board and lodging. There were no children under five years old, nor patients with severe infectious diseases or advanced consumption. There were many fundraising events for equipment such as invalid chairs. When Dr Hunter died in 1894 a new wing was built, which still bears a plaque to commemorate him: "Hunter Wing 1897".

Caroline Smedley visited every day to assess the patients, so she could be seen entering the building from her carriage. From her serious religious convictions, one would have expected her to be soberly dressed, but she believed in cheering people up by her appearance and manner.

> To this end, she nearly always appeared in a bright blue silk gown, a white lace shawl thrown over her shoulders, and a white front, with frills, and a flower therein. Her hair which was auburn, was done quite plain, and parted in the centre. Both hands were well covered with valuable rings, and her countenance was ever lit up by a cheerful and happy smile. Her consulting room was a sort of floral bower ...

She wore a fashionable crinoline hoop to render her dress cool in hot weather. Any visitor who struck up an acquaintance with Mrs Smedley might be invited to take tea at Riber Castle:

> You proceed by handsome corridors to the grand saloon, which is entered by a broad staircase. This noble room is about 35 yards long and ten yards wide. The staircases at each end lead to a wide gallery running all round, from which drawing rooms, bed-rooms, and dressing rooms are entered. The seating of the salon is arranged down each side, and divided into open boxes, each of which will accommodate some twelve persons. At one end are finely painted oil portraits [8] of Mr and Mrs Smedley. There is much coloured ornamentation of a somewhat Moorish style, and statuary, vases, mirrors, choice paintings and other works of art abound. The floor is covered with rich carpets. There is an organ, a grand piano and a bagatelle board. The lighting is chiefly from the roof and partially comes through pretty stained glass.

The other hospital on the Bank was the Derby and Derbyshire Convalescent Hospital, which opened in 1889 in the old Lime Tree View guest house. This establishment also depended on charity. For the payment of fifteen guineas, a subscriber could recommend a patient for up to three weeks treatment. The patient paid five shillings a week for board. The wards were named after benefactors such as Lady Cavendish. Visitors who expected a severe utilitarian building found a

---

8. These portraits were presumably the ones which were later hung either side of the doors in Smedley's Hydro drawing room.

Wombwell's Menagerie in Bateman's Park – in 1888 their visit resulted in the headline
"Man attacked by bear in Matlock".

[Glynn Waite]

moss-covered house with climbing roses, French windows with light curtains blowing in the breeze, shady gardens and lovely views.

There were events in the town which could be enjoyed by locals and visitors alike. Wakes Week in September involved athletics and cycling races on the cricket ground, a boat regatta, swimming races, bonfires on the hills and a firework display. From 1875 the Week had concluded with a brass band contest which was held in a field near the railway station, but from 1882 they used the grounds of the Old English Hotel. The bands played for £40 in prizes, including a silver cornet.

In 1880 the winner of this cornet, worth fourteen guineas for a solo performance, had to take the organisers to court. Two men had entered, but one heard the opposition playing a solo in the band contest. He promptly withdrew to avoid "making a fool of myself". The officials said a man could not win if he was the only competitor. The court disagreed – he had paid his entrance fee and performed: it was not his fault he was alone. The following year there were protests that the winning band contained a professional, so their prize was withheld pending an investigation. The organisers eventually decided to limit the entries to Derbyshire bands, to keep out these "crack" bands and musicians from Yorkshire and Lancashire. In 1885 there were seven bands from Chesterfield, Derby, and Birchover.

In 1888, there was the famous headline – "Man attacked by bear at Matlock". The stretch of land known as Bateman's park was named after the licensee at the Railway Hotel. It was across the road from the public house where the bus station

106

and supermarket now stand. Many fairs and circuses spent a day or two here. The headline told of a bear from Wombwell's Menagerie grasping hold of a trainer's hand. Cattle markets were held at Matlock Green, where the Red Lion public house served hot dinners from 12 to 2pm on market days.

THE DAY TRIPPER

When the springing year renews its pride,
And Special Trains commence at Eastertide,
The railway like a torrent pours its floods,
Into our valleys and among our woods;
And daily almost in the Summertime,
This scene continues till the Autumn prime;
And so throughout the varied circling year,
Thousands of visitors on the scene appear.

J Buckley, 1868

It seems part of the whole "duty of man" to do two things on Good Friday – to eat Hot Cross Buns and to go to Matlock".

The Visiting List, 1895.

Day trippers in Matlock Bath.
[Picture the Past]

At Bank Holidays the day trippers were used to coming to Matlock Bath in their tens of thousands. Between twenty and thirty special excursion trains from the surrounding cities drew up at the extra-long platform and disgorged their excited passengers – but the station could not shelter them when it rained. The exposed down platform was over two hundred yards long and the up 288 yards: twice the lengths at Matlock Bridge. On Good Friday 1890, thirty trains called "heavies" with over 800 hundred passengers each contributed to the estimated 30,000 visitors. One compartment from Birmingham contained nineteen passengers "packed like herrings". Sixteen trains ordered for Easter Monday were not enough – nine more were commandeered. Some people did not arrive until 4.30pm. A great mixture of accents would be heard, but many looked up at the hills and said, "'Ay, but that's grand".

Extra staff were brought from other Midland stations to assist Mr Richardson; in 1886 he was sent sixteen men. At home time there was a mad scramble. Men would grab the doors as the train came in so that they could "bag" a carriage for their party: this led to some nasty accidents. The trains did not necessarily come back in the expected order and the platforms could be full of the "wrong" people. The crowds had to be controlled by shouting through megaphones.

As soon as the trippers came out of the station, they were confronted by touts from the caverns and restaurants, who shouted at and intimidated the new arrivals. This was a real problem which the Local Board asked the police to deal with several times. They even employed a detective to track the worst offenders.

These boards greeted visitors arriving by train. Mr. Leggoe's skating rink can be seen as the long low buildings on the hillside. Behind is Clarence House Hydro.
[Peak District Lead Mining Museum]

For many restaurants and inns the weather at the Bank Holidays was a serious lottery which could mean success or failure in any one year. Cold and rain, strikes in the mills, coal shortages on the railways, exhibitions in London or other cities, deaths of monarchs, smallpox: all these things could spell disaster. But on a good day even the "cottagers threw open their doors" to provide refreshments. Families on low budgets brought their own sandwiches and ate them on the grass in front of the railway station.

Many itinerant traders arrived for the day from nearby cities. They were a mixed blessing because they could take trade from shops who had to pay rates. Many excursionists came for "street fun". The pavements were crowded with music hall artists who sang popular songs for the public to join in the chorus. Shows with "hanimated figgers" displayed wax models of famous murderers. One German brass band which visited in 1881 was described as "mostly women" and "horribly out of tune". In 1889 were reports of a steam roundabout, "land sailors" and shooting galleries.

A day-tripper to Matlock Bath on Good Friday 1886 wrote a colourful description in the *Visiting List*. He spoke of the usual immense numbers brought by twenty two special trains from Liverpool, Stockport, Manchester (3 trains), Leicester, Keighley, Birmingham, Sheffield (2 trains), Rotherham, Nottingham (2 trains), and Derby (4 trains). The Nottingham lace makers, distinguished by their dressiness, contrasted with the drawling accents and strong physique of the Manchester mill hands, "loose for the day from their 5-storey cotton spinning cages".

Mingling with the crowds were hawkers from Belper and Nottingham selling Grantham gingerbread from capacious baskets, lemon drop dealers, watch sellers from Birmingham, and fortune tellers from Italy whose dark complexion could wash off in wet weather. Great lady Samsons "in slack tights" provided a show near the Fishpond, grinding out waltzes by turning a handle on their hurdy gurdy. A man came with a monkey playing the cymbals, Spaniards brought love birds, children sold bunches of violets.

Some excursionists walked to Matlock Bridge where Sangers circus had set up on Bateman's park opposite the Railway Hotel, advertising the show with huge banners on every cliff top. Sangers had been before, in 1882. They featured a troop of elephants which had recently performed in Berlin for the German Emperor. Herr Hoffmann had brought his trained horse, Conway Seymour, named after a soldier in the Seven Years War. In 1887 Sangers were in the grounds of the Old English Hotel from where they paraded a cavalcade of 200 horses into the town.

Five thousand people paid to enter the Pavilion where Belper Band was playing for dancing. The ferry to the Lovers' Walk was manned by a "Falstaff-like individual". Several people fell in the river. The boats were full, the hotels were full and the tea rooms were full. Crowds of heads could be seen looking over the balcony of the tower on the Heights of Abraham.

There were not many reports in the 1880s of big factory outings to the Matlocks, but in 1882 three hundred came from W Walker & Sons, sand crushers from King's Lynn, to dine at the Albert Heights rink. In 1883 the Jacoby lace manufacturers (of Nottingham, Paris and Germany) brought 550 to eat at the Old English, in a tent in the garden. The meal was a celebration of the factory owner's wedding. A month later 750 iron workers came to the Bath from Russell & Co in Walsall.

On the Spring Bank Holiday in 1888 twenty thousand visitors came, but none from Sheffield where there was a smallpox epidemic. (The servants at Chatsworth were vaccinated in case visitors were infected.) Residents with long memories may have recalled three and half thousand men and their wives coming from John Brown & Co (Atlas Works) in Sheffield in 1863. Several men became drunk and the few police handled the situation badly. A fight ended with 400 men and five police-men injured. Thankfully in the 1880s the Local Boards were usually able to congratulate themselves and the police on a job well done.

Every Bank Holiday a handful of boaters ended their day at the gas works, having their clothes dried. There were sadly several fatal boating disasters involving trippers and locals alike. These were often in full view of the crowds. The newspapers were always calling for people to learn to swim or even for the lifebelts to be better positioned. There were life-saving demonstrations at the Fountain Baths. But often the trippers brought disaster on themselves by ignoring the warning signs before the Masson weir and even ending up going round the water wheel at the Mill. Bodies were generally laid out on the billiard table at the nearest hotel.

One such sad incident occurred in June 1888. A local couple were drowned in only four foot of water in front of a large crowd by the Boat House Hotel. However, one young lady angler was very indignant when some gentlemen tried to be gallant and save her. Two careless young men had accidently set her boat adrift. She calmly jumped out and floated on her back to the shore. She was a good swimmer and had not wanted rescuing.

As described in previous paragraphs, the citizens of Matlock Bath had made a collective effort in the 1880s to provide more for the visitor, with the Promenade and the Pavilion, and easier access to the Lovers' Walk. The Heights of Abraham, High Tor and the caverns were always popular. Mr Buxton, described at Whitsuntide 1890 as "the proprietor of the gigantic toy, the switchback railway" on which one could "feel all the sensations of sea-sickness for a penny" was turning his domain into the attractive Derwent Gardens. Things were definitely looking up for those who appreciated the day tripper and his spending power.

In June 1889 a young woman – who had been really cheerful and energetic all day – gave birth in the station waiting room. Mr Richardson said he was delighted.

FURTHER AFIELD

I was bound like a child by some magical story,
Forgetting the South and Ionian vales
And felt that dear England had temples of glory
Where any might worship: the Derbyshire Dales.
Eliza Cook, 1884

Visitors could see the boards advertising tours outside the various stables; the hotels and hydros also organised outings for their guests. There was a good choice of guide books. Jewitt's *Matlock Companion* established in 1825 claimed to be the first annual guide book in existence. He also published books of Derbyshire songs and ballads. "*A 6d Guide to Haddon and Chatsworth and how to get there from Buxton and*

H. HAND & SON,

POPE CARR LIVERY STABLES,
MATLOCK BRIDGE.

CHAR-A-BANC runs daily (during the Season) from Crown Square at Ten O'clock, for not less than four Passengers, to Chatsworth, Haddon Hall, Dovedale, Hardwick.

Booking Offices: Phillips, Hairdresser; Barnwell, Jeweller, Matlock Bridge.   62m

Matlock" by E Bradbury was published locally. Bemrose, a Derby publisher, issued a Matlock guide in 1869. Some guides were parts of national series such as Ward Lock's Red Guides published from the early 1880s. *Matlock and its environs* was published in 1876 as a Nelsons' Pictorial Guide Book: "The scenery here is singularly wild and to a traveller fresh from the southern counties of England will seem remarkable for boldness and even grandeur".

Many of the cab firms could hire out charabancs, landaus, Victorias, dog-carts and wagonettes of various sizes for groups who wished to explore Derbyshire, but visitors were advised to book ahead as there were not enough at busy times. Briddon's Stables in Matlock Bath, for example, took carriages to Chatsworth, Haddon Hall and Dovedale daily at 10am and returned about 6pm. There were several charabanc companies on the Bank including Joseph Boden at the Gate Hotel

Fish-Pond Posting Establishment.

Char-a-Banc, Landaus, Waggonettes, Private Carriages of every description for Hire. Wedding Carriages supplied. Hearse and Mourning Coaches.

The only Public Conveyances for Haddon Hall, Chatsworth, and Dovedale starts from this Yard at 10 a.m. daily.

Nat. Telephone 45. Telegrams: " BRIDDON, MATLOCK BATH."

HERBERT BRIDDON, Proprietor.

WAS BLONDIN HERE?

Charles Blondin was a famous tightrope walker born in France. Some sources say he went to the United States in 1851, some 1855. He first walked across Niagara Falls in 1859. He came to England in 1861 and stayed. His final performance was in 1896 when he was 72 years old.

In 1882 the *Visiting List* said that "ten or twelve years ago" the famous French tightrope walker Charles Blondin had walked on Pig (now Pic) Tor rocks. So many people came on special trains they could not all get out. Blondin had wanted to cross from the Heights of Abraham to High Tor, but Mr Arkwright refused permission.

A lady wrote in *Derbyshire Family History Society News* in 1997 that her grand-father had helped to strain the ropes across a Matlock gorge for Blondin.

Joseph M Severn in *My village: Owd Codnor*, 1935, wrote that as a child he saw Blondin walk down Codnor Park monument with a sack over his head. Severn was born in 1861. I can find no other reference to this.

Blondin did indeed perform at Derby Arboretum in July 1861, August 1862 and July 1872. He also went to Sheffield in April 1862. The Derby advertisement in 1872 said it was his first visit in ten years. A relatively small crowd of 2000 watched him because it was a Monday and the shilling entrance fee was expensive: many watched from outside. There was no report in the Matlock newspapers.

The *Matlock Bath Telegraph* reported in August 1861 that his rival Mr D'Albert wanted to walk from High Tor to the Heights of Abraham and challenged Blondin to a match for £500. Arkwight refused permission and Blondin declined. So D'Albert stretched a rope at Matlock Bridge half a mile towards Darley Dale, over a plantation, the river, the turnpike and a quarry. The performance began at 5pm. First he simply walked, for the second crossing he was in a sack blindfolded and performed acrobatics in the middle, the third time he walked with his feet in wicker baskets, the fourth time he walked backwards and performed more acrobatics. Thousands of people came to watch. The railway used the sidings for extra trains and built a temporary bridge over the river.

In September 1882 an American tight rope walker called Frank Gilfort, described as the only recognised rival to Blondin, performed 50 feet in the air above the Old English gardens as part of Wakes Week. He also had a trapeze hung from the centre of the rope and did all his descents holding the rope only by his teeth to loud applause!

Were memories at fault or confused? I cannot find a description of Blondin actually coming to Matlock – but I would love to see one.

The Peacock Hotel, Rowsley.

The Chatsworth Hotel, now the Edensor Institute.
Card posted 1909.

and H Hand & Son at Pope Carr. Mr Hand also later took over the stables at the Gate where the substantial premises at the back had room for seventeen horses, carriages and everything necessary for a good funeral turn-out. William Furniss arrived in the late 1880s at Cherry Holt on Wellington Street. His Duchess and Primrose charabancs were drawn by "splendid greys" and he had other teams of matching piebald and skewbald horses. Joseph Allen had cabs and a haulage firm on Hackney Lane, later moving to Dimple Farm.

In the summer, special stagecoaches, such as the Champion, ran to and from

Buxton: "the horses were in splendid condition when they arrived to the sound of a horn on Saturday". Another coach called "The Queen of the Peak" came twice a week for visitors to Buxton to lunch at the Royal Hotel. The horses were changed at Ashford on the two and a half hour journey.

Without the possibility of hopping into a motor car, people in the nineteenth century generally walked quite long distances. It was common for visitors to walk from Matlock to Rowsley, or even Chatsworth (which could be entered by the Beeley Gate) and Haddon Hall, although they might use the railway to return. The ivy-clad Peacock Hotel at Rowsley, described in 1884 as a "picture of comfort and old fashioned hospitality" was very popular for tea while waiting for the train. The tourists who stayed there often did so for the fishing, for which they did not even have to leave the garden.

Chatsworth House was open daily, except for Sundays. There were several restrictions: no group numbering over twelve persons, no school parties, no dogs, no litter from picnics, no flowers to be picked, no shrubs damaged. Visitors were asked to respect what they were allowed to see by "the kindness of the noble proprietors". Guides advised people to have their picnic as soon as they arrived, because the tour took an hour and a half and they would be hungry by four o'clock. Well-organised visitors to Chatsworth could send a telegram to order a carriage to pick them up at Rowsley station and convey them to lunch at the Chatsworth Hotel (now the Edensor Institute) where there was also a coffee room for ladies.

There were remarks that the tour of Chatsworth was a bit too thorough; a visitor to the gardens in 1884 complained that a "very communicative" gardener knew the date every tree had been planted and by whom. A flag flying from the Hunting Tower indicated the Duke was in residence. From 1882 visitors could see Lord Frederick Cavendish's grave in the churchyard: his assassination in Dublin had been well covered in the *Visiting List*. On Whit Monday 1888 it was claimed four thousand people visited Chatsworth, and a further three thousand on the following

Up Darley Dale, the wanton wind
In careless measures sweeps
And stirs the twinkling Derwent's tides,
Its shallows and its deeps.

O'er distant Matlock's lofty Tor,
A broken rainbow gleams,
While the last ray of parting day,
Athwart the valley streams.

The waving woods that crown the banks
'Bove Chatsworth's gorgeous pile,
Repose in greenest gloom nor catch
The sun's departing smile.

Written by Lord John Manners from his shooting lodge at Stanton Woodhouse

HADDON HALL, FROM RIVER WYE.

Hydro visitors walked to Haddon from Chatsworth, then returned by train from Rowsley or Bakewell. Card posted 1906.

Friday and Saturday.

Visitors short of time could walk from Chatsworth to Haddon via Calton Pastures, but the path "is not well defined, and is known only imperfectly, if at all, by the villagers". It was better to ramble along the river or even go by the very dusty road.

It was never clear how much of Haddon Hall could be visited at any time. It was usually described as uninhabited but in fairly good repair. Tourists could certainly wander in the grounds and visit the chapel. A guide book of 1872 mentioned the little room of curios, the Roman altar and the manacle in the great hall just as exist today. "Teas, buns and the like" were available in the cottage where the topiary was admired, although the main gardens were not particularly well kept. These topiaries of boar's heads and peacocks, representing the Vernon and Manners families, also survive.

A visitor in 1884 said, "Even in its ruinous state, the Hall looks charming". While he was there "carriages with their loads of many occupants were constantly arriving from Bakewell and elsewhere". He heard the "winding note" from the horn of a carriage and four which swept into the drive. From Haddon, it was easy to walk into Bakewell for tea and take the train back. (As hinted in the poem, the Dukes of Rutland used the lodges at Stanton Woodhouse and Longshaw for their visits.)

In October 1881 Joseph Whitworth rather grudgingly announced he would open the grounds of Stancliffe Hall two days a week the following season. He had landscaped his garden into an "immense natural rockery". However, he intended to charge five shillings per party, to include a guide booklet. The charge was to "exclude the rough element". A walk or drive through Darley Dale always

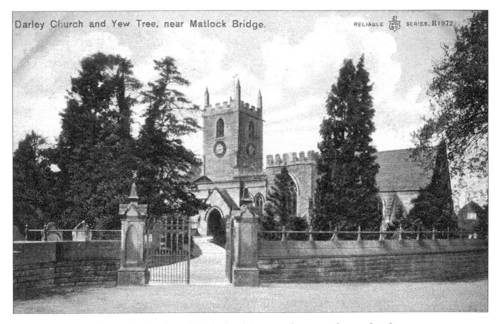

Darley Church and Yew Tree, near Matlock Bridge.   RELIABLE SERIES. R1072.

A short walk from Matlock, this scene has not changed today.

included a visit to the pretty St Helen's Church with its famous yew tree. Illustrations in guide books showed a view which has hardly changed today.

Lea Hurst, the home of the Nightingale family, was usually let to tenants. One of them laid out a short golf course, which was the nearest to Matlock for many years – men only of course. Mr Arkwright was President of the club. Wingfield (usually then spelt Winfield) Manor was famous for its romantic ruins associated with Mary Queen of Scots. One paid to enter at the farmhouse, where they also provided teas.

The Via Gellia, with its waterfalls and tufa cottage, was a favourite destination for picnics, particularly in the spring. It was famed for its wild flowers: kingcups, primroses, forget-me-nots, violets, and, above all, lilies of the valley. Local children would pick the lilies to sell in the villages on the Spring Bank Holiday, but eventually keepers had to be employed to stop tourists digging up the bulbs.

In 1881 a new guide book called *Rambles among the hills in the Peak of Derbyshire and the South Downs* was published by a Louis Jennings. The local press was horrified by its "cheap cynicism". They nicknamed it Derbyshire Dammed and said even Buxton had been libelled. The author certainly had little good to say about either Buxton or Matlock, or anywhere really. He said he had been up what he claimed the locals called "Via Jelly" once and would not bother again to "go pottering along in the company of nursemaids, cadgers picking wild flowers and objectionable persons on the bicycle".

The Via Gellia was also on the route to Dovedale, which was perceived then as now to be the valley to visit by trippers. The hydros provided picnics for the day's outing and donkeys or ponies could be hired to explore the dale. The journey over the hills was described by a visitor to the Royal Hotel as being like the west of Ireland: with stone walls and treeless but with splendid roads. "The curlews and

"Winfield" or Wingfield Manor was a popular charabanc destination. Card posted 1908.

The Via Gellia, famous for lily of the valley.
Postcards of this beauty spot were always uninspired.

Donkeys could be hired to explore Dovedale.

Black Rocks, also known as Stonnis – a good walk from Matlock Bath. Card posted 1905.

Matlock High Tor, a Random Sketch by Ambrose Lee, 1886

At Matlock there is a most wonderful rock,
That the nerves of the strongest will certainly shock;
It stands in a very romantic position,
But would puzzle the pate of an Eastern Magician
To tell what on earth it were placed up there for,
And this Adamite lump they have christened
High Tor.

One Sawney Macdonald, a tall brawny Scot,
A sight of this famed elevation once got;
Who exclaimed, "Hoot awa! Ye no ken Lochnagar!
'Tis a wee bit o' pebble, your famous
High Tor.

Ap Griffith ap Shenkin came over from Wales,
Having listened to numberless wonderful tales;
When he saw it he thought of old Snowdon afar,
And look'd up with contempt at poor
Little Tor.

A Cockney stepped over from London's fine city,
Pronouncing the Tor rather neat and quite pretty;
His sole exclamation's summed up in,"Oh lor!
We ain't nothink in town to come up to
High Tor!"

From Yankeeland, once, Brother Jonathan came,
Having heard of the Tor's cosmopolitan fame;
"Wa'al I reckon, folks, you ne'er saw Niagara?
Or you wouldn't swell out so about your
High Tor.

One fine summer morning a soldier passed by,
And up at the Tor cast a warrior's eye;
Saying, "Don't I just wish, in the Crimean War,
I'd been snug here in shelter right under
The Tor!"

A Russian, who hailed from the great Alexander,
Took into his head round the Tor to meander;
And jauntily said, "I must tell our big Czar
To pop over and look at your
Wonderful Tor!"

From gay France there popp'd down a most spruce Parlez-voo,
And the view of the Tor seemed to tickle Mossoo;
For he shrugged, and he writhed, and cried,"Sacre, mi Lor!
Vot a fine stone, by gar, you have make of
De Tor!"

blackbirds were the only living things."

Alderwasley Woods were famed for their bluebells, visible from the train. But again, fern gatherers were a nuisance. Also to the south were Black or Stonnis Rocks from which the view was spectacular. Visitors then probably had less interest in the High Peak Railway and Cromford Canal, whose remains fascinate us today. The climb up Cromford hill often forced gentlemen to get out of the carriages and walk, to relieve the horses.

VISITORS

Disappointingly few famous visitors were mentioned in the *Visiting List* in the 1880s. Some may well have taken great pains to stay anonymous. Census lists showed that the overwhelming majority of guests in the hydros were born in Lancashire, the West Riding of Yorkshire and London. There were also a fair number from Scotland and Ireland. The same impression was given in the *Visiting List*, where it stated their current home town. Perhaps surprisingly, there was no evidence of extra numbers of spinster ladies or widows – the sexes were fairly evenly balanced.

Several books claim Robert Louis Stevenson wrote *Kidnapped* at Smedley's Hydro. Stevenson came to Smedley's for just over a week in April 1886. He was not feeling well himself; but he came with his father who was developing dementia. Stevenson wrote in a letter that his father had exhibited "a dose of Hyde this morning". He also wrote, "We are (my father and I) stranded at Smedley's and at the tender mercies of Dr Hunter, who seems a capable fellow". I doubt he got much writing done.

In 1895 an American millionaire from Chicago called Mr Liebes came to Smedley's. He was the only licensed merchant for seal fisheries for the United States Government and also dealt in furs. He had been all over Germany and Italy for five years trying to cure his liver disease. After six weeks at Smedley's, he declared himself "practically a dead man restored to life".

One type of visitor who began to come regularly to the hydros was football teams. They often came to train before important cup ties and endeared themselves to local men by practising on the football pitch, which was then on one of the fields which later made up Hall Leys Park. They even played friendly matches with the town team.

In 1893 Newton Heath (later Manchester United) stayed at Prospect Place Hydro. They played Stoke on the Saturday but returned to prepare for a Cup match, before which they played Matlock on the Thursday. John Goodall, the famous England centre forward, came with them. He had played football for Derby County and cricket for Derbyshire. In October 1895 Manchester City came to Rockside and Sunderland to Chesterfield House. Manchester City came again in March 1896 for nine days because they were playing Liverpool on the Good Friday.

Stoke City arrived at Chesterfield House on Christmas Eve 1899 for a three week stay. They were not allowed out after 6pm so they played many games of billiards. Luckily several of them were musicians and they entertained the other guests. They played Bury, Aston Villa and Burnley during their stay.

In 1898 John Brinsmeaad, aged 83, stayed at Smedley's, bringing a piano for the drawing room at a cost of 300 guineas. John Brinsmead & Sons had already made forty four thousand pianos at a rate of two a day for sixty years.

In 1881 William Henry Perkin who invented the first aniline dye, Mauveine, stayed at Smedley's.

In 1892 John Tiplady Carrodus, a famous violist, was a visitor at the New Bath Hotel. He had recently given a concert at the Pavilion. He owned a very famous Guarneri violin, but the report did not mention this. In the same year Joseph and Mrs Chamberlain stayed at the Royal Hotel.

INTERLUDE

In 1893 the Manager at Smedley's, Alfred Douglas, died aged only 36. Despite being unwell for three years, he was still working a fourteen hour day at the end. He had tried cures abroad and seemed to be rallying, but he died suddenly on a visit to his brother in Lea. He was buried at Holloway. Until the closure of the Hydro in 1955, the management then became slightly incestuous. This did not matter because, by all accounts, all three men were efficient and well-liked. Mr Douglas was succeeded by his clerk, deputy and brother-in-law, Henry Challand, who had already been at Smedley's for twelve years. Mr Challand was a farmer's son from Southwell in Nottinghamshire whose sister Ellen had married Alfred Douglas. The widowed Mrs Challand senior also lived with the Douglas's at Beech Villa on Chesterfield Road, until her death in 1894. When Henry Challand died in 1925, Alfred Douglas's son and grandson became the last two managers.

Only just over a year later in December 1894, Dr Hunter died, just two months after the death of his eminent father at the Bridge of Allan Hydro in Scotland. Our Dr Hunter was being treated by doctors from Manchester and had seemed to be mending; he actually had a holiday to Cairo booked. He had been a great attraction in drawing visitors to Smedley's and his early death was a great loss to the advocates of hydropathy. In the same twelve months Smedley's also lost George Statham, the architect of its expansion, and a director called Jones.

Several hydropathists died in the 1890s: Thomas Davis in 1891, and his son Jesse in 1896, Ralph Davis also in 1896, Jonas Brown and his son Joshua at Old Bank House in 1897, and Mrs Thomas Davis at Oldham House in 1898. Mrs Barton of Jackson House and Dalefield Hydro died aged only 49.

There were other deaths of people known to visitors in the 1880s. Mr Mattocks, who had left the Old English, died in London in 1896. Mr and Mrs Pegler at the Crown Hotel both died young in 1898, as did Mr Abbott at the Queen's Head.

Other people moved on. Mr Leggoe joined the Salvation Army and his skating ring was replaced by new villas. He left the town for a while, but he was back on the Council by 1907. Mr Bramald of Elm Tree Hydro left to marry and settle in Blackpool. Mr Richardson moved to Buxton Station in 1898.

Several new substantial buildings appeared on the Bank. A new hydro was built on Chesterfield Road, which is described later. On Smedley Street East, The Matlock Concert Hall and Pleasure Gardens Company opened their new premises in June 1896. Several well-known local men such as Dr Moxon, Job Smith, Henry Challand, Arrow Smith and George Barton were on the Board. A bay-fronted assembly hall with ticket office, retiring rooms and a refreshment room was built with a 60 foot swimming pool at the eastern end, complete with seven dressing rooms. Four acres of gardens surrounded the buildings, landscaped with a bowling green and later tennis courts.

Victoria Hotel, Matlock Bank

A strangely named Victoria Hall in Smedley Street.

The assembly room was used for many theatrical performances. The stage was fitted with two large drop scenes with eighteen side wings. The stage property included thunder equipment and rifles etc. Pianists for dancing classes were paid ten shillings per week. An orchestra for a "long night" was paid £1-2-6d. What was the "acid for the floor at dances" which cost ten shillings in the accounts? This venue became known as the Victoria Hall to commemorate the Jubilee in 1897. However, like the Pavilion in Matlock Bath, it was very difficult to make a business such as this return a profit in a relatively small town. The Company was in liquidation by 1900.

The Princes Buildings just off Crown Square have the date 1894 and the next building, built by the Croft family of joiners and undertakers, is dated 1897. Opposite them in 1899 William Furniss built stables for sixteen horses as part of his livery business to give him a town centre location. At the front he opened a hairdressing business and his wife kept apartments. This building, with the top floor missing, is now The Crown with an appropriate date plaque. Furniss and Mr Bateman of the Railway Hotel also built houses on Bakewell Road. All through the last decade of the century Dale Road also filled up with shops and houses as far as the railway bridge.

However, during a snowstorm in February 1899, there was a dramatic fire on Dale Road. Else's double-fronted stationers and library was destroyed. Parr's Bank (late Brown's Temperance Hotel and then Derby & Derbyshire Banking Co) and Marsden's grocers (one of a local chain) on either side were damaged. All the neighbours at the Queen's Head, the Beehive Stores and the Post Office rushed round to help because, of course, the owners and managers were living above. Luckily the Else family had actually gone away for the night: their dog was brought out alive.

Potter & Co's office in the old Brown's Temperance Hotel
on Dale Road.
[Potter & Co.]

In June 1890 Matlock had its first Thursday early closing: from 4pm! Matlock Bath later decided on 2pm. Most shops at that time opened no later than 8am and closed at 8.30pm or even later. Shop assistants came second in number to servants in the occupations given in the censuses. Many young men and women were employed, not only to serve customers, but to frequently change window displays, sweep the pavements in front of the shop, take deliveries, keep the account books etc. When the early closing movement spread to Matlock Bath and other resorts, they applied for exemptions in the summer months. Many of the young men were organised into clubs and sports teams on their afternoon off, presumably so they did not roam about being a nuisance. (This trend for shop and factory workers to have a half-day holiday in the week is why many sports teams were named "Wednesday" or "Thursday" after the town.)

A report in 1891 had described "rows of good buildings erected and streets appearing in the once rural part" of The Dimple. A week later it was reported that only one new house had been built during the last ten years in Matlock Bath. Whether this was strictly true or not, it emphasised the contrast in the health of the two Board's rateable values. Matlock Bath's population actually declined between 1891 and 1901. In 1894 the Local Boards were demolished and their roles taken over by Urban District Councils (UDC in the following text), but the men in power stayed largely the same. Matlock Council began life in a new Town Hall: the Reverend

Nicholson's bankruptcy had conveniently allowed them to purchase Bridge House Hydro. A new wing was added to include a new assembly room, which opened in October 1900. The court was also moved over from the old Market Hall in Dale Road.

Two notable new buildings were built in Darley Dale under the supervision of the widowed Lady Whitworth. The Whitworth Hospital was opened in 1889 and the Whitworth Institute late 1890. While the Institute was being built there was a great deal of speculation locally as to what it actually was! In the event it contained a public hall, a swimming pool, a reading room, lending library and a museum of natural history complete with the stuffed animals and birds' eggs collections, as well as rooms for local clubs to meet and listen to lectures. Many of the trees in the Park were planted as quite mature specimens dug up from Darley hillside. When the Park opened in 1892, it soon became a venue for day trippers in the summer and in the winter locals skated on the boating lake.

One great boon to visitors was the tramway[9] which opened in 1893 between Crown Square and the top of Rutland Street. The idea of a cable tramway up the steep hill is always credited to Job Smith of Malvern House Hydro, who had seen a

Tramcar No.1 waiting outside the Crown Hotel.
Sparrow Park is on the left with the Town Hall behind.

---

9. For a history of the tramway, see *The Matlock Cable Tramway*, Glynn Waite, 2012.

SHOCKING EVENTS

Three times the citizens and visitors to Matlock were shocked to read of terrible events in their breakfast newspaper. The first murder involved visitors, the third devastated a hydro family.

FRIGHTFUL TRAGEDY AT MATLOCK:
A MINISTER MURDERED BY HIS SON, March 1883

The Reverend Julius Benn brought his son William Rutherford Benn to rooms rented out by the Marchants in The Cottage at the bottom of Steep Turnpike (now Harley House, it had been the toll cottage). William had clearly been ill and was very quiet, but they had been out walking every day. On the Saturday they visited the Heights of Abraham before retiring early to bed. The Reverend, a tall and powerful man, had insisted on his son sharing his room.

At 7am on the Sunday morning the Marchants heard a rapping noise. Mrs Marchant knocked on the bedroom door several times but heard a voice telling her to go away. When her husband returned from church at lunchtime, he knocked again. William opened the door in his nightshirt standing in a pool of blood. His father's body was on the bed.

Mr Marchant ran to the Else's house across the road at The Firs (now the library). They called the police and Dr Moxon. The Reverend had been clubbed several times with the chamber pot and stabbed with a penknife. William had stabbed himself in the throat; Dr Moxon stitched the wound on the spot. When cautioned, William said, "Yes, I did it".

William had been married the previous December, but had suffered a nervous breakdown and been in an asylum before being released into his father's care. After the murder, he was sent to Broadmoor but left in 1890 on the condition he dropped his surname. His daughter Margaret (the actress Margaret Rutherford) was born in 1892. The family went to India but Margaret's mother committed suicide and she was sent home to live with an aunt. William

Dr. William Moxon.
[Potter & Co.]

returned and died in Broadmoor. The politician Tony Benn was Margaret's cousin.

MYSTERIOUS MURDER OF A QUAKER LADY AT MATLOCK:
A HORRIBLE TRAGEDY, March 1891

Balmoral House, a large villa on Cavendish Road next door to Claremont, was lived in by an eccentric man called Michael Morrall and his wife. They had been there over thirty years but servants did not stay long.

Mr Morrall was connected to the family who founded the Aero knitting needle company in Studley, Warwickshire, where he was born. He was the author of *The History and Description of Needle Making* (1862) which contained several Matlock hydro advertisements.

One night Mrs Morrall stayed up reading the newspaper in the kitchen while her husband went to bed. He heard shots and found his wife dead with wounds in the side of her head. He ran across the road to Rockside Hydro, from where William Atkins sent a couple of his servants to help before going himself. Mr Morrall then ran all the way to Poplar Cottage Hydro to fetch Jesse Davis. Suddenly two of Mr Morrall's nieces arrived for Easter on the last train from Manchester! There were therefore many people tramping round before the police arrived. All this took place in a snowstorm.

The shots seemed to have been fired through a gap under the blind covering the window and through some plant pots. The room was lit by one small candle – therefore it was a very good shot. The window had shattered and the murderer must have been showered in glass. No-one could explain a poker and box of dominoes on the table in the next room, of which Mr Morrall and his servant denied all knowledge.

A few nights later, the nieces were woken by a loud crash: Mr Morrall had fallen head first down stairs. The police constable, still on duty in the house, sent for Dr Moxon and a bathman from Poplar Cottage. Mr Morrall was not sure if he had been pushed! Inhabitants in nearby houses began to lock their doors, but nobody suspicious was ever found.

The inquest was held at Rockside Hydro and the poor telegraph officer at the Post Office had to send ten thousand words to London for the newspaper reporters. No-one was ever accused of the murder although there was speculation when Mr Morrall soon announced he was to re-marry. He died later in 1891 before this could happen. In 1896 and 1903 there were confessions from men claiming Mr Morrall had hired them to kill his wife, but they came to nothing.

Balmoral House was re-named Bidston and lived in by George Knowles, a builder, and later Dr Christopher Orme.

TERRIBLE SHOOTING TRAGEDY, September 1932

The third murder would have really horrified the visitors who had known the Davis family of Tor House Hydro. George senior had retired to Hazeldene on Smedley Street, the house of his step-sister. He had just taken morning cups of tea up to his son George and daughter Winifred when shots rang out. George had shot his sister and himself in the neck. They were both taken to Whitworth Hospital but later rushed to Derby. Winifred died that night, but George recovered enough to stand trial. He was found guilty but insane.

mineral works cable tram in San Francisco. A newspaper report in 1884 mentioned a Mr Donaldson staying at Malvern House who had applied to the Board of Trade to construct a cable tramway up to Smedley's. He was a friend of Smith's who had come to survey the route, but the idea was abandoned at that time. The company was financed by Sir George Newnes, a famous newspaper proprietor who had been born in the manse at Glenorchy Chapel in Matlock Bath. Bank Road had been "steep, unyielding, un-sympathetic towards human frailty", but now even the infirm could get up the hill without calling a cab. The chimney on the power house behind the depot below Rockside Hydro was a new landmark on the postcards.

There were wonderful views of High Tor and Masson Hill from the open-topped tramcars on the descent.

Two other people familiar to visitors played a part in the opening ceremony: William Cocking was the toastmaster and Dr Moxon attended as chairman of the tramway committee for the Local Board.

There had been a very prominent gas lamp in the centre of Crown Square, but this was removed in 1899 when the tramway passenger shelter with the clock was erected. There were new lamps on the corners. The shelter actually became quite a traffic hazard, but buses found it useful to stop there too. It was paid for by Robert Wildgoose who lived at The Gables on Chesterfield Road. He had been the manager for Smedley's at Lea Mills and Chairman of the Hydro Company; when he died a few months later, Florence Nightingale sent a wreath. Some parts of the shelter are still a landmark in Hall Leys Park.

The inevitable passing of the pioneer hydropathists left the way open for new ideas and expansion on Matlock Bank. Matlock Bath needed to continue the entrepreneurial spirit shown by the builders of the Pavilion, the Jubilee Promenade and Bridge, the switchback railway, and the newly thriving hotels. How would both settlements respond to the prosperity and new freedoms of that age which we now look back upon nostalgically as the halcyon days of Edwardian England?

THE 1900s

THE VISITORS ARRIVE …

[Glynn Waite]

A Ward Lock guide book of the 1890s extolled the Midland Railway's carriages which ran so smoothly on double bogies that "we scarcely feel their motion". Even their third class carriages were luxurious compared with only a few decades previously and included their own dining cars and lavatories. The trains were well ventilated in the summer and heated by hot water pipes in the winter. From May to October one could buy cheaper tourist tickets at weekends, although the Matlock newspapers always grumbled that these were more expensive than similar tickets to seaside resorts. Thomas Cook's tours, for example, would charge one excursion fare, such as 3/6d return, from any station in the West Midlands to any station between Matlock Bath and Rowsley.

Arriving at Matlock Bath station was still a joy. Mr Porter, the new stationmaster, continued to receive money from the Midland Railway to finance the flower displays. Several stations were described and photographed for *Gardening World* in 1905. The garden at Matlock:

> …*extends along a well-sheltered bank, and consists of a number of circular, semi-circular and other shaped beds, which were filled this summer with calceolarias, Henry Jacoby pelargoniums, double stocks, variegated godetia, and white violas edged with, in some cases, pyrethrum, and in others with lobelia. There was not a great variety of subjects, but the plants were vigorous in spite of their dry situation, and blooming profusely, and the ensemble made a particularly gay and attractive picture. The edge of the bank was covered in rock plants, selene saxifrage being strongly in evidence. At the top of the bank were clumps of Drummondii (phlox), interspersed with tangled masses of climbing, many-coloured nasturtiums, and some standard roses.*

Sadly, the photograph of Matlock Bath was too poor to reproduce here. There is a

Belper station in 1905.

great deal of track shown and very few flowers. However, the image shows the bridge in the far distance and a paved crossing of the line opposite the booking office. There is what might be the tiny shelter provided in 1894 beyond the bridge and a vast stretch of uncovered up-platform, with a large telegraph pole and the gas holder behind. The flowery bank faced the station buildings. A photograph of the display at Belper station gave a better impression, complete with a stern-looking lady who apparently refused to move for the photographer. The alpine plants there were provided by Mr Strutt.

In 1902 a petition to the Midland Railway for more shelters received the reply that another waiting room would only encourage excursionists to congregate on the platforms in wet weather. Female day trippers, wearing the new fashionable flimsier summer dresses, did indeed suffer in the rain.

Visitors to the hydros were still getting wet at Matlock Bridge too, although a glass canopy was erected at the entrance in 1898. This was scorned as a "benefit more imaginary then real". A larger W H Smith's stall also opened in 1905: before it had been a subsidiary of the one at Matlock Bath. Another branch of the stationers opened at Cromford Station which was very welcome because of the distance to the village shops.

There was now an alternative to waiting for a cab at Matlock, if one was prepared to walk over the bridge. The cable tramway running up Bank Road had been opened in 1893, running close to several hydros, who soon added this convenience to their advertisements. If there was no room on the platform for luggage, it could easily be sent for later.

The Council's constant lobbying of the Midland Railway did pay off in one respect in 1905: Matlock Bridge Station changed its name to simply Matlock.

WHERE SHALL WE STAY?

The Bath boasts the best hotels. The Bank chiefly entertains its guests at its hydro-pathic establishments. The Bath, as the older resort, speaks of the Bank as an upstart, a haven of hypochondriacs… The Bank affects to look down on the hearty jollity of the "trippers" who make the Bath their own in the summer season. Perhaps the passing visitor would do best at the Bath, while for a longer stay the Bank would be the more airy sojourn. Precedence must be given to the Bank, as indeed the larger and more flourishing of the two, though the Bath now lays plans to recapture its lost superiority.

The Peak Country, A R H Moncrieff, 1908

A visitor returning to the Matlocks in the early 1900s, after a ten-year break, would be aware of an overwhelming change. There was no longer really a "season". Many people were now spending the winter months in the hydros and hotels. There were peaks at Christmas, Easter and mid-summer, but the bigger establishments were pretty full all the time. All the hydros had increased their numbers of bedrooms or had plans to do so. In spite of this, at Bank Holidays many visitors were forced to

*Tramcar No.3 near
the bottom of Bank Road.*
[Glynn Waite]

"sleep out", which was a boon for the increasing number of guest houses, or even for anyone prepared to let their spare room. By 1908 there were nearly sixty such addresses at Matlock Bridge and Bank, with another fifty-plus at Matlock Bath. This was in addition to the hotels and public houses.

Matlock House Hydro was reportedly so busy at Christmas 1899 that people slept in the bath cubicles. Some visitors must still have set off for Matlock without checking whether accommodation was available. Fred Byron, Smedley's coachman, told the newspapers he was glad at Easter 1910 to be told to stop going to the station once the hydro was full, because he hated telling people there were no places. At August 1900 Rockside broke its accommodation records and encountered the problem of visitors refusing to leave, which forced newcomers to board out. Groups of young people attending conferences took the fun option of camping out. For several years, the ladies attending the British College of Christian Union meeting at Matlock House stayed in the Hydro, while the men pitched their tents on Matlock Moor.

In order to keep increasingly large numbers entertained and occupied in all weathers, the hotels and hydros had been through a period of expansion and refurbishment, which was still in progress. To attract the winter patient, they needed the minimum facilities of a dining room, a drawing room, a sitting room for ladies, a billiard room, a smoking room for gentlemen, card tables, at least one piano, and various items of equipment for indoor and outdoor games. And, as T P O'Connor MP [1] tellingly remarked about his visit to Smedley's, a garden or terrace where one could simply lie on a couch in the sunshine and do nothing at all.

There were social reasons for the popularity of the hydros in this era, especially amongst those who welcomed a crumbling of old class barriers. With all the entertainment and sport on offer, everyone could find some opportunity to join in or watch in the company of others. A duchess could not stand on her dignity scuttling down to the baths with no make-up or *coiffure*. A shop girl who could sing beautifully would be welcomed by all the company. The lonely and the old, as well as single and widowed women, could find friendship which might be missing in a small boarding house or exclusive hotel. Families came year after year and grew up together. *Health Resort* in 1906 described Matlock's hydros as "hotels de luxe" with sumptuous furnishings and beautiful surroundings.

The *Visiting List* continued to chronicle all the arrivals; the lists themselves were taking up more and more columns. At Easter 1899 for example Smedley's had 319 visitors; in 1906 they had 401. Similar figures were recorded by Rockside Hydro: 160 and 210. Poplar Cottage, having become Jeffs' Poplar Hydro, showed an increase from 106 to 175.

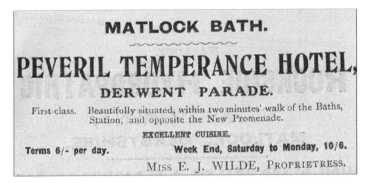

Prices in 1910 clearly indicated the hierarchy of accommodation. A full-board stay at Smedley's cost from 8/6d to 12 shillings a day, depending on the room. The Royal Hotel charges were similar but complicated, depending on the use of private sitting rooms (fifteen shillings) and suites. Rockside Hydro was on the next tier at 10/6d, and the New Bath charged 10 shillings. Chesterfield House and Matlock House both charged 7 shillings, as did the Old English Hotel, and the Devonshire and Hodgkinson's Hotels in Matlock Bath. Sycamore House Hydro charged 5 to 6 shillings, as did the Peveril Hotel in Matlock Bath. However, it must be remembered that a stay at the more expensive hydropathic establishments included many different treatments and plenty of entertainment – one need spend no more. Most places advertised reduced winter rates, except at Christmas. There were also cheaper rates for servants, presumably relegated to north-facing attics.

---

1. TP O'Connor, nicknamed Tay Pay, was an Irish Nationalist MP for Liverpool and a journalist. He founded the Star and Sun newspapers and became the first President of the Board of Film Censors.

The Heyday of the Royal – Hotel de Lux

Mr Thomas Tyack had been running the Royal Hotel from July 1889 on a twenty-one year lease from Maximilian Lindner, the German Consul to Birmingham. Mr Lindner died in 1898 shortly after the 87-bedroom hotel had been advertised for sale. Perhaps because of the uncertainty about ownership, Mr Tyack[2] decided to leave Matlock Bath to run the Rutland Arms Hotel in Bakewell, which he already part-owned. He auctioned his belongings from the Royal: the familiar hotel omnibus made £21 and the billiard table £90. Miss Lake from the New Bath Hotel and a Mrs Scott Shaw briefly managed the Royal for Lindner's son, but he was looking for a buyer. It was bought by Leonard Brigg of Keighley, Dr Sharpe's brother-in-law, but he sold it on to a London syndicate, headed by a Carlos Vetter (who died in 1910). The new owners spent £20,000 on the hotel's re-building and launch in early 1904 as a luxury hotel, spa and hydro.

The Royal Hotel. Card posted 1906.

The new manager was Emile Thoma-Badrutt, who some guests would recognise from his previous post at the Kulm[3] Hotel in St Moritz. He was described as the epitome of courtesy and urbanity. He decided to advertise Matlock as the "Carlsbad of England". Sadly his wife died at a very young age back home in Switzerland in 1905 and he left. The management role was soon taken over by Andreas Buttgen, a German. He married the daughter of the manager of the Hotel Rubens in Antwerp in 1906. An article in *The World* extolled Mr Buttgen as "a man of world-wide

---

2. Thomas Tyack died in 1907 aged 72. He appeared to have fainted while on an evening walk. He fell in the river and could not be revived.

3. This hotel was opened in 1864 by Johannes Badrutt, the founder of St Moritz as a winter resort. Presumably Emile was a relative, perhaps sent to Matlock to get experience abroad.

experience to whose courtesy and tact are due the perfection of detail and the smoothness with which the great machine works".

Guests entered the hotel's hall under a new cupola roof. In the centre was an artistic fountain splashing with thermal spring water like a private pump room. Here the *Health Resort* magazine said, "visitors may be seen at all hours of the day sipping the natural mineral waters". Bamboo chairs were provided for those waiting for friends or transport. The huge area below the staircase had become a lounge where Professor Lewis Avanzi (on the violin) and his Milanese orchestra, a sextet, played twice daily. They must have been very accomplished musicians. Afternoon tea at 4.30pm, accompanied by classical music by such as Schubert, Beethoven, Wagner and Verdi, soon became a local treat. The orchestra played again from 8.30pm. Evening parties began to come out from Derby at weekends to dine and dance. A visitor in 1905, who said they were the best band he had heard in all Europe, felt sorry for them playing endless waltzes all evening. There was also a Bechstein grand piano for guests and visiting artists to play. Professor Avanzi left in

The Royal Hotel lounge.

1911, but a "Bijou Orchestra" of the Misses Radford, violinists from Matlock, replaced him. They had been at the New Bath in 1910.

Mrs Buttgen was also a great asset to the hotel, not least because she had a powerful soprano voice which came in handy at celebrations. In August 1908 she and Dr Sharpe's wife sang in a charity concert in the old Pavilion. Mrs Buttgen sang arias from *Tosca* and *La Boheme* in French. Shortly afterwards, she and lady visitors began to sing with the orchestra in the afternoons. Was her beautiful voice really a restful accompaniment to tea-time conversation? In warm weather, tea was also taken on the terrace, where the light summer dresses of the ladies produced a colourful continental scene.

An article in *Gentlefolk* in 1905 enthused that the public rooms, "are models of what such rooms should be – artistically furnished, light, airy, spacious and comfortable to a degree". A similar article in *The Gentlewoman* in 1909 called the Royal, "a conspicuous example of a perfect modern hotel". There were two dining rooms, one serving a *table d'hôte* menu, one *à la carte*. These rooms were in Elizabethan style with ribbed ceilings, huge fireplaces, baronial furniture and oak dados. The wallpaper featured red lions on a straw coloured background. The billiard room had *art nouveau* Fabrikona canvas walls. The ladies' boudoir was pink. The drawing room, which could be used for dancing, had green wallpaper. Warings had been in charge of these decorations.

No expense had been spared. Although Mr Jaffray the architect was local, the suppliers were definitely not. Otis supplied the lifts, Waring & Gillow the furnishings, Sulzer Freres of Winterthur the central heating, Briffault Freres of Paris the kitchen equipment, Chalet & Parquet of Interlaken the floors. The salon and bed-room carpets were from Saxony and Bruxelles, and the corridor floor coverings were Turkish. The white damask tablecloths and bed linen came from Ireland. The beds in the newly furnished and heated bedrooms had silk counterpanes and bed-side lamps. Ladies were supplied with spacious wardrobes and easy chairs – the actress Mrs Patrick Campbell arrived almost at once (with maid).

The gardens were extensive and noted for the variety of old roses such as Dorothy Perkins and Mme Abel Chatenay. In 1906 the romantic view from the terrace at the Royal was described in *The Pall Mall Gazette* by Lieutenant Colonel

[Peak District
[Lead Mining Museum]

135

The Terrace of the Hotel.

The view from the Royal Hotel.

Newnham-Davies, their gastronomic correspondent and later author of the *Gourmet Guides to Europe* and *London*:

> *On the edge of the terrace and on the edge of the wrought iron rail which guards it, a yellow-leaved ivy sprawls luxuriantly; a long step below is a shelf of emerald lawn, gemmed with flower beds, and then sinks an abyss of foliage, a vast dip of rustling woods, in whose bosom is the glint of rippled water, and from the furthest wave of which rise great grey battlements of rock, creeper-hung, and with slim trees shooting sunwards from the crevices. The breeze which always moves gently on the gorge wakes the soft whisper of the stirred leaves, and from near at hand comes the music of falling water.*

More prosaically, he continued:
> *The Royal Hotel I found very comfortable and well managed. In the hall there is a marble fountain which spouts the mineral water continuously, and this and the shrouded figures descending by the lift to the baths, and the sticks some of the guests use to help rheumatic limbs, are the only reminders in the hotel that Matlock is a "cure" as well as a pleasure palace.*
>
> *The cooking is good, and the dishes as a rule simple, and on the menu of the dinner I ate there was only one dish, a vol au vent, which could not pass muster as a part of a cure diet.*

The chef in 1904 was Frank L Crohill, the brother of the chef at Smedley's Hydro, although by 1908 he had moved to Rockside Hydro and been replaced by Monsieur Tureczeck.

In June 1908 a new three-storey wing was opened at the rear to provide sixty more bedrooms and a lounge. The bedrooms were en suite with a bathroom and

A view from behind the old Pavilion with the Royal Hotel below on the left.

sitting room, opening through French windows to a Toraczo-paved balcony. On the ground floor was a new ballroom which could be entered from outside by non-residents. A winter garden extended the dining room on to the terrace. The magazine *Health Resort* noted that the Royal advertised itself as a winter resort for those "to whom a long and expensive journey abroad would be one of suffering".

In spring 1905 the Royal Hotel bought the failed old Pavilion building for a reported £7000, thus greatly increasing the acreage and interest of the gardens. There were plans to use the building as the basis for a new luxury hotel and sanatorium, reached by a funicular from the main road. Mention of this gradually petered out and the magnificent building became merely an indoor games facility, with archery, diabolo and ping pong. A badminton court was set up on the dance floor.

The other hotels in Matlock Bath

After Mr Tyack relinquished his lease on the New Bath Hotel in March 1898, the ownership devolved to a limited company who appointed a Mr Bertram Clulow from the Midland Hotel in Derby to be the manager – two hundred and fifty had applied for the post. The company also owned the Bath Terrace Hotel, whose basement had been turned into a palatial billiard room. Advertisements described the two as winter resort hotels, although it was suggested the Bath Terrace was for the less well-heeled – especially cyclists.

A sale catalogue in 1895 described a "new" restaurant and vaults belonging to the New Bath, built down on the main road. They were serviced from the hotel via an underground passage, which is still there – a very eerie addition to the basement

137

The New Bath Hotel, its great lime tree and roadside restaurant.
The Bath Terrace Hotel is at the end of the garden. Card posted 1904.

and pool.

The managers changed over the decade: Mr Rimmer in 1902 was succeeded in 1908 by John Cordell from Liverpool, but he died after only a few months, to be followed by a Miss Lakeman. Compared with its flamboyant neighbour and the booming hydros, the New Bath did not really receive much notice from the newspapers.

Indeed, in November 1910, the town was shocked by the news that the New Bath Hotel Company was being wound up. Apparently the business had been in trouble since March and several local tradesmen were owed money. There had been a fire in the stables in January, which had not helped. The stables were sublet to William Furniss. His horses had been saved, but the carriages were damaged. Luckily a Lanchester motor worth £600, belonging to a guest, had been rescued with the horses.

However, the business continued much as usual as far as the visitors were concerned. While still in the hands of the receiver in 1912, six thousand tons of tufa in their roadside quarry were offered for sale. This tufa was for sale in 1895 and 1930 as well – it but does not seem to have been a quick earner! In 1895 it was ten shillings a ton.

The Temple Hotel continued as a modest and quiet place to stay, except on trip days, when they specialised in catering for large parties of diners, as described later.

Clarence House Hydro on Holme Road had had several owners following the Reverend Nicholson's bankruptcy. For most of the 1900s, a widow and her young son ran the place as a boarding house. Eliza and Edward Theodore Aspey had worked for the previous owners as bath woman and servant. By 1911 Edward had

MATLOCK
BATH
HYDRO,

Holme Road.

∞✕∞

E. ASPEY, Proprietor.
∞✕∞

Is situated at a moderate elevation on
the ascent to Heights of Abraham.

TENNIS.   GOLF.   CROQUET.

Specially recommended for
Invalids, being sheltered from
North and East Winds.

———

Correspondence invited from those
in search of
Health or Pleasure.

Established nearly 80 years.

The Devonshire Hotel (on the left) backed on to the river. Card posted 1911.

139

moved to Borrowash, although he later returned to Matlock Bath, as will be seen.

There were two temperance hotels on North Parade: the Peveril and the Albion. The Peveril was above Parr's Bank next door to the church. The Albion was in the first building after the Fountain Villas, with the pretty first-floor railings. It was run by Mr and Mrs Albert Graves. Their restaurant served hot dinners from the joint for 1/- to 1/6d. The dangerous bottleneck persisted where the Devonshire Hotel met the road: ironwork on charabancs frequently hit pedestrians on the head. Hodgkinson's Hotel still had its popular licensed beer garden by the river: one Good Friday they took £117.

The Speed family continued to run the Old Vaults public house. Edward's son Frank died of yellow fever on board ship returning from the Gold Coast, but his monkey and a parrot made it home. Jacko the monkey entertained thousands in the bar before being sent to Belle Vue zoo in Manchester.

SMEDLEY'S HYDRO – MR CHALLAND'S KINGDOM
In 1895 Bulmer's *History & Directory of Derbyshire* enthused that on Matlock Bank, "from a mean and insignificant beginning has arisen perhaps the largest and most magnificent hydropathic establishment in the world".

Henry Challand.
[Jean Douglas]

The manager at Smedley's Hydro from 1893 to 1925 was Henry Challand. He had been Alfred Douglas's bookkeeper and deputy for twelve years; he was also his brother-in-law. Mr Challand must have had immense powers of organisation. Many times the hydro was compared to a small town or a military operation, such were the numbers of guests and staff and the quantities of food and fuel required to care for them. Even in the year to June 1892, it was reported that staff and guests at Smedley's had put away over eighty thousand pounds of flour, eleven thousand pounds of butter, nearly fifty nine thousand eggs, twelve thousand chickens, eighty five thousand pounds of fish and eighty thousand pounds of meat; this was before the huge expansion in visitor numbers in the 1900s.

By 1901 it was calculated that Smedley's had welcomed over 300,000 visitors

The smoking room fireplace.

since its foundation; each year the numbers were increasing by about five hundred. As the century dawned, the directors announced a £5,000 increase in receipts over the previous year to £40,000. After paying out the dividend, they were still able to bank £4,000 into the reserves. In 1904 the total income was £45,440, which equates to over £4.5 million in today's money. Expenses on provisions had been £14,587 and on salaries, £17,498. The average number of staff was two hundred. At Easter and Christmas, the number of guests staying regularly rose to over 400 and they had to refuse a further 300; office staff worked day and night answering enquiries.

The fourth phase of building at Smedley's had continued in 1892 with the opening of the billiard room on the main frontage, followed a few months later by the smoking room. (These two rooms are still largely in their original state, if one can ignore the modern lighting.) The hydro now had one long frontage with the drawing room, ladies' drawing room, reading room, billiard room and smoke room. There was no great ceremony when the billiard room opened, but a demonstration of Edison's latest phonograph was given, followed by entertainment by Nottingham Glee Club.

The billiard room had a mosaic marble floor and Sienna marble pillars, surrounded by oak-panelled walls. The main decorative features were the unusual stained glass top lights to the windows. These depicted women playing national sports such as golf, croquet, archery, cricket and skipping. Comfortable recesses for card playing were furnished with velvet sofas. Skylights and electric lights provided plenty of illumination over the two billiard tables.

Skipping and cricket.

When the new baths were opened in 1894 (described later) Mr Challand was able to say of the great building programme:

Thus we were occupied for the better part of a dozen years. Years of due discomfort, of toil and turmoil, but tempered by hopes of better things, and cheered by the steady growth throughout it all of the popularity of the place.

The alcoves today.

Further improvements were inspected by a *High Peak News* reporter just before Christmas in 1898. The old kitchens and store rooms were becoming inadequate to feed an average of five hundred guests and staff daily. Henry Challand went on a fact-finding trip to London to see the kitchens of the best clubs and hotels: the new facilities were on a par with these. A new grocery store could receive provisions hoisted by pulleys straight up from the railway drays in the street. The shelves held a ton of sugar and 600 pounds of tea. At that season, four hundred and sixty pounds of plum pudding were ready prepared. Flour was lowered from this room into the new bread bakery below at a rate of 30 stones a day. The new bread oven, along with meat and pastry ovens heated from the same furnace, was fired up continuously. It had taken two weeks to get them up to temperature.

Two new meat stores – raw and cooked – were kept at a temperature of 32 degrees Fahrenheit by a cold air pump and 10 inch thick walls insulated with charcoal. The larger raw meat store was stocked at that Christmas time with 2327 pounds of meat, including 56 brace of pheasants, eight hares, one haunch of venison, twelve geese, six dozen pigeons, four dozen chickens, forty hams, and 400 pounds of bacon. The white-tiled milk and butter larder was also ventilated with a cold air pump system.

Four old ranges in the main kitchen had been replaced with a new super-size one. The old spit-roasting apparatus in its six-foot fireplace, reminiscent of Haddon Hall, had been replaced by a new fuel-saving fire. New steam ovens, which kept the foods and their smells separate, could take whole turbots and six dozen cauliflowers at once with ease. A new gas cooking table had eighteen saucepan rings. The toaster in the stillroom toasted eighteen slices of bread at once.

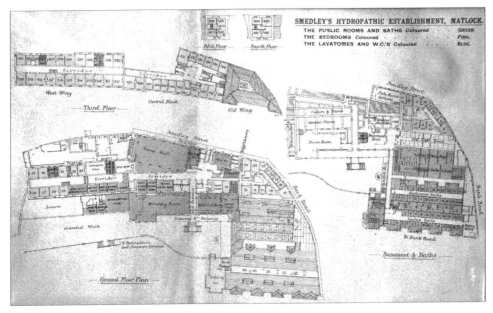

The improvements completed by 1900.

The *Visiting List* once said that the chefs at Smedley's knew a great secret unknown to London chefs: "How to provide a *recherché* repast which shall at the same time be healthful". In 1901 Alfred William Crohill arrived from Cambridge where he had been trained at King's College kitchens and where he had also been a choir boy. Three of his brothers were also chefs. Frank came to the Royal Hotel and Rockside, as already mentioned. Thomas was at Jesus College, Cambridge, where he was registered bankrupt in 1905. In 1901 Harry Robert was a chef in London, but he did come to Matlock, as we shall see later.

In 1905 Alfred was awarded a gold medal by the Universal Food and Cookery Association, which is perhaps why, soon after, a London couple chose to be married by special licence in Matlock and gave a reception at Smedley's. The bride's dress from Worth's of Paris was of pale fawn silk trimmed with skunk fur. She wore a chiffon picture hat. The flowers and cake came from London, but the couple trusted Mr Crohill with lunch! The next year Chef Crohill went to London's Horticultural Hall to compete against the chefs of the King and the Prince of Wales, as well as the top hotels. The King of Greece awarded him a silver medal.

There was always ongoing refurbishment in the hydro. In 1900 John and Caroline Smedley's portraits in the dining room were re-framed and moved to the drawing room. To the reading room was added a frieze of trees with ribbons listing authors and poets. The wood panelling in the dining room was re-polished and a deep-pile Irish carpet installed. Waring's were brought in to redecorate the walls, including a "beautiful picture".

By September 1901, a new suite of 45 bedrooms had been constructed on the north side of Smedley Street, connected by a double deck bridge to the main building. (The cabmen's shelter had to be moved to the Town Hall gardens.) These new lofty and spacious rooms were supplied with hot and cold water, electric lights

Ceiling decoration in a writing room.

The north bedroom block with its row of shops.

The Winter Garden today.

The Winter Garden fernery.

with a switch over the bed, radiators, oak furniture including a writing desk and ottoman, and a telephone. A pretty Wilton carpet covered the corridor floor. By Christmas week 1906 thirty nine more rooms were ready. The new three storey building included writing lounges with bay windows, still a feature of the street. These rather ornate sitting rooms had moulded ceilings and white walls touched with gold. The wicker tables and chairs were bright crimson. (The rooms are today decorated in garish colours and crowded with conference paraphernalia.) Seven shops including a bank were built on the ground floor; the first tenant was John Wildgoose the florist. Later the hosier Thomas Crowder Johnson opened a "blouse depot". A decade later the directors were planning more bedrooms to bring the capacity up to five hundred.

The last addition to Smedley's, which is still prominent today, was the glass conservatory known as the Winter Garden, opened in 1900. Previously, large balls had been held in the dining room; it must have been an organisational nightmare to clear a dinner away before dancing.

The long lounge corridor was extended to culminate in an anteroom which was decorated for parties in Turkish or Indian style with curtains and cushions. On the right of the new room was – and still is – a fernery constructed from seventy tons of Derbyshire tufa and planted with twenty varieties of fern. A small lagoon contained colourful goldfish.

There was room for one hundred couples to dance comfortably. The central floor was constructed on spiral springs, the same as used in the Tower ballroom at Blackpool. The surface was of oak, walnut and sycamore parquetry with a huge interlaced star in the centre. The surround was laid with patterned marble mosaic in a flower design. The heating pipes were hidden behind iron staging on which stood pots of palms. At the back was a stage for the orchestra, with a piano. To the right side was a "green room" and to the left lavatories. The room also had its own

MATLOCK, SMEDLEY'S HYDRO. (LOWER WALK.)

kitchen. The glass and iron roof culminated in an octagonal dome. At some point, probably during the First World War, the room was decorated with the flags of our allies, and these stayed in place for many years. (The County Council covered this beautiful floor, but a recent flood has provided the opportunity to scrape some areas clean and expose the marble. The springs are still underneath.)

Two new greenhouses were built so that Mr Knowles, the head gardener, could grow gloxinias, ferns and caladiums (a foliage plant with brightly coloured leaves) for the Winter Garden. This brought the total number of greenhouses to five. Mr Knowles, still keeping the family's music shop on Smedley Street, died in 1914 after 52 years' service. His son had already been his assistant for thirty-nine years.

In 1903 more grounds were added with the purchase of Yew Tree farm, just below Smedley's on Bank Road. The house was let out as a shop to a butcher called Charles Taylor. (This is now a private house, but remembered as Cobs and Cakes.) Some postcards from the early 1900s show quite rough fields still in Smedley's grounds, but soon there were smooth lawns. In 1904 a new bowling green was laid out, with a pavilion large enough to serve afternoon tea. This was a crown green, but it was made flat in the 1930s. Advertisements listed two grass tennis courts and two of asphalt. These tarred courts could be used for roller skating or flooded for ice skating in winter. The new drill room (which became the old Local Studies Library) was also used for roller skating and the bath's basement had two twenty-yard bowling alleys.

More land was bought for a different purpose. In 1899 the 160-acre Farley Farm was acquired for £5,000. Smedley's henceforth had their own source of fresh milk, eggs and meat. There was plenty of swill from the kitchens to feed the pigs: a donkey cart could be seen carrying the waste daily up the hill. The donkeys also still took fragile visitors on short outings along Hackney Lane.

Card posted 1907.

In 1892 the boiler room, with its tall chimney on Bank Road, was built as part of the new baths complex. From here the baths were heated and all the rooms kept at their prescribed temperatures. In 1901 John Smedley's disused church in the hydro grounds became a gas-fuelled engine house with dynamos humming in the aisles and smoke coming from the steeple. More electric plant allowed an increase of arc lamps in the Winter Garden from three to six. Above the end of the baths a band pavilion was built, which is still a prominent feature.

It was thought that lighting in the new bedrooms and extensions would require a greater capacity to store electricity, so the hydro bought the old mill with the red chimney by the railway station. It had also been planned to store water there, but the new sources found on Matlock Moor by the Council made this unnecessary. In 1906 the mill was leased out because it had never really been needed. It was taken as warehouse and stabling by William Pride, the game dealer in Crown Square.

Speeches given at Christmas and during other ceremonies always mentioned the happy working atmosphere created by Mr Challand. He was a familiar sight in the hydro with his waxed moustache and formal frock coat. His family lived at Norwood Villa on Lime Grove Walk, which is the semi-detached house on the corner now opposite the surgery. In 1905 a gas explosion caused a dramatic fire in the kitchen. In 1908 they moved into the newly-built Rockwood on Cavendish Road, but one cannot imagine Henry was often at home. After twenty-five years' service, he was made managing director of the Hydro in 1907. This action was praised in *Restaurant and Hotel Review* as a far-seeing move by the Board, which should be emulated in other establishments. They thought that managers were the best people to make business decisions. From 1897 Harry Douglas, Mr Challand's

Smedley's horse bus bringing guests from the station.
[Glynn Waite]

149

Sergeant Cocking's drill room.

nephew and the son of the former manager, became his clerk.

Harry's grandfather Alfred died in 1907. He had been the secretary for Smedley's Board of Directors for 33 years and the head cashier at Lea Mills for fifty years. He retired to Bradford Villa on Chesterfield Road. There were two other sad losses to the Board. In 1905 the Chairman Joseph Crowder was killed in car crash near Huddersfield and in 1906 their architect and clerk of works William Doxey died.

A visitor's first impression of Smedley's was up to Fred Byron, who for many years drove their horse bus up the hill from the station. He kept to a very strict routine by resting the chestnut horses at the same place half way up the hill. It was said he did the same with the motor car in later years. In 1908 Sergeant Cocking retired after twenty one years as a hall porter, but he continued with the drill classes.

With most of the planned great building works completed or in their final stages, the stage was set in 1900 for Mr Challand and his team to dazzle a generation who were prepared to enjoy themselves enormously.

THE OTHER HYDROS ON THE BANK

At Whitsuntide 1891 the hydros on the Bank had been joined by newcomer, built by an old hand: George B Barton junior of Jackson House Hydro. He had retired to live on Chesterfield Road in a house called Dalefield, on land below Cavendish School and behind the Congregational Church. He probably demolished this house to build **Dalefield Hydro,** the south wing of which was still his home. The new five storey building was in the Elizabethan style, with 40 *en suite* bedrooms. Pupils at the boarding school in the premises in the 1960s recall large mahogany wardrobes and silk-lined drawers for gloves. A huge metal framework on the roof proclaimed the name "Barton".

The magnificent hallway was decorated with stained glass windows, Minton tiles and grey stencilled walls. The dining room at the north end could hold 100 diners. The drawing room was fitted with novel sliding doors so that it could become two rooms. The morning room was decorated in chocolate and pale blue. There were billiard and smoking rooms which featured Bentwood chairs. (These were chairs using wood which had been steamed and glued, following an Austrian patent in the 1850s.) All the rooms were fitted with electric bells and speaking tubes. The atmosphere was kept fresh with Arnott's ventilation, which had been specially developed for medical premises. The baths in the basement included electric apparatus running off Leclanche batteries.

Outside was a promenade terrace and a second lower terrace with a tennis court. One could even walk on the roof. Advertisements tried to encourage family holidays with activities for children, who were kept out of sight and mind in their playroom in the basement.

George Barton retired in 1906 to The Beeches in Matlock Bath where he died at the end of 1908. He had been a chairman of the Urban District Council and the vice-chairman of the Matlock District Improvements Association (described later). The hydro was then managed by Mr and Mrs W L Booth. In July 1910 Mrs Hiles became the new owner, but the 1911 census has the third generation George Barton and his wife Hannah residing in an otherwise empty building. The reason for this downturn in the hydro's fortunes is unknown.

In 1892 William Atkins had left **Rockside Hydro** after twelve years, for three of

A new tower bedroom at Rockside.

ROCKSIDE HYDRO, MATLOCK.

VIEW OF INGLE IN LOUNGE.

Tennis (dry and grass) Courts.
Bowling and Croquet Lawns.

Card posted 1915.
[Glynn Waite]

which he managed the business alongside his own Darley Dale Hydro. Rockside was briefly floated as a company with Mr Rowland putting in £7,000 of the £21,000 needed, and Mr Bardsley, the manager, as managing director. Visitors were encouraged to buy shares. Mr Rowland died in 1902 aged 88 years.

However, the Hydro was bought for ten thousand pounds in 1894 by the Goodwin family from Wolds Farm, neighbours of the Rowlands on Cavendish Road. Mrs Goodwin, a farmer's widow, first ran the hydro with her daughters, but many members of this energetic family became involved over the next forty five years: they made a great success of the business. One daughter, Marie, was trained as a doctor in Manchester and she took over the medical side. In 1900 she married Dr Albert L'Estrange Orme, the surgeon at the Whitworth Hospital. They built the Red House on Dale Road, where their son Christopher was born, but Albert died aged only 45 years in 1909. His funeral procession was one quarter of a mile long.

In 1903 Rockside Ltd became a semi-private company with the share capital held by the Goodwin family and friends. At this time the Goodwin directors were listed: Eliza, widow; John Godfrey, who was then still working as a commercial traveller for his cousin G W Goodwin at his Odsall Lane soap works in Manchester; Thomas, an accountant in Manchester; Annie Eliza (Lilie) the Rockside manager, who had trained in domestic science in Manchester; James Henry, another Manchester accountant; Harriet Ada who was the Rockside housekeeper; and Dora who was the book-keeper.

In the early 1900s Rockside was described as comfortable and informal. The drawing room had a mixture of sofas, easy chairs, five o'clock tea tables, an organ, a piano and lots of books, all set out on a beautiful carpet. The piano was an up-to-date transposing model. The billiard room had velvet settees and wool rugs. The five acres of gardens were an "earthly paradise": in the summer of 1901 there was a splendid display of variegated poppies. But there were no longer enough bedrooms and the public rooms had become too small.

The Goodwin family chose two architects who were already well-known in the district and who were shortly to become very eminent nationally. Barry Parker was born in Chesterfield; he and Raymond Unwin, his brother-in-law, began working together in Buxton in 1896, where Parker had already designed notable houses. In Matlock they had altered Megdale Farm and Cawdor Cottage, which by then belonged to the quarry owned by Parker's father. In 1903/4 they also designed the houses at 79 and 81 Cavendish Road, followed by 87 Cavendish Road in 1928/9. The partnership went on to design Letchworth Garden City and Hampstead Garden Suburb.

In August 1903 their visitors gave the Goodwins a silver trowel to lay the foundation stone of the new wing. (The stone is still there but clumsily cut in half by a new wall.) Fifty workmen from John William Wildgoose's firm were given a substantial tea to get them started. The new turreted east wing contained thirty seven new bedrooms on four floors. The rooms, reached by elevators, had Arts and Crafts-style fitted furniture, radiators and fires, and electric lights controlled from the bed. There was a choice of vi-sprung or hair mattresses or feather beds. The rooms on the fourth floor had individual fireplaces with copper hoods in *art nouveau* designs and green-glazed tile surrounds. Many fittings were decorated with heart-shaped *art nouveau* motifs.

On the ground floor was a recreation and ballroom with a dance floor of

The stage and ballroom staircase.

153

Rockside dining room in 1906.

Rockside entrance hall.

"constructional woodwork, so arranged as to form its own springs". It was finished with seasoned Austrian oak parquetry. A hand-written note by a Goodwin said the guests "danced many miles on this floor without tiring up to the small hours of the morning".

A large stage was equipped with the latest lighting effects. This soon became very popular with local dramatic societies. On the next floor, a lounge took up nearly all the space, with an inglenook copper-hooded fire with green tiles, and cushioned window bays. The furnishings were by Johnson's of Leicester. A "well" in the lounge gave a view down on to the ballroom stage like a theatre gallery. There were a couple of very pretty staircases out of the room.

French doors led out to a new terrace and the remodelled grounds, with a carriage drive to the entrance hall. This had a Derbyshire stone staircase. Much of the decoration here and in the dining room was very similar to Charles Rennie Mackintosh's designs.

The Mather and Platt electric plant was housed in a separate building so the hum would not disturb the patients' sleep. The main rooms were lit by electroliers. In 1905 new kitchens were opened, lit from an octagonal roof, with tiled walls, and a telephone to the Misses Goodwin in their offices. A seventy foot chimney provided ventilation, cooking was done in steamers in order to retain the nourishment, and pastries were made on Hoptonwood stone slabs. Chef Frank Crohill was enticed from the Royal Hotel. At the opening dinner, John Barnes played his new march called "Rockside". Later another wing was built stretching back from the old building to provide more bedrooms and a laundry. Planning permission was given after a promise of money to widen Cavendish Road.

Matlock House Hydro was still a company, largely run by its secretary Robert Hall, who was also busy with many other concerns in the area such as the High Tor

Matlock House Hydro. Matlock. STATION:— MATLOCK BRIDGE.

Ideally situate, 700 feet above sea-level, and commanding a panoramic view of scenic beauty of almost unparalleled splendour.

Unequalled for Position.

Dowsing Radiant Heat and Light Baths— the only complete installation in Matlock, the Metropolis of Hydropathy.

For Comfort and Cuisine Unexcelled.

Baths of every description. Replete with every Modern and Approved Form of Appliance known to Medical Science, including Finsen Lamp, Massage Vibrator, Sinu Soidal Current, etc., etc., Conspicuously successful in the treatment of Rheumatism, Gout, Sciatica, and kindred ailments.

Terms, en pension, from £2 2s. per week.

pleasure grounds. In 1900 a new manager called Margaret Beard came from Colwyn Bay and Rhyl Hydro. Her motto was "Comfort, Cleanliness, Liberality and Pleasure". Advertisements were still aimed at the upper classes, with mentions of a *"bijou"* theatre where guests performed theatricals and a *"salle à manger* of the most up-to-date description" with a rich and luxurious carpet. However, Miss Beard's predecessor George Southern had been refused a liquor licence. The company was wound up in 1910, but a New York-born manager, Miss Cameron, was keeping the business going for the time being. The hydro's subsequent history can be read in "A Tale of Three Hydros".

Elm Tree Hydro had really ceased to be a viable business after William Bramald re-married and moved to Blackpool, where he died in 1901. John Wall and his wife took over; he was the son of Harriett Richards (by her first marriage) and grandson of Ralph Davies at Chesterfield House Hydro. His name was also linked with Wood View House and he was briefly a director at Poplar Cottage. By 1908 Mrs Lawrence Wildgoose was running Elm Tree as a boarding house, and the Walls had moved to a small hydro at Stanley House on Smedley Street. In 1911 Matlock House bought Elm Tree as an annex.

The drawing room at Chesterfield House.

Chesterfield House Hydro had been inherited by Mrs Harriet Richards [4] from her father Ralph Davis, who had died in 1896. She and her husband had already been running the business for many years. They had added a new west wing in

---

4. Mrs Richard's daughter Ann married a professional footballer. Alfred Priest played in two winning cup finals for Sheffield, and once for England. He then became player manager for Hartlepool United. Was this marriage the result of footballers training at the hydros? Alfred died in 1922, but Ann lived until 1976, dying aged ninety nine.

1895, which included new baths and billiard and smoking rooms. The old building had been updated with a new kitchen, drawing room and dining room. In 1898 the business became a limited company with Ellen Wood as manager and John Kay and his wife in charge of the baths. Soon after Arthur and Sarah Hitching took over; he had been a lace curtain designer in Nottingham. They extended the building with a ballroom and new veranda, as well as setting out improved tennis, croquet and bowling greens.

The 1890s saw the end of the link between Prospect Place and Poplar Cottage Hydros, when Thomas Davis died in 1891 and his son Jesse (Aaron Josiah) in 1896. There had been some modernisation of Poplar Cottage with new baths in 1895 and they now offered accommodation for two hundred and fifty guests. In 1900 the business was sold by George, Jesse's son, to Mr Charles Jeffs of Grimsby, who had made his money in the fishing industry. At the second annual meeting of the **Jeffs' Poplar Hydro Company** in 1903, he claimed that he had, "in two years brought this hydro from a chaotic state into a good payable concern". This was not a very tactful remark, as Jesse's widow and son George were still running the baths – she had been doing the job for forty years.

ABOVE: [US-Retro]

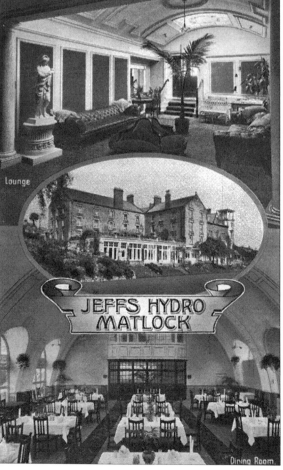

RIGHT: *The distinctive ceilings at Jeffs' Poplar Hydro.*
[Glynn Waite]

The first manager was Mary Williams, but she left in 1902 to buy Sycamore House Hydro. She was replaced by Miss Trolley from Grimsby. When she left in 1909 she was given an illuminated address and a purse of gold. Charles and Alice Wood were the next managers, but the company failed in 1911. The hydro was taken by a new company of businessmen from outside the area led by Alfred Knott and Francis Taylor and renamed **Chatsworth Hydro**. The first managers were Mr and Mrs William Hides; but, by early 1914, the chef Frank Crohill was named as manager. A document in the 1920s said that one party had backed out of the company and it had struggled ever since.

At April 1906 Mr Jeffs turned the first sod of a new wing. John William Wildgoose constructed new bedrooms reached by a new staircase and lift (the old dining room became a lounge and entrance hall). They built a new dining-cum-ballroom, recreation room, and lounge. The ballroom had a glazed a Holland floor, ornamental lead lights in an octagonal roof, Ionic columns and a plastered ceiling. The new kitchen was described as one of the finest in the county. Electric lights ran from nine tons of accumulators so there was no hum from engines at night. Photographs show the lounge and dining room had unusual barrelled ceilings, which can still to be seen, although ruined by modern lighting. The dining room also had a fanciful windowed gallery, reminiscent of German churches. By a small distance, the hydro was able to boast the nearest proximity to the new golf club.

Oldham House and Prospect Place Hydros were managed as one business by the Wildgoose family. Mrs Rachel Wildgoose, the daughter of Thomas Davis, had run Prospect Place after his death in 1891. Her husband John, the builder, town surveyor and Bentley Brook quarry owner, began a new career as a hydropathist about 1890. He lived in Arbutus Cottage, but this was inadequate. He built the substantial Oldham House, absorbing the cottage to provide a drawing room and

Oldham House and Prospect Place Hydropathic Establishments.

MATLOCK BANK, Derbyshire,
(Two Minutes' Walk from Tram Terminus).
STATION—MATLOCK BRIDGE.

National Telephone 0190.

Terms:
28/=, 30/=
and 32/6
per Week
Inclusive.

SPECIAL
WINTER
TERMS.

Hot Water Heating . . Apparatus .

Spacious Dining & Drawing Rooms, also Recreation & Billiard Rooms.

Magnificent Scenery. Splendidly Situated,
Southerly Aspect.
EXPERIENCED BATH ATTENDANTS.

Mrs. WILDGOOSE,
(Daughter of Mr. THOMAS DAVIS, late Proprietor of Poplar and Prospect Place Hydros).

Accommodation for over 100 Visitors.

Rachel Wildgoose.

billiard room. He chose the name Oldham because his son Edmund had moved there to manage a printing works. Finally John bought Prospect Place to make one viable establishment for over a hundred visitors. By the end of 1906, it formed one building with connecting corridors.

John and Rachel had seven sons still living, but their chief helpers in the hydro were Lubin George and James Anthony. Lawrence and John William were builders, Davis a stone mason and architect, and Francis a plumber. After Rachel died in 1909, Lubin became the manager of a new private company. James had been in charge of the bath house, but he promptly left for Winnipeg with his family of nine children.

Lubin became a Town and County Councillor, but his real love was music. He directed the very successful Matlock Prize Choir, although he tried to resign in 1903 because of pressure of business. The choir grew from his Primitive Methodist church choir. In 1910 and 1911, they won the first prize in their class at the Crystal Palace, and only missed the following year by one mark. More of his musical activities will be described later. He built a recreation room with a stage in the hydro. (Lubin's nephew Lawrence, the son of John William the builder, was equally famous for a pure tenor voice which won him many festival prizes.)

In 1904 the new dining room at Oldham House was decorated with panels of pale red wild roses with stems in green and brown. It had a cream ceiling, with blue stencilled paper above the picture rail. There were extensive gardens both sides of Cavendish Road. Photographs show an archway in a wall, with a sign "Oldham House Pleasure Gardens" and a huge pile of rocks on land now occupied by a County Council car park. There were ornamental walks and summer houses, tennis courts and a bowling green, stables and a garage.

Bank House and Church View Hydro continued to be managed by Henry Ward, although Mrs Ward died in 1901 leaving him with no housekeeper. A new block had been built in 1894 to provide a new dining room and billiard room, reached by a spacious corridor from the old buildings. Mr Ward claimed to be the only hydropathist taking real patients, rather than hotel guests. His no-frills approach was demonstrated by the Christmas dinner menu in 1899: plain roast turkey, goose and beef, cabbage and mashed potatoes. But the lights were seen to be on after mid-

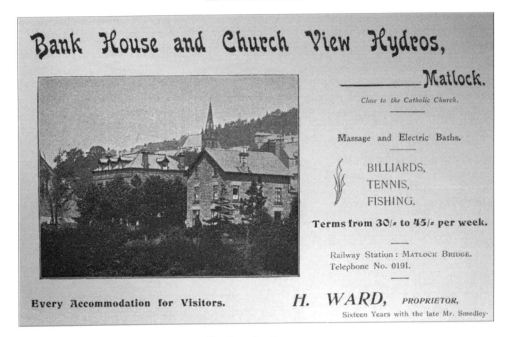

Bank House and Church View Hydros,

Matlock.

Close to the Catholic Church.

Massage and Electric Baths.

BILLIARDS,
TENNIS,
FISHING.

Terms from 30/= to 45/= per week.

Railway Station: MATLOCK BRIDGE.
Telephone No. 0191.

Every Accommodation for Visitors.

H. WARD, PROPRIETOR,
Sixteen Years with the late Mr. Smedley·

night because visitors were actually dancing!

Jackson House Hydro was still owned by Mr Barton until his death in 1908, but Mr and Mrs Leonard Bramwell had taken over as managers and they bought the business in 1913. They could take up to 60 guests. Their advertisement was usually a sketch showing the house with lofty mountains behind – were visitors disappointed by the reality? As at Bank House, home comforts were still their byword and the treatment was the basic mild water cure.

Sycamore House Hydro was bought from John Dawes in 1902 by Miss Mary Williams who had been at Jeffs' Poplar Hydro. There are very few photographs or details to be found: one view shows a group playing bowls under a large tree on the south side.

At **Tor House Hydro** George Davis could claim to be the last of his family trained by John Smedley and still in practice. He died in 1901 and his widow the following year. His sons George and William carried on, with their sister Mary Jane and George's daughter Winifred. The business was for sale in 1909, advertised as a going concern with seventeen bedrooms, but George was still there in 1913. (See the section "Shocking Events" for Winifred's sad fate.)

Malvern House was run by Job Smith, his sister Sarah and their nephew Herbert. Job died in May 1907: his huge funeral at All Saints Church reflected his standing in the town as a previous Local Board Chairman and Urban District Councillor, JP, County Councillor, promoter of the tramway, and member of many boards and committees such as the High Tor Company, the Whitworth Hospital Board, the Harrison Almshouses, and the gas company. He had always tried to make the town more beautiful for the inhabitants and visitors by improving streets and planting trees; he had recently organised gardens in front of the Town Hall. On the day of his funeral, the shops remained shuttered and the trams stopped. Sarah and Herbert carried on with the hydro until her death in 1919, when it was bought by Smedley's

Darley Dale Hydro.

as nurses' accommodation.

Rose Cottage Hydro had been sold to Charles Eyre, a retired cab driver. **BelleVue Hydro** was bought in 1902 by Mr and Mrs Herbert Warner; he had been a masseur at Smedley's for twenty years. **Spring Villa Hydro** was still known as Wheeldon's in 1908, but John and Louisa had both died, so it is not clear who was running the business.

Darley Dale Hydro was a short-lived enterprise between 1889 and 1903. William Atkins bought The Grove, a house, farm and kitchen garden in Darley Dale. He replaced the buildings with the Victorian pile seen today. An 1891 advertisement described a "splendid sanatorium" on a wooded site of 51 acres. Over seventy guests could enjoy country pursuits and golf on their own course (see the Golf section). William also decided to use his middle name, Montague: he must have thought it would attract the right kind of guest! Nevertheless, he was bankrupt by 1903, and he died in 1910 in Birmingham. He perhaps lost heart after his young son died in 1892 and his son-in-law was killed in 1902 in a cycling accident. The building became St Elphin's school for the daughters of clergymen: they held their first Prize Day in 1905. The site is now the Audley retirement estate, the house trebled in size with extensions.

A huge new sign painted on a roof could be seen from Matlock Bridge: "Boarding Establishment The Mount". This large guest house had been opened at the top of Steep Turnpike, across the road from Bell Vue Hydro. The first owner was a retired Scottish Congregational minister called J Beaty Hart, whose wife ran the business.

An even larger boarding house was built in 1906 by John William Wildgoose for Jane Houghton, a coal merchant's widow from Nottingham. This imposing building, on the corner of Henry Avenue and New Street, had fine views, balconies,

161

Golding House.
[Glynn Waite]

dining and drawing rooms, two sitting rooms and seventeen bedrooms. At some point, the business became known as Daysmill. (In 1922 the house was bought by the Teachers' Provident Society as a convalescent home and renamed Golding House after the secretary of the Society. In charge was Sister Eastland from the recently closed Derby and Derbyshire Convalescent Home.)

The Old English Hotel was extended in line with the original building before the fire. The publican from 1894 to 1908 (when he died aged 42) was a famous Midland athlete called Arthur Wall. In 1896 he won the 500 yard steeplechase at Notts Forest sports, but he was also a hurdler and high jumper. He encouraged Matlock Cycle Club to build a track in his grounds, described later. The Old English tennis courts and bowling green were also used by the town clubs. The football club called the hotel its headquarters and used it to change in before matches. Sometime during the decade, the two corner rooms were let to the Dalton family of Matlock Bath to open the Oriental Café. In 1914, the grounds were divided up into eleven building lots between the "New Road" and the river bank.

It was a sign of the times that in 1902 Arthur Wall shot and stuffed a waxwing he spotted in his garden – because the birds were so rarely seen! Sometime in the decade, the hotel became Ye Olde Englishe, for no very good reason. Their advertisements over the next forty years added and dropped the extra "e" on either word, and the "Ye", at random.

The Crown Hotel was managed at this time by William Tanzer. The Old Crown Hotel on Bakewell Road was being run as a temperance hotel by a Mrs Watts. There

Pic Tor promenade with the Derwent and Trevelyan hotels in the distance.

were many calls for its demolition to widen the road and remove the eyesore, which finally happened in 1906. The Queen's Head and Railway Inn were now Kimberley Brewery public houses.

Brown's Temperance Hotel had been bought by the Derby & Derbyshire Banking Company, which became Parr's Bank. The building was damaged in the fire in 1899. The bank built the impressive new brick and stone building next door which is now the NatWest. James Potter, the solicitor who lived at Dimple House, bought the old building as his office. It still then had a handsome stone porch with pillars.

However, this was not the end of Brown's. In c1891 the hotel moved to new larger premises at the bottom of Dale Road. It became known as the Trevelyan Temperance Hotel, with a long period until the mid-1900s when it was also called Taylor's Trevelyan after its owner John Taylor. The advertisements show the back of the building, which was very near the river with a garden. In 1910 the building was taken by the Matlock Club where gentlemen played snooker and cards – and

163

presumably drank alcohol! Henry Challand was the chairman. The Club is still there, but the ground floor is now the Sewing Corner, with French windows from what must have been the drawing room.

Next door was the Derwent Temperance and Commercial Hotel, now an accountant's office. This also advertised its position by the river and steps still clearly descend to a landing stage. In the 1940s the advertisement suggested the businesses had merged.

DOWN TO THE TREATMENT ROOMS

The chilling word "hydropathic establishment" has lost its terror. It does not convey the impression of an Inferno in fire and water where the visitor is alternately frizzled and frozen, fried and flooded, boiled and baked; now packed in ghastly sheets like an Egyptian mummy in process of embalmment; now treated as if he were a burning building to be played on by a hose; and anon regarded as a garden bed to be manured with mustard and squirted upon with a syringe. Bradbury, 1891

This is what we call the Cold Pilip, sir."

[Glynn Waite]

"See Naples and die" may be an Italian proverb, but "see Matlock and live" is a better plan, was written in guide book of 1900. Every hydro upgraded its baths during the 1890s and early 1900s. The basic treatments already described were still available, but the bigger establishments were investing heavily in electrical equipment and carefully watching developments abroad: they had to compete with foreign spas. The magazine *Health Resort* in 1906 thought they were succeeding: "Germany, once the first, has had to give place to Matlock for its hydropathy. Its staff of medical superintendents, bathmen and women are far beyond anything to be found elsewhere".

When Mr Tyack leased the Royal Hotel, he continued the work begun by his predecessor Mr Hinton in realising that a spa hotel was not enough – he had to advertise the hydropathic facilities which they had both installed. In 1891 he invited a group of London-based journalists from *Vanity Fair*, the *Illustrated London News*, the *British Medical Journal* and the popular dailies to spend the day with him. They visited the hotel's baths and the Pavilion, partook of a champagne lunch, and

THE ROYAL HOTEL
AND BATHS.

With the famous Thermal Spring, noted for its anti-acid properties and efficacy in the cure of Gout, Rheumatism, and kindred Ailments. Continental Baths in perfection, including Turkish, Nauheim, Carbonic Acid, Vichy, Aix, &c.

Electric Treatment: High Frequency, Four-Cell, Radiant Heat, "X" Rays, &c. Massage.

All the Baths are in the Hotel, and directly accessible by Lift. Resident Physician.

An Ideal Winter Home,

being sheltered from North and East Winds.

FANGO DI BATTAGLIA (Volcanic Mud Packs), the most effective cure for Gout, Rheumatism, Sciatica, Neuritis, and Nervous Disorders.

WEIR-MITCHELL TREATMENT.

The Hotel is conducted on the best Continental lines. It is situated in the most beautiful and sheltered spot in Derbyshire, in Grounds of over 20 acres. Milanese Orchestra, conducted by Prof. Avanzi, plays twice daily. Golf, Badminton, Fishing, Coaching, Billiards.

ACCOMMODATION FOR MOTORS.

For Particulars and Terms apply to A. BÜTTGEN, Manager.

drove up the Via Gellia. However, Mr Tyack overstepped the mark by describing his baths in his welcoming speech as the only ones in the district using a thermal spring; Mrs Howe at the Fountain Baths wrote an indignant letter to the *High Peak News*.

In 1904 Mr Thoma-Badrutt revealed the even more splendid baths in the basement of the re-vamped Royal Hotel, under the direction of Dr W Cecil Sharpe. This was really the ground floor, set into the hillside; the windows were double-glazed to further retain the heat. The thermal spring in the grounds, which is the only reminder now of the hotel's existence, had been restored and was connected to the swimming pool and drinking fountains. Reached from all floors by a lift, the baths included the latest treatments from European spas – the rich did not need to travel abroad.

The hotel's owners held the British rights of the Fango di Battaglio Company. Volcanic mud was imported from Battaglio, south of Padua, and mixed with spa water to make mud baths; in 1905 the Royal had 100 tons in stock. The radium it contained helped in the treatment of gout, rheumatism and sciatica. The idea for this introduction came from one of the hotel's directors who had broken his leg; but he was able to play golf and dance after being "Fango-ed". Straight after use, the hot mud was mixed with sand so it only had one application. Non-residents were soon queuing up for the experience. The Duke of Rutland, who suffered from sciatica, and Lord Burnham (who owned the *Daily Telegraph*) were described as regulars.

The management at the Royal must have been delighted when the famous

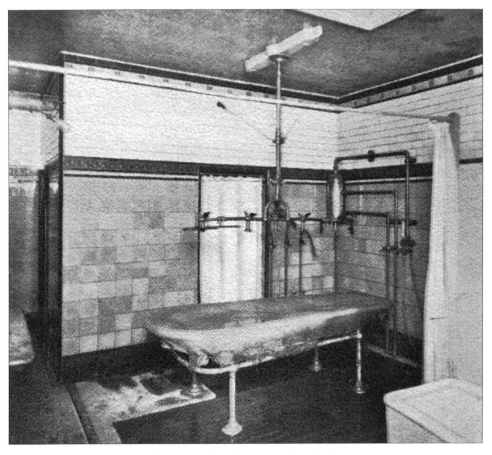

The Vichy douche room at Smedley's.

beauty Lady Colin Campbell spent Easter there in 1905, after her plans for a European trip fell through. She had been married to the youngest son of the 8th Duke of Argyll, but was the subject of a notorious divorce trial in which, unusually, her adulteries were described, and at the end of which she was still married! She re-invented her life by becoming a respected journalist writing for art, travel and sport magazines (she was a keen cyclist and fisherman). She wrote a very complimentary article about the Royal in *The World*. After only a three hour train journey from London,

> *I find myself seated on the wide terrace of the Royal Hotel at Matlock Bath. I own that I have found something worth discovery.*
>
> *But I have not simply come to Matlock Bath to admire its lovely scenery or to drink in its delicious invigorating air; so I leave the terrace and make my way down by the lift to the bathing establishment which that terrace covers. It is a white region to which I descend: walls of white tiles and white enamelled woodwork everywhere give it at once a most delightful impression of cleanliness. The baths are an embarrassment of choice.*

There are rooms for the Vichy douche and massage, the Aix douche, wave douche, needle baths, ascending douches, sulphur, pine, brine and soda baths, Russian vapour baths, Turkish Baths (both followed by shampooing), and a swimming bath. But what interests me more than these are the Nauheim carbonic acid baths, the extraordinarily complete installation for electric treatment, which includes an unusually fine electric radiant heat bath, electric mineral water bath, and the electric four cells bath where the patient sits comfortably in a chair, while arms and feet have each an electric bath separately, yet at the same time; and, above all, the far-famed Fango di Battaglia. This is the only place in England where this mud can be obtained. It is brought from Battaglia, near Padua, where the hot volcanic springs send up this mud instead of water.

Lady Campbell went on to describe the taps which gleamed like silver (all the metal fittings were plated in nickel silver); above each set were thermometers for constant regulation of the heat. A new machine had recently been introduced for inhaling eucalyptus to treat sore throats. She was tempted to try the "whole bag of tricks", but could hear the horses stamping outside and she "annexed her furs" to go for a ride up the Via Gellia instead. She concluded,

Where else can one find beauty and health so admirably combined within less than four hours from London?

The gentlemen's bath suite at Smedley's. The ceiling is still visible today.

167

The plunge pool at Smedley's.

The London-based reporter from *Health Resort* in 1906 was equally astonished that the Royal had "every bath appliance one could meet with at Marienbad, Nauheim or Mont Dore".

Smedley's was soon advertising Fango mud too; later they added Fango D'Agnano from a spa near Naples. The large hydros also installed Nauheim baths, mentioned above, named after Bad Nauheim in Germany. To relieve cardiac conditions, the patients took a course of twenty baths of increasing duration from ten to twenty five minutes. Then they rested for one hour, warmly covered. The water had carbon dioxide bubbled through and "flowed like champagne". In the second week the treatment was often combined with Schott exercises, developed by two brothers who were doctors at the German spa. These were movement resistance exercises, pressing different limbs against pressure from the therapist. By taking a Nauheim course in Matlock, the heart patient could avoid the strain of foreign travel.

New baths on the side of Bank Road were opened at Smedley's Hydro in 1894 by the Duke of Devonshire. The contract "to complete the colossal sanatorium" had been given to John Wildgoose at Christmas 1891. At the opening, they were described as a tribute to the architect George Statham who had recently died. The whole town joined in the celebrations with lavish street decorations and brass bands. Afterwards, the ducal party went on to the Matlock Bath Pavilion, where a *"café des fleurs"* had been set up to raise money for the Derby and Derbyshire

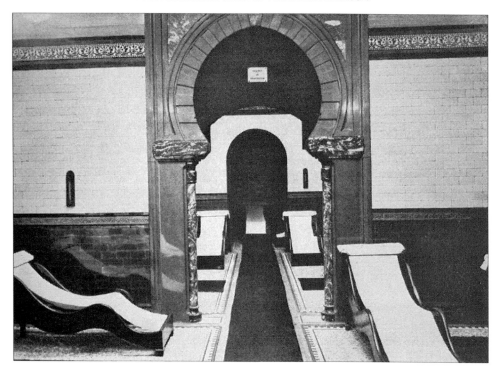

The Turkish Baths at Smedley's. The sign says "Silence is requested".

Convalescent Hospital.

The new baths, reached through the basement, consisted of four gentlemen's and four ladies' suites, each with dressing rooms. Each bathroom had its own attendant. The old baths became Turkish Baths for ladies and spare facilities for busy times. There was a new plunge pool, which still exists under a floor. The floors were paved with Italian mosaic tiles in ivory and amber with majolica borders, but covered with mats for the feet. The wide corridors were walled with Minton tiles and plastered above in bright adamant. [5] A later inventory listed dozens of mirrors, for example 26 in the ladies' corridor, 24 in the spray rooms and 13 in the gentlemen's cooling room! The mahogany couches in the Turkish Bath's cooling rooms were furnished with many cushions.

Each of the sixteen bathrooms had the basic needle (rain) sprays and head baths etc. The patients lay on a marble slab. There were separate rooms for douches. At one end were the electric baths and packing and drying rooms, where wringers with rubber rollers prepared the wet sheets.

Dr Sharpe had taken over from the late Dr Hunter as senior physician, with Dr Harbinson as his deputy. Dr Harbinson was appointed the Chief Physician in 1904 at a salary of £800. He and his wife lived in various rooms on the third floor of the central block; for most of the early twentieth century he and Doctor MacLelland

---

5. Adamant plaster was manufactured in the United States from 1886 as a substitute for lime plaster.

169

were in charge. The initial consultation still cost one guinea. The "consultation roll" kept by a footman gave the order of priority for cases during each day. The sixty bath staff included trained hospital nurses who wanted hydropathic experience. Throughout this period the matron was Sarah Louise Fox from Dewsbury, but the head bathman of twenty five years, William Wilson, died aged only 53 years in 1905.

> *Yesterday I had my first taste of massage, or I ought to say punch and poke etc., by such a dear little nurse, such a bright jolly little soul, who is blind, but seems to have such a wonderful sense of touch and very strong capable hands.*
>
> Round and Allen.

Several of the female masseuses were blind or partially-sighted. In the 1911 census it was recorded that two had been blind from birth, three from childhood and one from the age of twenty six.

There was a specific leaflet which doctors could order. It listed the all the facilities described above, but included one interesting paragraph concerning alcoholics. Whilst the treatment would be good for dipsomaniac patients anxious to be "delivered from their thraldom", Smedley's declined to undertake the "mere custody of confirmed drunkards". Tor View house on Jackson Tor Road was used for isolation cases and those with the DTs.

In 1900 T P O'Connor MP described his treatment, which still used the same bath books devised by John Smedley. He listed examples such as number 61C (a Russian Bath of two minutes), 85D (wearing a damp towel bandage next to skin), 64A (standing in a bath with hot water on the feet and a hot water lather). His lunch was fish, cold lean meat, green vegetables and stewed fruit. Dinner was the same with a little roast beef added. However, such simple fare left him "feeling a new man" and at a cost per week which would only pay for one day in the West End.

An expanding range of baths and sprays, or showers, could be specifically aimed at every part of the body: foot, head, eye, ear and nose baths; hot or cold, shallow or flowing sitz baths; ascending, vertical or horizontal, local or spinal douches; needle, wave, steam, box or vapour baths. There were more imports from Continental spas: *Aix le Bain* douches directed a nozzle of water to an area being massaged and Vichy douches consisted of a metal arm from which several shower heads were suspended over a treatment couch. At Rockside, the masseur at the Aix douche couch had a rubber hose over his shoulder, which continuously directed warm water on to his hands.

From the 1890s Smedley's, the Royal Hotel, and the larger hydros introduced the Weir-Mitchell treatment for nervous collapse. At Smedley's this cost an extra nine guineas per week, but that included a specialist medical attendant, electrotherapy and massage, and special diets. Dr Silas Weir Mitchell was an American physician who had developed cures for nervous diseases caused by the trauma of the American Civil War. The treatment involved isolation from other guests for four to six weeks; it was nicknamed Dr Diet and Dr Quiet. The patients at Smedley's had their own suite of rooms and were reserved part of the upper balcony.

Electric and radiant heat treatments were taken at the patient's own risk. The electrical treatments came in many forms, but usually involved applying electrodes to the body. Galvanic or direct current treatment used a low voltage. The positive electrode was held by a nurse, and the patient lay on or held the negative electrode to pull electrons inside the layers of skin. It could continue for thirty minutes. In 1891 there was an advertisement for Galvanism at Volta House on Bank Road. "Richardson & Wilkinson Medical Electricians" claimed to give treatments at Rockside Hydro with "No shocks".

Faradic high frequency treatment used an oscillating current, which left energy on the skin in the form of heat which boosted the metabolism and stimulated muscles. It could also destroy infections. Matlock House Hydro was keen on weekly demonstrations of their equipment as after-dinner entertainment. They used D'Arsonval apparatus, developed by Jacques-Arsene D'Asvonal, a French electro-physiologist, and still used today for cosmetic cases. In 1903 it was said to treat "almost every morbid condition of the human body" including diabetes, gout and rheumatism. "It is evident that the current is of a high frequency as an incandescent lamp held between the two hands of the patient becomes brilliantly illuminated." But thankfully, "The patient only evinces the most delightful of sensations".

In 1903, a young man returned home to London and described his treatment at Matlock House in the *Daily Chronicle*. He said it was nicknamed High Freak:

> Not being scientific, I can only say that you sit on one end of the electricity and hold the other in your hand. Then about 8000 volts are passed through your body with the aid of a little machine which revolves at the rate of about a million turns a minute, more or less. I remembered that 300 volts electrocuted people in New York, but was reassured to learn that the current would pass through me too quickly to do any harm.

Another visitor, Mr Peerless in 1908, watched a demonstration. The nurse stressed that the patient must not be touched. He was handed a metal cylinder and told to touch a frame of glass on the wall. He felt a tingling sensation and green fire flashed from his fingers. The nurse then placed her hand a few inches from his feet to induce more green flashes.

Smedley's used Franklinisation (named after Benjamin Franklin) which was the application of static electricity. The patient sat on an insulated chair or couch. There was a positive pole on the leg of the chair and a negative pole attached to the head electrode under which the patient sat, or the patient held one pole. It was used to treat neuroses and asthma. Smedley's also gave patients electric shocks from a small Leyden jar, a device for storing static electricity. The treatment was directed to the

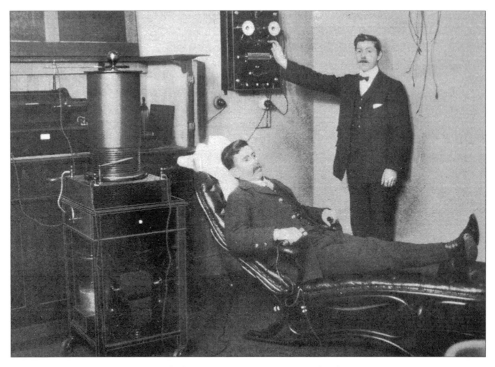

High frequency treatment at Rockside.

part indicated up to five times a sitting.

Patients could sit in electric baths with the current passing from their feet to their head, but not straight after meals! If their head felt full and throbbed, the bathman applied a cold wet towel. If the patient felt faint, the current was reduced. Sinusoidal electric baths used alternating electric current of low voltage. One zinc electrode was placed in the bath and the patient got in. When a second electrode was introduced "a very delightful electric sensation was at once perceived". These baths were used to stimulate weak and paralysed muscles or as a pain killer.

The Royal and Rockside Hydro introduced Schnee 4-cell electric baths, invented by German doctors. Photographs show a patient sitting in a chair dressed in a suit and tie, but with his sleeves and trouser legs rolled up, His arms and legs are encased in boxes. Next to him is an electric motor and a switchboard. According to a description, the current could "take any direction": Galvanic, Faradic, Sinusoidal or High Frequency. The treatment was for lameness, paralysis and hysteria.

The Royal Hotel soon advertised their D'Arsonval high frequency treatment and their diagnostic x-ray apparatus. On one visit to Matlock House, Dr Dowsing (see below) entertained after dinner with thought-reading and demonstrated Roentgen Rays – which we know as x-rays. In 1903 the local photographer W N Statham had taken the first x-ray image to be seen in the town. He meant it as a novelty, but it was of a patient here for treatment. Smedley's x-ray machine was once used to locate a brooch which a child had swallowed; the child was taken to Manchester for an operation to retrieve it.

In 1897 Smedley's purchased two Dowsing machines, but it was Matlock House

*The Schnee 4-cell electric bath
at Rockside.*

Hydro which was proudest of its association with Dr Dowsing, who visited several times to give lectures and demonstrations. Using "The Science of the Sunbeam", he advocated radiant heat which "bathed the whole body in luminous heat resembling sunshine". The treatment was chiefly for rheumatism and other diseases of the joints, but apparently proved efficacious for chronic alcoholism too. Dr Dowsing [6] claimed over one hundred establishments were using his system in Britain and Europe, curing twenty thousand people each year. He said his Radiant Heat and Light baths rendered Turkish Baths obsolete. He could supply heat to suit each

6. Dr Dowsing did not restrict his efforts to medical matters. His company also manufactured domestic radiators and cooking stoves. His memorial stone of 1931 is in Golders Green Crematorium.

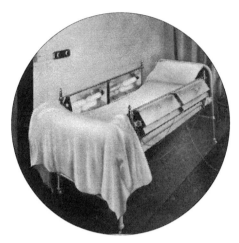

The radiant heat bath at Smedley's.

patient with mathematical accuracy up to 500 degrees Fahrenheit.

The heat was produced from up to ten lamps under an asbestos tent, or two lamps trained on a painful joint. The journalist mentioned earlier reported that he had sat in the asbestos tent, his heading poking out, with his body lying in a temperature of 280 degrees.

Mr Peerless, the patient writing in 1908, described a demonstration by Nurse Payne. He said the patient lay on a bed and was covered in a sheet steeped in a solution of "tungstate of soda" to render him non-flammable. Four powerful electric radiators were fixed along the sides. A coverlet was provided, supported on iron standards so that it did not touch the patient, with a hole for his head. Surely the skin turned very red? There was also a "Dutch-oven like" arrangement for heating a foot or an arm.

A similar arrangement at the Royal was described as an electric light cabinet. The patient sat on a glass chair bathed in light and heat. The large arc lamps had colour screens which could be changed. The heat had the same effect as taking a Turkish Bath, but without the patient breathing impure air from the boilers.

Matlock House also bought a Finsen lamp, equivalent to 30,000 candle power.

The Turkish Bath plunge pool at Rockside.

This was developed by a Danish doctor to use ultraviolet light to treat diseases of the skin. It especially destroyed the bacilli which cause lupus. (Professor Niels Finsen was awarded the 1903 Nobel Prize for Medicine.)

Vibrators were used for massage by hand, providing 10 to 12 movements per minute. Society ladies found they removed wrinkles and relieved headaches. Mr Peerless described a vibrator for stirring up the liver as being like sitting on a trotting horse!

The last new suite of luxurious baths was built in 1906 at Rockside Hydro, at the side of Rockside Steps. The separate male and female suites were decorated with white tiled walls and green Italian mosaic floors. All the fixtures had rounded edges to prevent dust settling. There were five Turkish Bath rooms: two hot, one cooling with couches, easy chairs and a green-tiled swimming bath, one shampoo, and one Turko-Russian bath. The pool room was decorated with hanging baskets, ferns, stands of bamboo, Turkish rugs and green curtains. Their inhalation treatments not only used eucalyptus, but creosote, pine oil and cinnamon. They claimed their Turkish Bath was the first in the kingdom to use a heated steam battery system (Row's patent), which kept the air pure.

STAYING IN – WE SHALL NEVER BE BORED...

The visitor who has once entered a modern hydro understands that it is in reality a luxurious hotel, a place of comfort and pleasure, where tennis and croquet woo the visitor into the sunshine, and music and theatrical performances enliven the hours between dinner and rest. The social life of the place is of such a description that a fort-night indoors during wet weather would do little to depress the spirits or lower the health.

Guide to Matlock and District, Ward Lock & Co., 1910

Visitors were certainly now going to hydros who had no intention of taking any treatment at all. At Smedley's in the 1890s, it was reckoned about a quarter of the residents did not have much wrong with them. These people had come for a good time and visitors on the mend also needed to be cheered up. The larger hydros, with over a hundred guests regularly in residence, realised that the committees of guests alone could no longer cope with all the entertainments needed. They appointed lady entertainment managers. Smedley's set the trend in the late 1890s with Gertrude de Soilleux Webster from London, known in Matlock as Gertie Webster. She had been a child prodigy on the piano, playing at the Crystal Palace when she was eleven years old. But she was really a budding author: as well as being able to perform at musical evenings, she wrote many plays and sketches. When she left to marry, she was replaced by Miss Brandon Hill, who was followed by Miss Tritton and then Miss Elizabeth Edgecumbe-Hobbs.

The *Visiting List* faithfully reported changes at other hydros. At Matlock House the lady entertainment manager in 1900 was Miss Linton who had been a member of the Carl Rosa Opera Company. Her successor Miss Montague was given an umbrella with a gold and mother of pearl handle when she left. Jeffs' Poplar Hydro employed Miss Mary Robertson. Rockside and Oldham House Hydros were blessed with family members who were very musical and talented themselves.

These lady managers did not replace the role of Master of Ceremonies at

A PROLOGUE BY MR CRUMMELL —
READ OUT ONE NIGHT AT SMEDLEY'S HYDRO

My Lords and Ladies, Barons, Dukes and Knights, Countesses, Primrose Dames and
    Women's Rights
Gentles and Simples, Misters and Esquires, MPs for Boroughs and for rural shires,
Good folk of common clay if such there be, lend me your ears and hearken unto me!
Lured by the fame which Smedley's Hydro bears, wide as the world and lofty as the
    spheres,
We have come here (My missus there and me) its cloud-capped towers and Turkish
    Baths to see.
For we have heard in regions far away: New York and Sydney, Tokyo and Cathay,
And such like places, stories grim and drear of rites mysterious which are practised here.
Of deeds so dread, so dire, so darkly deep, that just like Banquo's ghost they "murder
    sleep".
I says to missus there, I says, "Maria! Where there is smoke, there's bound to be some
    fire.
Let's pack and go – them stories is exciting. And if they turns out true, there will be some
    fighting".
"All right" says she, "And here's my hand upon it. Just wait a minute while I pack my
    bonnet."
And so we came. We came! – My cheeks grow pale. We have survived to tell the
    awesome tale.
At first all was plain sailing, for we found a sumptuous palace set with gardens round,
With lawns and terraces all gay with flowers, and everything to wile away the hours.
On every side, kind faces, civil greeting, amusements, papers and abundant eating.
In fact, a Paradise for man and woman, with just a grumble here and there to keep us
    human.
So much for first impressions; on the morrow, we found things topsy turvy to our sorrow!
For we, with many another visitor, were hauled before the Grand Inquisitor.
Oh my! Words fail to paint that interview – with ghastly stethoscope he pierced us
    through,
And ere we knew what we were about, he took and turned us quickly inside out.
Then to his Myrmidons, a gruesome horde, "Down to the torture chamber", loud he
    roared.
Swift to the dungeons we were carried off ("where now?" our merry jibe and heedless
    scoff.)
And to our Chief Tormentor given o'er – Forgive me friends, I really can no more!
What words can tell the horrors of that den, where we were boiled and baked and
    boiled again.
Where reeks of chilli, soap and steam, all blended in one horrid nightmare dream,
And not the least among its terrors ranking, re-echoed through the cells, the sound of
    spanking!
As if our childhood days had all come back and we were writhing 'neath a tutor's whack.
And yet we lived, and ate and drank again, as if life held no dangers and no pain.
Now my Maria's a girl of sense, and mighty keen on raking in the pence,
And so she says, says she, "I tell you Joe, I've half a mind to run a little show.
'Twill pass the time and cheer us up a bit, and if by luck we make a blooming hit,
We'll travel through the land and in a while retire from business when we've made a pile."
So here we are, for worse or for better, My Lords and Ladies etcetera etcetera,
It's only a scratch company, it is true, but when you've had a CRISIS, what can you do!!

A SPLENDID SUCCESS!

In the Derbyshire Record Office is a document from Smedley's Hydro which I had never dreamed could still exist. I was handed a very large and heavy grey package. As I undid the tape, the magic words "Recreation Committee Book 3" appeared on the spine of a thick, red-bound volume. Inside, on crumbling paper, were glued dozens of programmes and a few photographs.

The programmes – 3d or 6d each depending on their quality – were beautifully printed in colour with pictures and borders. (The money went to charities.) They gave the names of the guests on the recreation committee, the title of every drama and its cast, the name of every song and piece of music performed and their performers. They included scenes from famous plays, home-made sketches, recitations, *tableaux vivants*, wax works, pyrotechnic displays, lectures, mock trials, conjurers, charades, spelling bees, ventriloquists, brass bands, orchestral concerts – the entire world of Victorian entertainment.

The volume began in 1892 with the opening of the new billiard room. There is the programme for the Nottingham Glee Club and a demonstration of the Edison phonograph exactly as described in the *Visiting List*. Mr William Lynd, who gave the demonstration, gave several more talks on electricity and its application,

A mock trial programme.
[Derbyshire Record Office]

and appeared in many sketches. (He wrote a book called *The Practical Telegraphist*.) One of his talks, on Edison and his inventions, featured phonograph recordings of a choir singing "*The Holy City*" and a speech by William Gladstone – how exciting to hear the Prime Minister's voice!

Other guests gave lectures. An Indian visitor called Dr Ramaswamy Jyengar informed everyone about Hinduism; he also enjoyed taking part in the sketches – he was on one of the photographs. A recent traveller to Japan showed views painted by the "natives" using a limelight lantern. (The photographer William Barber was several times credited with supplying the limelight.) Another lecture, entitled The Dark Continent, was magnificent-ly illustrated by oxy-hydrogen apparatus, a kind of early projector.

Barnes Orchestral Band, Lea Mills Prize Band, Matlock Bath and District Military Band and later the Matlock United Brass Band conducted by Lubin Wildgoose, gave several concerts. Mrs Christie Murray, (whose husband features later) organised *tableaux vivants*.

Professional performers were brought in and commented upon: "splendid success", "very enjoyable", "moderately good", or not as good as so and so. Successful acts had left their contact address. Several claimed royal connections. David Devant, Royal Illusionist and Shadowgraphist, had recently impressed the Queen of Romania. (He went

Ramaswamy Jyengar, an Indian guest, (second left)
joining in a sketch. Photo by Frederick Barber.
[Derbyshire Record Office]

on to give Command Performances to our Royal family and famously made Queen Alexandra laugh a lot. He became the first President of the Magic Circle.) Mr Chillingham Hunt, a "public reciter", always boasted he had just given exactly the same performance at Sandringham.

James Pain & Sons, pyrotechnic experts to the Prince of Wales, (who claim they were involved in the Gunpowder Plot), gave a display which included rockets, shells, a Monster Glow Worm, Silver Saucissons, Mammoth Spreaders and a Flight of Seagulls with weird screams!

Towards 1898, the programmes became less elaborate, hand written on the same headed paper with views of the hydro's rooms. A familiar name from the *Visiting List* began to appear: Gertie Webster. Mr Challand had realised the guests could no longer manage a "Palace of Varieties" by themselves and appointed a professional.

VERY REFINED.

One of the best Entertainers that has appeared at Smedleys. £3.3.0

Smedley's, Matlock,

WEDNESDAY, JULY 5TH, 1893.

Special Engagement of

MR. R. A. ROBERTS,

FROM THE CRYSTAL PALACE, LONDON, WHO WILL APPEAR
IN HIS REFINED AND ORIGINAL

MONOLOGUE ✦ ✦ ✦
✦ ENTERTAINMENT,

WRITTEN AND COMPOSED BY HIMSELF.

To commence at 7.30.   Programmes 6d. each.

Comments added to a programme
by the Recreation Committee.
[Derbyshire Record Office]

An early mention of Gertie Webster. [7]
[Derbyshire Record Office]

celebrations. Time and again, the same names appeared at Christmas and Easter of gentlemen guests who undertook this role. They must have been larger than life characters, who presumably were long cured of what had taken them for treatment in the first place. There were also many references to talented guests who received gifts of appreciation. In 1900, for example, a Poplar Cottage Hydro visitor was given a meerschaum pipe for being a good entertainer.

By now the *Visiting List* was giving very detailed reports of plays and musical entertainments, with cast lists and revues – always positive! The larger hydros could afford to boost the casts with performers from London's theatres who were no doubt grateful to be paid for a weekend in some luxury rather than in their normal

7. In 1903 Gertrude left Smedley's and married Herbert Wentworth James, a journalist. She wrote over fifty rather racy novels, some with characters who underwent osteopathy and other treatments. One called *The Girl who wouldn't work* was made into a film in 1925. When searching *Mayfair* magazine in 1912, I noticed she was the author of the current serial.

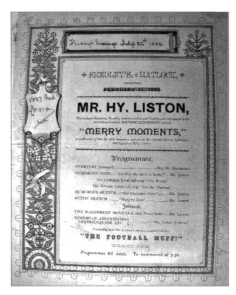

[Derbyshire Record Office]

boarding houses. Musical comedy and revue artists would do solo turns as well. Harry Liston was one frequent visitor – his signature song was *When Johnny comes marching home."*

Lubin Wildgoose, the manager at Oldham House, conducted Matlock choirs and brass bands, both of which he took to many competitions. He played the organ at the Primitive Methodist Church for over sixty years and conducted their prize-winning choir. He also played the double bass in the town orchestra. Aside from all this serious music-making, he could be relied upon to play dance music for his hydro guests.

Most of the hydros had concerts on Sunday evenings, with varying degrees of sacred content. Funeral marches were deemed suitable for pianists and hymns were sung. Some hydros invited the local church choirs, such as Lubin's, to perform. Many visitors joined the residents at the tram shelter in Crown Square on summer Sunday evenings for an all-denominational open-air service. This service later moved into Hall Leys Park. The tradition of conducting morning prayers in hydro drawing rooms persisted. At Rockside old Mrs Goodwin was still in charge of this in 1913 aged eighty. Every Christmas the Farnsworth family choir sang carols in the hydros to raise funds for the Whitworth Hospital.

This was the great age of country house parties with entertainments, so publishers produced long lists of short amateur plays and monologues. The Abel Heywood guide books offered "dramas, dialogues and operettas" and "recitations, dialogues and speeches, comic and otherwise" with such titles as "Ever-ready recitations of wit and humour," "Rhymes on Social Subjects" or "Poems and sketches in th' Lancashire dialect".

Some of these sketches and acts would be very offensive to us today, but they were a feature of the age. Visitors frequently blacked up and imitated Negro minstrels and comedians. In 1902 Parlato's Royal White Coons performed around Matlock Bridge for the season. Their variety act included La Belle Esma, a gymnast

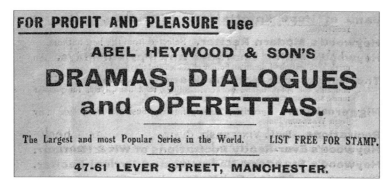

on a wire, the Musical Sevilles with over twenty instruments, Collett and Waldron Negro comedians, Mademoiselle Carola's miniature circus and a Japanese juggler.

Gertie Webster at Smedley's appreciated that it could be difficult for guests to learn long parts, so she employed readers in the wings while the actors mimed the actions. On the programmes in the Recreation Committee book, it sometimes said "characters will be sustained by" Gertie Webster and another, which presumably referred to this practice – it probably added to the fun. She wrote sketches with titles like "When ghost meets ghost" and "The statue and the picture".

There were favourite plays performed many times, such as one described as "a pair of lunatics in the ante room of a ball at an asylum".[8] Probably the funniest entertainments were the unscripted sketches. The first mention of one popular game was at Oldham House. They turned the drawing room into a law court and played out a breach of promise case: Lily Snowdrop versus Tom Jilters. At Jeffs' Poplar Hydro they staged a parliamentary debate: "Should bachelors be taxed" and if the amount should increase every year until they married?

Guests still loved dressing up for *tableaux vivants*. One at Smedley's, described as a symphony in black, white and green, appeared very dramatic in the lime light. Mr Peerless, visiting Matlock House, enjoyed the *tableaux*, although he complained about the long wait between scenes. He especially liked a series called, "Home they brought the warrior dead".

There was one frequent game enjoyed at all the hydros, which combined dressing up with a competition. A guest to Rockside described being met by Boots at the station and escorted up the hill on the tram. Miss Goodwin gave him a hearty welcome. Hearing music in the drawing room, he entered to find a crowd of Egyptian mummies! Using sheets and bandages the guests had wrapped each other up. Their fellow guests were given a list of those taking part and had to guess their identity.

There were many impromptu dances and more formal balls at holiday times. The band was invariably provided by John Barnes and his family, who were hosiers and drapers, but also sold pianos and other musical instruments on North Parade. Surely there must have been more than one ensemble, because they monopolized the dance scene in both Matlock Bridge and Bath from the early 1880s. John began

---

8. This is not as far-fetched as it sounds. At the West Riding Paupers Lunatic Asylum (later High Royds) male and female patients met every Friday night to dance.

A dance crowd in the Winter Garden.
[Picture the Past]

work as a schoolmaster [9] at Heage, but soon became a full-time musician. As well as having always to be up to date with the latest dance music from London, he composed tunes himself. In 1897 he was appointed as an orchestral composer to a London publishing house and toured all the watering places in England playing his own compositions. In the winter he ran weekly dances at the Matlock Bath assembly rooms where he had tried out apparatus called an *illuminaire*: presumably a lighting effect. At one time he was musical director at the Victoria Hall in Matlock. Later he played for weekly subscription dances at the Grand Pavilion in Matlock Bath. His brother Charles worked in their drapers shop, but often led the orchestra as a violinist until his death in 1927.

In 1904 John played for new promenade smoking concerts in the Winter Garden at Smedley's, but in 1910 this changed to the custom of playing every teatime. Although other musicians later took over this role, such as Mabel Miller's Ladies Orchestra, the late afternoon music and dancing sessions continued right up to the outbreak of the Second World War.

In 1907 the Barnes Orchestra was involved in an omnibus accident on the way to Bradbourne. The horse ran away, some passengers had to jump out of the rear door and the driver broke his shoulder. Nothing daunted, the band travelled on in another carriage and played their engagement.

Calico balls were becoming less frequent, although one at Jeffs' Poplar Hydro in 1905 had dancing from 9pm to 3am with two suppers at 8pm and midnight. Cinderella balls were now popular: many were run by a "Miss Candelette" in the Town Hall. These dances allowed girls to attend unescorted, but presumably they were home by midnight!

Matlock House Hydro was still famed for its fancy dress balls. At the New Year in 1900, the reporter enjoyed watching Mephistopheles dancing with nun and a sea-

---

9. It was revealed in John's obituary in 1932 that he had also written reports for the *High Peak News* and the *Visiting List*. Another brother Ernest was a career journalist, who had moved the offices of the *Visiting List* to their drapery shop at 9 North Parade in 1898. Advertisements could be taken to his house, Belmont, on Waterloo Road.

side minstrel, with a four foot high Union Jack on his head, swing round a simple country maid. At their August Bank Holiday fete, 500 lamps were lit in the gardens; they danced from 11pm to 1.00am.

The *Visiting List* exclaimed "They DO waltz at Rockside". A newly introduced waltz minuet was very popular. There were still reports of the lancers, polkas, Washington Post, *pas de quatre*, cotillions and quadrilles, but times were changing. The veleta was a very popular sequence dance in waltz-time introduced in 1900. The Victoria Hall held a veleta dance competition in 1905. When roller skating caught on again, they waltzed on skates.

In January 1904 visitors danced the cake walk, a dance evolved from Negro dance rhythms in the United States – rag time had arrived in Matlock! London visitors brought the latest records to play on Smedley's gramophone on the terrace.

There were four great crazes for the visitors in the 1900s: photography, cycling (described later), ping pong and, at the end of the decade, everyone was roller skating.

There were professional photographers in Matlock. Frederick Barber and his son William Harvey were employed by Smedley's to take photographs of their guests and their activities such as the *tableaux vivants*. They also made magic lantern slides for lectures. They had a darkroom in the hydro's basement where they printed guests' negatives. Later the guests could do the processing themselves. Most hydros eventually provided a small room or hut in the grounds for a darkroom. Other visitors could use the chemist shops: Mr Asbury allowed free use of his dark room in Matlock Bath. In 1907 enthusiasts visited the Grand Kodak Exhibition in Buxton.

Charles Colledge had a very useful shop next door to Bailey's chemist on Smedley Street, just outside the Hydro doors. As well as taking his own photographs, many looking down Bank Road, he sold stationery, needlework items and wool. The longest running business was William Nathan Statham's photographic studio in the last shop at the bottom end of Dale Road, until the Picture Palace was built. Statham was a trained artist, so stocked painting materials too.

"At Rockside it is ping pong morning, noon and night," reported the *Visiting List*. Ping pong originated among the upper classes in England during the 1880s, where it was played after dinner using improvised equipment such as a row of books for the net. The game manufacturer J Jaques & Son patented the ping pong trade mark in 1901, so other makers used the name table tennis. Celluloid balls were introduced from the United States, soon followed by the development of the modern bat with

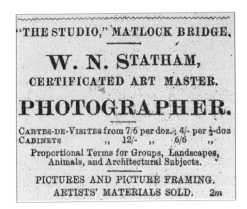

a sheet of pimpled rubber fixed to the wooden blade. An unofficial world championship was held in 1902. All the other hydros had to follow Rockside's lead and ping pong soon rivalled billiards.

The roller skating rink off Holme Road in Matlock Bath had been demolished in 1892 to become the site for Rockvale Terrace and Villas, but a fresh craze for the sport started at the Victoria Hall in autumn 1908 and a new maple floor was installed the following winter season. Soon visitors could skate there every day, and Monday, Wednesday, and Friday evenings. They held skating balls and hockey matches. The Royal Hotel prepared the floor in the old Pavilion, which could accommodate two hundred skaters. When the new Pavilion at Matlock Bath opened for business in 1910, roller skating was the first event.

The hydros and hotels now all maintained their tennis courts, bowling and

The bowling green at Rockside.

croquet greens in top condition. They were sports in which both sexes could compete, which made them very popular, although the women probably served under arm at tennis. Smedley's and Rockside introduced bowls, tennis, croquet and golf tournament weeks in August, with silver trophies and cups. The same guests came year after year to compete – the 1939 competitions had only just finished when war was declared.

Hydros with extensive lawns held cricket matches, although they also borrowed the town pitch. At one Rockside gents v. ladies match, the men batted left-handed with broomsticks, but they were all bowled out very quickly by one skilled lady who was presented with a silver purse. Rockside ladies also enjoyed playing football on the bowling green.

Unusual sporting events were often the only reason the smaller hydros got a mention in the newspapers. Oldham House set up a rifle range in the corridor during the Boer War. One croquet match at Bank House went on so long they had to strike matches to see the hoops. Chesterfield House Hydro guests played deck billiards on their drive. Belle Vue staged tugs of war. At Matlock House they played ninepins and the gardener often joined in the bowls matches: he was very good. In 1900 city dwellers at Jeffs' Poplar Hydro enjoyed helping a neighbouring farmer with his haymaking.

Smedley's were able to put their hard tennis courts to other uses. They flooded them for skating in winter, but also held cycling gymkhanas. In summer they floated paper boats for a regatta. One skipping competition drew 120 entries. They also staged a few walking races, but seemingly only for the staff. In 1904 several men were started on the nine miles to Rowsley and back by Mr Cocking, cheered by the guests. The race was easily won by W Dooley in one hour 26 minutes, for which he was given a gold watch.

Visitors and locals alike eagerly waited for a good snowfall. Until increased traffic made it too dangerous in the 1920s, the steep roads were turned into toboggan runs. One could set off from Jackson House Hydro and use Imperial Road, or take the faster and more thrilling Jeffs' Poplar, Steep Turnpike route. The way back up was easy once the tram was built.

Card games were played every day, particularly whist. A visitor to Oldham House Hydro was once dealt all thirteen trumps in one hand! Mr Peerless wrote that prizes for all the games played were typically silver pencil cases, match holders and china ornaments for the winners, with hat pins and boxes of cigars for the booby. Vouchers for local shops such as Evans the jeweler were sometimes given.

Rockside held penny purchase competitions – to buy the most interesting item, which it claimed were fun for the shopkeepers too – perhaps. Matlock House gentlemen were sent out to buy hat trimmings to decorate hats. They were also humiliated by needle-threading games. From every hydro came reports of familiar and long-forgotten parlour games: potato races, musical chairs, telegrams, guess the book, needle and thread, picking up marbles with pencils, picking up potatoes with teaspoons from a polished floor, fan and feather races, cigarette and tie races, hot handkerchief, coach and horses, secret society, singing proverbs, and dumb music.

Visitors also liked to be educated and informed. In 1903 Smedley's guests were given a lecture on the recently (1898) discovered element radium and shown the new spinthariscope. This device, which quickly became a toy for people to keep in

Tennis and bowls at Oldham House. Card posted 1910.
[Glynn Waite]

their pockets, emitted flashes of light from splitting atoms of a radium compound. A demonstration of Marconi wireless telegraphy in 1898 was followed in 1908 by a Marconigraph [10] brought in by the Post Office manager. (The first radio message across the Atlantic had been sent in 1902.)

Guests gave talks, such as "My experiences of New Guinea and its savage people" at Matlock House. Mr Palliser of India exhibited his postage stamps worth £1500. In 1906, after the recent dreadful news from San Francisco, David Christie Murray, a famous author and lecturer, gave a lecture on earthquakes and volcanoes. (Perhaps he really was ill: he died a year later.)

The *Visiting List* found a lady to write occasional fashion reports. At Smedley's Easter Ball in 1910, she noted a preponderance of white and pale shades. There were several dresses of, "soft white satin charmeuse, [11] veiled with chiffon scarves and draperies, varied by crystal or silver trimmings". One dress was in a soft rose pink, draped with a chiffon over-dress in blue-green, shot with gold. Another was in ivory silk with large gold spots.

For the first time in the spa's history, Matlock Bath had a Christmas season in 1904. Eighty guests at the Royal Hotel, including the Earl and Countess of Cottenham, enjoyed the sensation of entering a luxurious haven of warmth and

---

10. My grandfather received a marconigram in 1911 on a German ship crossing from Spain to England. Lord Kitchener was travelling on the same ship: the SS Feldmarschal.

11. A silk fabric with a satin finish.

Rockside's extensive pleasure grounds.

comfort. The cotillon – an elaborate ballroom dance for couples with a frequent change of partners – lasted one and a half hours on Christmas night. At midnight a twelve-course supper was served before dancing re-commenced. The pastry chef had made a replica of the hotel and Royal Well in coloured sugar. In subsequent years, an annual Easter ball was held too, and the special lady correspondent described some of the dresses worn in the *Visiting List* for 1906:

> *Mrs Walter Barrett's dress of black sequin net suited her admirably, and with it was worn a charming posy of choice flowers. Miss Bateman looked very well in pale yellow satin. Mrs Huish wore pale blue stain draped with tulle. A very pretty dress was of cream silk muslin with touches of pale heliotrope. Mrs Eccles's very handsome dress of black net pailleted with black and gold was much admired. Miss Howson in a lovely confection of pale orange crepe de chine was extremely "in the picture".*

All the hydros made their biggest effort at Christmas and introduced novelties. In 1903 Mr Jeffs presided over a dinner produced by visiting chef: Mr Stone from the Mikado Café in Nottingham. In 1904 Rockside held a *café chantant* with visitors dressed as waitresses. At Matlock House, "the *"viands"*, under the weight of which the tables seem to groan, whet the edge of the most jaded appetite". In 1902 they introduced a masked ball. But Mr Challand and his team at Smedley's really had no peers.

GOING OUT

In May 1908 a letter to the *Visiting List* asked where the water carts were hidden (a

Lord God to Thee we sing
Spare us our Noble King
Lord send him strength to rise
Now that he stricken lies

In 1902 the coronation of King Edward VII was postponed because he needed an appendectomy. A visitor at Matlock House wrote an extra verse to God Save the King.

new one was actually purchased for the Bank that year). The writer said the attractions of the Matlocks were the pure air and scenery, but against these the "dust demon is allowed to wage war unchecked". A letter in *Motor* magazine in 1909, signed by "Bumps", advised its readers to avoid the Matlocks. It claimed that one 250 yard stretch of the main road had three hundred potholes, some two feet across and three inches deep. The road seen at night, by the light of headlamps, resembled the surface of a rough sea. In 1910 a correspondent joked: "if you want a switchback ride, get on a bus and try the asphalt on Dale Road".

It seems the problem of dust and poor road surfaces remained as bad as ever. A deputation from the hydros to the UDC in 1901 complained that, in spite of the heavy rates they were paying, the dust down Bank Road was two inches deep and entering the shops. In fact, motor cars had exacerbated the problem. There were many complaints of thoughtless drivers "racing" through the towns kicking up clouds of dust. In Matlock Bath a new nuisance had appeared. There had been a find of basalt at Ible and the stone was being carted daily through the town on two massive steam lorries – snorting, smoky engines with massive grinding wheels. They were tall enough to catch on the gas lamps and damage the mantles. Another thirty steam lorries a day were passing through Matlock carrying stone from quarries or flour from Bailey's mill.

In 1904 Buxton and Belper councils experimented with a road surface called Westrumite, a mixture of ammonia and petroleum, but the remedy was worse than the evil. It had a horrible smell and the shops complained of black footmarks. In 1907 a competition was held in London for solutions to the "Great Dust Problem". One class was open to the best machinery to spread tar on road surfaces, but a Matlock firm entered the "best preparation of tar" section.

In July 1909 a Northwich company demonstrated a road covering of sprinkled calcium chloride, to absorb the moisture. *The Visiting List* conceded that the dust had not risen and the surface was not the dazzling white of limestone. Earlier that year they had published a letter from a Portsmouth visitor who said his council had been pleased with pre-formed ashphalt blocks.

Tar spraying was being tried out in Derby in 1909, but a Matlock councillor was worried a rain storm might wash tar into the river and kill the fish. Local trials brought complaints of an "oozy pitch-like stickiness", but it was agreed this was preferable to dust and mud. Tarmac, as we know it, was actually a local invention. In 1901 a surveyor for Nottinghamshire County Council, called Edgar Hooley, was walking in Denby when he noticed a smooth stretch of road close to an ironworks. Locals told him that a barrel of tar had fallen from a dray and burst open. Someone had poured waste slag from the nearby furnaces to cover up the mess. Hooley

CHRISTMAS AT SMEDLEY'S HYDRO – "AN ELYSIAN PLEASURE"!

At Christmas 1900 two hundred people had been turned away. For the lucky ones, "care flies to the winds under the aegis of the happiness which reigns supreme everywhere" and "it is simply impossible to be dull". The numbers of rejections steadily increased to over four hundred by 1910 and required extra secretaries to deal with the problem. Smedley's festivities had become, "a byword among the leisured classes of the kingdom". They even merited a report in *Le Matin*, the Paris daily paper.

Samuel Henstock, the house porter, had been in charge of the decorations since 1881.The planning and execution now took him six weeks, with the help of the "Ladies motto department". Then on Christmas Day it took him two hours to sort the half dozen sacks of post!

The visitors always wanted their traditional programme. The list of evening pastimes in 1905 was repeated with few changes for the next three decades: December 21st progressive whist, 22nd promenade concert, 23rd dance, 24th sacred concert, 25th Christmas banquet, 26th visitors' ball, 27th humorous entertainment, 28th concert and dramatic sketches, 29th fancy dress ball, 30th whist drive, 31st sacred concert; January 1st staff ball, 2nd progressive whist, 3rd concert and *tableaux vivants*. In the afternoons, there were sports in the Winter Garden, such as badminton, but also pillow fights, and clothes basket races, before dancing at teatime.

At Christmas dinner the popular Mr Talbot Cheesman [12] had presided since 1896. He was also the head waiter at the servants' ball. In 1901 there were 600 at the servants' dinner and 700 at the ball. Chef Crohill always wrote the Christmas dinner menu in sugar on the back of a real turtle shell; it was surrounded by electric lights and displayed on the sideboard. The traditional boar's head, hams, game pies and galantines of turkey were placed on pedestals under-lit with more electric lights. The four-tier Christmas cake weighed a hundred pounds.

Mr Crohill's best creations appeared at the Boxing Day ball supper: life-sized swans in trifle, a sugar polar bear whose head could swing from side to side, Eddystone lighthouse on a turbulent sea with boats, Nelson's column with lions. Often they were topical: in 1901 a sugar bust of the late Queen, in 1908 Wilbur Wright's airship – a bit strange as it had recently suffered a fatal crash.

The fancy dress ball was an innovation at New Year 1901. Some guests might have come prepared with beautiful costumes, but others used their imaginations. The bedroom corridors must have been alive with giggling guests borrowing and swapping clothing, or taking the tram down town to buy last minute trimmings.

There was a strange silence after dinner; but all was revealed as the guests came downstairs at half past eight. The characters entered the Winter Garden in pairs, through the "Indian lounge" to a march played by John Barnes orchestra. In 1902 they marched round the room to the recently published Rodolphe Berger's *Marche Electrique*. The dancers formed a perfect square, paraded again in single file, then, at a signal, broke into a polka. Viscount Tatters of Mildew Court, a lady in a genuine costume from the Harem of the Sultan of Morocco, a Saxon man at arms and many Marie Antoinettes, Napoleons and shepherdesses dance until 2am. In 1910 Mr Barnes had written a new waltz: *The Nun's Dream*.

12. He was an engineer on the Chilean railways, who must have made a real effort to return each year. He was always a lodger on the census – perhaps Smedley's was his family's winter home?

A rare view of Matlock Bath's narrow road taken looking south in 1906.
The sign to Hodgkinson's stables is on the side of the Devonshire Hotel.

realised this resurfacing had solidified the road – there was no rutting and no dust. By 1902 Hooley had patented the process of heating tar, adding slag to the mix and then breaking stones within the mixture to form a smooth road surface. Nottingham's Radcliffe Road became the first Tarmac surface in the world, but the Matlocks had to wait until the 1920s.

From 1910 the Council tried a scientific test for two years by the cricket ground on Causeway Lane. The road was not as busy as Dale Road, but over 400 vehicles a day did pass through. Different sections were laid with basalt, granite and limestone foundations. Limestone stood the test as well as the other two, and had the advantage of being much cheaper. From that point, tar spraying on the loose stones became widespread, but, for some reason, it was not suitable for steep sections.

The councils had another practical task. They had to name all the new streets. Postmen wanted house numbers, but there were often still too many gaps. St Joseph's Church were in trouble for putting up their street sign before a Council vote.

At the end of 1896 Matlock Bath UDC bought its gas works, but they, and the Bridge, were still stingy with the street lighting. In 1906 Upperwood was still in the dark. Nowhere had lamps in June or July, nor on darker August nights. Towards the north, it was said, "It is just as possible to break a limb on a dark night on the foot-paths of Darley as it used to be fifty years ago in the streets of Matlock". Ten cheap second-hand gas lamps were erected in Starkholmes and declared to look very

A loaded charabanc on a dusty road passing the Queen's Head Hotel.
The tall bank on the left opened in 1902.

pretty from the town. The outlying villages were also beginning to push for lighting because, "gas has a civilising influence on residents"! The councils had very little interest in introducing electricity, but in 1896 the first electric lights appeared in a shop: Mr C Kirkland, the plumber on Dale Road, installed his own plant.

Many postcards show the tall telegraph poles in the towns. Visitors were demanding more up-to-date information, such as news from the second Boer War, 1899-1902. The latest war telegrams were posted outside the newspaper offices and the *Visiting List* published a war section. There were special celebrations when Ladysmith and Mafeking were relieved, and much singing of *"Soldiers of the Queen"* in the hydros. (This new song had become very popular at the Diamond Jubilee.)

In October 1895 the first telephone lines were laid in the town. The company made an application to erect poles which were described as "presentable" with ornamentation on the top, but some thought they should go underground as at Buxton. When the exchange was opened behind the Town Hall a year later, there were 25 subscribers. The Police were given number 1, William Furniss, with his omnibuses and cabs, no.11, Dalefield Hydro was no. 7 and Smedley's no.17. (There could have been a large extension to the Town Hall in 1903. Andrew Carnegie, the builder of thousands of libraries in the United States and Britain, offered the Council £2,000 to build a library wing on the Town Hall; unbelievably they decided the 1d burden on the rates needed to sustain the project would be too much.)

However, telephone trunk calls, which had to go through Chesterfield, Derby or Sheffield, were a problem. In 1905 a Manchester businessman waited three hours to be put through, then telegraphed his office to phone him. Another Manchester gentleman took nearly two hours to call his office, and wished he had just gone on

Matlock old Post Office on a snowy day. Card posted 1905.
[Jean Douglas]

the train to speak to them. Even by 1922 evening trunk calls to the city were taking forty five minutes to connect, being routed through Birmingham – 140 miles instead of 50 – and the voices were indistinct.

Masson Mill had become part of the English Sewing Cotton Company in 1897. In 1900 the lease ended for the paper mill next door and the business was transferred to the Via Gellia. This allowed the ground to be cleared and the footpath and views to be improved. A new boiler and chimney were installed in Masson Mill itself by 1901, followed by the huge new wing to the south in 1911, with its red brick tower.

Caroline Smedley had died in 1892 and the contents of Riber Castle were auctioned. In 1894 her home became a boys' boarding school run by the Reverend John Chippett from Harrogate. It was not an easy building to heat, but the boys may have been pleased to find there was no fixed bath in the building.

It was not always possible to visit Willersley Castle grounds in this period: the house was sometimes let. However, every November the head gardener Mr Jeal proudly displayed his chrysanthemums in the conservatory.

After Mr Peters and his fellow subscribers had rescued land at Artists' Corner from the developers, it was handed over to Matlock Bath UDC in 1906. Several unsightly buildings were gradually removed such as the limekiln and Gregory's marine store by the Boat House. In 1911 the *High Peak News* commented, "It used to be said that Matlock was approached from the south by a rag and bone shop and from the north by a common lodging house (the old Crown)". Now was the golden opportunity to remove even more old property in Dale Road. Unfortunately Artists' Corner was frequently despoiled by advertisement hoardings: a poster for Hill's Brewery in 1904 was described as an American-type blight. In 1907 there was another, sadly unsuccessful, proposal – an aerial railway between High Tor and the Heights of Abraham!

Horse cabs were still being used to collect visitors from the station, but their days were numbered. In Matlock in 1903 sixty cabs were licensed, by 1908 fifty, by 1911 twenty three, and by 1926 only two. Some of them were still used in wet weather to carry patients boarding out in guest houses to the hydros for treatment.

Horse omnibuses were becoming more common, particularly along the Dale and between the different parts of the Matlocks. The cabmen were angry because buses were allowed to carry ten people with one horse, whereas they could only carry five. The buses were eventually allowed twenty five passengers with two horses. By 1902 there were buses running every twenty minutes from Matlock to Cromford provided by Hand & Son, Herbert Briddon and William Furniss. The problem was getting them to keep to anything resembling a timetable. The clock on the tram shelter was supposed to help, but even by 1908 it was deemed quicker to walk than wait.

In September 1912 the last blue tuppenny horse omnibus ticket was issued between the Matlocks: the next day it would be motor buses. William Furniss had purchased a big Pioneer bus, which he learnt to drive at the age of fifty. Mr Hand ran a smaller vehicle, possibly a Fiat. The timetable, which may or may not have been kept to, advertised buses between Matlock and Cromford every thirty minutes between 10.00am and 10.00pm, at a cost of four pence for the whole distance.

Matlock Bath

The Promenade with newly planted trees – when it was still free to enter!

Firth, in his *Highways and Byways in Derbyshire* of 1905, was wonderfully rude about almost everything. However, he reserved his greatest scorn for Matlock Bath. He imagined John Ruskin returning to witness the despoiling of Paradise. He would be, "bubbling over with fury and rage" and wanting to tell the people "in scorching words that they have suffered their beautiful country to become vulgarised". The railway companies had…

> …let loose daily in the summertime, among its sylvan beauties, a horde of callous rowdies, who envy Attila his destructive secret, whereby the grass never grew again where once his foot had been planted.

Every shop was either a cheap eating house or a cheap spar shop selling "a bewildering choice of perfectly useless and futile ornaments". In Firth's view, the gas works reeked, the shops and eating places were "frankly detestable" and the switchback railway was a "wooden monstrosity".

Mr A R Hope Moncrieff was a gentler critic of commercialism in *The Peak Country* in 1908, although he did say the "bit of garden" had been "vulgarised" by the switchback railway – a diversion which could as well be enjoyed in Glasgow or Wormwood Scrubs:

> The river now flows below a bank of wooded crags, the left side laid out in shady Lovers' Walk, while on the other crooks the long street, where trippers are appealed to by rival refreshment rooms and museums, bazaars of spar and other mineral ornaments that here answer to "a present from Margate". Pictorial postcards are as thick as leaves in Vallombrosa; and penny-in-the-slot machines make their mute appeal. Petrifying wells also vie for penny patronage in exhibition of curious and comical effects of incrustation by the mineralised waters. Another favourite sight is a fish pond of tepid water in which thrive chub, perch, goldfish and others, kept fat by contributions from an admiring public administered by means of an apparatus for putting in a penny and bringing out a packet of food for the fishes. On the slope behind are the chief hotels with their baths. On this height are gained caves and views, which will not fail to be forced on the notice of strangers; and each of them, according to its proprietor, who ought to know, is the thing most worth seeing in Matlock.

Moncrieff thought it a pity that the natural features had to be paid for: "cavern mouths shut up with cellar doors, cataracts under lock and key, precipitous crags compelled to figure in ornamental gardens".

The *Health Resort* in 1906, while praising the Royal Hotel, was disparaging about the town: "it should be clearly understood that Matlock Bath is little more than a large village, consequently amusements, so called, are conspicuous by their absence".

Extreme as these views were, people did worry about the future of the town. In 1904, the *Visiting List* conducted an interview with Mr Toma-Badrutt, the manager of the Royal Hotel. He had ambitions to make the town a true spa resort like those in Germany. He thought Matlock Bath had the necessary water supply and superior scenery. While acknowledging that some businesses relied on the day visitors, he felt that the balance was too far in that direction,

> Visitors get disgusted with the behaviour of the trippers. If a visitor goes into a shop on a busy trip day, he will be insulted, pushed about; he will see girls dancing in the street and that sort of thing.

Pearson's spar shop, the parish church and the Royal Hotel. Card posted 1907.
[Glynn Waite]

A local vicar claimed, "The hillsides of this pretty district are spoilt for self-respecting people by the behaviour of many of the trippers, young men and women". Most of the day trippers only flocked on Bank Holidays and summer weekends. To attract a better class of visitor, it was felt a pump room, baths, an evening venue and a superior promenade were needed. This was in spite of the fact that the old Pavilion, a splendid building with beautiful grounds, had been a financial failure from the start. Apparently, although the Fountain Baths were good enough for the hoi polloi, and had a drinking fountain, they could not satisfy "a fastidious public". The Council therefore embarked on a ten year saga, which at times descended into farce, but provided plenty of material for the newspapers and divided opinion all round.

The first steps were logical. Mrs Hannah Ratcliffe, who leased the Lovers' Walk and hired out boats, died in 1896. Matlock Bath UDC took over the lease for the land from Mr Arkwright, as far as Masson Mill, for 21 years at £40 per year. They erected new fences and chained off the weir. They put up notices forbidding rabbiting, bird nesting, and picking ferns and flowers. (This might not have included "rossum" or wild garlic. Visitors often first thought it was lily of the valley, but "the odour was enough to kill at ten yards".) They continued Mrs Ratcliffe's small entry charge for a while, shutting the gate by the far side of the Jubilee Bridge at dusk. A bell was rung fifteen minutes before closing; but they soon decided to throw the Walk open – at least for a short time.

The Council had also taken over Mrs Ratcliffe's twenty pleasure boats and a ferry. Messrs Buxton, Smith and Woodfield owned another three boats each. They all came to an agreement to charge 6d an hour with cheaper family and season tickets. After several fatal accidents, the boats became licensed; they had to be inspected

ON THE DERWENT. MATLOCK BATH

Derwent Gardens and the switchback railway are on the right. Card posted 1924.

and named, with the maximum number of passengers painted on the side. Their 1901/2 report showed that the Council had carried 14,422 passengers. The receipts were £214, but they spent £110 on wages and expenses. The Council also started a new ferry from near the New Bath.

As has been already noted, the Pavilion was failing as a business. There were visitors: thirty five thousand people listened to the bands and danced in 1899, but the manager, Frederick Downs, was still being refused a bar licence. In an effort to attract families, the entrance ticket included their children's nursemaid. In 1902 Charles Lax, the season's band conductor, died in post so the next year Emanuele Guidi brought his nine-man Italian Military Band. It is usually written in local histories that one musician in Matlock Bath, Romolo Tinti from Bologna, played for the orchestra in the Royal Hotel. However, in the 1901 census he and Signor Guidi were listed as musicians in Scarborough with several more of their countrymen; perhaps he was actually in the Military Band, which stayed in the town until the end of the decade. Romolo became a British citizen in 1907 and married a local girl; they opened a fancy goods shop on North Parade.

The musical director at the Pavilion, Harry Fieldhouse, was still booking prestigious acts such as John Dunn, billed as England's greatest violinist, and Julian Clifford, a pianist, but the audiences were meagre. There were popular acts like Flossie Behrens, an operatic souffleuse (whistler), who performed the obligato from Braga's *Serenata* written in 1898 – a dialogue between a mother and her daughter who hears an angel's voice. She appeared with Albert Chevalier, the famous music hall singer of coster songs such as *My old Dutch* and *Knocked 'em in the Old Kent Road*. He wore the traditional cockney costume with pearly buttons. Miss Behrens was also a frequent performer at Rockside and Smedley's Hydros.

A few businesses in Matlock Bath.

The mortgagees foreclosed in 1901 and the Pavilion was up for auction in 1902, but it was the Royal Hotel who made the purchase in 1905, as described earlier. Matlock Bath tennis club had to find a new home and the Victoria Hall benefitted from losing a rival, but it was a sad end to a beautiful idea. Nor were lessons learned.

Soon Matlock Bath UDC launched its ambitious plans. The 1905 Matlock Bath Improvement Bill was drawn up and presented to Parliament. It had clauses to improve sewerage and deal with the gas supply, but, from the visitors' point of view, it allowed the Council to purchase and demolish property, to extend the Promenade and to clear a site for a Kursaal [13] with a pump room. The owners of the Royal Hotel agreed that the spa water would come from their spring and guaranteed an income of £600 a year in the pump room, which they would control for ten years, before passing it to the Council. The Bill also allowed the Council to charge entry to any pleasure grounds.

Once the Bill was passed, the Council began to purchase the land on the river side between the Midland Hotel and Woodland Terrace: this involved thirty property owners. Mr Thomas, who owned the Ferry lands, and Mr Buxton, who owned the land and boating business facing the Fountain Villas, as well as several others, took their compulsory purchase cases to arbitration in London, which extended the Council's debts. Mr Thomas asked for £6,000 against the Council's offer of £3,000: they settled on £4,800. Another case was brought by Mrs Leston, the widow of Mr

---

13. German spas used the word Kursaal for a room in a health resort: it literally meant 'cure room'.

Woodfield, who had owned boats for forty years. He died in 1901 and his boats were sold to the Council for £27, but now she was claiming £349 compensation. The court was perplexed by her refusal to let anyone see her account books.

The Council had trapped themselves into a situation where they had enormous financial outlays and they needed an income. The Bill had itself had cost £3400, to be repaid in five years at £800 per year, but the interest on the loan was £400. The local rates were already very high and the population was not increasing. They had promised to build a Kursaal, which would require another substantial loan. They needed an extra source of money urgently. Their solution was very unpopular, and, some said, illegal.

In short, they proposed to enclose the Jubilee Promenade and charge visitors 2d to enter. They estimated 100,000 paying visitors a year would solve their problem. In spring 1906 the Council fenced off the Promenade at a cost of £333, planted a wall of shrubs, and erected toll booths at each end and at the entrance to the Jubilee Bridge. Although this move had been indicated in the Bill, people reacted with horror to this breach of faith against the original concept of free access. The Jubilee Bridge belonged to everybody: how could the Council charge? The residents eventually received free passes, but rich visitors would not demean themselves to purchase a 2d ticket and the trippers were equally angry. Cyclists no longer lounged by the river, but passed quickly through. The only bit of promenade left unfenced quickly became a cab stand. Petitions were drawn up, but the Council remained obdurate.

The cost of the railings was not the only charge. The Council built a rustic log cabin with a thatched roof by the bridge and bought turnstiles. The rent of the

Seats were only available to those who paid to enter the gardens.

Lovers' Walk had increased to £60 annually. The Council now felt obliged to provide entertainment for the public's 2d and provide some shelter for performers. Paying for a band had always been a problem. In 1905 the Excelsior Band, playing three times a day in the Lovers' Walk band kiosk, had cost £250 for twelve weeks. The balance owed had to be raised by holding a bazaar. In the 1906 season, the Council suddenly seemed to lose its head.

They began by erecting a tent for a 3d hop (dance) on the Lovers' Walk. The tent cost £35 to rent, and the floor for dancing £20. This was an eyesore and the music

---

A native in exile and a visitor were both moved to write verses about the fencing off of the Promenade at Matlock Bath. The native "denied access to the haunts of youth by the stern mandate of a copper custodian" managed sixteen verses, of which these are samples:

> No more to roam my native wilds
> (But sternly held at bay)
> No more to climb my youthful rocks,
> Unless I tuppence pay.
>
> I'll bear the rack, the thumbscrew
> Or the stake – without dismay:
> But, never, never, never – no!
> I'll never tuppence pay.

The visitor sent this to the *Visiting List* in the mid-season:

> Dear Pa and Ma, at Matlock Bath we've arrived
> As you per postmark plainly see;
> The Midland's tunnels we've survived,
> And so just after tea,
> We thought the beauties of the Bath,
> You oft to us extolled,
> We'd try to find – but Alack! Alas!
> We find that we've been sold.
> The Promenade is now fenced in
> With awfully ugly iron bars;
> We really think it is a sin –
> The wretched thing gives us the jars
> And Fred, though he is awfully nice,
> And sweet, and kind to me –
> Clenched his teeth just like a vice,
> And muttered, - Monstrosity!
> So, Papa dear, we're moving on,
> And hope it won't give you offence,
> But we won't stay to gaze upon
> That awfully ugly iron fence.

could be heard all over the town until 10pm. To the amusement of Matlock Bridge UDC, they had forgotten to apply to the magistrates for a music and dance licence, incurring a penalty of £5 per day. They did apply and the licence was refused because the tent was flimsy and dangerous. The hop was abandoned in August.

Then there was a time when a "mermaid" was exhibited in a little shed on the roadside by the Ferry grounds. It was suggested she was released into the river and taught to do tricks in front of the Promenade. A small boy was heard to explain that she had "gone for a bottle of stout" when visitors asked her whereabouts. The Council also allowed a helter skelter, which the town was not happy about.

There were many reports of the empty Promenade gardens, such as "four men and a boy" one Saturday in July listening to the brass band, while the Derwent Gardens, Pic Tor, Matlock Broadwalk and Belper River Gardens were packed out. At the end of September 1906, the band played the National Anthem for the last time that season at 8pm to a totally deserted Promenade.

In 1907, the Council removed the turnstile at the north east end of the Promenade to build a shelter for wet weather, described at different times as a "red-tiled monstrosity" and a "rickety ruin standing idle". Even when complete, for some strange reason the shelter was usually locked – there were still complaints about this in 1920.

When it rained, visitors had to abandon the Promenade and stampede for the station – where the Midland Railway was still refusing to extend the canopies. When the north gate to the Promenade had gone, people could not easily reach the toilets either. Later complaints mentioned the shelter spoiling the view of the war memorial.

There was another construction at that end of the Promenade: the corrugated iron open-air stage, used mostly by Pierrot companies. Will Mack's Minstrels and Parlatos, and Mr Drake's Pierrots, were the mainstay of public entertainment for the

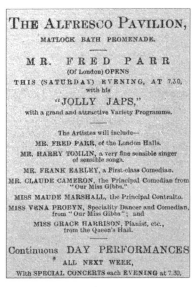

An entertainment in 1911.

The following are some of the Artists who will appear at
M ACK's COMPLIMENTARY BENE-
FIT CONCERT,
At the Pavilion, on MONDAY, Sept. 22nd.

THE FIVE ARTELLFS, in their Drawing Room
Acrobatic Entertainment.
BONETTI. the Tramp Juggler.
Mr. FRED CHARLES, Comedian & Laughter Maker.
Mr. TOM BARNSLEY, the favorite Yorkshire -
Humorist, in his latest success, 'The Curate.''
CARL FRITZ. Cartoonist.
Your old favorite, Mr. FRANK STANERT,
Laughing Comedian and Instrumentalist,
Miss JESSIE YONDI. Comed'enne and Dancer.
Miss M. RHHAN. Serio Vocalist.
Sergeant WEBB, Indian Club Performer.
Mr. FRED CHARLES, Comedian & Laughter Maker.
Miss FLO MERRY. Comedian and Descriptive
Vocalist.
And a host of others.   1173

A benefit concert in 1902.

whole decade. However, like the shelter, its appearance caused remarks such as "a glorified cart shed", and "for all the misplaced ugly objects ever erected in Matlock Bath this takes the biscuit". The audience had to sit in the rain. The Council in 1903 had tried to relegate Mr Mack to the Ferry Lands, where a stage was built, but a petition resulted in his reappearance on the Promenade. In 1909 John Wildgoose built Mr Drake a new Empire Pavilion, which was an improvement; it even had a cover for the audience. For several weeks the "Grand Opening" advertised three performances daily. There were mentions, and glimpses on photographs, of yet another eyesore – the Council could not stop the sound from a brass band or minstrel show drifting over the fence, but they erected tall canvas screens along the perimeter to obstruct the view.

In 1907 Mr Herbert Buxton, formerly vice-chairman of the Council, behaved rather provocatively. No sooner had he received his compensation for losing his boating rights near the Jubilee Bridge, than he seemed to be back in business. He had retained a private landing stage from which he was hiring out two new boats to visitors. Technically he still owned the "soil" from his shop on South Parade and under the river to half way across. The Council promptly roped off the river above and below and stationed what were soon nicknamed "gunboats" to keep him in check. The problem with this was that the river was deep near the landing stage and very shallow over the other side where the Council's boats were operating. The ropes were actually quite dangerous. In March 1910, the Council took Mr Buxton to Court. The hearing was entertaining, but he lost.

In 1908 Matlock Bath Improvement Association estimated the town had lost 50,000 visitors each year since the enclosure. At Whitsuntide, only 5,000 of the 25,000 visitors had paid to go on the Promenade. They suggested a compromise: open the Promenade and put the pay booth at the other end of the Jubilee Bridge. How could one have a health resort without a free seat? They suggested the Council would actually make more money from extra boating and the new public conveniences. When a child fell in the river in July, the rescuers had to climb over the fence. The *High Peak News* criticised unprofessional practice. There was nothing

South Parade in snow. Winter 1905.
[Peak District Lead Mining Museum]

at the entrance to tell visitors what they would get for their 2d, just a few crumpled cards, and a dirty rustic pay box manned by a scruffy unofficial-looking individual smoking a cigarette. The newspapers had taken to calling Matlock Bath UDC "Muddleton Council".

In April 1908 a report said the Promenade was to be managed by Major Ward, who would provide the entertainment and take 55% of the gate money, but it is not certain this happened. That August Bank Holiday a record amount of £74 was taken, as well as the best ever sales of mineral water and ginger beer – but this did nothing much for the debts.

In early 1910 the Council did relent and re-opened the Promenade for a trial period and it was prettified with new gravel on the paths. The pay booth was fixed to the end of the Jubilee Bridge instead, in spite of questions about the legality of charging only for the Arkwright-owned Lovers' Walk, which had not been sanctioned in the Bill. The new Pierrot company for the season, the Smart Society Cadets, were now free; they claimed they earned far more money by collecting from the larger audiences.

But in 1911 the UDC began to charge again because their income was down. The *Visiting List* pointed out that the previous year had not been a fair trial because it had been a very wet summer and the King had died. The bands had often taken shelter in the Kursaal (see below). Matlock Bath was once again the resort without

DAINTY! DELIGHTFUL!! DELICIOUS!!!

WHAT ?

Afternoon Tea

in the DERWENT GARDENS CAFE, or in the OPEN GARDENS overlooking the River Derwent.

DERWENT GARDENS CAFE.

ALSO AT THE

"EDINBURGH" Boarding House Restaurant.

BREAKFASTS, LUNCHEONS, DINNERS, TEAS, &c., &c.,
— ON THE SHORTEST NOTICE.

Personal Attention given to secure the comfort of Boarders.

Every convenience for Schools, Friendly Societies, Bands of Hope, Mothers' Meetings, Cyclists, &c., &c. . . . . Parties catered for, any number.

Terms, &c., on application to

J. W. BODEN (late of the Ferry Dining Rooms), Proprietor

a free seat while Belper River Gardens were thriving. The shops were further annoyed because the Council had allowed automatic sweet-vending machines. The UDC claimed a success at Easter: 6,000 had paid at the turnstiles. The *Visiting List* dismissed this: 14,000 more people had not. The streets were crowded, not the Promenade.

The Council was frequently asked about the non-arrival of the promised Kursaal, which was to transform the town into a successful spa. A sign next to the hop tent all through 1906 had said "Site for Pavilion". Some thought it a waste of money anyway. Buying the Ferry lands had already cost the UDC £4,800. The old Pavilion had lost money from the start and the Victoria Hall on Matlock Bank was often in financial crisis. Cafes and restaurants on the Parades had benefitted from the lack of competition, particularly in wet weather. Mr Buxton had improved the free Derwent Gardens, where concert parties performed daily. Most significantly, the Royal Hotel Company was now opposed to the scheme, for reasons never made clear in the Press.

In May 1908 the Fishpond stables were sold after being run for forty years by the Briddon family. Herbert Briddon had moved on to run the Peveril of the Peak Hotel in Dovedale. Thirty seven horses and forty one carriages were sold to William Furniss, who carried on the business until the Council made a decision about the position of the Kursaal. In the following January thirty men began to pull down the stables: "that venerable and hoary eyesore". The following year the Ferry House came down.

Then came a dispute about the Ferry grounds themselves: the "old mudheap" which the Council had bought at the time of the Improvement Bill. On the Ferry lands was the Providence lead mine, claimed by Herbert Buxton, who owned the Derwent Gardens on the old Orchard Holme. In 1906 he put in new door and started mining, because tradition said it should be worked or forfeited. The Chairman of the UDC, Charles White, [14] kept petitioning the Barmote Court to transfer ownership to him. In the end, Mr Buxton gave up and Mr White took over, although he had claimed there was no lead to be had. He gave the mine to the Council. Then the dispute became confused with Mr Buxton's need for access to the Derwent Gardens and ferries between the mine and the river. The Council petitioned for a Bill to remove traditional mining rights from the Ferry land, which did become an Act in 1910. (A later 1927 Act exempted the Pavilion grounds, High Tor, Pic Tor, Hall Leys and Artists' Corner from lead mining claims.) There were many column inches in the *High Peak News* as the Barmote Court in Wirksworth debated the consequences of such a breach in their ancient laws. Many saw it as a personal squabble between Messrs Buxton and White, which, although entertaining, cost the Council money it could ill afford.

When the Kursaal plans were finally revealed, the Council were using the same architect as the Royal Hotel Company had used for their recent extension. However, at some point Mr Hodge was put aside; later he took the Council successfully to court. His design had included baths, but this feature was dropped which many thought a mistake. The new architect was John Nuttall who had designed the original Pavilion. The building eventually began to take shape in early 1910, with criticism that it was a shame brick was being used in an area of famous stone quarries. Sadly, two workmen were injured in March when roof girders fell in. An engineer sent to sort out the problem also fell from the first floor into the basement.

The new building contained a dance floor at ground level and a large room with a stage above. There were public chambers on either side, one of them a Pump Room.

The Kursaal opened for business in August with roller skating on the ground floor, although they never held a proper ceremony. The building had cost £11,000, but, with the purchase of the land and expenses, the total was nearer £20,000. Professional roller skaters praised the floor and the type of music played. The Marquis of Granby and his sisters were among the first to try it out when they visited their father, the Duke of Rutland, on one of his frequent visits to the Royal Hotel baths. The first play in the theatre upstairs was *Cingalee*, a musical set in Ceylon. This was followed by the popular *Charley's Aunt* and *A Message from Mars*. The Council moved their offices into the building, although the legality of this was questioned.

The Pump Room never really took on the appearance of its continental rivals. The UDC had expected an income from the water at a penny a glass, but it soon turned into a tearoom, with sales of hot drinks and Whittaker's flavoured mineral waters. Lack of the right kind of publicity was blamed. Critics said the Pump Room attendant needed to smarten up and wear a neat uniform and apron like the ones at

---

14. Charles F White, and his son of the same name, were prominent local politicians. Both served on the local councils, the County Council and as MPs for West Derbyshire, breaking the Cavendish stranglehold on the seat. They had strong opinions which they were not shy of expressing on any occasion,

The newly built Pavilion in 1912. The gateposts led to the Derwent Gardens.
[Glynn Waite]

Harrogate. In 1916 they tried to promote bottled spa water under the trade name Hydrotherm. The label said, "a sparkling water from the natural warm mineral spring, Matlock Bath", but the venture only lasted a short time.

The newspapers now latched on to the fact that the Council had a new building with no real plans on how it was to be managed. The words "vacillation" and "hesitancy" were bandied about. The first discussions concerned catering. Mr Seymour at Victoria Hall offered to run the business and sublet the catering to locals. Mr Boden, with the dining rooms at Edinburgh House and the Derwent Gardens cafe, said he would not have supported the scheme if he had known there would be competition from serving food.

In November the Kursaal was handed over to a company (unnamed in the newspaper) for a £400 annual rent. They staged an opening with a free night of dancing and skating and a whist drive, attended by over a thousand people. But by December the next year, the Council were uncertain again and offering a rent of £200.

By 1912 the Kursaal was being spoken of as a burden on the rates. Attempts to let the room out to caterers met again with protests from the other dining rooms in the town. However, in February it was reported that Captain Casson of London, a reputable caterer, and Captain Welch, an entertainments manager, had signed a lease for £300 a year. Their company was called Theatrical Amusements Ltd. They opened with a concert by a ladies orchestra from London.

When a new Council was elected in 1913, the *High Peak News* estimated that the loan burden from the previous ten year's activities had reached £50,000. As the Kursaal and Promenade were both making a loss, they faced a "Herculean task".

Editorials and letters exhorted the Council to decide for whom they were catering. If for the upper classes, they needed to tidy up the river side and provide real pleasure gardens. If for the day tripper, they needed more thrills and sideshows.

Meanwhile the town surveyor had transformed the area around the Kursaal using tufa and shrubs along the path to the ferry and round the bowling green. New tennis courts were being used by the local club which had been thrown out of the old Pavilion.

In front of the Kursaal, the fishpond was improved in 1895 by widening the footpath and adding a fountain. The Council installed four automatic machines to dispense fish food, which varied in content over the years – in 1898 it was chopped meat. Did it not smell? In 1907 one of the huge chub died, aged about 30 years. It was accustomed to eating mice and small rats: it could be two days before rat tails disappeared down its gullet.

Herbert Buxton was still running his successful business on Derwent Gardens, with Boden's café and the switchback railway, all landscaped with ponds and flower beds. He hired minstrel groups and bands, such as the White Star Concert Party, and benefitted hugely from the Council's fencing of the Promenade. In 1907 he opened a fish hatchery and freed 5500 Loch Leven yearling trout into the river. He was also still a maker of spar and marble ornaments for sale in his Royal Museum.

Howe's Fountain Baths became Hall's. The swimming pool was used by visitors as well as local schools and swimming clubs. In 1911 the proprietor was James Fearn, the head bathman at the Royal Hotel, trained at Smedley's.

From 1892 there was a new cave to visit: the Whittakers at the mineral water works had opened the Long Tor Roman Fluorspar Cavern in an old quarry behind their factory. There were several galleries of sparkling crystals, toadstone and black marble. Mrs Whittaker also sold refreshments in the grounds. Mr Cardin, the proprietor of High Tor Grotto, brought out a *Visitors' New Guide* in 1907 describing the geology and flowers of the district, as well as several walks. It was printed (interestingly) by Mr Beaty Hart of The Mount guest house on Steep Turnpike.

In October 1898 Matlock Bath shops introduced their first half-day closing at 2pm on Thursdays, but they wanted this to be winter only. The Shop Hours Act in 1904 allowed County Councils to fix hours and decide which shops would be affected. However, closing could not be earlier than 7pm except for one day, from 1pm at the earliest. Friday closing could be no earlier than 8pm, and Saturdays 11pm. Two thirds of the shop owners had to come to an agreement locally. The Act also stipulated one seat per three female shop assistants! By 1912, pleasure resorts were exempt from regulation during the season, because, as they said at Matlock Bath, "if the shops closed at 9.30pm, visitors would think the place was dead". In 1899 was held the first annual dinner of the Matlock Thursday Cricket Club (Shop Assistants) Association.

The Parades in Matlock Bath were still a mixture of shops and restaurants, many still in business from the 1880s and before. The name "Derwent Parade" had largely been dropped in favour of today's North Parade. Barnes & Sons at the southern end was still a draper's shop, but, with the family's musical and journalistic connections, they seem to have sold all kinds of items. In 1901 they advertised new electric Christmas presents: "It is now possible to have perfectly

The Royal Hotel and the old Pavilion.
Note how near the switchback railway was to the parish church.

harmless electric novelties of the utmost utility and the prettiest design". It was not necessary to have a retail shop: Madame Alice Edwina Rowland was a *modiste* providing the latest *Parisienne* styles in trousseaux, evening gowns and motor coats from her home, Linacre, near the New Bath.

William Bryan's shop at the corner of Holme Road sold artistic millinery, mantles, hosiery, umbrellas, sunshades and boas. In a workshop at the back he made hats. But his significance to this work was his role as the "Busy Bee". He distilled the chatter he heard from customers into a column in the *Visiting List*: a mixture of criticism and encouragement for the powers-that-be, which has often been quoted on these pages. His brother Benjamin published the *History of Matlock* in 1903.

In the same block early in the decade was another draper and dressmaker: Henry Cooper had come from the mantle trade in Manchester. His rear showroom was decorated in black and gold. Many of his goods were imported from Ireland, where

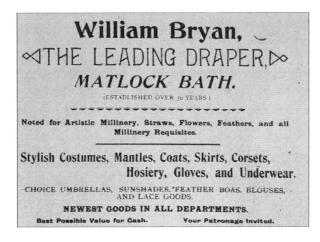

the Donegal "peasantry" trimmed the ladies' underwear with lace; he also sold "grass-bleached" linen from Belfast. Mr Cooper was a shirt-cutter himself and able to make a well-fitting flannel shirt in many colours for his customers. His experienced staff could turn out ball gowns, wedding trousseaux and mourning outfits "in high-class style, perfect in fit and finish".

Thomas Asbury the chemist left the Matlocks to open an "electric laundry" in Belper. His shop in Matlock Bath, next to the church, was taken by Alfred Newton, another pharmacist. These premises still retain his stylish windows with his name on the edge of the shelves. What would he have thought of his Otto of Rose cold cream pot lids being reproduced on Portmeirion pottery and traded on ebay? By 1909, the business belonged to Fred Slawson.

John William Boden was a retired grocer and caterer originally at Boston House on Derby Road, opposite Masson Mill. After twenty years, he and his wife moved to the Ferry House and ran the café there until it was demolished. Then they moved to Edinburgh House, a boarding establishment and restaurant. They celebrated their Golden Wedding there in 1925. They also ran the café in Derwent Gardens. John died in 1928 and his sons took over the businesses.

Another John William Boden was the son of John the baker on South Parade, who died in 1902. He continued to run the family bakery and shop and the dining rooms across the road where dances and whist drives were also held. His sister Kate ran a cake shop at the bottom of Bank Road in Matlock town centre.

GOLDEN WEDDING OF MR. AND MRS. J. W. BODEN.

The Bodens in 1925.
[Potter & Co.]

There were over a dozen refreshment rooms listed in the 1908 directory. The Dalton family's five hundred seat Central Restaurant on North Parade was said to be the largest in the county. (Mrs Dalton also ran the Oriental Café on Dale Road, which was on two floors on the corner of the Old English Hotel.) Next door in Matlock Bath was the Parade Restaurant. Between these two restaurants and William Bryan's shop was a large grocery called Wyvills. The Wyvill family also ran the Fishpond Hotel at the beginning of the decade.

New transport brought new business. F Ashby, who advertised himself as a maker of the French Gladiator bicycle, opened the Matlock Bath Cycle Works off South Parade. This was on the raised bit of road (near the current pedestrian crossing), where a large bicycle wheel could be seen on the roof. Mr Ashby claimed

North Parade: Wyvill's grocery store and the Central Restaurant.

209

to be able to repair any bicycle and could teach the sport. He also hired out motor cars and recharged accumulators for visitors, even on a Sunday. Unfortunately he was not a very good businessman and failed. Ernie Williams was another motor engineer on South Parade, on the same side as the Devonshire Hotel. After the Fishpond stables were demolished, William Furniss moved his booking office into a building by the side of the public house. He also used Portland House Mews and the New Bath Hotel stables. Later he opened a garage at the north end of the Promenade near the pierrot stand. The turnstile was moved and for a time visitors had to enter through the "unsightly and unsavoury yard of a garage".

MATLOCK BRIDGE AND BANK

Matlock Bridge certainly was thriving, if new building can be taken as a measure of success. One only need look at the solid stone buildings in the town around Crown Square, down Dale Road, up Bank Road and along Smedley Street to see how many were built in the last twenty years of Victoria's reign and the first ten of the new century. As well as shops, churches and public buildings, many of the houses were constructed in the same period: an estimated 300 were built between 1900 and 1905. One builder, John William Wildgoose, was responsible for the greater number. His advertisements offered houses built to "YOUR tastes and requirements". His offices were in the Industrial Works at the top of Rutland Street where some buildings remain. Many of his semi-detached houses in Matlock have a very attractive feature: a roofed porch spanning the two front doors. He lived in the end house on Rutland

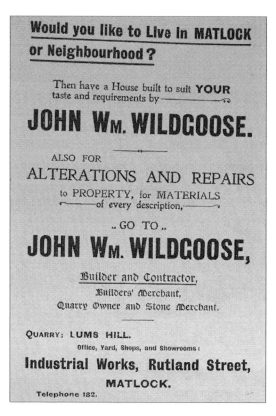

Avenue, then called Industrial Road, with his trade-mark porch spanning the double bay and fronted by an elaborate doorway.

In the 1901 census for the Matlock Bank, Bridge and Green areas, nearly 200 men worked with stone, either in the quarries or as dressers and masons. Nearly one hundred and fifty men were in trades such as joinery, plastering, plumbing and slating. Any visitor must have been aware of building sites all over the town, with their noise and dust, and the delivery of materials by horse drays and wagons.

Criticisms were now beginning to be voiced via the newspapers and travel journals about the first impressions a town made on the visitor. For at least the next forty years, one recurring theme was the unsightly entrance to Matlock from Darley Dale. Firth in his *Highways and Byways in Derbyshire* of 1905 unsurprisingly had something to say. The approach is "spoilt by aggressive limekilns, quarries and all the paraphernalia of industry in its ugliest form". He could also have mentioned the gas works and the tar boiler. He continued:

> *Matlock Bridge stretches away up the steep hillside to the left hand – a prosperous looking place of little interest, unless your tastes lie in the direction of hydropathy and the buildings where it is cultivated.*

In 1903 there were calls for the UDC to buy the land opposite the Railway Hotel where the road was very narrow and included the eyesore of the old Crown Hotel and stabling. The buildings were demolished three years later. There were still ugly advertisement hoardings both sides of Bakewell Road, by William Furniss's offices, and in Crown Square at the entrance to Causeway Lane.

William Furniss's Stables (now The Crown), a wet week and hoardings.
[Glynn Waite]

Firth described Smedley's Hydro as looming over the town like a gaunt Tibetan lamasery. To his way of thinking, hydros were a "quaint compound of hotel and nursing home" or "no more than a synonym for an unlicensed hotel". He dismissed Dale Road as a street of commonplace shops. He said Riber Castle compelled every stranger who saw it to ask who had built it and why, comparing it with the point-less coliseum at Oban.

The Matlocks & Bakewell: Famous Derbyshire Health Resorts (published by Rochard in Brighton in 1893) was more positive:

> *The whole Bank now bristles with handsome hydro establishments, villas and private residences, with churches, chapels and institutions, adapted to the requirements of a fashionable resident population.*
>
> *There are excellent modern shops, first class conveyances, and, in fact, all the resources of a prosperous modern town that is also a fashionable resort.*

The County Bridge was still a bottleneck at the beginning of the decade and the structure needed urgent repair. The narrow single pavement compelled well-dressed visitors to wait for an empty road to avoid being covered in dust or mud. It might have been a long wait: a day's survey one Friday in August 1894 counted one thousand vehicles and six thousand pedestrians – and this was before motor cars

Evans Jewellers. A shop still in business on Dale Road.
[Glynn Waite]

arrived. In 1890 it was said workmen had been "pottering" on the bridge for two to three years. There were calls to end the "patching and mending folly". Countless hours were spent wrangling over responsibility and cost between the UDC and the County Council. In July 1903 contractors finally appeared, only to be delayed by floods. A temporary footbridge was erected but there were accidents. Mr Walters, a traveller for Orme's grocers, was nearly knocked into the river by a dray which did not stop. The work to widen and repair the bridge was finally finished in late 1905.

By 1900 most of the space between the County Bridge and the railway bridge down the east side of Dale Road had been filled in with shops. The fire in 1899, described earlier, had destroyed Else's stationery shop and badly damaged Marsden's grocers; this left an ugly gap which was not cleared for several months. In February 1902 Parr's Bank opened their handsome brick premises with its stone front and cupola (now NatWest Bank). They sold their old building to James Potter, the solicitor, whose business remains there today.

Several new shops and cafes had appeared since the 1880s. Probably the best known, because it still thrives, was William Evans & Son, jewellers and watch-makers. William moved from Wirksworth in 1893 and erected his famous projecting clock. His son Charles was an optician and he advertised his eyesight testing rooms next door with a huge pair of spectacles. The next shop down was a chemist called Harker.

On the corner opposite the Old English Hotel was a grocer's shop called Hunter's. Next door was Basquil & Co, tailors. They were one of the firms contracted to produce the tramway uniforms. The Manchester Stores was a large shop selling drapery goods made in that city. The Thai restaurant, now in the

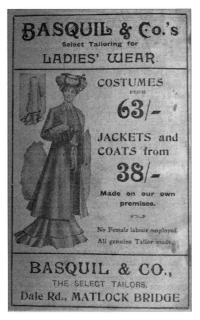

What was so awful about
female labour?

Dale Road with a crowd outside Marsden's drapery.
Barnwell's shop has been replaced by the Bank.

premises, has kept the shop sign inside. Marsden's clothes shop had opened a menswear department next door in the nearest part of the Parr's Bank building. Another bespoke tailor was James Wilby in the narrow shop below the stained glass window (now Fabrik). A dyer and dry cleaner called Stevenson specialised in colouring and dressing ostrich feathers.

On the west side of the road, Dr L'Estrange Orme, the surgeon at the Whitworth Hospital, who had married Dr Marie Goodwin of Rockside, was building the Red House (now with a fancy-dress shop in the basement). Next was the southernmost row of single storey shops, known as the Coronation buildings, presumably built after the accession of King Edward VII. One shop was W Pilkington's chemist, who stocked Kodak cameras and would develop films for the visitors. He also developed stereo views: two photographs which gave a 3-D image when viewed through a stereoscope. Next door was the International Stores, the nation-wide chain of tea merchants. The taller building next to the Coronation buildings was Frisby's Boot Emporium – the sign is still just visible on the wall. It still says "London store prices" as if this was to be recommended.

In the old Market Hall were several fancy bazaars: Emery's, Melville's and Mrs Machin's. They sold everything: pots, pans, candles, toys etc. at very low prices. They were joined by Wilfred Croft, who moved his long-established watchmaker's business from Crown Square.

Henry Barnwell's shop, on the corner opposite the Queen's Head, was still selling jewellery and china, but in 1914 it was demolished to build the London, City and Midland Bank, late HSBC. The last shop before the Bridge was still a chemist, run by Mr Arthur Davis. Like the others, he advertised photographic goods.

The main confectioners and tea rooms on Dale Road was run by W H Moore: "machine-made bread a speciality", with a large Hovis sign (a brand name registered in 1890). Moore's advertisement said they had been founded in 1863, but this must have been somewhere else. They were famous for their pork pies, bride cakes and funeral biscuits. Matlock Town football players were given a dining ticket there as part of their wages. (The building is currently an estate agent.)

Across the bridge, the shops against Hall Leys were joined early in the decade by a new out-of-place mock Tudor block, headed by Burgon's provision merchants, specialising in tea, coffee and butter. The elephant still visible on the back of the building was the tea brand logo. Inside would have been a wonderful aroma of coffee as they roasted beans every day on the premises. In May 1904 their window display featured all 57 Heinz varieties of tinned goods: soups, beans, and sauces. Inside were samples for customers. The famous Heinz slogan had first been used in 1896. The Pittsburgh-based company actually sold over sixty foods, but Henry Heinz thought "57" sounded lucky. In 1908 Burgon's promotion included Heinz's latest product: "evaporated apples".

Across the road, Mr Hartley now had a bicycle wheel hanging as his shop sign; but he left the area in 1908. The shop became Goodall's stationers with a lending library of 1300 books. They also sold fancy goods and continued supplying sports

A Heinz display in Burgon's window.
[Glynn Waite]

The well-stocked interior of Orme's grocery at Park Head.

equipment and fishing permits. Next to Kirkham's shoe shop, Hilton's had been replaced Mrs Addy's sweet shop and tearoom. (Her husband was a coach builder on Pope Carr Road.) On the other side of Goodall's was a shoe shop to rival Kirkham's: William Mottershead (now Wilsons the butcher) advertised very stylish boots. In Princes Building was Wrigley's bakery and dining rooms which had moved from Dale Road. By 1908 Peter Holmes' shop on the corner of Crown Buildings had become John Beard's drapery and hat shop.

John William Wildgoose the builder, had a showroom on Crown Square, but the location is uncertain. He was also a monumental mason, so photographs of the interior show a rather bizarre mixture, with two tiers of fireplaces mounted on the walls, and the floor space taken up with grave stones and memorial crosses.

There were still big open spaces around the Crown Buildings, behind the Crown Hotel, and along Causeway Lane. A long low wall led to a sparse grove of beech trees where Iceland now stands. Steep Turnpike had little habitation above The Firs (now the library) and all the land round the cricket pitch was fields. However, early in the next decade, the imposing Post Office building was built by John Wildgoose and opened in September 1912. Further up Bank Road was "La Patisserie", a high class confectioners with a room for private parties and whist drives.

In the Central Buildings on Smedley Street was Barnard's Post Office and lending library, with Henry Bailey's chemist shop to the left. Barnard's then became Colledge's shop, described earlier. Opposite Smedley's, with Wildgoose the florist, was a branch of Crompton & Evans Bank and F W Thorpe, tailor and outfitter.

A shop in Smedley's north block.
[Glynn Waite]

Another tailor called Ward & Toplis (later just Toplis) had a shop opposite All Saints Church.

The Dakin family ran a newsagents on Smedley Street East in the shop which was a Post Office until recently. Their son Arthur combined the business with a hair-dressing salon. William Phillips, of the long-established hairdressing business on Crown Square, had married Arthur's aunt, but they had no children, so Arthur took over his business in the town centre after the First World War.

William Crowder's hosiery workshop with four old hand looms on Wellington Street had been inherited by his nephew Thomas Crowder Johnson. He advertised ladies' and gentlemen's combinations, chemises, vests and drawers in silks and merinos. By 1925 he and his wife had overstretched themselves borrowing money to buy more shops and other property; they were declared bankrupt but carried on. Mr Potter closed his other workshops to concentrate all his hosiery work in his factory on The Dimple and moved to live in Holt House on Dale Road.

The main new attractions for the visitor at Matlock Bridge in the 1900s consisted of walks and park land. The handsome row of houses known as Knowleston Place

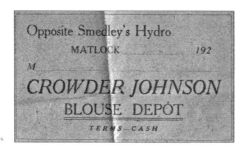

Pic Tor Walk & River, Matlock.

was built in the 1850s. Next to them, the area by the river, once used for lead mining and lime burning, was landscaped into a formal garden for public use, which was bought by the Council. They then leased the cliff known as Pic Tor (or Pig Tor on old maps) and the water meadows from Mr Arkwright and made a riverside walk to link Matlock Green with Dale Road. The promenade was opened in August 1902 and was soon advertised on tram tickets. Pic Tor summit was later chosen as the location for Matlock's First World War memorial, because it could be seen from all over the town.

In 1898 Henry Knowles donated a strip of land by the river from the County Bridge to Knowleston Place as another promenade called the Broadwalk. At this time the old football pitch still occupied one field to the side and Henry Ward of Bank House Hydro farmed the other. There were many discussions in the newspapers at the time about the correct name for these fields: Haw Lees, Hall Leys, All Lees and variations. The Council had also discussed trying to purchase the land, but were put off by its frequent flooding.

In 1904 the twelve foot wide Broadwalk was asphalted and fenced; eventually old tramway cable was used as linking rope between the posts. The footbridge giving access to Dale Road belonged to the Old English Hotel, but the public had free use of it. It was sold to the Council and rebuilt a few yards downstream early in 1921.

In 1907 the UDC approved the purchase of the Hall Leys fields for £3750, although many people pointed out they could have bought them more cheaply if they had not dithered when Henry Knowles died. The price on completion in 1908 added to the Council's debts, which meant they had to make a revenue from the park. Luckily they had more sense than to follow Matlock Bath's example.

Hall Leys Park (the name on old Ordnance Survey maps) was opened formally on 23 June 1911 as part of the Coronation celebrations, but had been drawing in the

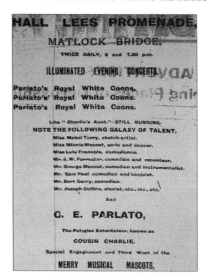

An entertainment in 1902.

crowds for some time before. Matlock Bridge did not want trippers, but it was recognised that visitors to the many boarding houses needed somewhere to enjoy themselves. Minstrel groups were booked straight away: the first was George Pitt's Pierrots. The bandstand, described as looking like a Chinese pagoda, was built in 1910 by an iron foundry in Kirkintilloch in Scotland. There was a small charge for chairs to listen to Matlock United Brass Band and others. In the next couple of years, tennis courts, a bowling green, and a refreshment pavilion were provided – the building still in use today. By 1912 the park was described as a hive of activity, much better than the old "ragged-looking" football field. The football pitch had been moved to its present site on the cricket field: the cricketers were pushed to one side.

Just before the war, a stage was erected at the Crown Square end of the park for pierrot shows. Mr George Davies and his Scarlet Debonnaires were a great hit in the 1913 season, with audiences of over eight hundred.

There were two other outdoor entertainment venues. The old Bateman's Park area, where the bus station now stands, was still in use. In 1906 Mrs Stacey and her Thespian Theatre Company of eighteen artistes arrived in March for three months. Audiences were kept warm with "combustion" stoves. In Wakes Week the area was used for merry-go-rounds and cinema exhibitions. The ground in front of the Town Hall was laid out with a promenade and gardens which included blocks of stone labelled with their names and origin. Troupes of minstrels performed there in the summer months. There were also concerts inside: in 1902 Joshua Dyson's Diorama and Gypsy Choir were booked.

The path to the Wishing Stone was a popular short walk: visitors were advised to "not fail to visit this curious and popular stone". From the tram terminus, a stroll led to the field path past Chesterfield House Hydro and Hurst Farm. One could return by a wooded lane to the top dam of Lumsdale and down "beautiful and sheltered glades to Matlock Green". A shelter with a seat was erected at the Stone

The new shelter built by John Wildgoose.

by John Wildgoose, but there was a problem: in 1901 there was a report of a refuse heap and rats; similar complaints continued for many years.

Apart from entertainments in the hydros, many visitors and the townspeople could attend concerts at the Victoria Hall on Smedley Street East. As with both Pavilions in Matlock Bath, the owners and management struggled to make a profit. In January 1900 the manager Mr Webb went off to fight in the Boer War, but he returned to buy the business. In 1907 it was bought by James White, a former brick seller and speculator from Rochdale, who accumulated over a million pound's worth of mortgages; unsurprisingly he was declared bankrupt by 1909. The manager was J Franklyn-Thomas. The next owner was a Mr Everett, with a manager called Seymour, although John Barnes was mentioned as the musical director. Then the business was floated as a company, with the intention of building a holiday camp in the grounds

All through these changes, the locals maintained bowls, tennis and swimming clubs, with galas and lessons for children. On Thursday evenings in winter they held dance classes. The dance floor of Victoria Hall was re-laid in maple for roller skating in 1909. Each August the Matlock Floral and Horticultural Society held its annual show. Evening classes were held for young men in the winter. In 1908 Matlock Operatic Society performed *The Mikado*, with *HMS Pinafore* the following year. Yum Yum was played by a professional from Covent Garden, Miss Lily Crawford. The Operatic Society committee contained many familiar names: Henry Challand, Dr Moxon, Mr Buttgen, Mrs Sharpe and Miss Goodwin.

When famous brass bands performed, the hydros did not need to provide their own Saturday concerts: the Coldstream Guards came in 1899, the Lifeguards with Violet Ludlow from Covent Garden in 1901, Besses o' th' Barn in 1905, and Black Dyke won a band contest there in 1908.

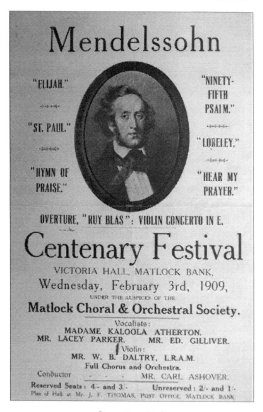

Mendelssohn

"ELIJAH."

"ST. PAUL."

"HYMN OF PRAISE."

"NINETY-FIFTH PSALM."

"LORELEY."

"HEAR MY PRAYER."

OVERTURE, "RUY BLAS": VIOLIN CONCERTO IN E.

Centenary Festival

VICTORIA HALL, MATLOCK BANK,

Wednesday, February 3rd, 1909,

UNDER THE AUSPICES OF THE

Matlock Choral & Orchestral Society.

Vocalists:

MADAME KALOOLA ATHERTON.

MR. LACEY PARKER.   MR. ED. GILLIVER.

Violin:

MR. W. B. DALTRY, L.R.A.M.

Full Chorus and Orchestra.

Conductor   -   -   -   MR. CARL ASHOVER.

Reserved Seats: 4/- and 3/-.   Unreserved: 2/- and 1/-.

Plan of Hall at Mr. J. F. THOMAS, POST OFFICE, MATLOCK BANK

[Jean Douglas]

There were educational lectures. In 1901 a famous war artist called Rene Bull spoke. He had been in the Sudan and South Africa until he was wounded in 1900. In 1904 E Gooroo Prasatham Cotelingam, a famous journalist, gave a talk with lantern slides. No subject is recorded, but it was probably about Burma.

In 1908 the Victoria Hall witnessed a semi-comic episode. A political meeting was held attended by the Duke and Duchess of Devonshire and many other local dignitaries. Because the main hall was taken over for the speeches, the emptied swimming pool had been boarded over to serve tea. The floor collapsed: everybody fell down six or seven feet with the tea urns and crockery on top of them. Colonel Brooke-Taylor from Bakewell made light of it in an interview, but he was actually the only person to be quite badly scalded.

In 1911 the first "living picture" show by Oxo Cinema Films at Victoria Hall attracted crowded houses. By 1912 they were giving two shows a week, but the Picture Palace on Dale Road was already being built. In M J Arkle's *Tuppence Up, Penny Down* is a memory of the Victoria Hall cinema. The projector was acetylene-lit and cranked by hand. The films might have six or eight reels, which meant intervals while they were changed. An attendant rushed to light the gas lamps and play gramophone records each time.

At the bottom of the town, the Market Hall assembly room was still in use. In 1902, Will Mack brought his minstrels nightly in December with a ladies night on

CELEBRITY ACTS AT MATLOCK'S VICTORIA HALL

1908 Gertrude Lonsdale, a contralto who had recently performed at the Proms, with Margel Gluck, an American violinist from Sousa's band.

1905 George Grossmith who performed many of the comic characters in Gilbert and Sullivan operas, such as Ko-Ko in The Mikado. He wrote "See me dance the Polka".

1908 Wilhelm Backhaus making his second visit. In 1905 he beat Bella Bartok to second place in the Rubinstein piano competition.

1908 Arthur Newstead, a pianist just returned from his European tour. He became a teacher at the Juilliard School in New York.

1909 Jan Kubelik, a violinist with his Stradivarius. He attracted the largest audience seen at the hall.

1907 Louie Freear, comedy actress.

1907 Ada Crossley, an Australian singer, who had given several command performances for Queen Victoria.

1908 Ada Forrest, a South African soprano.

Thursdays. In autumn 1905 it briefly became the Theatre Royal with several plays staged including Grace Warner [15] in a musical East Lynne – a sure crowd puller adapted from the 1861 novel. It included the famous line: "Dead, dead, and never called me mother!"

In 1902 the newspapers gave a brief mention of the Matlock Concert Control and Entertainment Bureau, with F W Oates of Smedley Street as secretary. He could supply vocalists, humourists, bands, and an Edison's concert phonograph, as used at the London Hippodrome. Its sound could fill a hall of ten thousand people.

In 1912 the trees in the last remaining space on the east side of Dale Road were felled to build the Picture Palace. The cinema could hold five hundred people seated on a sloping 1 in 10 gradient. There was a stage for concerts, a fire-proof operating room over the office and pay box, and electricity supplied from a gas engine working a dynamo. They opened in 1913 with three performances a day at 3pm, 6.45pm and 9pm. The silent films were accompanied by a piano, and sometimes a violin and drums, with sound effects for storms. Many people did their shopping before the second show and expected to be able to collect it afterwards. (Until recently this building was Bamford's auction house, but is currently unoccupied.)

Also in 1912 William Deacon's Bank, in the old house by the railway station, was extended and a new porch built. Inside were added new plaster ceilings, a Sicilian marble floor, pine clad walls, and mahogany fittings, some of which remain in today's RBS. In 1920 the wrought iron gates at the bottom of Snitterton Road were removed and the present portico installed. (This building had belonged to the Nuttall family, probably related to John, the architect of the two pavilions.)

In 1914 the Conservative Club bought the old assembly room above the Market Hall, which for a few years had been the drill room and ammunition store for the Territorial Army. After giving themselves a fright in 1912, when a fire nearly exploded the ammunition, it was decided they needed to build a new premises.

THE DAY TRIPPER

Nature was kind to the dwellers of the working regions of the Midlands when she placed Matlock in so central a position. The ironworkers of the Black Country, the toilers in the dingy district of the Potteries, the cloth weavers of Yorkshire, and the cotton spinners of Lancashire, are all within from forty to sixty miles of this miniature Switzerland; and from any of the four great manufacturing districts a Saturday afternoon excursion to Matlock and back allows time to explore all the main features of the neighbourhood.

Guide to Matlock and District, Ward Lock & Co, 1910

The debasing influence of the day tripper is everywhere visible in Matlock. His trail is unmistakable. His litter is omnipresent. He has tastes which must be catered for – the ugly phrase is here appropriate. His eye is supposed to be dim; therefore nothing but what is gaudy will attract him. His ear is so accustomed to the roar of machinery and the din of streets that there must be a bawling salesman on the pavement to shout crude invitations to buy.

Highways and Byways in Derbyshire, J B Firth, 1905

15. The sister of a future famous film star: HB Warner.

It was reported in September 1900 that Llandudno had had its worst season for 5 years and Douglas on the Isle of Man was 40,000 visitors down, but the Matlocks had seen a 25% increase. However, this success was seen more at Whitsuntide and the August Bank Holiday then at Easter. Many factories now worked on Good Friday and Easter Tuesday did not see as many trippers, although extra trains were still needed.

At Whitsuntide in 1901, twenty two special and fifteen regular trains brought 25,000 visitors, packed fifteen to a compartment. One caterer had received a booking for 1100 dinners back in January. The Postmaster reported that six thousand postcards were posted on Whit Monday in 1905. The following year, an excursion train direct from London was so crowded that it was followed by a second: over a thousand trippers had arrived by 2.50pm, to return at 8pm. A half day "corridor express" ticket cost 4/6d; the usual fare was 23 shillings. However, Whitsuntide 1910 was a disaster because of Edward VII's death and funeral: all the shops were closed.

There were several attempts in Matlock Bath to extend or enhance the season with fêtes and regattas. For many years, national and local events in Matlock Bath had been celebrated with lanterns illuminating the rocks and on boats floating down the river. There had been many spectacular firework displays.

In the Jubilee year of 1897, the two Councils co-operated with a beacon bonfire on top of Masson and a flight of sixty rockets at 10pm. Down in Matlock Bath pensioners were given their dinner at Boden's and children had tea in the Pavilion. After dark, the Lovers' Walk was illuminated with Chinese lanterns and the Promenade with one hundred crystal fairy lamps. The celebrations came to a triumphant close with two processions: a single file of a dozen illuminated boats was rowed upstream from Woodland Terrace, while a torchlight procession processed down the Lovers' Walk. As they crossed, two hundred coloured fires (provided by Mr Asbury the chemist) were set off simultaneously. The two lines returned, but this time the torches were high on the summit of the cliff. The Masson Mill and the Military Bands played.

Everybody was so pleased with the organisation of this celebration that in September they held another regatta which they called a Venetian fête: it was suggested this should become an annual event. However, the next year it was actually held in July.

The first official Venetian Fête therefore was held in September 1899 and was a great success. The organiser was John Speed, the son of Edward who had done so much for the town in the 1880s. Ten thousand fairy lamps were set up on the Lovers' Walk with Japanese and Chinese lanterns. Matlock Bath Military Band and Mack's Minstrels entertained the crowd before the illuminated gondolas sailed down the river. The sight was hidden from the non-payers by a canvas screen.

The following year thirteen thousand lights were used. A letter in the newspaper from a visitor, who had recently watched the Republican Fête in Paris, said Matlock Bath was a much better setting because of the reflections in the water; some candles were hung from strings stretched across the river. At nine o'clock the rocks were illuminated with coloured fire. Lea Mills and Masson Mill Bands played.

The thirteen boats in 1901 included a lady of the harem in a Turkish *caique*. This time Matlock Bath was compared favourably with Venice itself: the latter a place of

MATLOCK BATH REGATTA
AND AQUATIC SPORTS
(Under A.S.A. Laws),
SATURDAY, July 27th, at 2 p.m.

BOAT RACES, including Fours, Pairs, Scullings, Lady and
Gent.'s Double Sculling, etc., etc.
QUARTER-MILE SWIMMING CHAMPIONSHIP OF
THE DERWENT.
50yds. SWIMMING HANDICAP.
SWIMMING WITH FOOTBALL, FANCY DRESS SWIM-
MING, etc.
GRAND WATER POLO MATCH.

Admission 6d.   Enclosure 6d. extra.

All Events Open.   Entries close July 20th.   Official
Starter and Handicappers.

Particulars from   Hon. Sec., E. SMITH.

"desolate banks, with ruined palaces full of Cook's tours, and full of rheumatism which brings on morbid feelings" whereas the former was "a wonderland, and the people for the nonce fairy dwellers of a sphere where all is light and gaiety". In 1902 ten thousand people saw a boat-chariot with revolving wheels win first prize. Mr Arkwright donated a cup for the best boat, which is still competed for today.

In May 1901 a second annual springtime Fête was tried with equal success and later they added a land-based competition. In 1905 the committee gave each competitor 300 lamps and one hundred lanterns with stakes. The winners on land had depicted Haddon Hall and a Japanese tea garden. The winners with boats were a Chinese junk and a Chinese gun boat. Matlock United Prize Band provided the music. In 1907 the May Fête fireworks were supplied by C T Brock's of London, another old British manufacturer, founded in 1698. The Jubilee Bridge was lit for the first time by gas – a "living fall of flame" like water.

However, the impecunious Council noted the success of these events. They had been happy to loan the Promenade for free, but in 1906 the May Fête was cancelled. The UDC had demanded a commercial rate from an organisation which only just managed to pay its expenses. They did not learn their lesson. Again, in 1910 they demanded 50% of the receipts on the Lovers' Walk: both Fêtes were cancelled in a year which was already a disaster with bad weather and the King's funeral. Everybody lost out and empty properties were appearing on the Parades.

Another annual event began in August 1902 when two new rowing clubs were formed: the Derwent Valley Rowing Club and the Matlock Bath Senior Rowing Club. They held their first regatta and water carnival. By 1904 they were attracting crews from Manchester, Newark and Burton. The only criticism each year was the dreary wait between heats. In 1906 twenty nine events, which should have been completed between 2pm and 6pm, took until 8pm. The Council did loan the Promenade free of charge, but a plea to the Venetian Fete committee for help with prizes fell on deaf ears. Mrs Buttgen gave out the trophies in 1909. As well as the rowing, there were swimming races and life-saving demonstrations.

Life-saving lessons were always a theme in the papers, as well as pleas for the life belts to be more accessible. The one near the central ferry was on a tree projecting over the river where one could easily fall in trying to reach it. There was a steady stream of accident reports. Usually the victims ended their day feeling foolish having their clothes dried at the gas works, but there were tragedies too.

On Good Friday 1897, not long after the Council had become the major boat

The Fountain Bath with a class, perhaps from Riber School.

owner, four over-confident young people hired a boat being steered by an un-fortunate local boy on his first day in the job. The river was very full after heavy rain but the two young men ignored both the wire across the river above Masson Mill weir, with its warning notices, and the boy's pleas. Luckily he was rescued from the boat, but the other four jumped out and drowned. The Coroner had every

sympathy with the traumatised young employee, but the accident led to more calls for regulations.

On another Good Friday in 1901 two brothers were drowned. Five excursionists and a boatman sank for no apparent reason. Of three brothers called Brown from Selston, one was taken alive to the Royal Hotel, but the other two were laid out on the New Bath billiard table. In July a sacred concert was held at the Pavilion to provide funds for a bereaved father who had lost two wage earners.

There were two other attempts to launch an annual festival. In July 1908 was held the first Floral Carnival in aid of the Improvements Association, and organised by Mr Aspey. The Promenade was decorated with garlands, which were also strung across the river. Once again there were decorated boats and land-based garden competitions, but accompanied by water polo, life-saving demonstrations, and a battle of flowers and clowns in canoes throwing soot and flour at each other. Later the crowds danced to an Auxetophone. This was an early phonograph invented by an Englishman called Charles Parsons in 1903 and on sale from 1906. They were very expensive, but could replace the cost of a band. This one was supplied for the day by Mr Dalton at the Central Restaurant, but he may have just hired it.

The following year, Mr Henry Drake arranged an Old English Carnival on the Promenade with 25% of the takings going to the Council. The entertainment included brass bands, a maypole, a Punch and Judy show, the Winster Morris Men and – incongruously – a six mile Marathon. This was all rounded off with a Brock's firework display.

At the beginning of the decade, the chief variety entertainment on the Promenade was provided for several seasons by William Mack's Minstrels and Parlatos. They employed a mixture of acts, which were supposed to change over the weeks, giving two or three performances per day. As well as the resident singers and dancers, Mr Mack's artists included Will Kinglsey, a champion handbell soloist, Leonard Ankers, a Yorkshire boy comedian, performing dogs, and patter comedians. Every season a benefit concert was given for the performers. In 1902 this included Sergeant Webb from Matlock, who gave a "wonderfully neat performance with Indian clubs", and Mr Wilde, a local tenor.

By 1908, Mr Mack had been replaced by Henry Drake's Pierrots who gave a two hour show. One act was Knoto the magician who drank a glass of "poisoned milk". His assistants pumped his arms and the milk drained out of his finger ends into a bucket.

They liked to involve the audience with singing competitions voted on by the crowd. One competition was won by George Smith of Matlock Bridge. There were baby shows, and treacle- and bun-eating contests for boys to win a pocket knife. In August 1908, a Mr Taylor sang standing on his head in a bucket. (I sincerely hope this was not my grandfather, Gladstone Taylor: this was the week he was staying at Malvern House Hydro.)

The other entertainment organised by the Council was the band employed to play each season. There were long discussions about quality, but chiefly, of course, the cost. It was reckoned to cost about £200 a season for decent musicians in 1900, but this cost crept up.

For several years the music was supplied by Matlock Bath & District Military Band, founded in 1891 by John W Hilder, the photographer on South Parade. Their

A temporary bandstand on the Promenade. Card posted 1909.

committee petitioned the Council for a permanent bandstand or kiosk. This was erected in 1893, paid for by public subscription, on the Jubilee Grounds at the north end of the Lovers' Walk. As well as their fee from the Council, the band had a collecting box and charged 1d for chairs. However, after a series of internal rows, the Military Band resigned and disbanded in 1900.

After this, several bands came and went. In 1905 the Excelsior Band cost £250 for twelve weeks of three concerts a day. A bazaar was held to make up the shortfall in money needed. Luckily, once the Pavilion closed, Signor Guidi's nine-man Italian Military Band became available, including Sundays when allowed (see Never on a Sunday) at a cost of £22 per week. In 1910 there was mention of a new moveable bandstand where Matlock United Prize Band played for the first time. Postcards do show a wooden bandstand on the Promenade, with a striped canvas roof.

In 1900 the 20th annual meeting of the High Tor Recreation Ground Company was held, still with Mr Robert Hall as secretary and Job Smith as chairman. In 1902 the grounds were improved with new planting of gorse and other flowering shrubs. However, real progress came with the opening of a new suspension bridge in May 1903 and a new serpentine walk to the summit. The new bridge was built to give access to the grounds from the main road near Tor Cottage. Firth, as usual, objected to the admission fee (3d) and the large signs erected at the turnstile. The opening ceremony was performed by Victor Cavendish MP, who became the 9th Duke of Devonshire. He had to walk to the summit, followed by a large crowd. After lunch at the New Bath Hotel, he toiled further up the opposite hill to open the new Matlock Bath golf club. The bridge was demolished in the 1970s, although its footings can still be seen at the roadside.

As well as visiting the caves, High Tor visitors could take tea in the café, play

The bridge to High Tor.
[Glynn Waite]

cricket on the summit, and quoits and tennis on the slope now occupied by the cable car station.

The day tripper no longer spent all his money in Matlock Bath. There were new attractions at the Bridge and Bank. Omnibuses took visitors along the Dale to the Bridge and it was easy to reach the top of the Bank by tramcar. In 1903 Mrs Mack's Merry Makers were advertised on the Old English grounds or in the assembly room when wet.

Victoria Hall and gardens, described before, benefitted from the closure of the old Pavilion. Brass band contests were still taking place in the Old English Hotel grounds, but the Black Dyke Mills band won a competition at the Victoria Hall in 1908.

Matlock United Prize Band was revived from a previous military band in 1893; they still wore uniforms with peaked caps. The busy Lubin Wildgoose was a conductor. They raised money for twenty-five new instruments in 1897, which were displayed in a shop window on Smedley Street. They often played in the Town Hall and Knowleston Place gardens before becoming regulars on the new Hall Leys bandstand.

A circus on Hall Leys fields in 1899 advertised a football match for a silver cup between the Matlock Town captain and an elephant. The human won, but, as the *High Peak News* remarked, "What more could the tripper desire?"

The same year a party from Belle Vue Hydro went down a lead mine off Snitterton Road. They were afraid of meeting dangerous wildlife, so they took firearms.

[Glynn Waite]

There once was a pretty new bridge
From Dale Road to the opposite ridge:
By the Board's wise intention
'Twas wire and suspension
And, in aspect, light as a midge.

There once was a gay day in May
When that bridge could be crossed without pay.
No doubt you remember
Our popular Member
Walked over to show us the way.

Limericks written by F S King for the opening of the new High Tor Bridge, May 1903.

In July 1909 a day out in Blackpool for the workers at Smedley's Lea Mills was ruined by train delays. They spent thirteen hours of their precious day's holiday not moving much at all – at one point they all climbed out and played cricket in a field!

There was another annual day trip which only passed through. Early one morning each June a procession of fifteen trains would pass through the Matlock stations at ten minute intervals. All other railway traffic was suspended: the Bass Brewery was on its way to Blackpool.

NEVER ON A SUNDAY

During the first decades of the twentieth century, there were many debates about what could and could not be done on a Sunday. Music on the Promenade at Matlock Bath came and went several times. Was it permissible if the music was sacred? What was sacred music? Was it just the words? Could one play any serious compositions by the great composers? If there was no music, the Council missed out on important income. The vicar of Matlock Bath spoke against the music, not because his parishioners were being corrupted, but because he was losing congregations and the afternoon concerts had wrecked his Sunday school attendance. When Mr Arkwright was asked his opinion concerning the new bandstand on the Lovers' Walk, he always vetoed Sunday concerts. In 1904 a Councillor confidently stated in a debate that, "the Music Committee should remember that visitors to Matlock have a religious tendency". Another vote in 1907 vetoed anything of "a rollicking description". This certainly included dance music. However, Signor Guidi's Band at the end of the 1900s was contracted to play on some Sundays.

There were many debates as to whether boating should be allowed on a Sunday, but while Mr Arkwright held jurisdiction over the river, this also was forbidden. He would not even allow a new Council-owned ferry crossing below the New Bath Hotel to operate on a Sunday. This attitude was described in the *Visiting List* as "tommy rot". If Mr Arkwright took a carriage to church, why should others not travel by boat? A letter from a visitor in 1912 scorned Matlock's attitude, describing the wonderful scenes as 2000 boaters crowded Boulter's Lock on the Thames on Ascot Sunday. Were they all dammed?

In August 1908 a club applied to Matlock Council to play a Sunday cricket match. They were refused. As the *Visiting List* exclaimed, "What are we coming to?" But the members at Matlock Golf Club voted in favour of Sunday golf in late 1910. (The lady members were naturally not allowed to vote, although they paid subscriptions.) Sunday play was already allowed at Matlock Bath and many other clubs. The smaller hydros were in favour, as proximity to the course was one of their selling points. Seven days of golf might also encourage city dwellers to build villas on the Bank. The Club committee met and overruled the vote; perhaps surprisingly Mr Challand and John W Wildgoose both voted against. By 1925 Matlock was the only golf club in Derbyshire with no Sunday golf, so they finally gave in that December – it snowed.

Even fishing was forbidden by all the Derbyshire angling clubs. Sunday afternoon trains were criticised by the Lord's Day Observance Society. The newspapers sometimes mentioned regrettable incidences of Sunday gardening, and workmen seen mowing and rolling tennis courts. The vicar of Matlock Bath, deploring the drunkenness of trippers, including women, asked for public houses to refuse to serve on Sundays.

As will be seen, Sunday boating and other sports caused more heated debate in the 1930s.

MATLOCK DISTRICT IMPROVEMENTS ASSOCIATION
In February 1902 the proprietors of the larger hydros called a public meeting to decide how they could promote the Matlocks. The first meeting was badly attended, especially from Matlock Bath, but the Improvements Association was launched. There had actually already been an association in Matlock Bath, but its existence was intermittent. At Matlock Bank, Henry Challand of Smedley's Hydro became the first chairman, with George Barton from Dalefield his deputy. They fixed the subscription at five shillings for the hydros and 2/6d for lodging houses.

The main aim was a sustained advertising campaign, as well as lobbying the

Council for improvements to the environment: planting trees, removing eyesores, dealing with dust etc. Mr Challand and his colleagues maintained the town was largely dependent on the visitors and their spending power, particularly when the fortunes of traditional occupations such as stone quarrying and textile manufacture could fluctuate. However, some Councillors refused to acknowledge this.

Mr Challand had a good point. Whereas the censuses showed a stagnation in the numbers employed in trade and manufacturing, the numbers of people in service rose steadily. Smedley's staff bill alone was £250 per week. The Hydro employed 120 householders as well as many wives and daughters of quarrymen and tradesmen. Over one hundred workers in the town called themselves hydrotherapists and bath attendants. Each decade there were rises in the numbers of those employed as dressmakers, laundresses, gardeners and shop assistants: all basic occupations in any town, but vital in a holiday resort. In 1908 the *High Peak News* calculated that between 800 and 1000 girls worked seasonally in the hydros, many from elsewhere in the East Midlands.

There were also professions which spoke of work in hotels and leisure industries: lift attendants and page boys, musicians, a golf professional, green keepers and caddies, several youths who were billiard score markers, and two skating instructors!

In spite of no financial support from the UDC, the Association was soon printing coloured posters for Midland Railway stations and carriages and other hoardings. One hundred thousand albums of twenty high class views of the Matlocks were produced for visitors to take away at a cost of 6d.

Matlock was prominent at a 1902 exhibition on health resorts at the Crystal Palace. In 1904 500 posters of Matlock Bank seen from Pic Tor, labelled the "Metropolis of Hydropathy" were sent out all over the United Kingdom, with other posters depicting the "Switzerland of England", plus 700 view albums.

There were hydro posters at the 1908 Franco-British Exhibition, in the location which became known as the White City. (There were also views of Matlock Bath, but unfortunately they were labelled simply Matlock.) The new campaign was pushing Matlock as a winter resort. Five thousand posters were printed, with ten thousand souvenir books and 50,000 handbills for distribution by Thomas Cook.

The Matlocks had always been able to boast a low death rate. In 1901 the *Daily Mail* reported it was the lowest in the United Kingdom at 10.5 per 1000. Now it was decided to advertise the climate too, with weather statistics published in the national press. The Association bought instruments which were tested at Kew and then set up in Rockside Hydro's garden. It was soon claimed that, at Whitsuntide 1902, Matlock had 14.4 hours of sunshine, Brighton 9.9, Southend 10.8 and Blackpool and Margate only 4. In 1907 the apparatus was handed to the Council and placed on an elegant stand outside the Town Hall. Later it was returned to Rockside and the readings were taken officially by Mr Davis, the chemist on Dale Road, who had free tram travel up the hill when on this task.

There were sometimes excited reports in the newspapers of spa water being found at Matlock Bridge, but only one spring was used regularly. Allen Hill Chalybeate Spaw can still be seen at the bottom of The Dimple from which locals collected the yellow-brown water to treat eye complaints. *The Matlocks & Bakewell: Famous Derbyshire Health Resorts*, published in 1893, had exhorted the Council to develop the spring, with a pump room and promenade by the river: all "enlivened by high-class music", but it was never to be. In earlier times unhealthy cattle troughs had been located close by. When the Improvements Association suggested cleaning the area up, they found the water was still polluted by effluent from Allen Hill Farm. (In 1936 borings were taken on Pic Tor for a "radio-active" spring and near the bandstand in Hall Leys Park for a thermal spring, but the initial excitement soon died out.)

There were, of course, national endeavours to boost British tourism against competition from Continental spas. In May 1914, the Health Resorts and Watering Places Bill was one such bid, promoted first by Pwllheli Council. The clause which most interested the Matlocks was the power to allow an amount equal to a penny rate to be used for advertising outside the local area. The Bill was revived after the War and became an Act in 1921.

In June 1914 the Improvements Association commissioned the Gaumont film company to film the town in Whit Week. The production, called "Picturesque Matlock" included scenes of the panorama from Masson, the Golf Club, Crown Square and the trams, Pic Tor, High Tor, and tennis, bowls and croquet being played in Hall Leys Park. *Bioscope* magazine said "the quality is first rate and this beautiful scenic should be very popular". The Gaumont film is now available to watch on the British Film Institute's website, but the nitrate base has suffered damage. Sadly, apart from a glimpse of Riber Castle and High Tor, only scenes in Dovedale survive. Many people went to see themselves at the Picture Palace before the film was distributed all over the country. In 1915 it was shown to soldiers at the Front. A second film was commissioned in 1919, made by the Sheffield Photo Company, showing the

MASSON FROM BANK ROAD, MATLOCK.

Ladies toiling up past Yew Tree Farm.

railway station, Crown Square and the Park. This was still touring the country a year later when 70,000 people were estimated to have seen it.

Matlock Bath Improvements Association came and went. In this decade the secretary was Edward Aspey at Clarence House boarding house. The occasional ball or other fund raising event was reported. In 1896 William Bryan and the UDC had met with the Midland Railway to ask for a photograph of Matlock Bath on their timetable, as had appeared the year before. They were promised one on the back of *Holiday Towns of the British Isles* instead. In 1905 the Association brought out a new brochure and the following year ten thousand books of local views, but they were constantly criticised for not doing enough.

In 1925 Matlock Bath joined with its neighbour on the Bank to form the Matlock Publicity Association, with Mr Ernest Bailey in the Chair. Their office, of which more later, was in the Town Hall. In 1927, the Chairman J G Goodwin of Rockside Hydro announced a new book of views. He called for more townspeople to join the Association: shop owners, charabanc proprietors, and other small businesses. He said those guest houses who had joined were always full because most queries to the office were about the smaller establishments. In particular, they needed more input from Matlock Bath.

One of the main aims of the Matlock District Improvements Association from its first inception was the provision of a golf course. After considering several sites, they settled on the fringes of Matlock Moor beside the main road to Chesterfield.

A ROUND OF GOLF

Matlock Golf Club was relatively late on the scene. In the 1890s there was a flurry of new clubs in easy reach of Matlock: Ashover (1895), Baslow (1890), Bakewell (1899) and Chesterfield (1897).

The earliest local green was a nine-hole course at Lea Hurst, the Nightingale's house at Lea, which was usually let out to tenants. There was a report in 1890 that the park had been closed to walkers because of their behaviour. Shortly after, the golf club was formed after meetings of the local gentry at Bridge House in Cromford. Mr Frederic Arkwright was the President; he presented a challenge cup made by the Goldsmith's Company in London, valued at £10, and promptly won the first competition himself. Mr Woodman from Buxton was hired as the professional. The thirty or so members met socially at the Yew Tree Inn, but the hoi polloi were never welcomed – and certainly no ladies. The course closed by 1901.

From 1901 to 1904, Darley Dale Hydro advertised a nine-hole course open to the public. It was opened with a match between two very famous golfers: James Braid and John Henry Taylor. With Harry Vardon, mentioned below, the three won the Open Championship sixteen times between 1894 and 1914.

Matlock Bath and District Golf Links was opened formally by Victor Cavendish MP in May 1903, on high ground in Upperwood. The nine holes, with "very sporting natural hazards" had actually been played since the previous September. The advertisements spoke of good turf and "easy" access – only fifteen minutes from the station! Arrivals could probably see the club house from the station, 800 feet up on the opposite hillside, but walking there in a mere fifteen minutes would have defeated most people. In 1909 there were forty members, but the club was running at a loss: the date of its demise is uncertain. There was a report in 1920 that land was being bought to extend the course, but it is doubtful this happened.

Henry Challand was the driving force behind the Improvements Association's determination to build a golf course for Matlock Bank. From 1893 with a subscription of 18 shillings the Goodwin family had had a kind of course on Wolds Farm for their friends. But the new site chosen was on Matlock Moor, on land which the UDC owned as a catchment area for the town's water supply. The golf committee asked for a 14 year lease on one hundred acres of Cuckoostone Grange Farm at £70 per year. They assured the Council they would need no help from the rates.

The 18-hole course at 900 feet was described as a good sporting one with hazards of gorse and trees. The course was designed by Tom Williamson, an expert from Hollinwell Club in Nottinghamshire, supervised by his father Edmund who became the first professional. It was also apparently "an easy walk", this time from the tram terminus – but a fair distance nonetheless. The first clubhouse contained simply changing and drying rooms with lavatories: the golfers played and went home.

The club was open by Whitsuntide 1907, but the official ceremony took place in September on a day with a "tropical sky". Colonel Brooke-Taylor, the Bakewell solicitor standing in for the Duke of Devonshire, struck the inaugural drive, followed by four famous golfers playing exhibition matches: Harry Vardon, Sandy Herd, George Duncan and Tom Williamson.

A lunch of salmon, beef ribs and lamb was served in a marquee behind the new clubhouse by Mr John Francis Chapman De la Court, who had recently opened a new temperance hotel and restaurant on Smedley Street. (This gentleman was known as Chippy Chapman, because he had worked in a fish and chip shop. His new name, curling moustache, check suit and cravat did not fool the locals, even though he looked "every inch a Frenchman".) The drinks had to come from Mr Tanzer at the Crown Hotel.

The President of the club was the Duke of Devonshire, who presented a challenge cup. Alfred Sykes, the chairman of Smedley's Hydro Company gave another cup, and there was eventually a Goodwin Memorial Trophy. Henry Challand was the first club Chairman, with John Goodwin from Rockside and John W Wildgoose on the committee. Dr Harbinson was the first Captain, followed by Ernest Bailey. Drs Harbinson and MacLelland of Smedley's Hydro soon found leisure time to get on the trophy board. Visitors could purchase daily, weekly or monthly tickets. From 1930 they could compete for the John Smedley Visitors' Cup. Ladies played from the beginning, although they were not an official section until 1912.

All the hydros advertised their proximity to the golf course. By the 1920s, the clubhouse had a common room, with radiators and gas lights, where refreshments were served.

NEW WAYS OF GETTING AROUND

Three ages of transport round the tram shelter – motorists were never sure where to go.

By 1900, travelling was becoming much easier. The "modern" bicycle had been around since the mid-1880s and was now very popular and affordable. At the same time motor cars with internal combustion engines were coming onto our roads. Women could, of course, use both means of transport on their own and embraced the new freedom this allowed.

In March 1900 the *Visiting List* praised the councils towards Derby for steam-rolling the roads ready for the cycling season. However, the surface in Matlock itself came in for criticism all year. The road in Darley Dale had been covered in sharp "loose chippings" and it was feared there would be punctures until heavy traffic had smoothed them out. North Darley District Council bought storm-proof lamps to erect at road works to warn cyclists of patches of new macadam.

A favourite trip was the level jaunt to Ambergate, in springtime passing the blue-bells in Alderwasley woods. On windy days, canny cyclists took the train to Ambergate or Bakewell and came back with the wind behind them. A South Darley councillor in a meeting wanted to tax cyclists as they were a nuisance on the roads and would not move out of the way. Just like dogs, came the riposte. The chairman ruled both men out of order.

In July 1893 a Matlock youth called Herbert Hodgson had achieved an heroic feat for a cyclist without gears "on a pneumatic". A crowd of people watched him cycle up Bank Road non-stop. He reached Smedley Street, and probably could have attempted Rutland Street, had not a tramcar got in his way.

Matlock Cycling Club had its headquarters at the Old English Hotel where they had been allowed to build a track. It was where the Derwent Gardens apartments now stand. The track was egg-shaped, to give straight runs down the sides, and

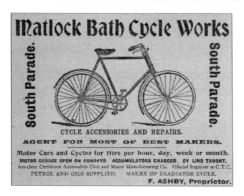

*This garage was on the raised area off
South Parade.*

banked at each end. Eight laps measured one mile. A reporter watching the 1912 Cycle Club five mile race was amazed the cyclists did not become mesmerized and fall over.

Visitors could enrol as Club members. There was also the Matlock Wheelers Club which included ladies. During Wakes Week each September from 1902, the clubs staged a fancy dress procession in aid of Whitworth Hospital. Cyclists and their machines were decorated as yachts, lighthouses, and Japanese flower ladies. This was the forerunner of Matlock Carnival.

As already noted, several shops, such as Ashby's Matlock Bath Cycle Works on South Parade and Hartley's on Crown Square, rented out bicycles and did repairs. They even offered to teach cycling. The hydros provided bicycle sheds; but the cheaper hotels and restaurants recommended themselves as being more suitable for those who could afford a bicycle rather than a motor car. Both the Trevelyan and Derwent Temperance Hotels on Dale Road offered "Every Convenience for cyclists". From 1902 the *Visiting List* published cycling notes.

The guide books issued pocket maps and routes with dire warnings, some of which we would not even think about today. For example, Abel Heywood & Son's Guide warned that at Rowsley, after one turned left at the station, "descend with care, nasty corner under railway bridge, river bridge adjacent generally very uneven". The route to Chesterfield was "the hardest of all" in the neighbourhood; the descent of Slack Hill "so dangerous that no cyclist should ride it".

They were also wise to caution the road into Millers Dale where,

If allowed, your wheel will attain such velocity that when the steep portion of the descent is observed, it is too late. The road is extremely dangerous, and the acute turn to left exposes rock, very dangerous road and precipice.

Sadly two brothers set off down Taddington hill in April 1900 on a brakeless tandem and were "picked up at the foot dead". A warning notice was placed at the top of Winster Bank after another fatal accident. When Fred Wright of Matlock Cycling Club was thrown on to his face cycling to Nottingham in 1904, he was brought back to Whitworth Hospital in a cab. In September 1902 the son-in-law of

XIII. TO CHESTERFIELD.

This is the hardest of all the road routes in the neighbourhood. From Matlock Bath to Matlock Bridge ; cross bridge, and follow the steep road to right of that up which the cable tramway runs. At top of hill the road is undulating, followed by a descent into Slack so dangerous that no cyclist should ride it. The route lies through Kelstedge and Walton to New Brompton, where turn to right for Chesterfield (11 miles from Matlock Bath).

Ward Lock's Guide warning of Slack Hill.

William Atkins, the owner of Darley Dale Hydro, was killed cycling in Cornwall.

In April 1900 came an intimation that cycling would soon have a rival. A councillor at a Matlock Bath UDC meeting asked if motor cars would come under the local byelaws. He received no real answer. A month later, the townspeople, visitors, and many spectators who had flocked down from the villages, had a real treat. The log book for All Saints' School recorded that the children were given half a day's holiday for the occasion.

On 27 April, sixty seven motor cars trundled into Matlock Bath on a stage of the great "1000 Mile Trial": the Automobile Club had organised a tour from 23 April to 12 May driving from London to Edinburgh and back to test the current speed and stamina of the motor car.

The bigwigs had lunch at the Royal Hotel. They included Alfred Harmsworth (later Lord Northcliffe) the newspaper owner. Charles Stewart Rolls drove a Panhard which won the final Gold Medal. Herbert Austin was in a Wolseley. There were several very competent lady drivers, including Mrs Bazalgette. After lunch everyone drove to the base of Taddington hill where another large crowd had gathered. Each car was allowed to set off in turn at full speed (the official limit was 14mph) to reach the top two and half miles further on. The winner was an Ariel tricycle which took eight minutes at an average speed of 18.91mph. Some drivers had to get out and push, taking over half an hour to reach the summit – jeered by cyclists. Bystanders also found the petrol smell objectionable and it was noticed that many motors vibrated excessively. Later in the tour, the cars crossed Shap Fell and underwent speed trials in Welbeck Park.

In 1909 there was a similar rally to test the reliability of motor cycles. Many locals and visitors watched them drive through the Matlocks on a circuitous route from Macclesfield to Shrewsbury. Hill-climbing was an important strength of motor cycles at that time.

A visitor had brought a motor car to Smedley's in 1898: a Daimler, which locals reckoned must have cost its owner £350. By 1901 the *Visiting List* reported that quite a few cars were to be seen locally: Dr Sharpe had a "splendid" motor. Each edition carried an advertisement for a powerful motor car taking tours from Hackney's Household Stores in Matlock Bath – "hills no difficulty". Mr Barton at Dalefield Hydro soon purchased a Daimler to take guests on trips. His son Tom advertised

A motor rally c1912.

himself as an experienced chauffeur, but in 1904 he managed to overturn the car in Tuxford, Nottinghamshire, pinning eight of his friends underneath. In 1905 there was a craze of moonlight motor trips through the romantic Peak: one such came to grief near Beeley.

A motor cyclist in Belper was charged with "furiously driving a motor" at 26mph and fined £2. The police constable at Taddington rashly stood in the middle of the road and waved his arms at a car seen racing round the village at 25mph. It brushed past him. At the driver's trial, the owner of a charabanc carrying nineteen passengers said his horses had been very frightened. In 1906 an American millionaire called J Russell King skidded on Dale Road and hit a lamp post.

As 1904 opened, the Motor Car Act raised the speed limit to 20mph, although Matlock Bath UDC would have preferred a 4mph limit through the narrow main road. Matlock Bridge also asked for a reduction of the speed through the town to 6mph. When cars raced through illegally at 30 or even 40mph, the pedestrians were, "blinded by dust, poisoned by the stink", and the cars were, "a confounded nuisance to everybody besides those who use them". In August 1905 police were seen taking every car number which passed over the County Bridge; motorists were told to beware of vindictive fines.

Cars now needed number plates and "R" had been chosen for vehicles registered in Derbyshire. Drivers had to buy a five shilling licence but did not need a test. The numbers of motors seen in the Matlocks gradually increased through the decade, but the *Visiting List* still thought it worth remarking that 305 cars had been counted driving through the towns on Good Friday 1911.

The guide books now gave simple motor routes, with complacent phrases such as "the road cannot be mistaken" and "the way is easily found". The directions from Leeds to Matlock suggested following the telegraph poles, once the tramlines had disappeared, to reach Wakefield. They seemed confident that a few direction posts and spotting of public houses would make the remaining route perfectly clear.

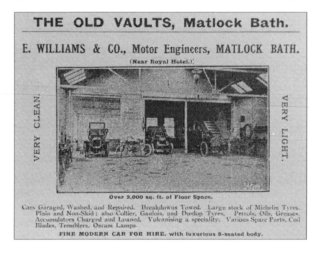

THE OLD VAULTS, Matlock Bath.

E. WILLIAMS & CO., Motor Engineers, MATLOCK BATH.
(Near Royal Hotel.)

VERY CLEAN.

VERY LIGHT.

Over 2,000 sq. ft. of Floor Space.

Cars Garaged, Washed, and Repaired. Breakdowns Towed. Large stock of Michelin Tyres, Plain and Non-Skid; also Collier, Gaulois, and Dunlop Tyres. Petrols, Oils, Greases, Accumulators Charged and Loaned. Vulcanising a speciality. Various Spare Parts, Coil Blades, Tremblers, Osram Lamps.

FINE MODERN CAR FOR HIRE, with luxurious 5-seated body.

By 1903 Mr Ashby at the Cycle Works at Matlock Bath was running a Daimler for trips. In 1909 Hand & Son bought the first motor car to hire out. A few weeks later it was used for the first "motorised" wedding, bringing the bride to church. Hand and W Furniss, the two main excursion companies, purchased Belsize Landaulettes, a kind of charabanc. A Hall & Co expanded their ironmonger and plumbing business in Dale Road to open a motor spares and appliances garage in Crown Yard.

The hydros began to advertise garages and parking. The Royal provided a garage from Easter 1906 which was "RAC appointed". The guests were still thrilled when a new motor whirled up the drive and,

> *a general air of thank-goodness-we-have-got-here-safely-and-now-we-can-breathe-again pervades the automobilists as they disembark and disencumber themselves of their wraps.*

Smedley's opened a garage on Smedley Street in July 1908. Guests had a key to their own rolling shutter door. There was a stove room to warm the chauffeurs and dry rugs and aprons, a wash bay and inspection pit. Oldham House Hydro had a garage for fourteen cars. Sycamore House Hydro built a garage and inspection pit and charged two shillings a day for its use. The New Bath was recommended to AA Club members.

By 1912 *The Car Illustrated* was writing of cars being affordable for the "better class of artisan". Caravan cars with sleeping berths were available for long journeys: the first modern towing caravan was designed in 1914.

Further Afield

The scenery around here is indescribably grand – a varied combination of hill, dale and cliff, and wood and river … There is perhaps no place in this country, or else-where, where so much romantic scenery can be seen within so limited an area.

Bulmer's *History & Directory of Derbyshire*, 1895

A visitor could still travel to Chatsworth and Haddon Hall by train, with a walk at the end. One could even now reach Dovedale on the London & North Western Railway via Buxton, alighting at Tissington or Thorpe Cloud stations. But most people used horse charabancs or carriages – it was all part of the day's fun to squash in with a couple of dozen others in an open-air vehicle with little brake-power on Derbyshire's hills. Gentlemen sometimes got out on steep gradients and pushed. Most of the hydros organised weekly charabanc trips; groups of guests could also book their own outings with picnics or tea in one of the hotels in Bakewell or Rowsley.

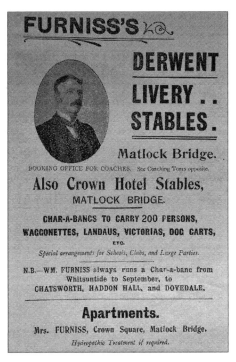

William Furniss claimed he had enough carriages and horses to "work a party of 500". He spread his business over several premises: the Derwent Livery Stables and

Crown Hotel on Crown Square, his original premises at Cherry Holt below Rockside Hydro, and Portland Mews and the New Bath in Matlock Bath, with a booking office next to the Fishpond Hotel. When driving his old four-in-hand "Times" coach William wore a long jacket and riding breeches with a red waistcoat. In 1911 he used nearly all his vehicle capacity by taking 400 staff from the *Manchester Guardian* up the Via Gellia in smart vehicles with an "excellent array of horseflesh". He kept a special team of grey Belgian horses for weddings and funerals. Joseph Allen at Dimple Farm still had cabs and supplied hearses for funerals.

The Gate Hotel was sold to Hutchinson's Brewery in 1903, and Hand & Son took the livery stables from Boden's to add to their Pope Carr business. Eventually they built the little one-storey office behind the public house which still stands. In 1900 they were taking out over six hundred visitors a week in their charabancs and could cope with 200 a day. Town centre bookings were taken in Phillip's hairdressers. Their advertisement was often headed "Funerals! Funerals!" In 1911 Mr Hand provided the first motor taxi cab at the railway station.

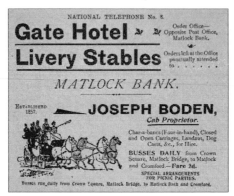

In 1902 Benjamin Talbot, a retired policeman, advertised stables on Crown Square and accommodation with his wife at Bradford Villa on Chesterfield Road. Every afternoon in the summer months a mail coach drawn by four "fine steppers" picked up guests from the Royal Hotel for a drive out.

Chatsworth was still the main attraction for a day's excursion. Firth, crabby as ever in his *Highways and Byways in Derbyshire*, complained that a "guide shepherds you from room to room, and the tired finger indicates and the uninterested voice describes, the things in which you take not the least concern". Abel Heywood's *Guide* warned that the House was, "crowded to excess in fine summer weather" and advised an early arrival.

Mr Peerless, a visitor on Whit Monday 1908 described a mass of charabancs, wagonettes and traps and the largest number of bicycles he had ever seen in one place. He joined a long queue, four abreast. Near the entrance was an enclosure like an animal pound, with a bar at each end. Fifty visitors were allowed through this at a time. The guide, who seemed to be a "superior-looking maid servant" hurried them through the house, because so many were waiting.

Lady Colin Campbell, who had been so enthusiastic a visitor at the Royal Hotel, did say that, "The presence of the tripper and his charabanc is a very big drawback to the enjoyment of Haddon", but she found the garden peaceful. The Hall was still described as being in a fair condition. Mr Peerless was charged 6d to visit, although the guide book had stated 4d, but this was a Bank Holiday. A petition from the Matlock District Improvements Association was sent begging the Duke of Rutland not to close Haddon Hall in 1913. He did so for five months and gave the reason as suffragettes!

From Haddon, the indefatigable Mr Peerless proceeded to Bakewell for tea. The usually quiet town was alive with people. Horses for sale were being run up and down the square. There were piles of pottery on the ground, with cheap-jacks calling out the price of knives and razors. He could hear the crack of rifles from the gypsy shooting galleries.

On another day, Mr Peerless visited Wingfield Manor. The farmer's daughter sold him a nicely written guide book and he was left to wander about. Afterwards he was given lunch in the farmhouse parlour and shown curios laid out in the next room.

NEW OPERA HOUSE, BUXTON

Buxton was sometimes perceived as rather superior to Matlock, so many visitors took a trip to see what they were missing. A band played twice a day in the Pavilion Gardens and there were plenty of shops and tea houses. In 1903 the new Opera House was opened. In the opposite direction was Derby, "where old-world belongings have almost been cleared away by the inroads of modern times". The Arboretum was popular and at nearby Royal Crown Derby the whole manufacturing process was shown to visitors with "willing courtesy". In 1901 the Council asked for late trains so people could go to the theatre. Until then, one could only buy a "market" ticket on Fridays and go to a matinee.

In 1903 Matlock House Hydro introduced the idea of short tours for their long-term patients. They might stay away for a couple of nights, perhaps visiting the Dukeries or Alton Towers, which was advertised as "The Fairyland of the British

Isles" but with only "adequate catering".

With the increasing numbers of bicycles and motor cars, visitors could tour local villages further afield. Previously they had been restricted to those within walking distance such as Crich and Bonsall. Eyam was described in Heywood's guide book as "a little mountain city overshadowed by the spirit of the old" because of the "awful circumstances" of its history. A description of a tour in 1908 said Hartington had become an important centre for day trippers, but Longnor was a "dead and alive place" with grass growing in the streets. Village pubs were receiving a fresh boost to their incomes: the Chequers Inn at Froggatt was famous for Derbyshire ham and eggs.

Rarely mentioned in guide books, but surely worth visiting, were the nurseries of James Smith & Sons on Darley hillside: "one of the marvels of the present age".

> As you whizz past in the Midland express at 40 or 50 miles per hour, you catch simply a bird's eye view of an enchanting picture of brown and green, grey and white, purple or red, just as the season of the year is, but what a gigantic panorama it is – 250 acres in extent.

The nurseries were not one block, but consisted of about twenty plots in and above Darley Dale. They were named for their position or speciality: Home (conifers), North Siberian[16] (spruce and heathers), Canada (cranberries and bilberries), Wheatley (hollies), Hall Dale (ornamental shrubs), Charlestown (rhododendrons), Station (Austrian pines and ornamental willows). It was claimed that millions of plants were grown: 40 acres of rhododendrons, half a million heathers in fifty varieties, three million larch trees, 150,000 spruce trees, 500,000 privet bushes, 50,000 sycamore trees etc. At the higher levels were pears, apples, cherries, plums and laburnums, all bred to withstand cold temperatures and strong winds. The colours in late spring and autumn must have been wonderful. An advertisement in 1908 said white "Scotch heather" was a speciality. In spring, gentians created "bands of blue running up the hillside".

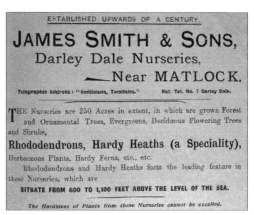

The Smith family had been in business since 1827, and now employed 150 to 200

---

16. It is not easy to find all these nurseries on maps, but Siberia and North Siberia are easily identified as the area now exactly occupied by Darwin Forest Country Park.

men and boys. Arrow Smith, Job Smith's friend, died in 1904 and his son James took charge. At one staff tea in 1908 it was reported that the packing shed was decorated with Canterbury Bells! The same report described over 8000 packs being assembled the previous winter and over 40,000 loose bundles of trees being sent down to Darley Dale station. However, late frosts had damaged two and a half million larches and rhododendrons.

The nursery supplied all the botanic gardens and Kew. The King was a customer, so he must have told his cousin the Kaiser: in 1908 six wagons of trees were sent to Potsdam to the Imperial Palace. In February 1911 eleven railway wagons of conifers were sent to British Columbia. Hotels and private houses could hire plants to decorate their rooms for balls and banquets. Visitors were taken round the thirty miles of roadway in the firm's motor car.

Accustomed as we are to regrets for lost meadows and woodlands, it was strange to see in the newspaper that carpets of white marguerites along the Derwent valley were described as "a horrid weed" of no benefit. Moreover, the rhododendrons at Alderwasley and Lea Hurst "made the landscape lurid". However, a description of the Matlocks in *Mayfair* in 1912 said there was "no district in the United Kingdom which offers a greater profusion of wild flowers", which they attributed to the variety of rocks and soils.

VISITORS

Many histories of the Matlocks list the same few famous visitors. Without the visitor books of the various hotels and hydros, these claims cannot be substantiated. It is certain some important people did not give their names into the *Visiting List* for obvious reasons, and they may have been dismayed to find them-selves spotted. A few names have already appeared in the previous text; below are some others who definitely came. They are often more interesting than the "usual suspects".

Apart from the influx at Christmas and Easter, the end of the London season in July and August brought the better classes to Matlock and other spas and resorts. When there were events such as the 1900 Paris Exhibition, more Americans arrived on their European tours. Wealthy Indians and others from our Empire toured the "Mother Country". As already described, entertainers came and performed, some while undergoing treatment themselves. Because hydropathy probably really did help with joints and muscles, it attracted many sportsmen.

Football teams continued to undergo fitness and physiotherapy regimes. In 1898 Sheffield United used Chesterfield House Hydro as their base for whole season. In 1903 they followed Nottingham Forest to Jeffs' Poplar Hydro. They were kept largely separate, only meeting other guests at meal times. Grimsby Town stayed at Elm Tree Hydro in 1900; they were seen up very early taking a six mile walk. Some teams were brought in the midst of cup ties for extra toning, as was Liverpool at Jackson House before replaying West Bromwich. In 1908 Bradford City stayed at Dalefield and narrowly beat the locals at billiards. Less successfully, Liverpool stayed there before a match at Nottingham. Their special railway carriage became accidently uncoupled at Derby Station, so they arrived in a fleet of cabs very flustered five minutes before kick-off, and lost. In 1909 Derby County's victory in the English Cup was hailed as a credit to their stay at Oldham House.

There were cricketers too. Leicestershire used the Temple Hotel as their head-quarters for a month in 1902. The same year, W G Grace and Billy Murdoch, an Australian batsman who played for London County, came for the match between that team and Derbyshire. In 1901 Prince Ranjitsinhji, one of greatest batsmen who played for England and Sussex, stayed at the Royal Hotel.

There were other eminent Indians. In 1906 Smedley's treated Sir and Lady Dinshaw Petit from Bombay. His father had founded the first textile mills in India and their daughter married Jinnah, the founder of Pakistan. A month later, another famous Bombay Parsi arrived: Sir Cowasji Jehangir Readymoney. His family's wealth had derived from the opium trade, but his generation were great philanthropists. He intrigued the people of Matlock by wearing his native costume around the town. In 1908 Sir Bampfylde Fuller, who had briefly been the first Governor of East Bengal and Assam, stayed at the New Bath Hotel. (He went on to invent a gas alarm in the First World War.) His fellow guest was the 3rd Lord Ellesmere.

Famous stars of the stage came: Charles Wyndham and his leading lady Mary Moore stayed at Smedley's. Famous for acting with Ellen Terry and Henry Irving, he had opened his own Wyndham's Theatre in 1899. The couple eventually married in 1916 after their spouses had died. In 1907 the actress, artist's model and socialite, Lillie Langtry stayed at the Royal Hotel for Derby races; owning race horses was one of her many activities. In 1908 a quartet of famous actors stayed at the Devonshire Hotel: Herbert Beerbohm Tree (the grandfather of Oliver Reed, he would be knighted the following year), Edward Terry, James Welch, and Tom Davies. Sir Herbert did stay in the Royal during the First World War.

In the same week at the Royal, they could have met Mrs John Pierpont Morgan, the wife of one of America's greatest financiers. Alfred Vanderbilt continued his family's tradition of coming to Matlock Bath when he stayed at the Royal in 1908 – he was destined to perish on the Lusitania. In 1903 it was reported in the *Daily Mail* that Mr Jeffs had written to Mr Rockefeller, who was offering a million dollars to anyone who could cure him of dyspepsia. As far as is known, he did not come.

Long-forgotten authors, who were obviously famous at the time, came to Smedley's. Horace Wyndham was author of a book called *"Soldiers of the Queen"*. His most famous book would be *"The Magnificent Montez: from courtesan to convert"*. Six months before his death, Sir Walter Besant, a prolific author of books on working class life and the history of London tried hydropathy. Others were the Reverend Charles Swynnerton who was the author of *"Folk Tales from the Upper Indus"* and *"Romantic Tales from the Panjab"* (sic) and Max Pemberton, the editor of magazines such as Chums and Cassell's, who also wrote adventure stories, the best known being *"The Iron Pirate"*.

Two authors came under their pseudonyms. John Strange Winter was actually Henrietta E V Stannard, but she wrote military stories which society would not accept from a woman. Richard Marsh, who was actually Richard Heldmann, had changed his name after a prison sentence. He wrote supernatural stories: *"The Beetle"* actually outsold *"Dracula"* when both were published in 1897. A famous lyricist called Edward Frederick Longton stayed at Matlock House under his stage name Edward Teschemacher. He sang his own sentimental songs there, such as *"Until"* and *"Because"*, which are still being recorded today.

> Because you come to me with naught save love
> And hold my hand, and lift mine eyes above,
> A wider world of hope and joy I see,
> Because you come to me.
>
> First verse of *Because*, words by Edward Teschemacher,
> a guest at Matlock House Hydro.

There were captains of industry. Mr Symington of Symington's food company stayed at Chesterfield House. The firm was famous for producing dried foods which just required water to be added. There were eight varieties of dried soup powder in the 1900s, but the most famous was Pea Flour which Scott took to the Antarctic in 1904. Jesse (still plain "Mr" then) and Mrs Boot stayed several times: they were at the Royal in 1905 and 1915. In July 1903 Sir John Blundell Maple MP, his wife and four valets and maids stayed at the Royal, "his health broken down". He died that November, leaving over £2 million. He was heir to the famous business which furnished palaces and luxury hotels all over world.

Soon after Dr Crippen's arrest in 1910, it was remarked that some may have remembered his murdered wife Cora appearing as an "artiste" in Matlock eight or nine years previously. She was a music hall performer with the stage name Belle Elmore. It did not say where she had performed – perhaps she was with a minstrel troupe.

A Royal visit in 1913.
[Glynn Waite]

As far as I am aware, British Royalty did not use the hydros. There were regular aristocratic patients such as the Duke of Rutland, Lord Scarsdale and the Duchess of Bedford. The King and Queen did come to Chatsworth on occasion with due pomp and ceremony, but more interesting were their private shopping trips. In 1899 the then Duchess of York made a visit to Matlock Bath. She came in a special carriage attached to the Blackpool train with only Sergeant Burgess and his constables as a guard of honour, before going on to Chatsworth. In 1904, and twice in the following years, Queen Alexandra came quietly by car to shop at Bryan's in Matlock Bath and Burgon's at the Bridge.

The hotels and hydros were increasingly keen to attract large parties, either coming for the day, or, better still, a conference. This was one reason why, especially after the First World War, the councils felt they had to provide large meeting rooms.

In 1893 two and a half thousand trippers from the Liverpool Gas Company had a picnic in the Pavilion gardens in three batches of 800 per time. Sadly for the dining rooms, they brought their own caterers: the Liverpool British Workman Temperance Public House Company. (This body was founded in 1875 and had sixty seven Cocoa Rooms in the city feeding 30,000 daily.)

In 1902 forty employees from Messrs Royce met at the Royal Hotel. (Rolls-Royce was formed four years later.) The same year, the manager and officials of Thomas Cook & Son met at Matlock House Hydro: it was said they had done well for local tourism. In 1903 the Royal hosted a convention of the New York Life Insurance Company, with representatives from all over the world – but they were not named on the *Visiting List*.

The Temple Hotel at this time specialised in providing substantial dinners and teas to large parties. One week in July 1900, they entertained 60 employees from Eastman's in Liverpool, 20 from Derby Post Office, 60 from Peel & Co, 55 from Waller & Co (both Manchester), and 49 from Masons & Co, Liverpool. The following week they were expecting Southport church choir and the Walsall

Licensed Victuallers. In 1902 Rochdale Wine and Beer Association brought 115 trippers and the North Staffs Bakers' Association one hundred and thirty. One visitor from Stockport wrote in the visitors' book after allegedly enjoying ten plates of lamb, "Just as I am without one plea, your mutton has nearly done for me".

Sometimes there were conferences elsewhere and the Matlocks were on the itinerary. In August 1900, seven hundred Liberals came from Salford to meet their candidate, J E Lawton MP. Tea was provided at the Pavilion, where Barnes Orchestra played, then Mr Lawton and his wife gave a dinner at the Royal for the people they needed to impress. In 1908 the Royal provided a meal for the British Medical Association during their annual conference at Sheffield; the delegates were very impressed with the baths. In 1912 the Royal hosted a meeting for seventy members of the National Medical Herbalists Association of Great Britain.

For several years the British College of Christian Union held conferences in different hydros, including Matlock House, Dalefield and Belle Vue. Over 170 men camped on Matlock Moor, while a similar number of women stayed in the warm and dry.

Mr Thomas Bramald, the son of the old owner of Elm Tree Hydro, had opened Matlock House Turkish Baths on Padiham Road in Burnley. He also started a travel business. Each year he brought a conducted tour of forty or fifty to Jackson House Hydro for a week. Unfortunately in 1909, he and Nelson Church Choir were in a charabanc which crashed at Plaistow Green on its way to Crich. A telegram was sent to Matlock Bath to fetch a carriage to take to the twelve injured to Derby Royal Infirmary. The driver cracked his skull and lost part of his leg.

INTERLUDE

In 1910 it must have seemed like the end of an era when the inestimable Mr Buttgen and his family left to manage the Abernant Hotel in Llantwrtyd in Wales. (Shortly after, it was announced that Mr Avanzi and his orchestra were also leaving.) While in Matlock Bath, Buttgen and his wife Anna had had two children. For several weeks, the Welsh hotel had a large advertisement in the Matlock newspapers. Sadly all did not go well. In 1912, the Buttgens took the tenancy of the Osborne Hotel in Langland Bay near Swansea, where another son was born in December. By May 1914, Mr Buttgen had amassed debts of £2861 through hotel refurbishment expenses and medical bills: he was declared bankrupt. The family's subsequent history has not been possible to find. I wonder if he was interned or they went abroad?

At the Royal Hotel, the Buttgens were replaced by a Mr T A Matthews, followed by George Storey in 1914. He had been at the Hotel Imperial in Blomfontein, South Africa.

In 1913 Smedley's also lost a key member of staff when Mr Crohill, their award-winning chef, retired to Blackpool to serve up his delicious menus in the Empire private hotel. His brother Harry replaced him, but it is not certain exactly when.

Dr William Moxon, the most prominent doctor as far as the townspeople were concerned, died in July 1911, aged only 56 years. He had been the Medical Officer and chief vaccinator for Matlock, as well as working at the Whitworth and Convalescent Hospitals, and acting as consultant for several hydros. Perhaps he was exhausted? He lived at West View on Lime Tree Road.

In the next few years, several hydros changed hands. Henry Ward, the last of the

Ernest H Bailey
[Potter & Co]

original bathmen, was now in his eighties and wanted to retire. In 1914 his recently refurbished Bank House and Church View Hydros were bought by Joseph Hales of the Wyvern Hotel in Leicester and renamed the Wyvern Hydro. The next proprietor, J Burley, died suddenly in 1922. The buildings were bought by Ernest Bailey, from the flour mill in Lumsdale, to give to the town as a co-educational grammar school, opening in September 1924. Mr Bailey had already donated Cliffe House to the Waifs' and Strays' Society as a boys orphanage. This was called St Andrew's Home, being opened on the Saint's Day in 1901. Every Christmas Mr Bailey made an appeal for public donations to give the boys a good time.

Dalefield Hydro seemed to close for a couple of years, but was re-opened by a Mrs Cowood on Christmas Eve 1914 with a new name: Lilybank. The manager was called Woodruffe. Just before Easter 1919, a recently de-mobbed John Kay took over as manager for a John Harvey of Barnsley. Before the War the Kays had been in charge of the baths at Chesterfield House.

Even during the War, Lubin Wildgoose was making improvements. In 1916 he bridged the remaining spaces between Oldham House and Prospect Place Hydros with a new dining room with a glass and beamed roof. He added a new entrance, lounge (decorated in white and buff), writing room, billiard room and a roof garden over the stage in the recreation room.

For the first few years of the First World War, the Royal Hotel seemed to be continuing as usual. A ladies orchestra played twice daily and the "recherché" after-noon tea was a speciality. But behind the scenes all was far from well. The problems arose from two sources. First, several of the directors of the company who owned the hotel were of European origin. The most prominent name when trouble started was Carlos Vetter, a German who had actually died in 1910. Mrs Vetter was British and her two sons and son-in-law were fighting for their country, but this did not matter when accusations started flying.

The second problem was George Storey, the new manager at the Royal. He had been born in Alsace of an English father, but he had no proof of his father's birth. He was not actually interned, but when it came to renewing the licence in May 1915, the magistrates would not accept him. The licence was transferred to the Company Secretary with Mrs Storey as merely a housekeeper. Mr Storey left for London, but not unreasonably he was seen sometimes visiting his family in Matlock.

Then in February 1916, Mr Charles F White called a public meeting at Matlock Town Hall which seven hundred people attended. Even allowing for the strong anti-alien feelings prevalent at the time, he gave a remarkable speech with little care for truth or the libel laws. He claimed, "the hotels and restaurants had been infected by these enemies against whom they were fighting today". He said the mainly German waiters at the Royal had listened to sensitive conversations between army guests at table and reported home. The many German visitors had sketched the district and spied on our defences. He wanted no licence to be held by an alien or his wife as she would be "infected by him". The speech was greeted with cheers and the National Anthem sung. Afterwards many Councillors tried to distance themselves and were obviously embarrassed they had let Mr White use their premises for free.

A letter in the newspapers from the Company refuted all Mr White's claims. Of the eighteen directors, only two had been German, and they had become British citizens. The "foreign" waiters were Swiss and Belgian. Mr Vetter's son-in-law came to the next licence meeting when a noisy Mr White heckled every unusual name. The head waiter Cecil Morris was granted the licence for one month, then a Mr Morrison was appointed manager.

Mrs Storey moved to manage the Temple Hotel, where her husband eventually joined her. They later took over the George, so presumably Mr Storey made his peace with the locals.

Then came another setback, as far as visitors to Matlock were concerned. The Royal Hotel was annexed at the end of November 1917 as a Canadian Officers' Convalescence Hospital, in which they planned to put 227 beds. A survey to list the fixtures and fittings painted a picture of a building and grounds well past their best, presumably because of the War and uncertainty about management. The old glass pavilion, for example, was described as very dirty and dilapidated. The heating system in the hotel was on the point of collapse and the cooking arrangements were "in a very deplorable condition". One wonders if the guests had noticed that the building was in such a poor state. It seems very strange when everything had been so expensively refurbished only thirteen years previously.

Mr F C Arkwright immediately placed Willersley Castle at the disposal of the military; it became a convalescent hospital run and financed by his wife. Their son Captain F G A Arkwright was killed in October 1915 flying in Scotland.

The Royal Hotel annexation aside, Matlock Bath actually welcomed many visitors during the War. One reason given for its wartime success was the distance from the east coast and the danger of zeppelin attacks. There were fewer lighting restrictions until February 1916 when all lights were reduced and shaded and blinds fitted on trains. Advertisements in London and the Midlands brought crowds at the Bank Holidays, in spite of there being no excursion trains or cheap fares. The Government had taken control of the railway companies and wished to discourage non-vital rail travel. Ordinary fares were greatly increased from 1917. Petrol rationing affected the use of motor charabancs and horses were in short supply even if the old carriages could be resurrected. But generally good weather helped throughout the conflict; huge numbers were recorded on the August Bank Holiday 1918.

Matlock Bath UDC also managed the Promenade more professionally and Mr Randle at the Grand Pavilion (renamed from the German-sounding Kursaal) had a successful record of providing concerts and plays. He converted the upstairs room into a cinema, which had a Pathé machine.

251

South, Parade & Heights of Abraham, Matlock Bath   *N° 1983*

A card posted in 1917 to a military hospital. The servicemen are looking in the fishpond.
Boden's dining room had become a glove factory.

By the end of the War and into the early 1920s, the Lovers' Walk was described as being in a shocking state. In 1920 land called the Shrubbery next to Fishpond, where a petrifying well had become derelict, was taken by the UDC for public toilets. The shelter and lavatories at the other end of the town were still often locked! From 1921 drivers had to pay to park by the Pavilion – the beginning of another long-running debate. Two hostelries lost their licences in 1917: the Old Vaults and the Prince of Wales.

A new industry to employ a couple of dozen young girls in a clean and light occupation was started by two local men involved in colour manufacture. George H

The Matlock Patriots in 1914.
Stanley Cocking is on the right.
[Potter & Co}

A group of Smedley's staff joining up in 1914.
Sergeant Cocking stands on the right.
[Potter & Co]

Key and Henry Hetherington opened the Spa Glove Company in the rear ground floor of the Grand Pavilion in 1917. Before the War, over one and a quarter million pairs of gloves had been imported from Europe and the demand continued even though the sources had dried up. Boden's dining room next door also became available and was used for finishing and packing. A shop window at the front displayed the gloves. In 1922 the business was transferred to Mr F Perry, but in January 1929 fire destroyed Boden's old building, including Worth's fancy goods store in a lock-up. The building was well alight before the fire brigade turned up and the roof had collapsed. The brigade was much criticised for its lack of effort, which soon led to a reorganisation.

In August 1921 there was a tragedy at the central ferry behind the Grand Pavilion. A soldier on leave from the 9th Indian Lancers took a ten shilling bet. He tried to cross the river hand over hand on the ferry rope. As his father watched from the far bank, he fell in and disappeared from view, calling, "I'm done Dad". A military funeral was held in Derby.

The *Visiting List* became a strange publication for the duration of the First World War because the Matlocks as places to visit were actually thriving. The front page continued to display a huge advertisement for the area as a health resort. The next two pages, as usual, listed visitors in the brim-full hydros, hotels and guest houses. The entertainments pages still described tennis, whist, music, outings, billiards etc. going on as normal, with the additions of occasional fund-raising, knitting for troops and entertainments for convalescent soldiers and refugees. Then came the grim pages of deaths and military tribunals – in Matlock chaired by the public-

Smedley's kitchen staff who joined up
by November 1914.
[Potter & Co]

spirited Mr Challand.

The only reports which combined the fun and horror were criticisms of youths playing tennis and football in full view of local soldiers being drilled by William Cocking. Aged 72 as the War began, William drilled soldiers in the Home Guard for five evenings a week until he retired as Commander in 1916. In 1919 he and his wife held a remarkable reunion in their home at Alma Villa on Cavendish Road. One soldier son had died in South Africa in 1910, but the seven others had survived their service in the army, although one was still in Cairo.

Smedley's Hydro wartime annual reports continued to describe a strong business. At the announcement of War, Mr Challand had entered the dining room and told guests they could leave without a penny charged. He lost about eighty staff to the forces, of whom seven had been killed by September 1917. He employed extra women, triumphed over the lack of fuel and the vagaries of food supplies and kept the huge machine going. From November 1916, they did charge an extra 6d a day, because of the rising cost of provisions, which increased to 1/6d a day if the guests stayed less than a week at Christmas and Easter. The daily average number of guests remained over 300. Looking at the lists, there did not seem to be any change in the balance of men and women. Many servicemen visited on their leaves, especially at Christmas. All the hydros were reported full at Christmas 1915. There were no jolly speeches at Christmas dinner, just toasts to the King, the armed forces and the Empire.

A later reminiscence of wartime at Smedley's described giving in ration coupons at the office on arrival and receiving a little bag of sugar each week; this continued into the 1920s. There was the sound of the hooter on the engine house warning of zeppelins over Derby; the visitors sat in the dark in the bottom corridor until the danger was over. Another memory was the clumping of the convalescent officers from Rockside and Chesterfield House "dancing over our superb floor in the Winter

Garden in their heavy boots".

Rockside Hydro flourished too during the first years of the War. In 1918 the Goodwin family were approaching their quarter century as proprietors. The beautiful flower beds had been dug up to grow crops of onions, leeks, parsnips, beet and carrots, although the gardener Mr Brown kept the famous arches of rambler roses and a few corners for chrysanthemums to decorate the rooms. In November 1915 the hydro guests helped to entertain many wounded soldiers from the battle of Loos, with a sports day at which many were able to take part. In February 1918 old Mrs Goodwin died aged 83, much loved by the town and hydro guests. Only weeks later John Goodwin's son Godfrey was killed flying in France. The family also took their part in helping out at the Red Cross hospital in the Whitworth Institute, especially Dr Marie Orme.

In 1909 the War Office had issued a scheme for the organisation of voluntary medical aid. The British Red Cross was given the role of providing supplementary aid to the Forces medical service in the event of war. In order to provide trained personnel for this task, county branches of the Red Cross organised units called Voluntary Aid Detachments. These VADs were trained in first aid and nursing. Dr Orme organised a hospital in the Whitworth Institute under this scheme and became its Commandant. Smedley's undertook the laundry and carried soldiers to and from the station.

The Goodwins added a whirlpool bath to the Rockside treatment rooms. These were effective in treating nerve-shocked soldiers, of which they took thirty or more per week, free of charge. In August 1918, the Goodwins became the victims of their own success. Rockside had frequently been inspected by the military, but they had hoped their relatively small size kept them free from being commandeered. Not so. One Saturday lunchtime John Goodwin had the dreadful task of telling his guests, some of them permanent residents, that they had to leave by Tuesday: the fate of the visitors is unknown. There was a farewell meal and a concert with speeches, one deploring this "disaster to its frequenters". Tired business men and convalescent soldiers were losing their haven. Miss Dawson, the entertainments manager, was given a farewell purse. She had recently been congratulated on coping with a lack of young ladies, as they left to take up men's work. A large family party of Goodwins gathered and had the strange experience of enjoying all the facilities to themselves for a few days.

The RAF convalescent hospital moved in to treat nerve cases among its officers. In November, they held a house-warming dance. The Goodwin's continued their hydro advertisements in the newspaper, using the take-over as a compliment to the facilities and position. The Hydro reopened in June 1919 after a complete redecoration and the installation of central heating in the original bedrooms. In 1920 Dr Marie Orme's work for the Red Cross in the War was rewarded with an MBE.

The Derby and Derbyshire Convalescent Hospital on Lime Tree Road released two thirds of its thirty six beds for soldiers. In 1918 Claremont (Mr Rowland's old house) became the Sheffield Workpeople's Convalescent Home; they also took Chindrass House in Starkholmes, next to the White Lion Inn (since demolished). Claremont is today called Golding Grange. The Convalescent hospital itself became a NALGO home in 1923. Latterly it became the Lindens rest home and is now a private house.

Rose Cottage Hydro kept going through the War but was sold in 1925 to a painter and decorator and divided up. Part of the building became Rosegarth bed and breakfast in the late 1930s, which is in business again today. Spring Villa Hydro on Smedley Street re-opened as nursing home run by Sister Dorling.

The Victoria Hall had been running at an irretrievable loss. Visitors preferred the in-house entertainment of the hydros and artists were not touring. In 1916 a Mr Frederic Broome bought it to make woollen goods for the war effort; it stayed a factory for the rest of its existence. (In 1911 he had been a guest at Rockside, the manager of a spinning mill from Leicester. Other sources say he had worked at Lea Mills. He had been using the old mill building at the station for some purpose.) The new business became known as Derwent Mills and made fine woollens.

Just as his flock was getting used to more peaceful times, the vicar of Matlock Bath cheerfully forecast that the second coming and the End of the World was due in 1934/5. Otherwise, events gradually returned to normal. The Venetian fete was revived and excursion trains ran again. Matlock UDC bought Pic Tor from Mr Arkwright and chose the summit as the site for the war memorial, which brought many complaints about its inaccessibility for elderly mothers and widows. Matlock Bath chose a very central location on the Promenade.

Post-war tourism faced problems. Prices were high: the cost of wages and food provisions at Smedley's had almost doubled. In general, the cost of living had increased by 150%, but the Company only increased the tariff by forty percent. The 1920s were marred by coal strikes, the General Strike and poor weather.

John William Wildgoose,
the builder.
[Wildgoose Construction Ltd.]

Several very prominent citizens died in the 1920s. John William Wildgoose, who had built so many public buildings and houses, died in 1923 aged 61. A huge funeral procession was followed by an address given by Charles White MP. Mr Wildgoose had lost his sight four years previously, but his last big undertakings were the new cinema and more extensions at Smedley's, which are described later. His family building firm is still in business today, with offices in Alfreton.

The death of Frederic Charles Arkwight in 1923 precipitated huge death duties. Much of his estate was sold to sitting tenants or auctioned: Matlock UDC bought the High Tor grounds. His heir Richard moved to Worcestershire, so in 1927 another sale took place at the Royal Hotel. Willersley Castle was bought by Sir Albert Ball of

Nottingham, but soon resold to Wesleyan Methodists as a guest house. They kindly announced that this was primarily for Wesleyan Guild members, but that they would not object to "decent people of any denomination". The Lovers' Walk and fishing rights were sold to G H Drabble, the timber merchant. This immediately caused scares about whether he would cut down the trees. The UDC knew they would one day have to purchase the land, rather than lease it.

Mrs Mary Challand died aged 58 at Rockwood, the family home on Cavendish Road, on 30 December 1924, which must have been a grief and nightmare for Henry during Christmas week. She had kept a very low profile in the affairs of Smedley's, busying herself with church matters. In June came further news which must have shaken to town to its core. There had certainly been no premonition in the newspapers that Henry Challand was ill, so his death left not only Smedley's Hydro, but nearly every committee and public body in the town, bereft. (A memorial leaving scholarship was set up at Ernest Bailey School.) His will named Harry Douglas as his executor. He left him his diamond and pearl pin and gold sleeve links and studs. Elsie, the Challands' daughter, stayed in the family house until 1930, when it was sold to Herbert Giles, a Matlock Bath quarry manager. After his death, the house became a student hostel for Matlock College.

It was lucky for Smedley's Hydro that once again an able man was able to step into the breach. Captain Harry Douglas, his nephew and near neighbour at The Rowans on Cavendish Road, had been Mr Challand's assistant for six years, but had been employed as a clerk since 1897 and knew the business inside out.

Dr Marie L'Estrange Orme MBE (née Goodwin) died suddenly one Sunday in March 1929. After tea at Rockside, she had gone for a walk. Witnesses saw her catch the Chesterfield bus, but she got off at the top of Slack hill, then spoke to a woman near Flash Dam. Her body was found in the water next morning. The inquest decided she had not committed suicide because she was a cheerful woman and had behaved quite normally all day. Her doctor in Derby was treating her for heart strain and diabetes, so it was assumed she had had a heart attack near the water's edge. This was a strange echo of Thomas Tyack's death in 1907.

Strange to report, Dr Orme's death was not mentioned in the *Visiting List*. Nor was there any hint in that week's Rockside entertainments round-up, despite the

Dr Marie Orme.

fact she was seeing patients up to the evening of her death. Many guests must have gone to her funeral, unless they were excluded in some way. Like Mr Challand, she left many public bodies mourning her loss. As well as her War work, she was President of the Women's Unionist Club, a District Commissioner for the Girl Guides, President of the Women's section of the local British Legion, and President of the Wakes charity carnival. She had been a widow for about twenty years. Her son Christopher at this time was a doctor at Kings College Hospital in London.

Reeling from the shock of Dr Orme's death, the town soon suffered one of its greatest disasters...

The Royal Hotel had been de-commissioned in July 1919 and the next year the Hydro Hotel Syndicate announced its sale. (A strange report in October 1919 had said that rats swarming from the empty hotel onto the river banks had eaten all the damsons from a tree.) Mrs Hocker became the lessee. She was the part-owner of

A DISASTROUS FIRE.

Extensive Damage at the Royal Hotel.

ABRUPT END TO HAPPY EASTER FESTIVITIES.

Two Fire Brigades' All Night Task in Hail and Snow.

seven hotels, including the Washington in London. She began by renovating the old Pavilion, now known as the Palais Royal, and its grounds, to re-open for the 1922 season. The "Royal Salon Orchestra" was engaged, which gave Matlock Bath residents a free concert one Sunday afternoon in June as a taster. Weekly balls resumed and a group of pierrots performed. By September, the renovations in the hotel itself were complete. There was a new ballroom for 160 dancers on the main first floor, which could be entered directly from outside by non-residents attending new weekly dinner dances. The sprung floor copied one built at the Portman Rooms in London. At one end of the room was a buffet with costly settees. The hotel was well booked for Christmas. A New Year ball was held in aid of St Dunstan's charity for blind soldiers and sailors, at which the patrons danced until 4.00am.

Not much was written about the Royal in the newspapers for a few years. In 1923 the Palais Royal held tea dances and evening sessions, with music from the Gordon Williams syncopated orchestra. There was a report of one hundred coffee tables being ordered for the building, of which 87 had to be immediately repaired. In 1927 Mrs Hocker, now Mrs McArthur, died leaving £179,000.

A Mr Bray, who owned Hotel Riposo in Bexhill-on-Sea, bought the Royal from her executors in October 1928. He raised the money with a loan from Lloyds Bank. He set up a company registered in November as RJB Syndicate Ltd and seemed set to make a success of the business by employing "a small army of painters and electricians" who were going to resume work after Christmas. The baths were in use again and advertisements for tea and dinner dances reappeared. A weekend package, including all the dances, cost thirty shillings. Just before Easter 1929 the *Visiting List* announced, "unique arrangements for the enjoyment and comfort of visitors during the Easter vacation" with a "galaxy of entertainments". There would be a concert on Sunday afternoon, three Cinderella dances, tea dances each day, and a grand ball on Easter Monday. Two hundred guests were in residence.

As guests danced to the "latest foxtrot" on the Monday evening, a man appeared at the ballroom door shouting alarm of a fire on the top floor. Dancers thought nothing of this until Mr Bray came and ushered everyone outside. Some people were lucky to grab their coats because outside a snowstorm with a high wind was blowing. Fortunately no-one was in bed on the upper floors. The fire brigade was called at 9.30pm and they were joined by Chesterfield firefighters at midnight. There was a delay when it was realised water would have to be pumped uphill and across the main road from the river. The lights fused all over the village, so dances in other venues were abandoned as people rushed to watch the disaster. Guests on the lower floors were allowed to collect their bags before they were parcelled out between the other hotels.

The strong winds fanned the flames and by morning a dreadful picture emerged. "The once luxurious rooms were completely wrecked. Sodden furniture, carpets and costly rugs were piled in heaps, wallpaper hung in strips from the walls, and through the ceilings the water came dripping in showers."

No real cause for the fire was ever found. People speculated that a curtain in a servant's room had blown against a gas flame. Modern authors have wondered if Mr Bray was trying to reap insurance money, but the efforts he was putting in suggest to me that he really had meant to make a success of the hotel. He only settled with the insurers in January 1930 and used the money to pay off the initial loan

The smithy and hoardings at Park Head.

from Lloyds Bank. This meant raising new money to undertake the necessary repairs. It must have seemed a daunting task.

In 1924 the two Urban District Councils merged and absorbed Cromford and Tansley. From that point, many Press reports remarked on a perceived resentment by Matlock Bath councillors of their richer neighbour. Whether it was true or not, they thought the money seemed to be spent at the Bridge and Bank, rather than at the Bath. Moreover, in the 1920s hours of Council time were taken up with the failure of the tramway company and the schemes for replacement buses. One of the chief champions of the tramway was Lubin Wildgoose. The Matlocks Publicity Association even suggested that, as the hydros and hotels were the large ratepayers, their opinion that the tramway should be retained was of the greater importance – but they were defeated in the end. The engine house chimney, a landmark on many postcards, was demolished in December 1926. It had become unsightly and dangerous, so the Publicity Association shared the cost. One of the steeplejacks danced a Charleston round the top – presumably there was an admiring crowd. (Barnes Orchestra had played the new dance for the first time at the Cricket Club only a few weeks earlier.) The tramway closed nine months later.

Matlock UDC decided to improve the appearance of the town centre by making a proper entrance to Hall Leys Park. They had already demolished the unsightly smithy and billboards behind Phillips' hairdressers before the War. In 1919 they purchased the row of three shops at Park Head for £3,500 in order to demolish them. They had to compensate and re-house the businesses.

In 1923 Orme's asked for the transfer of their licence to their new premises on the corner of Crown Buildings, where Beard's drapery had latterly become Reay's (Costa Coffee today). Castle & Hurd the draper had become Margerrison & Co, then Gessey's, a confectioner and stationer, who also moved to the bottom of Bank Road. William Phillips the hairdresser had died in 1921, but the shop had already been transferred to his nephew Arthur Dakin. In 1924 Burgon's building was extended with a new shop for him. The Council was supposed to demolish the old shops by March 1925, but actually began in February the following year. When they had gone, it was commented that the bridge now looked very narrow and the "death trap" of a tram shelter looked silly stranded in the empty road.

The Matlocks had begun new sewerage works before the War, but the conflict caused delays, even though they kept on working. Indeed, in 1916 the appearance of South Parade reminded men on leave of the trenches. In 1921 an old lady fell in the excavations on Dale Road and died; but by 1925 the new sewers were working "at last".

In 1923 the Derbyshire and Nottinghamshire Electric Power Company began laying electric cable in Matlock, with a few experimental street lamps going up the following September. The gas companies rallied with a large showroom and offices at the bottom of Bank Road, which still displays the 1925 date plaque. The gas showroom, to the right of the arched doorway, and its neighbour Gessey's stationers became known as the "Gassy-Gessey Parade". Matlock Bath was "electrified" in 1925 and businesses in both towns began to convert. It must have been a marvel to see the brightly lit shop window displays.

A TALE OF THREE HYDROS

Matlock House Hydro Company was wound up in 1910, but continued as Matlock Hydropathic Company. Miss Cameron, an American lady, was manager, but unfortunately their consultant Dr Moxon died. They bought Elm Tree Hydro as an extension and installed electric lighting. In 1915, the hydro was refurbished and referred to as Tilley's, after a new owner Mr William Tilley. Two years later, a Dr Frederick Kincaid was using the building as a sanatorium for TB patients.

One patient was Srinivasa Ramanujan, a celebrated young Indian mathematician, who had been brought to Britain to study at Cambridge University, after demonstrating his brilliance to professors there. It is still not certain what illness he actually had, but he returned to India and died in 1920 aged only 32 years.

In 1920 Chesterfield House Hydro was for sale, including its fixtures and fittings, and was offered to the same Dr Kincaid, who was now engaged in treating ex-servicemen and women. In 1919 it had been purchased by a Mrs Smith-Wilkinson who had recently married "a very youthful husband", according to Dr Kincaid's solicitor, and left the neighbourhood.

This Mrs Smith-Wilkinson was an early celebrity, known variously as the Countess of Monte Cristo, Madame Aladdin, or the world's best or worst dressed woman, depending on one's point of view. Born Margaret Wilkinson in 1866, she had married a Frank Dunk, with whom she managed the Victoria Hotel in Nottingham. In 1910 she married Thomas Southerns (or Sutherns), an hotel valuer, who was 16 years her junior. He died in 1913 aged only 31, leaving her a widow at 47 years old. The pair had managed another hotel at The Poultry in Nottingham. It may have been in connection with Thomas's work that Margaret purchased Chesterfield House Hydro. Her actual input at the hydro before her third marriage is unknown.

Aged 54 Margaret married a young man in his twenties in Matlock, after insisting he change his name to Edward Henry Smith-Wilkinson. The pair then embarked on a spending spree, breaking into a startled Society scene. Reports vary, but they allegedly spent three weeks at the Paris Claridge's Hotel, where she had their suite redecorated and bought many dresses and some spectacular jewels, possibly to the tune of £150,000, but probably less. She also ordered limousines with upholstery to match her costume. She was shunned on a visit to Longchamps racecourse, where she was described as resembling a zebra in a tasteless black and white outfit. Her accessories were a six foot high sunshade and a black and white poodle dyed to match! A similar extravagant stay at London Claridge's added to her reputation.

Margaret then left for South Africa without Edward and he decided to give interviews to the Press. He claimed Margaret had promised him £1000 and a cheque book on their marriage, but he had been given nothing. Indeed, she had treated him like a servant, and between their hotel jaunts he had eaten bread and dripping. Their wedding breakfast had been a cup of coffee at Derby Station. Now he only had his army pension. They were a strange pair in other ways. Apparently he was tall and thin and she was short and dumpy, fond of wearing horn-rimmed glasses. Edward's fate is unknown, because his true identity is uncertain, but Margaret died in London in 1924 after an operation.

Dr Kincaid had Chesterfield House Hydro valued at £33,000. It was a fine building set in 13 acres and eminently suited to his purpose because there was room in the grounds for army huts to use as officer quarters. But, in May, the bank cancelled the sale because Dr Kincaid could not pay the deposit. He had to cancel staff and workmen. By November he had still not completed the purchase, but he was running a successful sanatorium there.

Dr Kincaid had already bought Jackson House Hydro from the Bramwells when they retired in 1920. He also had another property: he lived at Tansley Wood House. So what was he trying to do? His plan seems to have been to manage several sanatoriums to treat TB and shell-shock and retrain his patients to return to civilian life.

There is a huge file of correspondence in the Derbyshire Record Office of Dr Kincaid's struggles with banks and bureaucracy, mostly between him and his solicitor, Colonel Brooke-Taylor in Bakewell, and various government departments. As Brooke-Taylor commented, they were in the Gilbertian situation of the Government demanding his help, but refusing him the money he needed. Indeed, the Government had confirmed that he was running THE sanatorium for all the tuberculosis cases amongst officers who had been infected during the war.

He would have liked to use Jackson House for neurasthenic cases (shell shock), but the Ministry said he had to use the beds to treat nurses with rheumatic conditions. He certainly did use the building as a staff hostel

Tansley Wood House was used as a training centre and hospital for forty men. The training was in agriculture, fruit, flower and vegetable cultivation, and poultry farming, plus estate law and bookkeeping. There was also brief mention of using a house in Ashover for training and treating thirty women.

It was then proposed that a Trust of three companies take over from Dr Kincaid, with him as a director at Chesterfield House. But he soon had to sell Jackson House; his son needed school fees and his wife was an invalid (she died in 1924). In March 1921 it was re-opened as a hydro by the Hallamshire Coffee House Company of Sheffield, with Mr and Mrs Peat as managers.

Dr Kincaid also suffered a falling off of patient numbers at Matlock House because of the unspecified "disloyalty and unprofessional conduct of a resident

Medical Officer". Neither did the town like tuberculosis cases so near to the other hydros. Matlock House sanatorium, intended to treat thirty men and women, was eventually abandoned in 1925.

In 1922 a Dr Hanway at Matlock House sanatorium went for a walk up Salters Lane with a doctor friend. They took a German Mauser .35 revolver and played at shooting tossed coins. Somehow Dr Hanway was shot in his lung from the back and was dangerously ill for many days.

In the end, only Chesterfield House continued for several years as a sanatorium for officers run by the Ministry of Pensions, but with no further mention of poor Dr Kincaid. Some patients slept in huts in the grounds. The Colonel in charge occasionally organised concerts and sporting events for the town. It was the last of the old hydros to get electricity in 1922; passers-by suddenly noticed brilliant illumination in the recreation rooms and the chalets in the grounds.

In 1925 there was a scandal when one of the soldiers was accused of getting a nurse pregnant – she was dismissed of course! Another nurse came forward to say the same had thing happened to her, but the men closed ranks and denied everything. Stories of "pyjama parties" were dismissed.

Chesterfield House sanatorium closed in 1926. The building was bought by Presentation nuns from Liverpool, who opened the Convent boarding school, specialising in educating girls from India. They now use the house as a nursing home.

In 1926 Mrs Albert Law established Matlock Modern School in Matlock House. She had run Matlock Garden School in Tor Cottage, which she continued to use for boarders and games on the tennis courts. The new school was opened by Sir Henry Hadow, the Vice-Chancellor of Sheffield University, who was also busy writing his Government reports on primary and secondary education. Mrs Law's eye-catching advertisements extolled her natural, open-air methods, avoiding any overstraining, and with no punishments. There was plenty of healthy dancing and self-expression via the drama department, as well as public

Tor Cottage and High Tor suspension bridge.
Card posted 1906.

speaking classes. The girls could bathe in artificial sunlight via a large sun lamp, probably left over from the hydro, under the supervision of a trained nurse. The pupils were soon seen in the town dressed in their beautiful grey and lilac uniform.

The girls were not the angels Mrs Law liked to believe. One eminent ex-pupil described to the author how they competed to aim missiles from the windows on to the top of lady's hats as they rode on the open top deck of the trams on Rutland Street.

Mr Law also ran an accountancy business and Matlock Health Centre in the building.

The 1930s

Introduction

The first issue of the *High Peak News* in January 1931 had a bold headline: "The hydro is dead"! Apparently Buxton Hydro had changed its name to the Spa Hotel on New Year's Day. The manager explained that the number of invalid visitors was now very small. People were arriving in their cars for a short visit on a touring holiday. No-one stayed for several weeks. Ladies languished no more: "Women nowadays are out playing games and trying to imitate men; they have no time to be ill"!

The expanded Lilybank Hydro with The Gables linked by the new ballroom.

Only a handful of hydros now survived in Matlock, but they did appear to thrive. As the "*Come to Derbyshire*" guide pointed out: "Nowhere are there more hydros, nowhere are there hydros combining in so great a degree EXPERIENCE with PERFECTION OF EQUIPMENT". There was no shortage of customers, whether they needed treatment or just wanted a stay in a good hotel with congenial company. John Kay of Lilybank Hydro, giving a talk to the Rotary Club in 1938, admitted a decline in hydro visitors; but the younger generation were now coming for holidays. He was full for Christmas, with guests sleeping out.

At the first New Health Society summer school, held at Matlock Modern School in 1932, Sir William Arbuthnot Lane described Matlock as being, "one of the most beautiful, healthy and attractive spas in Great Britain". He could imagine no greater paradise. "How anyone can be ill in a place like Matlock goodness only knows."

For the town as a whole, the fact had to be faced that there was huge competition from seaside resorts and foreign spas. On the other hand, there was a new market to tap. The unions were fighting for paid holidays and even lower paid workers could travel long distances by motor cycle or motor coach. Matlock Publicity Association was told in 1938 that 600,000 more workers had received a paid holiday the previous year, bringing the total to 2,750,000. Even Matlock UDC granted six days paid leave, plus Bank Holidays, to its own manual workers. Eight hundred men who worked for Derbyshire Stone were allowed a week's paid holiday in 1939.

The dreaded day tripper was still a force to be reckoned with. Cyclists and ramblers were out and about. Families were touring the countryside in their new motor cars. The Matlocks had to advance and ADVERTISE!

In 1935 a few typical enquiries to the Publicity Association Office were published:

Not having been at all well lately, my doctor recommends Matlock as a place where people don't die easily, so let me know if he is right, and, in case the worst comes to the worst, is the cemetery in a sunny position?

I understand you have petrifying wells in Matlock Bath, and I wonder if it would be possible to get a duck-egg petrified whilst we walk around as we shall be there for the half-day.

I am bringing a party of adults three weeks come next Saturday and we intend to visit the caves, but if so we would like to know if some of them are lighted by gas. I am told that in some of them the guide carries a candle, and it would be awkward if this went out as my party is a "mixed" one.

Hearing that you have a snowy winter in Matlock I should like to come if you can find me a toboggan, but, as I cannot come for pleasure alone, I wonder if you can find me a place as a manageress of an hydro hotel, failing which can you provide me with a small bedroom in some humble dwelling where in exchange for keeping the room clean I should have free board and lodging. I am 37 years of age and of an even disposition unless I am roused. (The Association recommended the workhouse.)

I write these few lines hoping to find you well as it leaves me at present. We are having our annual Mothers' Outing in June and we think of coming to Matlock. There will be 40 of us if Mrs Wiggins comes, but if she doesn't there will be only 39. It is her washing day and she won't put it off. Last year we went to … and had a beautiful ham tea for nine pence a head, but as Matlock is a smaller place, we wondered if you could do it for seven pence.

From a German: To come to Matlock is my intent and it will me much interesting if you will kindly let me know if the livers in your city speak the language English as to study is my wish.

FIRST IMPRESSIONS MIGHT NOT BE FAVOURABLE!

In 1937 the Derbyshire edition of Arthur Mee's *The Kings' England*, [1] a very popular travel series, was first published. Matlock Urban District Council and Publicity

---

1. Arthur Mee and a team of researchers spent five years travelling around England to produce county guide books, which he described as a "New Domesday".

Association were furious about his opinions:

> *Matlock has sold its beauty for a mess of pottage or a pot of message. We remember it*
> *as one of Nature's lovely places; it has sunk to the level of a place of many hoardings,*
> *cheap houses, and mean sights.*

This does seem a bit harsh, but it was not the only example of such criticism. An article in *Motor Cycle* in 1929 by Oswald Frewen (a famous journalist and cousin of Winston Churchill) reported,

> *We ran north through Nuneaton and Ashby de la Zouche, and thence via Matlock*
> *and Buxton, through beautiful scenery polluted by gas and sewage works, and iron*
> *bandstands and Victorian villas …*

At a Rotary Club lunch in Derby in 1930, a member of the Committee of the Council for the Preservation of Rural England said Matlock was a disgrace. Why? What might have displeased the visitor to the Matlocks?

There was the perennial problem of the approach from Darley Dale. At various times over the years there had been complaints about quarries, railway sidings, advertisement hoardings, the gas works, tar burners, lime kilns, heaps of scrap iron, gypsy caravans and their occupiers, decrepit wooden buildings, and before its demolition in 1906, the old disreputable Crown Hotel.

However, many of the untidy buildings had gone. The only improvement which would not hurt local employment or services would be the removal of the hoardings. The Midland Railway Company had merged into the London Midland & Scottish (LMS) in 1923. The station still needed its sidings to move stone, coal, tim-

The Bakewell Road approach to Matlock: the quarries, the gas holder,
advertisement hoardings and piles of scrap iron.
[William Twigg Ltd]

The Matlock gas holder and more hoardings.

ber, flour, and steel for William Twigg's works, although the siding yards were apparently becoming very dusty with disrepair. Admittedly, the piles of metal in Twigg's yard were unsightly, but it was a busy reclamation and engineering works. The gas works could not be moved.

It was said that the quarries were slowly becoming hidden by trees, but there were constant complaints about dust from those on Dale Road, particularly Greatorex's Harvey Dale workings. They had problems with the equipment which was supposed to suppress the emissions. The Dale was also an eyesore with tips of quarry waste. There was already the riverside car park on land which it had been hoped would form a pleasant walk between the two resorts. In 1937 the Publicity Association also complained about smoke from the mills in Lumsdale and the colour works in Matlock Bath. They called for more regulation.

Although some areas had more camouflaging woodland, fifty trees had been felled or had fallen on the summit of Masson and the owner was asked to plant more. In 1939 the land was for sale, but the Council could not afford the purchase.

There was still the old obsession with dust on the roads. A letter in 1922 claimed, "you could hardly breathe, see or smell and all the wondrous beauty of the hillsides was nearly blotted out". However, the main routes were being tackled, as described later.

There was one huge problem, which hopefully the visitors might not notice, unless they explored certain parts of the town. Ratepayers in Lumsdale complained again and again about the nearby refuse tip. In 1933, of the 1045 vermin killed by the Council rat catcher between January and July, 500 were caught on this area during one five week period. The Smedley's Hydro correspondent described another refuse site above Farley as an appalling spectacle; he joked that all the tips should be floodlit for the Coronation in 1937. There were seven local refuse dumps; in 1938 the rat catcher asked for, and was refused, a pay rise.

A party of councillors went to Brighton in 1934 to see a rubbish incinerator or "destructor", but nothing had been purchased three years later. Each November for several years, the Council held a "Rat Week" to encourage householders to exterminate their pests. In 1938 they showed a public information film called *Your enemy, the rat* at the Cinema House. There is no reason to suppose this was particularly a Matlock problem: the tip in Bakewell was described as a "moving mass of rats, like an ant heap". But it did not look good for a health resort.

Most of the above complaints seem aimed at Matlock. However, in 1933 a gentleman stayed for Christmas at Matlock Bath and thought it a mistake. He objected to Cromford pond choked with weeds and decaying rubbish. He did not like the look of Masson Mill. In Matlock Bath were the dilapidated ruins of an amusement park and a municipal building labelled "pump room", but which "resembles more the begrimed corn exchange of an industrial town". On the other side of the road were numerous tumbled-down houses, unpainted and unwashed, and "conspicuous untidy garages". Shop windows and the goods they displayed were "such as would destroy the business of any tradesman in a London or Birmingham slum". During the holiday, the only entertainment provided had been a second rate film.

In 1939 a letter from the vicar of Dartmouth in his parish magazine even dammed the people with faint praise: they "have but little graciousness of manner, but once one gets under the surface and accustomed to what one might regard as uncongenial mannerisms, they become pleasant, kindly and even talkative".

> When its springtime in the Matlocks
> Life seems just a pleasant song,
> By the winding river Derwent
> You can wander all day long;
> You may play at golf or tennis,
> You may hike or fish or row;
> If you want to cross the river,
> In the ferry boat you go.
> From the *Matlock Publicity Association Official Guide*, c1934

"Come to Derbyshire"

You will find in Derbyshire
Charming views and bracing air,
Homely folks and wholesome fare,
Baths to charm your aches away,
Come to Derbyshire today.

E Powell in *The Derbyshire Guide*.

Why did the people of the Matlocks care what anyone thought about their town? Perhaps they were afraid tourists would no longer be happy to see evidence of industry or real life in their holiday resorts. City dwellers were paying to enjoy a rural idyll, which many thought was under threat.

In the 1930s architects, town planners and lovers of the countryside were becoming very worried about certain trends. They wanted to preserve all that was traditional and beautiful in Britain, but not at the expense of rural unemployment, which was increasing during the Depression. Several bodies were set up to tackle the issues. Their remit also involved encouraging responsible tourism.

The Council for the Preservation of Rural England (now the Campaign to Protect Rural England) had been formed in 1926. Its first President was Sir Guy Dawber, the architect of St John's Chapel in Matlock Dale. There was a growing concern about ribbon development from towns and the idea of green belts was introduced. There had already been a committee based in Sheffield and the Peak District trying to control building along main roads.

Derbyshire Rural Community Council (now Rural Action Derbyshire) was established in 1924, part of a nationwide movement to support the populations of villages and market towns. In line with the CPRE, they saw threats to the Matlocks and the Peak District from inharmonious buildings, petrol stations, American-style advertisement hoardings, electricity overhead lines, litter, and ill-conceived town planning schemes.

A conference was called by the Community Council at the County Council offices in Derby in 1930. Over fifty delegates accepted Matlock UDC's suggestion of setting up a committee to promote the beauties of the county; this resulted in the "Come to Derbyshire" campaign. The aim was to foster pride in Derbyshire, and take active steps to preserve such areas as Kinder Scout and Dovedale, at the same time as publicising its appeal as a holiday resort worldwide. The head office of "Come to Derbyshire" was in St Mary's Chambers in Derby. There was eventually an enquiry bureau on the Haymarket in London.

There was an element of goading Matlock at this meeting. The chairman of Buxton Publicity Committee said he was glad Matlock had some "pricking of conscience" as the approach from the west had "an avenue of old iron and tin shanties: it was enough to rouse the indignation of every Derbyshire man". To laughter, the Matlock men indignantly pointed out that the shanties were no longer there, although they could not deny Twigg's existence.

One of the first directors of "Come to Derbyshire" was Ernest Bailey (he died in 1938). He and the other members of Matlock Publicity Association worked to produce a guide to the Matlocks and Darleys which were sent all over England, Europe and the United States, often distributed on ocean-going liners. In 1935 five thousand Matlock guides were printed. Mr Bailey reported a request from Baghdad! A very substantial *Come to Derbyshire Guide* was published annually from 1931 with lists of accommodation and places to visit.

The Rural Community Council began a quarterly newsletter called *The Derbyshire Countryside* in 1931 which was edited by Dr L du Garde Peach and cost two pence. At first the content was produced by volunteers, who only wanted to cover their costs. In 1933 the price increased to 6d and, shortly afterwards, it was announced that the magazine and the work of "Come to Derbyshire" had been taken over by private company: The Derbyshire Countryside Ltd. The amount of advertising increased dramatically, but had always featured Smedley's and Rockside Hydros, Wildgoose the builder, Bailey's flour mill and Matlock Modern School. (In 1964 the magazine became monthly and was renamed *Derbyshire Life and Countryside*.)

One important introduction by the Community Council was the employment of voluntary countryside wardens. By 1934 there were eighty, often recruited from the Ramblers' Association. They regularly removed large amounts of litter from Dovedale and tried to discourage visitors from picking the wild flowers.

John Goodwin of Rockside Hydro had his portrait in the *Come to Derbyshire Guide* as President of the Matlock Publicity Association. In 1934 the Publicity Association had a hundred subscribing members in Matlock and 39 in Matlock Bath, which was encouraging. They had placed advertisements in forty three national newspapers and magazines and 1025 posters had been distributed by the Manchester Bill Posting Company. The following year, the *Morning Post* featured Matlock in a *Spas of Britain* series and the Matlocks featured in the weekly *Telegraph* holiday guide and the *Townswomen* magazine.

The enquiry and holiday booking office was in the Town Hall, managed by J E Guy-Bray. In 1931 the Association sent out two thousand souvenir books with a list of accommodation. In spite of the Depression, they reported increasing numbers of enquiries: in July 1932, 133; in July 1933, 270; in 1934, 487. In the single month of May 1936, there were over 800 enquiries and in May 1938 over a thousand. That year leaflets were sent to the Glasgow Empire Exhibition.

The Association was described as doing "splendid work" using its subscriptions,

John G Goodwin.

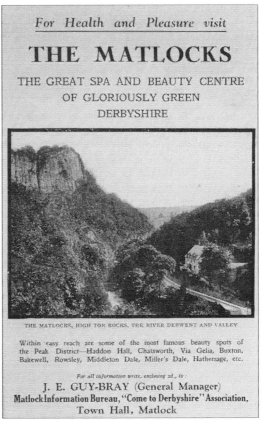

but they wanted extra help. The LMS railway company was providing funds, by going 50/50 with some publicity. In 1931 they jointly spent £300. In 1929 the LMS cigarette cards of Beautiful England included a view of High Tor: there were four million in circulation. The Matlocks were still depicted in a good percentage of the posters in railway carriages.

Typically, the UDC had agreed to support the "Come to Derbyshire" movement if it did not cost them anything. However, they were now on the brink of spending money on publicity themselves. In 1930 they very belatedly adopted the Health Resorts and Watering Places Act of 1921. This gave them the powers to raise a penny rate towards advertising outside their own area, or to use the profits from tourism (e.g. renting out chairs or park admission charges) if this amount was not greater.

The Publicity Association welcomed the news, hoping to receive some funds. Not surprisingly there were arguments: some councillors thought that publicity spend-ing was a waste of money. The situation was complicated by the newly-formed but short-lived Matlock Bath Spa Advertising Association, led by Edward Aspey who had returned to the area as the proprietor of the Heights of Abraham and resumed his role as a promoter of the town. He was soon a town councillor. He thought the age of the poster and bulky guide book was over and wanted to produce a concise leaflet in five languages.

Mr Aspey and other Matlock Bath councillors were convinced only Matlock Bank would benefit if a grant was given to the Publicity Association. They wanted the UDC to control the all funds themselves. In 1934 Aspey actually wrote to the Ministry of Health to dispute the legality of sharing the money. He also claimed that, because the Council always lost money on its pleasure grounds (£3369 in 1931 – a very bad year) they had no profit for comparison purposes anyway. The District Auditor ruled that all was above board.

In 1932, by seven votes to six, the UDC agreed to grant £100 to the Publicity Association. This increased to £150 in 1934. Perhaps Councillor Jacques's poem swung the vote:

> You want pleasure seekers in the Matlocks,
> Besides invalids sent by the fat docs,
> But it's simply tommy-rot
> If they don't know what you've got,
> To hope for an invasion of the Matlocks.
>
> The proposal on the table isn't shifty,
> Helps south west of England to be thrifty,
> Tell the world of Matlock's beauty.
> As a Council do your duty:
> Back Publicity by contributing fifty.

The UDC then negotiated their own 50/50 deals with the LMS. By 1936 three annual amounts of £500 had been spent on 25,000 folders and 7,500 posters. Mr Aspey even went to help choose the designs.

There were other moves. The LMS was asked to provide more trains back from Manchester in the afternoon. If businessmen could commute from Blackpool and Colwyn Bay, why not from Matlock, which was nearer? The Chamber of Trade was founded in 1928, chaired by Mr Bailey with John Goodwin and Harry Douglas on the committee. It inaugurated shopping weeks and trade exhibitions, using the slogan VIM – Value in Matlock. In 1933 the *Matlock Visitor* was re-launched after it had more or less dwindled away in the late 1920s. The new circulation was 1000 copies; each advertiser received a free copy and it was given out in the hydros.

There were other movements in the Derbyshire countryside which affected visitors to the Matlocks. The Ramblers' Association, the National Parks movement, the Youth Hostel Association, and the National Trust will all be mentioned in later chapters.

In 1935 *The Derbyshire Countryside* ran a competition to design walking wear. The judges concluded that, "contrary to popular belief all women can wear shorts if they will only study their individual figures and have the material cut accordingly. It is fatal to buy ready-made men's wear and hope it will do".

WHERE SHALL WE STAY?

The Matlocks did make immense efforts to make themselves more attractive to visitors in the 1930s, and to advertise their amenities. The full page advertisement in the *Visiting List* boasted that Matlock is:

> *A unique centre for the motorist, cyclist, hiker, artist and geologist – the tired man or woman – the robust and the delicate.*

The Publicity Association office at the Town Hall would do all the booking necessary for no fee, given the number in the party, the dates and the price range. The number of guest houses had reduced: in the 1932 *Kelly's Directory* there were only 13 addresses apart from the hydros, hotels and public houses. In Matlock Bath there were eight. However, many of these were quite substantial houses which were new to the lists. They included three on Henry Avenue: Ingledene, Clarendon, and Dalemount. Others were Heatherbank above Smedley Street West, which had been the manse for the Congregational Church minister, and Glendon on Knowleston Place, which is still in business. One substantial guest house, which lasted from the 1890s until the 1970s, was Thornton House on Bank Road. In the 1930s it was run by

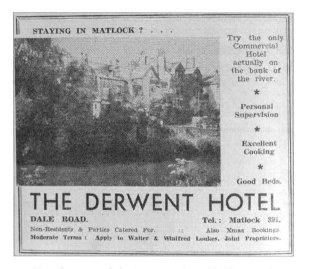

Trevelyan's and the Derwent Hotel had merged.

Mr and Mrs Frank Smith.

To cater for walkers and cyclists, several farmhouses offered accommodation such as Thacker's at Wolds Farm, Portland Grange on Matlock Moor, Ash Tree on Hackney Lane and High Leas at Riber, which also had a camping ground. Riber Hall advertised itself as an "Old World House". Some offered refreshments: Castle Farm at Riber, Oak Lea at Oker, and the Woodlands Tea Garden on Matlock Moor.

Tor Cottage, the house in the Dale opposite High Tor, had several identities during the decade as a school annex and Hostel, but by 1938 it was the High Tor Guest House. The Brunswood Hotel also described itself as being opposite High Tor: "commercial gentlemen specially catered for".

The advertisements for the hotels and public houses changed subtly to encourage a new breed of holidaymaker who expected as standard indoor sanitation, electric lights and fires, hot and cold water in the bedrooms and a motor garage. Some offered special terms for parties because clubs began to take several days away instead of the old day trip. The Temple Hotel became AA and RAC accredited as a centre for motor tours, as did the Queen's Head and Ye Olde Englishe, which was still capriciously adding and subtracting its extra "e"s. Most hotels claimed to be ideal and reasonably priced for cyclists and ramblers.

(The AA and Motor Union started classifying hotels in 1912. They issued locked boxes to their chosen premises to keep in the cloakrooms. With their AA key, visitors then had access to a small pile of towels and a brush and comb! The AA said it was waging war on insanitary roller towels.)

The remaining hydros flourished. The novelty of hydropathy was long over, but there were plenty of people wanting the combination of a jolly good holiday with some healthy treatment thrown in. The advertisements now blatantly emphasised sports and entertainment over the health element. As the clouds gathered over Europe, the reports in the *Visiting List* often praised the hydros for providing a haven from the real world.

There were still many of course, like my grandfather, who were seriously ill and hoped for respite and improvement when conventional medicine had failed them. One might wonder how they felt observing from the side-lines the relentless programmes of tennis and golf tournaments, drawing room entertainments and increasingly frenzied dancing to jazz music. "Come to Derbyshire" did offer special advance treatment for invalids by supplying trained nurses and companions for visitors who might otherwise have difficulties arriving by train.

Matlock Bath

*The last advertisement for the Royal
with Mr Bray as manager, 1929.*

Mr R J Bray's problems following the fire at the Royal Hotel were hinted at in the previous Interlude. He tried to start with a clean sheet financially by using the insurance money to pay off his initial loan from Lloyds Bank. The main old building of the hotel was a ruin; only the annex at the back had really survived the fire. Bray now had to raise fresh loans.

His progress was chronicled in the Press every time he turned up at the Brewster Sessions to renew his bar license. Between 1930 and 1936 his license for an empty hotel was renewed, even though the Bench said their patience was being "sorely tried". In 1937 no application was made.

In 1932 Bray submitted plans to rebuild. His ambitious ideas included a London architect called Ernest Schaufelberg, who built the Fortune and Adelphi theatres. His "roadhouse de luxe" would have a palatial swimming pool, with a sliding roof and winter garden below the existing terrace. On the main floor would be a dining room, tea room, ballroom and new kitchens. Twenty-six new *en suite* bedrooms were planned with a staff of fifty servants. J W Wildgoose & Sons won the contract to demolish and build.

Unfortunately a Mr Stevens promised money and then failed to produce it. In 1934 a Mr McCarthy said he could form a company with capital of £50,000, but something went wrong. Work began, then stopped. Mr Bray owed money to the builders and the architect. He now announced that he would use his own money for a modest scheme costing £25,000. In 1935 the owner was listed as Modern Hotels Ltd, but in 1936 the agents Knight, Frank and Rutley offered the freehold to the UDC for £10,000. There was no chance of them raising the money. In 1937 the hotel, old pavilion and grounds were auctioned at the Crown Hotel. It was reported that Councillor Wheeldon on Chesterfield Road was the buyer, but no-one knew why. This was the sad end of any hopes for the Royal. It gradually fell into even more disrepair and was eventually demolished. Children in the 1950s can remember looking through broken windows at the remains of the baths.

In 1930 the New Bath and Bath Terrace Hotels were sold to Trust Houses Ltd. The sale catalogue described the New Bath as having 41 bedrooms, a roadhouse bar and a garage for fifteen cars. The new manager was Mr Charles Herbert. The bar on the main road became popular with motorists on a tour through the Peak District. Weekend guests could enjoy a break from Friday to Monday in the hotel, inclusive of music and dancing, for 37/6d. In the 1920s the Bath Terrace had been managed by Dick Coates, a popular local comic singer, but by the early 1930s it was only being used as an annex and staff bedrooms for its neighbour.

In 1930 the previous manager of the New Bath, Mr Mace, had closed the pool in the basement because of rowdy public behaviour. Trust Houses came up with an ambitious plan. On the large level lawn, where the famous lime tree had blown down in 1912 and finally expired in 1920, they constructed the first open-air swimming pool in Britain to use natural thermal spring water. It is a large pool 120 by 42 feet and nine feet deep at one end. There was a four-stage diving board, spring boards and a chute. Spring water flowed into the shallow end over an ornamental cascade with coloured lights. The whole pool was floodlit for moonlight bathing. The swimmers and spectators taking refreshments round the edge were entertained by a radiogram – more noise near the church! The Bath Terrace Hotel was used as changing rooms with 400 lockers, cubicles and showers.

The pool opened in June 1934 with a diving display by Mr and Mrs Burne ("national champions"), a water polo match and a mannequin parade of swimwear.

UNIQUE
SWIMMING
POOL
fed by a
NATURAL
WARM
SPRING

NEW BATH HOTEL, MATLOCK BATH

Hot and Cold Water in Bedrooms.   Outdoor Pool and Indoor Plunge
of Thermal Water.   -   Tennis.
Tel. Matlock 39.

**UNIQUE OPEN-AIR
SWIMMING POOL**

Constant flow of Thermal
Water from Natural Spring

OPENING JUNE 21st

4-30 p.m.   (Gate 4 p.m.)

at

**NEW BATH HOTEL,
MATLOCK BATH**

The approach is at the southern
end of Matlock Bath, on the left-
hand side travelling north.

TRUST HOUSES LTD.

A month later clowns from Bertram Mills Olympic Circus gave a cabaret in aid of Whitworth Hospital. Strangely a few fatal drowning accidents were reported: in 1939 the wife of Dr Ryan of Ripley drowned in odd circumstances surrounded by her husband, friends and several staff. The pool was used by the inhabitants of Matlock Bath, as well as many day trippers. It is still there, abandoned, but remarkably fresh looking, presumably because of the constant flow of water.

The other hotels in Matlock Bath carried on as usual, with little news but appearing in the visitor lists. The Temple was AA and RAC accredited. The Fishpond claimed to be "the ramblers' rendezvous". Hodgkinson's Hotel was managed by Warren Boden, the son of John William at Edinburgh House and the Derwent Gardens.

In 1932 Woodbank House, the previous home of John Lawton, sometime manager at Masson Mill, was bought by the Friendship Holiday Association of Ilkley and renamed Cromford Court. From 1911 it had been a Co-operative Holidays Association guest house.

In 1922 Matlock Bath had been startled by several loud explosions. The proprietors of the Midland Hotel were clearing rocks from the garden by the river. They constructed flowery terraces with apples, hops, raspberries and pears.

In 1926 William Freckleton of the Devonshire Hotel fell over his balcony into the river and was taken to the Whitworth Hospital with head injuries, but the outcome is unknown. In 1931 the hotel lost its licence through lack of trade. The bar closed in 1932 and was referred for compensation at the Brewster Sessions on grounds of

The old Devonshire Hotel before its demolition.
[Doreen Buxton]

redundancy. The last tenant was Mr Hutchinson. On the final Saturday night, he held a competition for someone to be the "last drinker", and kept the last bottle of stout as a souvenir. Matlock & District football league meetings moved to the Midland. It was thought the building would be demolished to remove the narrow bottleneck and, "over its once well-filled cellars will pour the traffic of the future". However, the premises continued as a café for many more years. In the old visitors' book was written:

> For attention and comfort the Devonshire Arms,
> Is filled with many dear homely charms,
> So when you like, and wherever you steer,
> You'll find the best landlady and landlord here.

MATLOCK BANK AND BRIDGE
SMEDLEY'S HYDRO

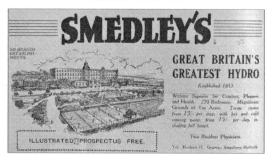

Smedley's now confidently advertised itself as "Great Britain's Greatest Hydro" and open "for health and pleasure". An article in the magazine *Truth* in 1926 endorsed its status as "the largest and most famous hydropathic establishment in the United Kingdom". The writer went on to attribute the success to being "fortunate in the character and personality of the founder and the enterprise, vision and sound common sense of its management". The visitor was impressed by the "self-contained completeness of the organisation. He finds himself in a well-ordered, self-supporting community of happy and contented people of all ages". Anyone could live there happily for the rest of their days – some had already hoped to do so, until their rude eviction in 1939.

Captain Harry Douglas was the capable manager, the third of the Douglas-Challand family to be so. He lived at The Rowans on Cavendish Road. Like his predecessors, he took a full part in the life of the town as a committee member, councillor and JP, but he also had a remarkable variety of interests which took him away. In 1924 he had competed in the Paris Olympic Games in the 600 metre free rifle shooting team. In the 1930s he was the captain of the English team at Bisley. Locally he helped to run the rifle club at Cuckoostone on Thursday afternoons. He was a church organist and Deacon at the Congregational Church. He also composed music under the pseudonym Robert Masson which was published by Novello and Company in 1914 and 1922. He bred and exhibited Large White pigs and Friesian cattle on Smedley's farm in Farley. In 1934 a 22 year old cow called Clifton Express became the oldest breeding pedigree Friesian in the country.

LEFT: *Harry Douglas with his rifle.*
[Jean Douglas]

RIGHT: *Harry Douglas.*
[Jean Douglas]

Harry's son Henry was being educated to take the role of deputy manager; some of the details here are taken from his memories. (He lived later at Tor View on Jackson Tor Road.) Another source has been an account of a stay at Smedley's which was found in a house in Hagley in 2010. Mrs Olive Allen and Miss Maggie Round visited for a month in 1920; their joint diary is quoted several times in this book. A third invaluable source has been the inventory the Army was given of every item in the building when they took over in 1939 – down to the last teaspoon. From this one can almost draw a picture of each room.

The hydro was no longer subject to the major building projects of previous decades but the guests still witnessed alterations and improvements. By 1920 the kitchens were becoming inadequate once more. The Directors of Smedley's took the opportunity to buy and demolish the last of the neighbouring cottages between the hydro and the Winter Garden to build a new kitchen, a lounge and some more bedrooms. The kitchen itself was on the first floor. Downstairs was a spacious service room tiled to the ceiling. It contained a new hot plate with nine carvers and heated cupboards down the centre, with cold benches down the sides. The food came down in lifts. Automatic dish washers were installed.

The chef was Harry Robert Crohill, the brother of Alfred who had held the post in the 1900s. He had his own office and kitchen on the first floor, where presumably he dreamed up his Christmas extravaganzas. In the warren of rooms below were a suite of chambers reminiscent of the basements of stately homes: a stillroom, bread room, bakery, make-up room, raw meat larder, butchers' shop, vegetable store, milk house, knife cleaning room, and refrigerated room for cooked meats. Guests must have been fond of ice cream, probably served at dance buffets: there was a special freezing room, over seven hundred ice cream plates and nearly three hundred sundae glasses.

Fresh fish was delivered from Grimsby each day. Kitchen staff went to Manchester every Tuesday to order vegetables, meat and game; the produce often beat them back to Matlock on the train. Groceries were ordered from Orme's on Crown Square or Charles Mason in Chesterfield. Cheese came from Derby, coffee from Nottingham, and tea was specially blended in London to suit the water. Indian tea came in 100lb plywood chests and China tea in cardboard boxes. (One story recounted a time the storekeeper found a cat using the China tea as litter!)

The under chefs were all men: meat, fish and pastry specialists. There were about three dozen waiters and waitresses. The men wore black jackets and grey trousers, while the women wore long-sleeved black dresses, white aprons and pleated caps. Before the gong for lunch and dinner, they lined up to be inspected by the head waiter, especially their hands and nails. Then they stood to attention while the guests filed in, before a nod from the head waiter meant the food could be served – each plate was watched for spillages round the edge. Tipping was forbidden, but they could earn bonuses called "talent money" for smartness, deportment and expertise in laying tables. Some of the girls saved this up to buy a dress for the staff ball.

The main dining room was redecorated in the 1920s with pastoral tapestry scenes of the Napoleons and mirrors between the pillars. In 1922 a new dining room called the Empire Room, with Adam-style decoration, was opened to seat 120 visitors. Here were tables of four for families to lunch or dine *à la carte* in the evening, sometimes with French cuisine. This cost an extra shilling per day. The room (now a large office) was near the Winter Garden and used for evening buffets. Both dining rooms were carpeted in green and brown Wilton and the Empire Room had brown figured silk curtains. The chairs in the Empire Room were walnut with leather seats; in the main dining room they used the cheaper Rexine, made from a cloth impregnated with cellulose to look like leather.

New mirrors and tapestries in Smedley's dining room.

The Empire dining room.

In the 1939 inventory of cutlery, the Empire Room silver was counted separately from the EPNS used elsewhere. Apart from the hundreds of ordinary knives, forks and spoons, guests were still using the correct cutlery for fish, grapefruit, mustard and butter etc. There were over a hundred sugar tongs and 117 silver egg hoops – egg cups which could be used both ways up for different sized eggs. Different dishes also had their own pottery: there were 555 new cheese plates, 263 old porridge bowls and 426 new ones.

> *It's real funny, half an hour before the dinner bell goes, to see a queue waiting before the hot water tap, glass in hand, they await their turn like a butter queue, then up and down the corridors they walk sipping.*
>
> Maggie Round and Olive Allen

Meals were served punctually, but the duration was not fixed: "The medical direction deprecates all hurry, for which there can be no valid excuse". There was now more choice at breakfast with fruit juice, porridge, two sorts of fish, fried or pickled herrings, eggs and sausages. A substantial lunch was followed by afternoon tea and dinner at 7pm. This regime was thought quite adequate – eating between meals was not encouraged! Smedley's remained teetotal: the 1939 inventory included nearly eight hundred tumblers, but only six wine glasses.

Entering from Smedley Street, the vestibule had two brass door stops and two

Indian & China Tea

Coffee   Cocoa

Porridge   Corn Flakes

Bloaters
Grilled Fillets of Haddock

Grilled Bacon
Scrambled Eggs
Sausage Noisettes
Sauté Potatoes

Honey   Marmalade

Apricot Jam

Smedley's breakfast menu.

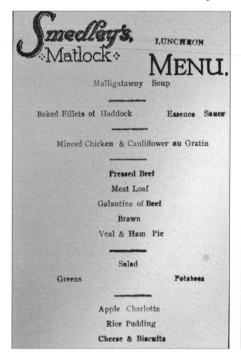

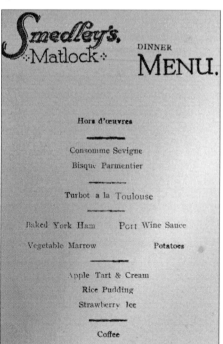

A light luncheon to stave off hunger before afternoon tea!

large brass jardinieres. In the centre of the entrance hall was the huge marble pedestal holding a copper vase containing a tall palm, which my mother remembered in 1936. Round this was the circular teak seat on which my grandfather was awaiting his son and prospective in-laws. Henry Douglas said there was an immediate whiff of cigars, dinner cooking and a "strange" smell from the baths. The porter's lodge had a 25-pigeonhole rack for the post and several scales to weigh anything from heavy parcels to postcards. From here, messages were delivered:

We are much amused at the "little Buttons" who suddenly pops up in the different rooms and with a queer little voice, which Maggie says sounds like pop gone flat, calls out the name of anyone he has a telegram for. Round and Allen.

This boy was appropriately named: photographs show the porters, lift girls and page boys in uniforms displaying several rows of brass buttons.

W H Smith's had a newspaper stall. The free *Visiting List* was posted to each guest the week after they left, in case they were mentioned performing or winning something. The hydro's own shop, with clothes displayed in a window, had become as much a gift shop as a hydro equipment supplier. From 9am guests could hire a wheelchair and buy bandages, bath apparatus, knitted sportswear, dressing gowns, silk hose and Jaeger[2] goods.

The entrance hall, stairs, corridors and offices in the main building were all carpeted with a red and blue Turkey carpet. The long corridor down to the Winter Garden, today so bleak, had almost a hundred yards of this in 30 yard lengths. It was known as the lounge corridor with sixteen comfortable settees upholstered in crimson velvet or red and green plush, a dozen oak standard lamps and nine jardinières. On the walls was a bold wallpaper of leaves on which were hung over thirty framed prints with such subjects as "Cattle", "The First Parting", and "Morning on the Isle of Arran".

All the sitting rooms were very crowded with furniture – dozens of chairs and occasional tables everywhere. The drawing room received a "make-over" in 1935 and became the lounge. Mr Douglas wrote to Waring & Gillow, Maples, and Cole's of Sheffield to ask for schemes; embarrassingly they all turned up on the same day, but Waring & Gillow won the contract. The colour scheme was still blue and gold, reflected in the three eight yard squares of very boldly flowered Donegal carpet and the heavy gold velvet curtains. The stage curtains were also in a gold plush material. On the stage was a three quarter size Steinway grand piano. The alcove curtains and comfy cushioned chair arms disappeared. The cosy fire in the alcove became gas or electric. There was also a great deal of patterned brown moquette on the settees and chairs, with brown Wilton carpet in the alcoves. The full-length portraits of John and Caroline Smedley were removed. This was presumably all very up-to-date, but somehow on a par with a "lounge". There was a disturbing number of new, unused lace chair backs ready in the store room when the Army took over – fourteen dozen – were they about to be spread round too?

Before the real fire was removed:

Instead of going to church again we got into a cosy little corner by the huge fire in the

---

2. Jaeger was founded in 1884 by Lewis Tomlin, using the advice of a German Dr Gustav Jaeger who advocated wearing animal fibres next to the skin. Their long-johns were worn by the army and explorers. In 1919 they introduced camel hair coats and more fashionable clothes. They made uniforms for the opening of the 1936 Olympic Games.

The new lounge at Smedley's.

drawing room where all the old ladies sit, which we found out was called the "Chamber of Horrors" and I do not wonder about it for the chatter and gossip and the personal remarks that go on, well, it's too funny for anything – to sit pretending to read but listening to the chatter.

Sometimes it is very interesting for quite a good number of these ladies are people who have been abroad and talk of their experiences and the life at the various hotels and on board ship. It is really surprising where some of these old ladies have been and the things they have done and the stories they tell.

Round and Allen

Another small lounge, across from the Empire room, was redecorated in shades of green and fawn, with Liberty curtains. It still had a coal fire, with an electric one hidden in the sideboard. The Bridge players immediately took this over. New cloak-rooms were provided with modern green and black Vitrolite (glass) tiles and chrome fittings.

The Winter Garden was painted in orange and cream, with a new orange awning on the roof. The reflected light was very becoming to a lady's complexion. There were one hundred and fifty wicker chairs in shades of green, orange and yellow arranged around the room, interspersed with over forty palm plants. The gramophone and wireless were kept on the stage with the full-sized Steinway grand piano. When the room was ablaze with lights at night, the building glowed visibly from a great distance.

The "Chamber of Horrors" at Smedley's: the large fireplace alcove.

The new orange awnings in the Winter Garden.

285

A detail of the Winter Garden floor.

(The Winter Garden is) a very large room with a sprung dancing floor, the centre of which is covered up in the daytime. All around the room are big settees with nice high backs and heaps and heaps of basket chairs. On one side through the glass is a fernery and looks exceedingly pretty, and then plants and huge palms everywhere, while flags hang in abundance. On the platform is a grand and each afternoon from 4.40 to 6.00pm, we have music, two violins and a piano, so most afternoons we get comfy in a settee and write, work and, above all, watch.   Round and Allen

It was a telling sign of relaxed social attitudes that smoking was allowed in the lounge. There were actually so many smokers harming their health that Dr Barnado's charity congratulated Smedley's in 1935 for being the hotel which sold the highest number of their match books in the UK. There was a cigarette machine in the Winter Garden, one hundred and eleven ashtrays among the bedroom china, and six brass spittoons in the Billiard Room. The Smoking Room itself had a worn Indian pink flowered carpet, and eleven Axminster doormats! The walls displayed sporting prints and cute animal subjects such as "For He's a Jolly Good Fellow" and "The Pekinese tells One".

The Hydro could accommodate over 400 guests. The 1939 inventory described the contents of every one of the 270 bedrooms. The passage of time had resulted in a lack of conformity in the furnishings. By this period, the overall impression must have been of a slightly tired and crowded homeliness. The inventory used the words worn and chipped quite frequently. The floors were covered in a lino surround and a flowery carpet square. All the windows had nets or lace curtains and chintz or figured cotton drapes. In the stores were forty seven yards of cretonne, fifty five yards of figured and gold casement, and twenty yards of netting ready for replenishments.

Each room had one or two beds: brass, oak or iron framed. In the old west wing the mattresses were still stuffed with hair, but the later rooms had Vi-spring mattresses. There was at least one wardrobe, a chest of drawers, a wash stand and a couple of easy chairs, all in a mixture of woods. The bedroom linen store had

One of the last batch of bedrooms.

another 600 lace chair backs. The old rooms had brass fenders and fireplaces, but the newer rooms had gas or electric fires.

Each bedroom had a framed picture or a blue and white oriental flower plaque. The pictures were very varied: "Return from the War", "Pyrenean Shepherd" or "Marlow Ferry" for example. I wonder if frequent visitors brought unwanted prints from home?

In the upstairs cupboards were twenty Ewbanks to sweep the bedroom carpets and nearly three hundred chamber pots. I doubt there were nearly enough lavatories. Four dozen chambermaids' new aprons and caps and two dozen frocks waited on shelves.

There were several changes outside. A new bridge was built to replace the old one across to the steam laundry, where visitors' linen was "expeditiously" washed at moderate charges. Below the laundry in 1934 a short new row of shops was fitted out by Pollard of London. The first tenant was John Wildgoose the fruiterer and florist, who had also been first into the previous row built under the 1901 bedroom wing. He supplied many bouquets and corsages to the guests. In the evenings, he brought a stall into the entrance hall to sell nosegays and buttonholes. One could order a bouquet to be placed at a dinner setting – tricky when a lady received competing offerings. John died in 1935, but his son Arthur took over. (Eventually he moved into the old Post Office, which is now Fleur.)

The last of the stables was converted into garages, which cost 1/6d a day. In 1920 Smedley's bought the empty Malvern House Hydro as a staff annex of twenty three rooms. (In 1955 this was sold to Mickey Morris as a furniture store.)

It had always been the custom at Smedley's to charge nothing for a visitor's last day. Henry Douglas noted that in the 1930s visitors were leaving later and later on that day. The substantial brochure was ordered in five year batches: it did not occur to the management that inflation would change prices. However, one does find brochures now with crossings out and bits of paper stuck over the numbers. The average weekly tariff was four to five guineas.

To the Manager:

Oh! bear with me, kind Manager,
You'd understand, I'm sure,
Could you guess one tiny atom
What we visitors endure?

'Twas yesterday, in deep distress,
My world was all awry,
When that most arresting notice
Caught my ever-roving eye.

"Suggestions for improvements;
The Manager would be glad
To make this good place better,
(Or this bad place not so bad.)

Not quite perhaps that wording,
But that of course was meant;
So lend your ear, good Manager,
(Or is it Management?)

We'd like a brighter Smedley's
And we'd like it very soon.
So to light the darkened terrace,
Would you please to hang a moon?

There had better be some shadows
Or that might cause a bother.
We may wish to see our friend-in arms,
But not, perhaps, our brother!

We shall come in very thirsty,
So remember if you please,

To grow refreshing fruits upon
The Winter Garden trees.

Please instruct the good night
watchman
(As we steal upstairs to bed
A little past our usual hour)
To turn away his head.

Our neighbour should be gently
warned
He must not cough or snore,
Nor when he leaves his bedroom
To dare to bang his door.

Perhaps you'd just remind our waiter
WE are the people who matter
And clear the corridors a bit
Of those who stand and chatter.

We might – if you provide a list –
Suggest perhaps some day,
The amusements WE should like to
have,
And what the band should play.

A thousand things there are,
But there's one deadly ill,
Pray command them at the office
Not to present our bill!

Written by a visitor
to Smedley's Hydro in 1932

The Other Hydros on the Bank

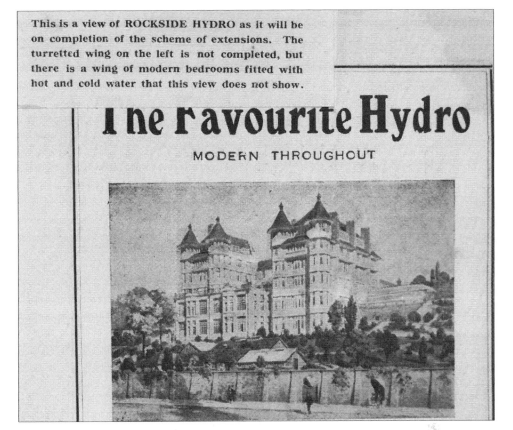

This is a view of ROCKSIDE HYDRO as it will be on completion of the scheme of extensions. The turretted wing on the left is not completed, but there is a wing of modern bedrooms fitted with hot and cold water that this view does not show.

The Favourite Hydro
MODERN THROUGHOUT

An optimistic sketch with the projected second tower.

In September 1923 the Goodwin family began improvements to **Rockside Hydro**, although a proposed second tower was never built. A new entrance was made through a long glass conservatory, which was full of chrysanthemums right up to Christmas. At the front they built a dining room to seat two hundred people at small tables. In the summer the windows opened to the sunshine and in winter the tables looked cosy with shaded lamps. The flat roof provided another terrace, but contained domes to light the room below. Unlike Smedley's, they did serve alcohol at meals, but the head waiter needed fifteen minutes notice and had to be paid in cash at the time. A new "concert room, *en suite* with the old ballroom" was built, extending the sprung dance floor to both. The new room had a stage and dressing rooms. The proscenium was draped with gold and blue curtains. Thirty more bedrooms were provided at the side of Rockside steps, with a choice of Vi-sprung, hair or feather mattress, and an electric or coal fire.

The turret windows in the lounge were fitted with vita glass to transmit ultra-violet rays. The well which had given a view of the previous stage had been filled in to provide more floor space. Outside a producer gas plant and workshops were installed in Furniss's old Cherry Holt stables. The garages were described as having

The new ballroom.

doors with latest Henderson fitments, electric lighting and heating. The long-serving gardeners were still the Brown brothers, now in their seventies.

The hydro's advertisements became very 1930s in style with the phrase, "Run down? Then run down to Rockside". Miss Annie Eliza Goodwin and her brother John announced their retirement at Christmas 1933. Annie had been in charge since

1894; she died in 1937 aged 80. Thomas, the chairman of the family company, died in 1936. John had been widowed and re-married in 1928; he lived at Kianga on Cavendish Road. Jennie Goodwin, their niece from Wolds Farm, took over the management and Lilian Goodwin did the accounts.

Lilybank Hydro was managed by Mr and Mrs John Sidney Kay from 1919. The building they took over had been completely empty, but a week later they welcomed eighty three guests. In October the business became a limited company with Mr Kay as director.

The Kays made several improvements. In 1921 they bought The Gables, the home of Mrs Robert Wildgoose, when she moved to Stoneycroft on Cavendish Road. They linked the two houses with a new ballroom, which looks like a square conservatory on exterior photographs. This room had a lantern roof with stained glass, a coloured frieze above the picture rail and a gallery for spectators, although orchestras soon took this over to make more room for dancing. Against two walls were commode tables surmounted by huge gilt mirrors. Guests danced on a Morton's patent Valtor sprung floor, like the one at Gleneagles Hotel. The mechanism could be "locked" when not in use. In 1922 they became the first business to take electricity directly from the Derbyshire & Nottinghamshire Electric Power Company via a cable from Ambergate: the house was fully lit for Christmas. Their visitors presented the Kays with a grand piano at Easter 1923. Busy Bee writing in the *Visiting List* said the ballroom was brilliantly lit by dozens of electric lights.

He went on to describe the dining room with a "Wedgwood" décor. The cosy drawing room had a large bay window overlooking the bowling green and the valley beyond: the only room with a smoking ban. The billiard room needed an electric fan to clear the air. The Kays copied Rockside by installing vita glass in a new sun lounge – in theory one could get a tan indoors. Three thousand new rose

THE
LILYBANK HYDRO
MATLOCK

Stands in its own beautiful grounds of six acres

Accommodation for 150 visitors. Tennis, Bowls, Putting Green. New Sun Lounge (Vita Glass). New Ballroom, Spring Floor. Hydro Baths. Hot and Cold Water in every Bedroom. Passenger Lift to all Floors. Cards, Dancing and Music Every Evening. Good Table. Garage for 22 Cars, Free.

Terms from £3 10 0 to £4 11 0 per week inclusive

Illustrated Booklet from

Mr. and Mrs. SIDNEY KAY

Telephone: 81   Telephone: 81

The ballroom, Lilybank Hydro.
[Glynn Waite]

Lilybank's new sun lounge.
[Glynn Waite]

trees were planted in the gardens and orchids flourished in the conservatory.

Oldham House and Prospect Hydro continued under Lubin Wildgoose and his musical family. They had rooms for only 120 people, but could seat more in the dining room, so they used some houses in Wellington Street and Cavendish Road as extra accommodation. A new garage could hold fourteen cars. (Henceforth, this hydro will just be called Oldham House.)

The entrance hall, Oldham and Prospect Hydro.
[Glynn Waite]

The 1931 brochure for **Chatsworth Hydro** had mottos such as, "The world is a great book of which they that never stir from home read only one page. Come to Chatsworth Hydro and see another page" and, "The best physicians are Dr Diet, Dr Quiet and Dr Merryman".

The hydro had had an uncomfortable time in the 1920s with the Taylors. One of Francis Taylor's syndicate had backed out and the business ran at a loss. Mrs Taylor managed the hydro, but her husband died in 1928 and his creditors put the building up for sale. She died only three months later. The vendors even suggested a change of use, as Matlock was "overdone with hydropathy". The price was low, but the property was withdrawn at £10,000. The manager for this period was Captain J Wilkinson. A re-auction only brought one bid of £6,000.

In 1931 the new owners were reported as Mr W Evans, the jeweller on Dale Road, and two directors from the colour works in Cromford: George Key and Henry Hetherington, who have already been mentioned in connection with the glove factory in Matlock Bath. They appointed Mrs E Dawson as manager; she had trained at Smedley's. She was the widow of Charles Dawson, the managing director of the Stancliffe Estates, who had died after a car accident. In 1939 the manager was Fred Turner, also from Smedley's.

The new owners received an AA accreditation and were keen to advertise a complete reconstruction, redecoration, and refurbishment. The ninety bedrooms all had hot and cold water. Even after the modernisation, some of the items from the 1930 sale catalogue may have been retained. Notable were Lloyd loom[3] chairs in the

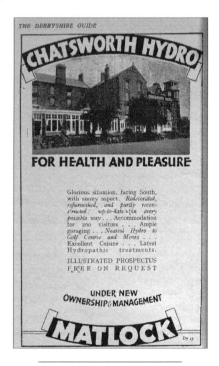

---

3. Made by a method invented in 1917 in the USA. Paper was twisted round wire and then woven into an imitation of wicker, but it was allegedly much stronger.

A lounge at Chatsworth Hydro.

The dining cum ballroom.

Chatsworth Hydro – not afraid to mix patterns!

The recreation room.

long conservatory recreation room at the front. The bedroom furniture was mostly satin walnut. In the ballroom was a Panatrope gramophone, two revolving ballroom lamps on stands and a mirror globe for lighting effects. The 133 dining chairs had Rexine seats. The stores included 192 apostle spoons, 175 pink coffee cups and saucers and 236 bone serviette rings. The garage could hold forty cars.

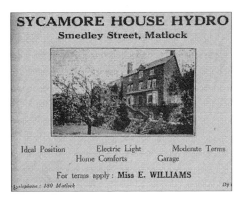

SYCAMORE HOUSE HYDRO
Smedley Street, Matlock

Ideal Position   Electric Light   Moderate Terms
Home Comforts   Garage

For terms apply : Miss E. WILLIAMS

Telephone: 180 Matlock

Sycamore House Hydro was still managed by Miss Williams, but, for reasons unexplained, the initial changed in the *Visiting List* from M to E one week in December 1928. Was this a younger relative?

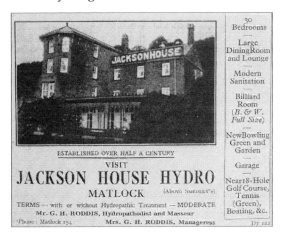

30 Bedrooms

Large Dining Room and Lounge

Modern Sanitation

Billiard Room (*B. & W. Full Size*)

New Bowling Green and Garden

Garage

Near 18-Hole Golf Course, Tennis (Green), Boating, &c.

ESTABLISHED OVER HALF A CENTURY
VISIT
JACKSON HOUSE HYDRO
MATLOCK (Above Smedley's)
TERMS — with or without Hydropathic Treatment — MODERATE
Mr. G. H. RODDIS, Hydropathodist and Masseur
Phone: Matlock 154   Mrs. G. H. RODDIS, Manageress

Jackson House Hydro had brought itself more up to date with a tennis court and a new billiard room and bowling green – and a wireless! They had introduced "weekend parties" for guests staying Saturday to Tuesday. The hydro had several managers: Mr and Mrs F Seal in 1930, who moved to Fair View guest house, followed by Mr and Mrs G H Roddis and Mr K Hofton from 1937. Although the other hydros were open until the outbreak of war, Jackson House stopped recording visitors after January 1939 and disappeared from the *Visiting List* in March.

Tor House Hydro was for sale in 1927 because George Davis wanted to retire. There were advance bookings into the following year. His name stayed as proprietor until the first week of December 1928, when the business disappears from the *Visiting List*. There had been no guests for several weeks. This is the only hydro to have been completely demolished and built over. It possibly existed as a staff annex to Smedley's for a time.

DOWN TO THE TREATMENT ROOMS

After breakfast I had to see the doctor and after being pinched and pummelled received a bath book which contains the most curious things and they include all kinds of pickling and spicing recipes. I am sure after I have finished I shall be a walking mixture of Bengal Chutney and Heinz best mixed pickle. I have had my first dose of mustard today which I must confess has eased my shoulder a great deal for which I am devoutly thankful. I had my first taste of massage, or I ought to say punch and poke, by such a dear little nurse, such a bright jolly little soul, who is blind, but seems to have a wonderful sense of touch and very strong capable hands.

Olive is now stewing in a lovely warm bath, like a dolly's bath. In it is hot water and "pickle" while her hand is put in an iodine pad, like a saucepan scraper, which is bound on her shoulder and an electric battery is attached and turned on. I sit on a chair enjoying it all and watching for her to jump, but alas ... she has just jumped, hooray now for some fun!

Round and Allen

Several Smedley's bath books survive from the 1930s to show that little had changed from previous decades. Doctors Harbinson and MacLelland had consultation mornings once a week. A footman kept a "consultation roll" for the order of patient priority. The head bathman and matron still had the main responsibility for treatment. The bath attendants worked in shifts between 7.30am and 10.00pm, with one day off in three months. The women wore a blue uniform, a white apron and a cap with a bow tied under their chin. A seriously ill patient might have a dedicated nurse, who had to wheel them around the hydro in a bath chair.

Despite the delicious foods available in the dining room, some poor souls were still on strict diets: 6 ounces of Bengers (an easily digestible milk product), beef tea or chicken broth every two hours, with stale brown bread, and boiled spinach for lunch were listed in one extant book. Patients were weighed each week, preferably in the Turkish Baths, with no clothes.

... the ladies! Oh for a pen to do them justice. Ninety nine out of a hundred is of course fat, fat, fat, great lovely, barrelly, tubby, bay window, rotundy, jelly-like little dears and a few, a very few, like Maggie and I "elegant and thin". Now here's an amusing question, I really must ask the doctor before I go home. Is it that hydropathical treatment is so obliging for the majority come to get thin and a few like yours truly and Maggie come to get fat and all the various stews and pummel and packs are guaranteed to do all things. Nice and cheerful sort of doctoring anyhow.

Round and Allen

There were new treatments advertised, some of which helped with rheumatism, gout and sciatica. Dr Christopher L'Estrange Orme, who joined the staff at Rockside after his mother died, was a specialist on rheumatism. He ran a clinic in Harley Street, which he attended every Thursday. The problem occurred when patients

A Plombiere bathroom at Smedley's.

were otherwise in the prime of life in their mid-forties, but Dr Orme advocated heat and massage, for which hydros were pioneers in the field. Moreover, as the Chatsworth Hydro brochure quipped, "Rheumatism is bad – but it's something to be thankful for that we still have a back to have it in"!

The Chatsworth Hydro brochure described their Crystal Bed, or radiant heat bath, for rheumatism, which avoided the depressing after effects of Turkish Baths. The patient lay in a recumbent position: "the portion upon which the patient lies is fitted with glass cross-bars bent to the shape of the body". Treatment could be "tri-colour" for twenty to forty minutes, followed by a tonic needle bath or a rough towel rub.

Smedley's and Rockside had a Plombieres department for colonic irrigation, with couches and commodes. The treatment was named after a French spa. (In Harrogate it was politely called "intestinal lavage".) Smedley's also had a Studa chair for the same purpose.

High frequency short wave diathermy was another new treatment. The 1939 inventory at Smedley's described the equipment: "6 meters by Siemens, with 7 Schliephake electrodes, 4 soft rubber electrodes with cables, 2 belts and 1 valve". There was also a machine with two telescopic arms, 2 sets of electrodes for same, vaginal and rectal electrodes, and a furuncle electrode.

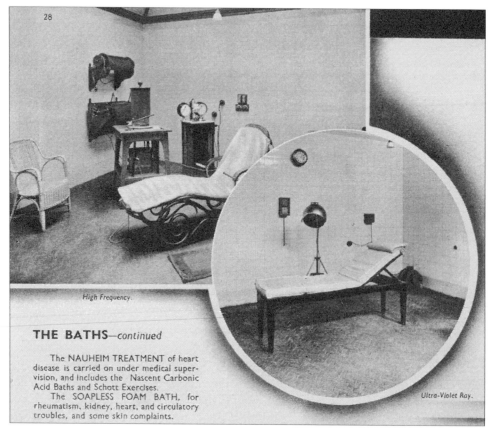

28

High Frequency.

THE BATHS—continued

The NAUHEIM TREATMENT of heart disease is carried on under medical supervision, and includes the Nascent Carbonic Acid Baths and Schott Exercises.
The SOAPLESS FOAM BATH, for rheumatism, kidney, heart, and circulatory troubles, and some skin complaints.

Ultra-Violet Ray.

A page from Smedley's brochure.

The idea was to deliver electrically-induced heat deep into a patient's tissues. Rubber electrode pads with felt spacers were placed either side of the part of the body to be treated. The high frequency waves travelled through the skin and tissues between them, converting their energy into heat. A furuncle was a boil or infection round a hair follicle, which needed a special electrode, if, for example, it was on the nose. (Schliephake electrodes are still used for diathermy.)

Chatsworth Hydro and Smedley's described their new ionic medication or cataphoresis for neuralgia and sciatica. This was the transference, by a weak electric current, of measured doses of drugs such as lithium, iodine and sodium "in active condition", from a pad impregnated with the elements, into tissues lying beneath the skin surface.

The hydros had artificial sunlight rooms. Ultra violet rays were used for the treatment of "cardiac derangements", insomnia, spinal curvature and arthritis. Sulphur baths were given for skin diseases such as eczema and psoriasis. Pine baths helped with chest infections. Soapless foam baths helped with rheumatism and skin complaints. Smedley's had a Berthelette treatment room, but its use is now a mystery.

Dr George Harbinson and Dr Robert MacLelland were still in post at Smedley's until 1939. Dr Christopher Orme at Rockside Hydro has already been mentioned. He lived at Bidston on Cavendish Road. He had been a doctor in the Royal Army Medical Corps. (In the Second World War he served again, then had practices in Sheffield, Dorset and Hampshire. He retired to Malta and died in 1979.) He sometimes worked with a Dr Mary Drabble, who was also a consultant at Chatsworth Hydro. She was the public vaccinator and lived at West Lea, Dr Hunter's old home.

Chatsworth used Dr Edward Crarer, who had been Dr Moxon's partner, but he died in 1934, after thirty years in the town. He lived at West Mains on Lime Tree Road. Dr George Meachim also saw many hydro patients. He lived at the Red House on Dale Road (built by Dr Orme's father); his partner was Dr Clifford Sparks, who lived in Dale House. In 1932 George Davis, a long-serving bathman, died. Originally at Jeffs' Poplar Hydro, he had latterly worked for his cousin Lubin at Oldham House Hydro.

There were advertisements for Masson House Hydro, opposite the mill, where S W Daley-Yates gave electrical treatments and massages. By 1939 he had moved into one of Smedley's shops as an orthopaedist and chiropodist: "Matlock Foot Comfort Service". Mr Law, whose wife ran Matlock Modern School in the old Matlock House Hydro, ran Matlock Health Centre as a naturopathy clinic, harnessing the healing power of nature.

Staying In – Safe from the World

It was still being claimed that the hydros could cure ills of the flesh, but "synonymous with much that is brightest in life, the festive programme provided is making life a round of pleasure and happiness". In Smedley's brochure they now admitted

ROCKSIDE HYDRO MATLOCK

ALTITUDE 800 FT.—
THE LOCAL LANDMARK

GOLF
TENNIS
MOTORING
DANCING
MUSIC

THE FAVOURITE HYDRO
Famous resort for health and holidays. Latest Hydropathic Equipment, including Diathermy and Ultra-Violet Rays. All treatment *inside* the Hydro. Well warmed throughout. Entertainments, Sports and Golf. Extensive Grounds. Moderate terms.

Telegrams: Rockside, Matlock.   Telephone: Matlock 312 (2 lines).

WRITE   FOR   ILLUSTRATED   PROSPECTUS

[Glynn Waite]

that, "one half at least of those residing in the place are other than invalids". Hence, "the social atmosphere is not by any means depressing". A stay in a hydro compared favourably with a cruise: all the entertainment provided meant one need never leave the building, but the experience was more enjoyable because there was no seasickness and one could get to sleep!

As the decade progressed, the festivities were often portrayed as providing an antidote to the sinister happenings unfolding outside in the wider world. At Smedley's, Edna Downing, and at Rockside Muriel Thompson, assisted by Ena Sangwin in the ballroom, filled their guests' days with a non-stop programme of sports, games and music, all of which was described in detail in the *Visiting List*.

Some activities occurred most days. From Monday to Friday, Smedley's provided a tea dance at 4pm. The musicians were usually a ladies trio consisting of Edna Downing, "our own pianist", Margaret Hampson (late of the Halle) on the violin and Marion McMillan a cellist. Another popular violinist was Maud Knowles, whose father and grandfather had been Smedley's gardeners. She also taught the violin and cello to the girls at Matlock Modern School. Other tea dance players were the Misses Radford from a music shop on Bank Road. In the evenings, these ladies were joined by a saxophone and drums.

John Barnes, the stalwart of Matlock's dance scene for nearly fifty years, died in August 1932. One of the four sons of Samuel Barnes, the hosier and draper in Matlock Bath, John had also written articles for his journalist brother in the *High Peak News* and the *Visiting List*. On his coffin his family placed a floral violin made of violets with strings of white silk cord, constructed by Arthur Wildgoose in the Smedley's building flower shop.

His death left a gap filled by several new orchestras led by Horace Holmes,

George Farmer, Will Leah, Billy Short, and Fred Slater with the Matlock Brotherhood. In 1937 Smedley's introduced Max Chappell's swing band from London. He brought the first "crooning" and the Lambeth Walk, from the musical *"Me and My Girl"*.

There were still times when the visitors were asked to play:

On Thursday evening the orchestra had their holiday from playing for the dancing and volunteers were called for. One lady we call "the lemon or acid drop" was one capturing the piano stool, but from her face you would never suspect her of having any music stowed away in her heart. When she did get an opportunity at last the poor dancers got into such a pickle; first it was like a funeral march, each person having one foot up in the air waiting for the next note before they could put it down; then it was like a merry-go-round where all the people turned and twisted in and out, up and down – no, decidedly "the lemon" was not a success.

Round and Allen

Music for dancing also came via the wireless and various types of gramophone. Rockside used a Panatrope, a type of phonograph, and an orchestrolian and amplifier, with the music recorded on rolls. Every dance featured a Paul Jones when one changed partners, and statue and spot dances to win prizes. Cinderella dances were still held; one described the dance finishing at midnight, when every-

The lounge at Oldham House. Card posted 1921.
[Glynn Waite]

one had to try on slippers from a pile at the front. The New Bath Hotel held a dinner dance every Saturday evening.

The Goodwin and Wildgoose families at Rockside and Oldham House Hydros were able to provide their own in-house talent. There was a Rockside theatre group and choir. The new Mrs Goodwin senior played the piano and other members of the household formed the Peakites 4 or 5-piece band. Oldham House Hydro had its own dance club band and choir under Lubin Wildgoose. His son Harold was an accomplished soloist and accompanist. Lawrence William Wildgoose, the son of John the builder, was known as "Wireless Willie" to friends, owing to his radio broadcasts from Manchester as a tenor vocalist.

Harry Douglas the manager of Smedley's Hydro wrote songs under the pseudonym Robert Masson, sometimes using his own verse, other times setting poetry to music. One of Harry's own poems, which seems to hark back to the First World War, was called Sing me a song:

> Sing me a song at daybreak,
> Just when the birds awake,
> Sing me a song of courage,
> Ere to the road I take.
> Sing me a song of comfort,
> Sing me a song of truth;
> Sing me a song of thankfulness
> In the hope and strength of youth.
>
> Sing me a song at noontide,
> Just when the sun is high,
> Blazing with all its glory,
> In the great azure sky.
> Sing me a song of gladness,
> Sing me a song of mirth,
> Sing me a song of happiness
> In the joyous things of earth.
>
> Sing me a song at sunset,
> Just when the day is done,
> Sing me a song of triumph,
> In the battle fought and won.
> Sing of welcome harbour,
> Wherein is peaceful rest,
> And of the one great Father
> Who willeth all things best.

At Oldham House Hydro, Sunday evening concerts were advertised as a feature. All the hydros invited local church choirs to perform. Prayers were taken by whichever reverend gentleman happened to be staying. Smedley's still had morning and evening prayers daily, taken by local ministers in rotation.

Local artists were also keen to be asked to perform: at Smedley's particularly on

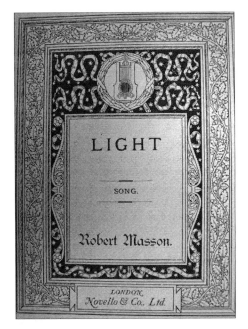

[Jean Douglas]

Captain Harry Douglas.
[Jean Douglas]

a Tuesday. One act was the teenager Herbert Siddons from Darley Dale, who did impressions of Gracie Fields in drag, "with her permission". Guests did still perform at Smedley's and in the smaller hydros they remained the mainstay of the entertainment. But sophisticated visitors here on holiday expected professionals at Smedley's and Rockside, at least at weekends and Bank Holidays. Some of these artists stayed for a few weeks, probably receiving treatment; many returned year after year. Most were well known at the time because they performed on the radio, but their names mean little to us now. At Christmas 1932, Esther Coleman, famous for *Songs my mother sang*, and Arthur Cox,[4] principal tenor at Covent Garden, performed. "Breathes there a wireless set that has not heard of these broadcast stars?" enthused the *Visiting List*. One performer who went on to become a household name even into modern times was Violet Carson. She was a well-known pianist and singer before her television career.

Another popular act was Cecil Harrington and Noreena Feist, drawing room entertainers. One can still see Mr Harrington perform today on *Youtube*; amongst other skills, he played the piano with his nose. In 1933 Nora Gruhn came from Covent Garden after recently performing on the radio. In 1937 Ivan Mellodew, a famous bass from Oldham, was engaged.

Rockside Hydro held amateur dramatic weeks in January and February. Groups from all the hydros took the train to theatres in Derby, Nottingham and Manchester. Eminent guests still gave serious lectures. In June 1935 Sir Henry de Mel and his wife gave a very entertaining display. Sir Henry was a politician and industrialist

---

4. Also known as Arthur Carron, he moved to the Metropolitan Opera in New York soon after.

A circus performance at Smedley's.
[Glynn Waite]

Henry Douglas and his brother (Alfred)
George dressed up for theatricals.
[Jean Douglas]

from Ceylon. After a slide show, they changed into native costumes to dance and sing for the other guests. (Sadly Sir Henry was murdered on one of his coconut plantations the following year.)

There were organised trips down to the cinemas in the town, but, from the 1920s, Smedley's had thought it important to entertain their invalids with Pathe Pictorials, to keep them in touch with the world outside, and cartoons to cheer them up. Thursday night was "film night". In 1934 they showed their first "talkie" film using large slow playing records, one per reel; but in 1935 they installed proper sound equipment.

For mature ladies, the main occupation was still playing card games: bridge, progressive hearts, military and Klondyke whist, which involved a different scoring scheme and bonus points for each hand. On their visit, Mrs Allen and Miss Round went into the drawing room to watch the progressive whist:

Some of them looked so serious over it as to give the idea they were almost in pain and some of the gay old darlings were having a ripping time. One dear huge lady looked just like a nice big mess of happy jelly, especially when holding a hand of trumps, while nearby Mrs Lippett knitted a jersey for "orphany" with a huge red geranium on her stiff upright high virtuous dress and looked on most disapprovingly. But oh the gay old colonel, one of the old boys, with a real "good life in the old dog yet" sort of air, quite a giddy old party sporting a huge buttonhole of lilies of the valley, which later on he presented to one of the young girls during the dancing in the Winter Garden... where are what appears to us to be the remnants of the British fleet, coming along in full sail, nice, huge ladies looking like grand old Dreadnoughts, and the only thing they would dread would be if the doctors told them there was nothing the matter with them.

MATLOCK. SMEDLEY'S HYDRO & GROUNDS.

The entrance hut, changing room and diving boards at one end of the pool.
Beyond are tennis courts

It was the variety of sports that were the main feature of the larger hydros. Indoors they offered billiards, golf-croquet, carpet bowls, deck quoits, skittles and ping pong. Outside guests played tennis, croquet and bowls. The hard or *"en tout cas"* courts meant play was possible even in the winter: Christmas day matches became a tradition.

Smedley's and Rockside held annual bowls, croquet and tennis tournaments in August. Challenge cups and trophies were supplied by the directors and former guests. The town pitches were used for fun matches. In 1933 Rockside staff played cricket against their visitors, whose side collapsed under the onslaught of Lilian Goodwin's bowling. Hall Leys tennis courts were needed for American tennis tournaments where everyone played everyone else. There were inter-hydro sports events, such as bowls matches:

> *Rockside is a hydro that's set on a hill.*
> *Its turrets look down on the valley so still;*
> *But far down below it, stands Smedley's – a house*
> *So vast that the largest feels just like a mouse.*
> *From Rockside to Smedley's the challenge went out*
> *"O send up some bowlers for us to rout".*
> *From Smedley's to Rockside, the answer came back,*
> *"We'll come and defeat you – eight woods to each jack."*
> *Now soon after breakfast, without further talk,*
> *They made ready the green with tape, roller and chalk.*
> *And at three precisely the visitors came,*
> *All grimly determined to put Rockside to shame.*

Poem written by a visitor in August 1932. She included the
name of every player in the rest of the poem – Rockside won.

The garden at Chatsworth Hydro – parts of it survive.

The visitors could be spectators. In 1934 a dinner dance at Chatsworth Hydro was followed by a demonstration tennis table match. Many went to watch the 1933 English table tennis championship in Buxton: an over-confident Fred Perry was knocked out in the second round. In 1934 one could have glimpsed the first lady to wear shorts on a Smedley's tennis court, described as "well-tailored Viyella". Further afield, tobogganing was now confined to Imperial and Woolley Roads for safety reasons. In 1933 there was a report of skating on Flash Dam, where the bank was lined with spectators. Smedley's offered horse riding up at their farm. There was also the Gwyther Jones stables on Cavendish Road. By the 1940s Yew Tree Farm, just below Smedley's on Bank Road, was also calling itself a riding school.

There were still activities purely for fun. At Smedley's the Winter Garden was used for "basket balancing": a guest in a basket suspended between two chairs had to perform tasks with a walking stick. At Lilybank the ballroom was used for obstacle races. Rockside used their ballroom for indoor polo matches and they played bottle golf in Oldham House Hydro.

Christmas was still the holiday to be booked well in advance. In 1935 all the hydros reported turning away more people than ever before. Ladies would bring trunks of evening dresses and the maids remember great rivalries to be in the latest fashion. Locals would linger round the door at Smedley's in the hope of seeing guests in evening dress, perhaps as they sneaked out to the Gate public house for an illegal drink. Dr Orme at Rockside found a use for the vacuum cleaner: blowing up balloons. John Goodwin usually dressed up as Father Christmas. The smaller hydros emphasised the traditional family Christmas, with guests returning year after year. The entertainment at the bigger hydros mirrored Smedley's programme; but, as ever, there was really only one place to be....

CHRISTMAS AT SMEDLEY'S

Older natives of Matlock still remember being taken as children to see the dining room at Smedley's decked out for Christmas. Some still keep a souvenir menu: every year a new one was printed with a different festive picture and verse. Many visitors had been coming to the celebrations there for almost their entire lives.

Planning began weeks ahead. As the *High Peak News* commented, even had the hydro been six times its size, they could not have accommodated everyone who wished to come: in 1927 there had been 1600 applications. The office staff were over-worked sending out thousands of "sorry we are full" letters. The house-keepers spent the week before in a "perpetual snowstorm of sheets and pillow-cases". The entertainment department had a hundred and one details to settle. The gardeners carried hundreds of plants in from the greenhouses. The hall porter braced himself, ready for the hundreds of cards and parcels he would have to sort, even on Christmas morning.

It is difficult to imagine how the kitchen staff coped. They had to prepare the Christmas menus at the same time as keeping the regular guests and staff fed. They knew they would be judged on their set pieces of confectionary art, especially at the fancy dress ball buffet supper.

The guests began to arrive each day up to Christmas Eve:

> There is no nonsense about arriving here for Christmas. In some hotels you are bowed all over the hall and corridors by obsequious gents with patent leather hair. There is a vague air of cathedral about. At Smedley's, immediately you enter you are engulfed in a tideless river of cheerfulness.

The entrance was full of old friends greeting each other. There was a mass of luggage, despite the never-ending flow of trunks into the elevator. Items of baggage showed the guests were ready for anything: tennis and badminton racquets, golf clubs, billiard cues, skates and even skis. The LMS sometimes played one of its "annual jokes", accidently taking cases on to Millers Dale or even Manchester.

On Christmas morning, whispering and door noises began very early as parcels and stockings were delivered, followed by excited voices. Guests in a variety of dressing gowns rushed round to each other's bedrooms. When the post arrived, the hall porter was besieged.

Dutiful guests attended crowded church services around the town, but several played badminton in the Winter Garden or tennis on the all-weather courts, which were specially treated against frost. After lunch, the King's speech was broadcast on the radio in the lounge. Those with very strong stomachs managed an after-noon tea while dancing in the Winter Garden. Parents of young children could deliver them to a party in the coffee lounge for games and a huge supper.

"Even the coloured pictures in *Mrs Beeton's Cookery Book* are a mere paltry shadow besides the staggering effect of the Corinthian Dining Room."

Dinner was at seven sharp. The dining room was a picture: decorations and foliage on the walls, long tables covered in snowy white linen, gleaming cutlery, and bottles of non-alcoholic drink with gold foil collars. The centres of the tables were filled with flowers, crackers, fans, fruit, chocolates, almonds and raisins. Add to this the men in their white ties and tails and the women in their beautiful dresses and jewellery. Each place setting had a copy of the souvenir menu. The Empire Dining Room was similarly decorated, but the smaller tables were used by families with children.

Once the crackers had been pulled, the music commenced and the food arrived. After the soup and fish, there came every meat imaginable: veal, pheasant, turkey, mutton, beef, venison and duck. This was followed by trifles, Christmas pudding, Chantilly creams, ice creams and gateaux. The noise was deafening. Whenever the band played a tune with a chorus, everyone joined in. They blew whistles from the crackers, banged spoons on glasses and rattled tureen lids. There were speeches and toasts.

> We do not recall ever hearing a more spirited rendering of After the Ball is over* arranged for voices, orchestra, dessert spoons, tumblers and vegetable dish lids. It would have been a credit to Stravinsky.
> *(This was the first song to sell more than five million copies of the sheet music.)

Stamina was then required for the Gala Ball at 9 o'clock. As dancers entered the Winter Garden they could pick up a hat – Spanish, Mexican or cowboy – a squeaker, whistle or hooter, and synthetic snow balls to knock the hats off. One really has to admire the musicians: they played from seven until one with two short breaks. For many years these were Miss Margaret Hampson and her quartet, but in the late thirties Max Chappell's swing band took over at night. For the first time "crooning" was heard at Smedley's.

On Boxing Day, there was a "scrounge". Visitors were given a list of items to find: a particular book, a flower, a wellington boot etc. The shopkeepers down in the town were ready for this. In 1937 the contest was expanded into an Auto Scrounge. Motor cars full of jolly guests set off at 2.15pm with their list. This included a list of green fees from the Golf Club, a ticket to Crich Stand, the inscription on Cromford Bridge, ditto on Little John's grave at Hathersage, the name of the licensee at several public houses, a piece of lead ore and a piece of Blue John. Chaos ensued in Belper as several cars blocked a narrow lane down which lived a Mr Moss, whose calling card was one item. A wall was accidentally demolished. After a round trip of about 75 miles, the excited competitors arrived back for tea and marking. That night there was usually a Cinderella Ball – bed by midnight.

The next night was the fancy dress ball. In the old days, visitors probably had great fun improvising, but by the thirties one suspects many had packed their more exotic outfits. There were still fun costumes. Alongside the many French and English queens (with and without heads), Spanish dancers, gypsies, cowboys, cardinals and pierrots, were a 12-legged Loch Ness monster in a kilt and smelling strongly of seccotine (fish glue), Belisha Beacons, and a robot (first mentioned in a play in 1921). One clever idea had caused a delay as the perpetrators struggled to descend the stairs in one piece: three men dressed as washerwomen with a length of washing line, complete with washing, strung between two posts and a prop. In 1938 there was even a tableau called the "*Judgement of Paris*". Several visitors in white togas led a cart containing Hitler, Mussolini and Chamberlain, wearing a placard saying "Mein Kampf".

Non-competitors, armed with voting cards, waited with great anticipation in the Winter Garden as bagpipers led a noisy procession down the corridor. As the first couple entered the room, the band (usually dressed as Japanese maidens) struck up a suitable march, such as the *Entry of the Gladiators*. The competitors marched twice round the room to be judged before the music changed to a dance.

At 10pm, Chef Crohill entered with his staff carrying an eight-tiered Christmas cake and the buffet was revealed to gasps of admiration. Over the years, the chefs concocted trifle and cream swans, wagon and horse yule logs, marzipan yachts in cream seas, and a garden of tulips made from painted eggshells. Unusually in 1937 they also made a seascape of yachts out of mutton fat and a basket of gilded chicken bones.

New Year meant another Gala Dinner and Ball, but by this time many guests would have walked and played various sports to counteract the over-eating. The whole holiday jamboree was rounded off with the staff dance and buffet; many of the girls had saved their bonuses to buy a party dress. The staff and their families were waited upon by the guests, who willingly donned aprons to rush about with trays and try their hand at washing up. The real chefs, who were surely flagging by now, still had to cook and the inept washers-up were often slaving in the kitchens into the small hours. The staff dance began with a chosen "Belle of the Ball" doing a round of the Winter Garden with the Manager.

Chef Harry Crohill's buffet at New Year 1925.
[Derbyshire Record Office]

THE MODERN TOWN

Had the Matlocks got to grips with their dusty road surfaces in the years since 1910? Yes and no. Reports in the 1920s were still discouraging. In 1927 Causeway Lane was described as a quagmire after rain, with slime several inches deep. The local roads were still being tar-sprayed where their gradients did not make this unsafe. Tarred slag on Dale Road in 1923 only lasted six months. The road through Darley Dale was very poor and the County Council was asked to take it over. At first they refused, but when the London to Carlisle trunk road was designated, they agreed to replace the surface with six inches of modern Tarmac over a two year period. The rest of the present A6 through the town was Tarmacked piecemeal, beginning with the stretch between Cromford and Glenorchy Chapel. Not everyone was pleased: some said the surface damaged horses' hooves. The process took a long time because they had to wait until the second stage of the new sewers was finished in 1931. In that year, tyres disturbing the old method tar spraying on Dale Road caused the pebbles sprinkled on top to "rattle on shop windows like hailstones".

Tor Cottage and High Tor. Note the steam roller behind the lorry.
Card posted 1928.

Quarrying firms benefitted from the new road surface workings. Hadfield's were Tarmacadam manufacturers on Dale Road. Constable, Hart & Co Ltd at Cawdor quarry were road surfacing specialists producing slag tarmacadam and "coharvia" bituminous road surfacing. In 1935 these and other companies were merged into Derbyshire Stone. The old Megdale Farm, mentioned in the 1880s, and the current RBS bank building, became their offices.

Local roads were still a drain on the local councils; many remained narrow and potholed. In 1933 a sarcastic letter from a resident of Hopewell Terrace thanked the UDC for providing them with free paddling pools for forty-six years. In 1937 there was anger in Darley Dale about the state of roads and pavements in Churchtown.

A view of Matlock from today's Edgefold Road.
There is a rubbish dump behind the United Methodist Church.

Sadly, road widening meant the removal of the lime trees from The Dimple and Lime Grove Walk. The old tree on Lime Tree Road had been removed in 1928. The big sycamore tree on The Dimple near Tor Hosiery had to be cut down to make the road wider for the buses which replaced the tramway. However, the Rotary Club planted fifty ornamental pear trees in the Dale in Coronation year.

Dale Road was improved in 1927 by the removal of some boundary walls to relieve congestion and improve visibility on the bend near the bottom of Holt Lane. The road at Artists' Corner was narrow and dangerous, particularly for motor cycles, owing to a bad camber. It was widened in 1935 from thirty to forty five feet. In 1937 the new traffic island in Crown Square was laid with turf from Carsington and fenced with ornamental railings. The tram shelter was replaced by a large gas lamp standard which was, "hardly as powerful as could be desired".

From the mid-1920s, there had been calls for another bridge over the river, crossing to the bottom of The Dimple. In 1935 the Council surveyor, John Simpson, put forward a formal plan as part of the town planning schemes in the Peak Region. It was reported that, "many new roads are suggested, including one to Riber, others from Bonsall to Matlock, and a third very desirable improvement to avoid the congestion and awkward turns at Matlock bridge by continuing Dale Road past the railway yard and across the Derwent over a new bridge to Bakewell Road". Also, "a possible aerodrome is mentioned on the flat ground by the river side east of Oker". Again, in late 1938, plans were lodged by the County Council to build the Matlock bypass, as an improvement to the London-Carlisle-Inverness trunk road. We had to wait nearly seventy years for Sainsbury's to provide the bypass – thank goodness the aerodrome idea was abandoned.

Car parking was a big issue for residents and visitors alike, and one where Matlock Bath felt badly done to. In Matlock Bath the main car park run by the

Council was round the Pavilion and subject to a charge. Old buildings, such as a spar shop and coal weighing house, were demolished to make more space. Postcards often show most of the area taken up by coaches. The vicar allowed parking in his vicarage grounds to raise money for the church. However, residents wanting to pop into a shop could not stop on the main road. The police turned up in under ten minutes if they tried! In Matlock, shoppers could park on Dale Road on different sides on odd and even dates. Up to eighty cars were also often parked for nothing on Causeway Lane, although forbidden on Imperial Road.

The Council was comparing costs between gas and electric street lighting as the contract with the gas company was near its end. It had been reported in 1924 that electric street lamps were being erected, but that was a short-lived experiment. In 1931 the Derbyshire and Nottinghamshire Electric Power Company asked to tender for replacement lamps and in 1935 two electric lights were trialled on Bakewell Road and Causeway Lane. By September 1937 new lamp posts were "springing up like mushrooms", beginning with Bank Road. Local youths could no longer enjoy themselves throwing stones at the glass panes round the gas mantles, which by this stage numbered 240.

The transformation was not universally welcomed. In 1932 the manager of the Gas Company gave a talk to the Rotary Club. He claimed that the City of Westminster and Birmingham Councils had recently signed new contracts for gas lamps. He also made the point that, in the home, the dirty ceilings which resulted from gas lights come from burnt dust – but better cremated on the ceiling than in our lungs.

The gas works had by now changed hands for a good profit. In 1933 Matlock Bath gas works were sold to Matlock & District Gas Company for £17,500. The works were dismantled, but the holder retained. A new mains carried gas over High Tor. Five men and a lamplighter were transferred. In 1935 the Matlock gas works were sold to the Sheffield Gas Company, who opened a showroom on North Parade to supplement the one on Bank Road, where an electricity showroom was opened next door. The battle for supplying domestic power was a fierce one.

There were calls for coloured lights on Hall Leys, the Promenade at Matlock Bath, and floodlighting for High and Pic Tors. Some thought this was a "cranky idea", but others thought it would pay for itself very quickly from increased Lovers' Walk entrance money and visitor parking. At the end of 1934, money was actually spent, although the next gripe was that the lights only came on after most of the trippers had returned home. In all other resorts, the lights were lit at dusk and stayed on.

The telephone exchange was updated and moved from behind the Town Hall to the Post Office, with three operators: there were now over 250 subscribers. New kiosks in the town meant visitors and residents could call the "rest of the world" if they had "enough silver coins". On Christmas Eve 1928 a visitor at Rockside had been the first in the town to call New York. A nine minute conversation cost him twenty guineas.

In 1934 the Urban District Council expanded again to include North Darley and Bonsall. The last act of the old Council was to approve 137 new houses along the main road between Matlock and Darley Dale. The aspect of the whole area between Matlock and Rowsley was changing with the kind of ribbon development criticised by the town planners. There were, however, still many trees on the roadside which

*Smedley's Hydro from Imperial Road showing houses built c1912
on land sold by the Wolley Dod estate.*

have since been felled. Darley House estate and South Park behind Broad Walk had recently been built; the row of shops was opened in the 1930s. Many more houses were appearing on the hillside. Huge new locomotive sheds and marshalling yards for stone, timber and the Express Dairy had been added adjacent to land where the Alcoa (previously Firth Rixson) factory was later built; that site was still the sports field for railway workers.

In Matlock itself house building was encouraged because the rateable income available from the hydros and shops had stagnated. In 1934 Wildgoose & Sons were advertising new sites, such as the "Asker estate" in the "healthiest part" of the town. An advertisement for "Houses of the Future" featured the art deco homes at Matlock Green, built and designed by E Sadler & Co. In 1940 John Addy began the Mountain View Estate, but this did not seem to extend beyond the row of semi-detached houses at the top of Dimple Road.

MATLOCK BATH

Matlock Bath wears a jaded look as if it had given up the struggle to make people drink its waters. I resent paying money to cross bridges and climb High Tor, I resent the presence of shacks of ginger beer and postcards, shops of Blue John hour glasses and photographic frames and petrified birds' nests.

So wrote a despondent S P B Mais in 1939 and he was an enthusiastic native of the town. The *High Peak News* and *Visiting List* in the 1920s and '30s reported a constant struggle by the Council to keep the town attractive to visitors while combatting

Card posted 1923.

infighting within its ranks. There was the ever present jealousy of the Bank's perceived wealth and spending compared with the Bath.

While Hall Leys Park was thriving – and free – to several hundred visitors each weekend, Matlock Bath councillors made remarks such as, "We have a few monkeys (see Monkey Business) and a few coloured birds and a glorified Prom with penny in the slot machines". By 1930 there were complaints that they lived in "a deserted village" with no indoor place of entertainment. Moreover, the Promenade was locked up and surrounded by canvas, the approach to the Heights of Abraham consisted of old cobblestones covered in sludge and the switchback was lying idle with no tenant or repairs.

The proprietor of one Bath hotel offered to put up councillors for nothing so that they could hear complaints about the Lovers' Walk and Promenade: "The contrast in the appearance of the Hall Leys and Matlock Bath pleasure grounds is so marked that one is forced to the conclusion either that the former is receiving special care and attention or the latter is being purposely neglected or inadequately super-vised".

The Promenade and Lovers' Walk were still subject to an entrance charge. There were often reports that both were actually closed on some days, even in the height of summer, thus, "killing the goose that lays the golden eggs". Free days were an unexpected treat. In July 1927 Busy Bee[5] reported, "Matlock Bath last Saturday had a quite overwhelming surprise. The lovely Promenade was thrown open FREE and

---

5. William Bryan, the columnist in the *Visiting List* known as Busy Bee, died September 1928.

was crowded with visitors, who, in addition to free access, were favoured with the provision of an excellent band, without being bored and annoyed by a demand for the eternal sixpence". But that August the gardens were closed nine days in succession. This left visitors with nowhere to sit down.

Everyone wanted the removal of the unsightly canvas screens which prevented non-payers from seeing the shows: "At present the place looked more like the outside of a circus than a health resort". There were more mentions of the so-called shelter being full of junk. In 1930 there was even a car barring the entrance, which spoilt the aspect of the war memorial. The old acrobat stage was demolished, and the boards used to mend bird cages in the aviary. The pierrots, who still gave concerts, presumably used the band stand.

However, there was a new ferry landing stage and the rockeries had been replenished with rhododendrons and ferns. Mid-decade, new public conveniences were provided near the Midland Hotel and on Lovers' Walk. To the annoyance of shopkeepers, there were fifteen automatic vending machines, but they only brought the UDC an income of £30. In 1930 the Venetian Fete committee paid for electric lights to be erected on the Promenade, but they mysteriously turned up illuminating Hall Leys! In 1932 a Columbia gramophone was placed in the Jubilee Bridge ticket office. After a couple of years, the records were rather scratched: a man on one disc "laughed for five minutes" and one tune was repeated three times an hour. There was no money to replace them.

The sale of Matlock Bath gas works provided a windfall, which allowed the UDC to buy the Lovers' Walk in 1934. This move had become urgent because Mr Drabble had been removing trees. The Council now owned all the riverside from Crown Square to Matlock Bath school, except for the colour works site and some railway land. The Walk had been free to residents for a few years; but from 1931 the visitors to Willersley Castle were also given free entry. As war loomed in 1939, the UDC spent meetings discussing whether this was fair when 40,000 others were paying their 3d.

Why was the Pavilion not thriving? A report in September 1930 said, "practically deserted, rapidly becoming derelict, and serving few useful purposes, the Matlock Bath pavilion presents an ever-present problem for its owners". The loss to the Council in 1927 was put at £300. In 1928 the room used by the glove factory needed its floor repairing. Other rooms were damp, especially the Council offices. The outside walls were bare and dirty. There was talk of closing the building or selling it.

However, in the summer there was still dancing and roller skating in the lower room. In 1930 seventy new pairs of roller skates were purchased. A Brunswick Panatrope was installed to attract young people by playing dance records four evenings a week and on wet afternoons. There were occasional entertainments. In 1934 J Fletcher Ray gave a series of lectures on electricity and psychology with a sermon and hymn singing. (In 1942 he wrote a best seller entitled *The hand that drove the nails*.) There was a library with 500 books.

In the upper room in winter was a cinema, but Mr Randle the manager resigned in 1928. The musicians who accompanied the films were dispensed with, except for the pianist. The UDC decided to book the films by committee.

> As we sped through Matlock Bath in the motor we saw advertised Ethel Dell's "Keeper of the Door", so on Friday we set out on the bus to have tea there and go over to the pictures. However, we must have fancied we were in London for evidently we expected too much from Matlock Bath. When we read the bill to our amazement the show was once nightly at 7.30pm. What a giddy place it is to be sure.
>
> Round and Allen

This was one of the drawbacks: the trippers did not stay late enough to go to the cinema. Moreover, the two other Matlock cinemas had "talkies" from 1930, using expensive equipment. The car park outside the Pavilion earned nearly as much as the film tickets. A Mr Flint took over management of the Pavilion and gardens, but a report in 1932 spoke of a band concert to raise money for his widow.

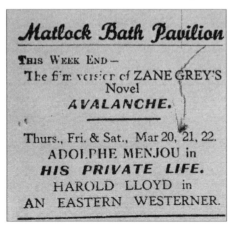

Advertisement March 1930.

In late 1929 the Council discussions about the cinema became very heated with "destructive comments" from Mr White. He accused other councillors of using it as a private club for their families. The *Visiting List* spoke of "detestable and unnecessary personalities". In March 1930 the cinema closed, for which many blamed Mr White – the last night was packed out.

The Pavilion saga then quietened down while Mr White was indisposed and then temporarily moved his political ambitions elsewhere. Instead it was noticed that the

Fishponds, Matlock Bath. No. 820.

[Glynn Waite]

revenue from selling fish food from the machines at the Fishpond in front of the Pavilion had nearly halved. The UDC had previously employed a boy to fill the machines, but in a cost-cutting move had left this task to the car park attendants. One councillor moaned that the fish-food outlet was the "finest asset they had in Matlock Bath" which speaks volumes!

> *Councillor Jacques has no axe to grind,*
> *But lost revenue he bears in mind,*
> *So when fish their food lack*
> *At officials he'll smack*
> *In attempting the culprits to find.*

Visitors paid 1d for fish food from the vending machines. The Council had bought raisins to fill the boxes, but the fish declined to eat them. They tried dog biscuits, but then settled on ordinary broken biscuits. They also paid boys 6d for wasps' nests and grubs. One councillor thought they should provide shrimps "which are cheap". Did these machines smell?

They still had to deal with the Pavilion. Mr Jacques, who liked to bring a poem like the one above into Council meetings, exhorted his fellow councillors to advertise the facilities properly. The letting terms were £200 for the large rooms, but there was no sign anywhere to say so.

> *If you would let the Grand Pavilion – Advertise*
> *Make the matter known to millions – Advertise*

Coaches and charabancs parked at the Pavilion.

From the slumber you've been taking,
It is high time you were waking,
Cut out your fear and shaking – Advertise!

But each applicant had to run the gauntlet of three Council committees: finance, pleasure gardens and the whole Council. This was criticised as no way to treat businessmen. However, the cinema was re-opened by a Mr Thompson of Bakewell in 1932 with talkie equipment. When the Operatic Society staged a very successful *Yeoman of the Guard*, the room was advertised as "warm and cosy". The business was taken by Matlock Cinemas in 1936, but it did not really thrive. In 1938 takings were only ten shillings a night and the acoustics were described as poor. They needed a false ceiling.

In 1939 the repayment of the loan to build the Pavilion finally ended. The interest paid had been £6661. The income, including rates, was still negligible.

In 1937 the UDC was united in anger at the action of the County Council. The time had finally arrived when part of the bottleneck on the main road was to disappear. The County bought the last old garage building to demolish – but instead they opened a "cheap funfair" inside! As Mr Aspey said, "what little bit of good is left in Matlock Bath should be spared any further humiliation". Objections about lack of planning permission fell on deaf ears.

By 1930 Derwent Gardens and the switchback railway were tenantless and in disrepair. Herbert Buxton had died in 1912, one son had emigrated and another died in the War. The third, Harold Buxton, was not well. In 1932 the Spa Amusement

Company, run by Messrs L A Hackett and J Sutton took over. They were manufacturers of fairground equipment, so they demolished the switchback and installed new rides. A toboggan run of 600 feet with two-seater sledges replaced the former railway. New amusements such as "Flash-O-Ball" and "Chair-O-Plane" were installed, although a young girl soon broke both ankles on the latter. There was a bowling game which delivered nine balls and scored automatically. They advertised car parking (cars sixpence), new electric lighting effects, orchestral concerts, grottos, a petrifying well, fish pools and the tea gardens, still run by a Boden – Mrs Warren Boden was John William's daughter-in-law. (He had died in 1928.)

Unfortunately, those who had been glad of quiet times with no switchback railway, were dismayed by the installation of £200's worth of loudspeakers. Mr Hackett promised to angle them away from the church and not play music during services. By 1936 the managers were named as Boden and Hardy: Warren and his son-in-law George Hardy. As well as running Derwent Gardens and Edinburgh House, Warren also took on Hodgkinson's Hotel.

The Fountain Baths pool was still used by the public and classes of school children. Frederick Godfrey also ran a wholesale hair products business on the premises, advertising hair pomades, tonics and dandruff lotion.

Romolo Tinti and his family ran refreshment rooms at Riversdale in the Dale. His son Remo began a coal business which is still remembered. There were a dozen other cafes and restaurants in Matlock Bath, some of which were survivors from an

*South Parade: there is an ice-cream seller behind
the horse and cart. Card posted 1930s.*

earlier age: the Central Restaurant (established 1887 and still the "oldest and largest" in the Midlands), Edinburgh House, Wyvill's and the Fountain Baths. Mobile ice cream vendors were accused of undercutting sales in the shops, but the UDC were powerless to intervene if they were not a nuisance.

Below the New Bath, their roadhouse restaurant (demolished in the 1950s) was popular with motorists. Next door tourists could fill up their cars at Dyson and Clough's petrol station. This was built on the site of a ruined building called Win Tor, and next door to Hartle's Bazaar, one of the old museums which had sold tortoise-shell combs as well as spar ornaments. Both were demolished in the 1930s.

MONKEY BUSINESS

The Council decided to add an attraction to the Lovers' Walk just before the First World War. In the area now occupied by the children's playground was an old bandstand, which was converted in 1913 into a home for seven monkeys. A few weeks later birds arrived to begin an aviary. Not everyone welcomed the move. A member of the Improvements Association complained in January 1914 that at 4am in the morning the parakeets were screaming and the monkeys screeching – he had hoped they would perish in the winter.

The problem of winter temperatures was a continual one. The monkeys – usually rhesus – were sold every autumn and re-purchased in the spring. Surely the same animals came round again and again? The permanent birds and animals were housed for warmth in the infamous non-shelter on the Promenade or even at the back of the Pavilion. In December 1928, for example, twelve monkeys were sold at thirty five shillings each (they had cost fifty shillings), but a lemur, an opossum and the macaws were moved to the glove factory for the winter. The vulture had died, so was not a problem. The RSPCA was not always happy with the living conditions.

Every so often news came of escapees. They lost one of the first monkeys almost immediately, last seen in Willersley Castle grounds. In 1927 a parrot flew away. In June 1922 the town was entertained when a "pack" of wolves was delivered by train from Manchester: one escaped his cage and took possession of the guard's van. The passengers were delayed for twenty minutes.

By 1925 the lone remaining wolf was unhappy. He howled at night, disturbing the sleep of visitors to the hotels. His neighbour the fox was moved, so they could not see each other, because "they were not good friends"; but this did not solve the problem. The town's dogs began to join in the nightly concert. Several people signed a "petition of regret", and the UDC were offered £7 10s for the animal, but the buyer "wanted the Council to pack it". The wolf was offered to Manchester and Blackpool zoos, but they declined. The UDC eventually sold the animal to a Mr Rodgers for £3 – buyer collect.

Two bears were bought for £25 each in June 1930, but they only lasted one season. No-one seems to have realised how big they would become. In November they were sold for £28 10s to George Mottershead for his new Chester Zoo. They did not like the look of the travelling cages he brought. Mr Flint, the Promenade manager, and his staff had to arm themselves with hefty staves and zinc roofing to use as shields before the animals were enticed into the boxes.

Each autumn the UDC did an inventory of the zoo. In 1931 there were 5 budgerigars, 30 foreign birds, 12 doves, 2 plumed doves, 1 diamond dove, 6 Astral parrots, 4 green parakeets, 2 guinea fowl, 1 crane, 1 peacock, 3 pheasants, 2 macaws, 10 rhesus monkeys, 2 lemurs, 2 Indian pigeons and 1 cockatoo.

When war was declared the monkeys were sold immediately, but many of the birds were offered to ratepayers "for the duration". Unbelievably at this crucial period, the UDC spent time discussing who would actually own any birds hatched during the hostilities!

MATLOCK BANK AND BRIDGE

Visitors in the 1930s would see several new facilities at Matlock Bridge, which roused the envy of the Matlock Bath councillors.

Hall Leys Park was developing into the bustling facility we see today, although it has had to be revived and brought up to date in recent times. In the 1920s, there was already a crown bowling green, a children's play area with swings and a seesaw, five tennis courts, a skittle alley and a croquet green. One day in 1928 a thousand people paid to play clock golf. In 1935 £450 was spent at Park Head on a low wall, crazy paving, and the formal flower borders around the old tram shelter. The towns-people asked for a replica war memorial because the elderly found it difficult toiling up the slippery path to Pic Tor each November. In 1930 a second bowling green was opened in front of the Town Hall.

MATLOCK PIC TOR & RIBER CASTLE

The war memorial on Pic Tor – a long climb.

Hall Leys landing stage.
[Glynn Waite]

The UDC decided to reintroduce boating on the river, although conditions were always tricky where Bentley Brook comes in and when the water was high. In 1925, under a headline "the Pirates of Pic Tor", the *Visiting List* chronicled the heroism of six councillors in a motor boat testing the safety of the river between the County Bridge and Artists' Corner: "these brave men with hearts as big as their girths". They encountered rapids, with the "laden boat rushing along at incredible speed into a whirling vortex". Then they returned into the "arms of anxious relatives, who are weeping with joy at their deliverance". A boat hut and steps were constructed from the Broad Walk opposite the back of the Old English Hotel. Five boats were provided, but rowers were advised not to venture downstream past Knowleston Place, so the experience was rather limited.

In 1929 the Rotary Club offered to pay for a surveyor and architect to improve Matlock's parks. Some quite grandiose ideas were discussed because it was felt the town lacked a large enough conference hall. Lubin Wildgoose suggested building a T-shaped glass and iron pavilion on Hall Leys as a venue for meetings, brass band concerts and dancing, and to provide somewhere dry for day trippers.

In 1933 it was reported that councillors were visiting Wicksteed Park in Kettering to price up new play equipment. Then came mention of plans for a boating lake, which were paid for by the Rotarians. A cost of £800 was quoted for a lake with five small islands, a paddling pool and shrubs. The Playing Fields Association offered £250 towards the costs of a paddling pool at least; but the UDC then deferred the whole idea, citing the problem of finding a source of clean running water.

The following year, the Playing Fields Association repeated their offer; this time

Card posted 1935: the flags remain from the Jubilee and lake opening.
[Glynn Waite]

the UDC accepted, asking for more donations via the newspapers. Messrs Aspey and Tinti, both Matlock Bath councillors, protested that money should also be spent on their children, but the grant was specifically for Hall Leys. The Ministry of Health sanctioned spending £2,000 and in December work began using un-employed labourers.

The opening of the boating lake and paddling pool was timed to coincide with the Silver Jubilee in May 1935. Crowds assembled in Hall Leys to praise the King and Queen and congratulate the Council and Wildgoose & Sons on a job well done. The Matlock United Prize Band played on their new instruments, paid for by public donations.

The final cost of the lake and pool came in just under £2000. The lake appeared much as it does today, a water-filled concrete and stone shell with islands planted with shrubs, and the whole surrounded by seats. The lake is two feet deep and the paddling pool was one foot three inches in depth. Public toilets and changing rooms were also provided. Six paddle boats had been purchased at £10 each; they cost 6d per half hour to hire.

The weather that June was exceptionally hot. Children were soon swimming in the boating lake which was not very hygienic, and the boats were impeded. In contrast, the following winter was very cold and the UDC made money charging skaters to use both new facilities! Coloured lights were placed on the islands for skaters at night.

Takings were £78 in the first three months. In 1937 eight motor boats were bought for which the charge was 6d per five minutes. Matlock Bath did get a new paddling pool, but at Easter 1938 Hall Leys received far more visitors because of the boating. The pay booth took £163 against £42 the previous year. Parents obviously felt their children were much safer here than on the river.

Councillor Lubin Wildgoose opening the paddling pool.
[Potter & Co.]

The sight of visitors bathing in two feet of dubiously clean water in Hall Leys convinced many councillors that the town needed a swimming pool. It was felt that Matlock was losing its attraction for young people and they "could not carry on with middle-aged visitors for ever". This was the era of the lido: in Britain more than 160 large open air swimming pools were built in the Art Deco style with diving boards and sunbathing areas. "All over the country prudish ideas are being put aside", wrote the *Visiting List*. New styles and materials for bathing costumes helped the trend.

The UDC also planned to provide "slipper baths", where the public could pay to have a bath. In 1933 the Matlocks had 2670 houses, but 1831 had no bathroom. The problem was actually worse in Matlock Bath, with only 153 baths in 874 houses.

The idea of a lido courted substantial opposition as a waste of public funds. The New Bath had already built its new swimming pool and there was still the Fountain Baths. Locals were perfectly happy risking their lives swimming in Flash Dam and Ladygrove, as well as other small ponds in Darley Dale

Two sites for a lido were suggested. In 1933 the UDC had bought the three acres of Dean Hills, behind the football pitch. However, the more level site was Sparrow Park (also called Imperial Road Gardens) opposite the Post Office. This area had once been a town rubbish heap, but the landowner Mr Wolley had given the land to the town as a garden, albeit rather neglected by this time.

The first real plans for the lido appeared in September 1935 and by the following March the UDC was ready to go to the Ministry of Health for their approval to

327

Bank Road c1930 with Sparrow Park on the left.
[Glynn Waite]

borrow £11,000. An enquiry was to be held at the Town Hall. To the fury of the Council there was a flurry of last minute objections, partly because the plan included four lock-up shops on Bank Road and a café.

The Chamber of Trade weighed in saying the scheme was too ambitious and would damage local shops who already could not make a living. However, their spokesman Mr Twigg was roundly rebuffed by exasperated councillors for not only failing to provide attractions for the town, but also encouraging "the fostering of vermin-breeding refuse dumps and the erection of scrap-iron heaps". The Imperial Road United Methodist church (opened in 1911 next to the Town Hall) objected because the lido would be just across the road and the noise would be unpleasant. At a ratepayers meeting Dr Sparks objected to the tripper element: we would soon have "tripper dances" outside our houses and property values would drop. He asked for a referendum. Others said the lido should be in a spot "where no annoyance would likely to be caused" and where visitors could "disport themselves without restraint". However, a letter of praise in the *Visiting List* congratulated the UDC and told shopkeepers they should be encouraging their efforts to improve a "shoddy and dilapidated" Matlock.

At the enquiry it was decided to drop the shop plans and forbid Sunday dancing in the café. Matlock Lido opened in May 1938 with a water polo match between Derby Swimming club and Sheffield Police, but rain forced the planned bathing costume fashion show into the Town Hall. There were several swimming galas that summer featuring champion swimmers and divers.

The complex was built by Frederick A Roberts, from New Street in Matlock, for a cost of £12,000; extra costs had been incurred because the old rubbish dump beneath the park caused problems. The large open pool was tiled in cream and pale green

Workmen putting finishing touches to the Lido in May 1938.
[Potter & Co.]

MATLOCK'S LUXURIOUS LIDO

Official Opening: THURSDAY, MAY 26th, at 2-30 p.m.
by
Brig.-General C. M. JACKSON, D.L., J.P.
(Admission by Programme, 6d.)
To be followed by

SPECIAL BATHING BEAUTY PARADE
AND DIVING EXHIBITIONS.

Centrally situated, the "Lido" offers a delightful rendezvous, with Matlock's crystal-clear water, constantly heated to 72 degrees, and always perfectly pure and safe. Ample SUN-BATHING facilities — Fashion Costumes for hire — Evening Floodlighting — Café, and many other amenities.
"IT'S NEARER THAN THE SEA!"

with three vermillion diving stages. It could hold 500 swimmers. At one end were two artistic cascades or fountains and a water chute was planned. In addition there was a smaller enclosed pool, five slipper baths, a sun terrace (advertised as "bathing beaches"), and a café with a balcony and roof garden. The water was claimed to be very pure and kept at a temperature over 20 degrees. The site was surrounded by trees rescued from the old park and decorated with flower boxes on the roofs. Many of us remember the baths, but the café and entrance was eventually replaced by Wilkinson's store.

There was floodlighting and amplified music – rather too loud for weekday worshippers at the church and clearly heard by visitors at Smedley's. A path to the Lido was made down from a bottom gate in the Hydro grounds, which is still used by Council employees. The café, which could be hired for dancing, had already taken £987 by October.

Matlock still had two cinemas: the old Picture Palace on Dale Road, until 2013 Bamford's auction house, and the new Cinema House, renamed the Ritz in 1955 and now Maazi Restaurant. In the 1930s they were owned by Matlock Cinemas Ltd, as was the Matlock Bath Pavilion film business.

In 1929 the new owners allowed the Picture Palace to be used to stage Matlock's first pantomime: *Babes in the Wood*. In November 1930 came the grand opening of the talking installation. The film *No, No, Nanette*, which included the song *"Tea for two"*, featured talking, singing, dancing, and technicolour sequences. The diary of the pair from Hagley in 1920 included a visit to the old facilities:

> In the evening we had another bit of fun for we went to Matlock Picture Palace to see the picture "Quinneys". The picture was splendid but the thing that made us laugh was a youth who every few minutes marched first up one side and then the other "squirting fresh air" out of a big syringe and it made such a queer noise and the noise came in at the most inappropriate moments. Fancy as the young man declares his passion and we are all feeling nice and "love me quick and let me sigh", you suddenly heard the squawk, squawk of the fresh air department.
>
> Round and Allen

The more up-to-date Cinema House had been one of the last projects of John William Wildgoose. It opened just before Christmas 1922. The talking picture apparatus was installed in July 1930 for a film called *Holiday Revue*. The following week they showed *The Broadway Melody*. There was a café and a fish and chip supper room, already called the Ritz, open until 10.00pm and on Sundays.

The Cinema House was also used as a large venue when Matlock Operatic

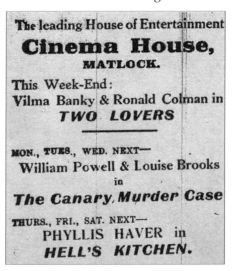

Advertisement March 1930.

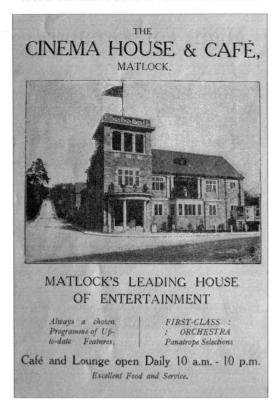

THE
CINEMA HOUSE & CAFÉ,
MATLOCK.

MATLOCK'S LEADING HOUSE
OF ENTERTAINMENT

| *Always a chosen*
Programme of Up-
to-date Features, | *FIRST-CLASS :*
: ORCHESTRA
Panatrope Selections |

Café and Lounge open Daily 10 a.m. - 10 p.m.

Excellent Food and Service.

Society was revived in 1927. They gave annual shows, beginning with a run of Gilbert & Sullivan operas. However, this arrangement had a hiccup when part of the Cinema House was destroyed by fire in June 1931. Luckily the blaze was discovered when an employee let himself back in at 3am to recover a pair of shoes before a trip to London. The balcony, talkie apparatus and stage were beyond repair. The manager blamed the disaster on customers dropping cigarettes on their seats. The rebuilding took a remarkably short time – only a couple of months – but the stage was out of commission for much longer.

After their performance of *The Mikado* in 1929, the Operatic Society held a ball at the Royal Hotel: one of the last events to be held there. After the cinema fire, a couple of operas were performed at the Pavilion, before they returned to the Cinema House with *The Chocolate Soldier*.

Most old photographs of Matlock town centre show a tall chimney outside the railway station. This had been a rag or paint mill, then an electricity store for Smedley's Hydro, followed as tenants by Mr Pride the greengrocer and Mr Broome of Derwent Mills. The owners in 1931 wanted to sell the building, but the Council was worried a purchaser might want to install something unpleasant. In the meantime they created nasty smoke themselves by using the building to burn paper and trade refuse.

In 1914 the *High Peak News* had shown a photograph of George Poyser, who had invented a type of lawnmower. He and his partner were employed by Hall & Company, the ironmonger on Dale Road. A trade exhibition in 1928 said Poyser

*The three tall chimneys of Smedley's, the tramway and
Derwent Mills. The shops at Park Head have yet to be
demolished.*

worked at Spa Engineering on The Dimple, employing twenty men. He produced
the "Daventry" lawn mower, mangles, tennis markers, a hygienic milk can with a
porcelain lining, and tongue and beef cutting machines. However by 1932 he was
probably involved with the Curtis Cultivator Company located in the station mill,
where the chimney was demolished in August 1933. In November 1937 the works
was destroyed by fire, in spite of the fire brigade arriving within three minutes of
the alarm bell sounding. The jobs of forty men were under threat, so the management asked to move into the old tramway depot, but the factory eventually moved
to Manchester.

Derwent Mills Ltd continued production in the old Victoria Hall, with Frederick
Broome as managing director. The old Spring Villa Hydro on Smedley Street had
become part of the works. In addition, they were using the old Cavendish School
building, although this was sometimes listed separately as the Matlock
Manufacturing Company. The 1922 OS map also labelled the old Belle Vue Hydro
as a "glove factory". At the town's 1928 trade exhibition, Derwent Mills was
described as producing "Furida" angora rabbit jumpers, Indian cashmere, alpaca
wool goods and golf wear. Arkle in *Tuppence Up, Penny Down* recalls a nationwide

Furida knitting competition which resulted in thousands of packages arriving at Matlock Post Office. The mill sent a £25 cheque in appreciation, but the Post Master declined the gift, to general disappointment.

Paton and Baldwin, the manufacturer of knitting yarn, had bought Farnsworth's bleaching works in Lumsdale in 1929. In 1931, they bought Derwent Mills and vastly expanded the business, eventually building a factory which dwarfed the Victoria Hall. In 1933 a report said they were laying out gardens, but also laying off eighty workers in Lumsdale. (During the Second World War, the largely female workforce at Paton and Baldwin's was retrained to manufacture taps and dies.)

There were still hosiery works on the Bank. Mr Potter's Tor Hosiery on The Dimple employed thirty people. Crowder Johnson was still using his Victorian looms at his works on Wellington Street. Samuel Skidmore & Sons (established 1784) was now managed by S W Turner and had moved into one of Smedley's shops, as well as keeping a branch in Matlock Bath.

Smedley Street was now a very busy shopping and business area. Several names appeared which remain or have only recently disappeared. Bailey's chemist (later Broome's) across from Smedley's had a licence to sell alcohol. American guests staying in the teetotal hydro were very adept at smuggling whisky into their bedrooms – they had practised during the Prohibition. Michael Wright, who had supplied so much hydropathic equipment over the years, died in 1935 aged 89 years. Two of his sons carried on the ironmongery, known to us all as Tinker Wright's. Walter Ash had a boot and shoe shop in both East and West Smedley Street: the name W Ash has only recently disappeared from the tiny shop near the crossroads.

Caring for visitors' cars and hiring out vehicles was now an important occupation. Farmer Brothers had garages in Smedley and Wellington Street. They were specialists in repairing Morris motor cars and hiring out charabancs and landaulettes. One son, Charles Farmer, began selling chargers for the lead acid batteries which powered radios in a hut adjacent to the garage. Soon he was selling radios and bicycles. This electrical goods business is now on Causeway Lane.

Harold Bradbury hired out cars from his West End Garage. Fred H Slater developed from being a plumber and electrician into being an automobile engineer and selling Hillman motors. William Furniss's sons ran a motor haulage business from Field House on Smedley Street West; they had sold their buses to the North Western Road Car Company. Gladwin motor cars were listed at Woburn Cottages.

Opposite Sycamore House Hydro, the John Higgs alms houses were built in 1930. Mr Cobb, a jeweller on the street, was famous for making the world's two smallest working engines, one smaller than a fly, one than a match head. He took the second one to the Chicago World's Fair in 1933.

One business had an upper and lower premises. The Goodwin family opened the Rock Café in George Statham's old confectionery shop in Wellington Square, the wide area by the tram depot. This allowed them to claim it was established in 1844. They also took over Boden's old café at the bottom of Bank Road next to Orme's grocery. They called themselves "hydro supply specialists" for cheeses and cooked meats, which they displayed in a refrigerated BTH Coldrator show counter. In 1932 their baker was "highly commended" for his Dundee cake at the National Bakers' and Confectioners' Exhibition in London. In 1937 he was awarded honours for

The Rock Café today.

The Co-op in Crown Square. Mottersheads was a shoe shop.
[Glynn Waite]

Dundee and "slab cake": a large flat fruit cake.

Crown Square was a mixture of old and new faces. During the First World War, the Goodalls left their shop to work for the Red Cross. The Derwent Valley Co-operative Society expanded from its Smedley Street base and opened a drapery store in the premises, followed by food departments in neighbouring units. In 1934 Arthur Dakin, who had moved his salon and newspaper business into the shop next to the bridge, won the "Eugene" golf cup for hairdressers at St Anne's-on-Sea.

The gas showroom on Bank Road was joined by an electricity office next door. As well as the Rock Café, there was another tearoom called Evans and Dewhurst's butcher's shop. The big premises on the corner opposite the Post Office was built in the late 1920s. Two ladies ran a millinery and dress shop, which had to be sold by 1938 because of the terms of a will. T Greaves the house furnisher moved in, but Haydn Stanley, the current owner, still found huge irons in the basement.

The garage built by William Furniss (now The Crown) had been taken by Joseph Allen who had begun business on Hackney Lane, but moved to Dimple Farm. He began as a haulier, carting coke to the gas works, but he had also driven his hearse for hundreds of funerals. Joseph died in 1933, but he had three sons to carry on. Their advertisement mentioned shillibeers, which were horse-drawn mourning coaches.

In 1914 Hand's Garages Ltd had built new premises between Furniss's and the Crown Hotel, in a space previously occupied by Robert's the printer and some messy hoardings. They advertised garage accommodation for a hundred cars, as well as their own first class landaulettes and motorised charabancs. They sold their buses to the North Western Road Car Company. Hand's were replaced by Kenning's Ltd by 1936. This building (now Greggs and Holland and Barrett) was also occupied

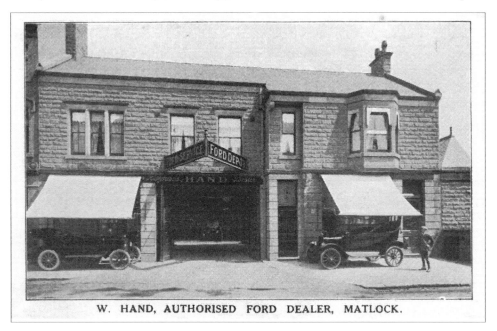

W. HAND, AUTHORISED FORD DEALER, MATLOCK.

[Glynn Waite]

THE GASSY-GESSEY PARADE

The showroom opened in 1925. The date is still on the building.
[Glynn Waite]

[Glynn Waite}

for a time by Stanley Fearn, who began his business in Darley Dale. Hand's also had a booking office across the road under the archway.

Stanley Fearn's cycle shop moved to its current site in 1926. Stanley's daughter had a second shop nearer Crown Square in the premises with steps and iron hand rails. Between them they offered bicycles, wirelesses, HMV gramophone records, Carter's seeds and fertilisers and ironmongery; Mr Fearn often provided prizes for local competitions. Bicycles could be purchased on hire purchase from 2/6d a week and motor cars could fill up with petrol. There were two other cycle shops on Dale Road: Mellor's and Raynes & Son.

Established in 1905, William Twigg's works expanded their site on Bakewell Road. They were metal reclamation specialists, for example buying the tramcars and cable when the tramway closed. (Parts of the tramway shelter were used as bus shelters next to the Railway Hotel and Burgon's shop.) In the 1920s Twigg's bought Wingerworth Hall for demolition and in 1933, Ilam Hall, although they re-sold that building as described later.

Bertram Mills Circus on the cricket pitch probably in 1934.
[Glynn Waite]

The land opposite the Railway Hotel was still being used for fairs. Chapman's zoo came in 1934, but the cricket and football grounds provided bigger sites. A market was being established, which survived outside until the bus station and market hall were built. Next door the North Western Road Car Company erected its art deco omnibus depot.

On Dale Road, the new bank on the corner became the Midland in 1938, until 2015 HSBC. W N Statham's photographic studio had diversified with a china depot. Pilkington's chemist shop had become J E Hadfield, but he used the same advertisements. Annette's hair and beauty salon opened in Hall's ironmongery, offering marcel waving and the "perfect perm". Noel Wheatcroft opened his auctioneer's office in the old market hall, which still contained several bazaars – not much different from its present use. Wallis's shoe shop sold "K" shoes, which in 1940 were labelled as "value for war-time".

One big name had arrived by 1916: Boots the Chemist, which was in the distinctive shop now occupied by Indigo. During the 1930s, Woolworth tried to build a store next to Dr Meachim's home in Red House. They were refused several times because there was not enough space behind the building line, which depended on the road width. (Woolworth opened on Causeway Lane in 1956.)

The Town Hall continued to be used for local balls and concerts, the "hills and dales" of the dance floor having been improved in 1927. The following year they held a shopping week display, which became briefly an annual event. A branch library opened in the evenings with five hundred books. (The library moved to its current site in 1944.)

In 1930 Riber Castle was for sale, but did not reach the asking price. Captain Lionel Garthorne Wilson had been the headmaster of the boys' boarding school since 1924, but his wife died and he wanted to move away. The UDC were in a quandary. They would be equally criticised if they spent money on "Matlock's Folly", or if they let it fall down. In 1936 they bought the empty building for £1,150. But what could they do with it? A museum was one possibility because for several years the Council had been given donations of historic items, including prehistoric relics donated by a grateful hydro patient. To these they planned to add the bedstead used by Florence Nightingale in the Crimea and Arkwright's frame from his old mill.

They did recoup some money before the War by throwing the grounds open and charging admission: 3d for adults, 1d for children. A surprising number of people went to take a look: eight thousand visitors in the first year brought in £100. The Council even rigged up some floodlighting for the Coronation – the fifteen large lamps cost £43 – but the effect was disappointing. During the War, the building was requisitioned by the Ministry of Food as a store.

In 1934 the Wishing Stone was given to the UDC by Ernest Bailey on condition the area was landscaped, for which they spent £123.

In 1935 the ladies of the Townswomens' Guild were asked their opinion of Matlock. They did not like the litter left by tourists, especially on Pic Tor: they wanted litter baskets; they wanted seats in the Dale; they wanted a crossing place in Crown Square, a public clock in Matlock Bath, a better footpath to the war memorial, a playing field, and a better market ground. They asked for the music festival to be revived (see below), for shops to close on Sundays – and, of course, for the hoardings to be removed on Bakewell Road.

In the coronation year of 1937, Harry Douglas proposed a formal town "attraction committee" of men and women in order to spruce up the town and bring in visitors for specific events. They would work with the UDC pleasure grounds committee. They issued a portfolio of dates, not all new, but with the intention of producing a cohesive programme. This included knockout cricket, an open tennis tournament on Hall Leys and the Darley Dale courts, and open bowls and golf tournaments, all with UDC trophies. They wanted to reintroduce the floral fete and swimming galas at Matlock Bath, and a second Venetian fete and band contests.

They intended to book variety performances split between venues and hold open-air whist drives. They wanted to stage county cricket and an agricultural show. Having seen what Willersley Castle had prepared for the coronation, they tendered for illumination schemes. (A huge floodlit crown did appear on the top of Rockside Hydro.)

As described later, several of these plans did briefly come into fruition, but world events intervened before they could really get started.

THE DAY TRIPPER

In *Derbyshire* A R Hope Moncrieff wrote in 1927, "One may be a little put out by the way in which the Matlock (Bath) people exploit their beautiful curiosities, fencing in the finest bits, and levying a "gate" on the performances of nature while everywhere the scenery is disfigured by flaring boards to attract custom. The trail of the tripper is over it all".

During the '30s there were usually twenty to twenty-five excursion trains at Whitsuntide and August Bank Holidays. But now the trippers could come by motor coach or even under their own steam. Guests at Smedley's observed through their field glasses an endless procession of motors, cycles and coaches as the "holiday caravanserai" passed along the valley floor. In 1934 a shopkeeper in Dale Road counted the passing cars on Whit Monday for ten minutes at 6.00pm. They came by at a rate of twelve per minute. There were complaints about cyclists parking their machines "anywhere". 1937 was a typical year of mixed fortune. Easter brought 27 excursion trains, but it rained all Whitsuntide and the Promenade was empty. At the August Bank Holiday, 24 trains arrived and tents were pitched on the hillsides.

Some of the visitors were still coming on works outings. In 1932 more than two thousand came from the Birmingham Co-operative Society; they were charged half price to visit the Lovers' Walk. In 1934 the Publicity Association arranged for the "biggest party ever", from Montague Burton the tailor. Mr Aspey at the Heights of Abraham negotiated a shilling ticket for railway travellers to visit several

High Tor refreshment rooms.
[Glynn Waite]

339

attractions: his own, Lovers' Walk and High Tor.

The UDC pleasure grounds committee agreed that Hall Leys and the Promenade should take it in turns to plant new spring bulbs. They installed some illuminations in both centres and floodlights on High Tor, but were criticised for being foolish to try to rival Blackpool. However, the visitors to the hydros could see the lights in Hall Leys and expressed their appreciation. On the other hand, visitors to the Venetian Fete were cross when the lights were turned out before they went home.

Music festivals were very popular at this time. Entries included both solo singers and village choirs, with elocution contests and country dancing. Newspapers filled whole pages with the results. From 1923 until the early thirties Matlock Bath ran such an event each summer, organised by Captain Wilson from Riber School. In 1931 there were thirty-six classes and 440 entries. In 1932 there were 700 competitors. For two or three days the contestants performed in the Pavilion, the church hall and at Masson Mill.

There was a strange report in 1930 that stewards had been needed because the terrible noise made outside by newsboys and people with tin whistles and trumpets had made the judges' task difficult. After a few years it was decided that money prizes were no longer affordable: the winners would have to be satisfied with certificates. In 1933 the whole thing seemed to fizzle out, even though similar contests, for example in Buxton, went from strength to strength attracting international choirs.

Brass bands were also having mixed fortunes. The UDC discussed the viability of hiring Matlock Prize Band, at £93 for twenty concerts, because live music was no longer a great attraction – people had the wireless and gramophones at home. Brass band competitions were in the doldrums and the trophies were given to the Venetian Fete to hold a smaller competition. In 1936 the Venetian Fete committee

The band stand in Hall Leys Park. The chimney of Paton & Baldwin is on the hillside.

held the first musical fete on the Lovers' Walk. In 1938 the band contest judge said he "did not think he had ever heard worse playing"! Because of rain, they had adjourned to the Pavilion and the instruments did not adapt to a different atmosphere.

However, Matlock's own Prize Choir and Band, usually conducted by Lubin or Lawrence Wildgoose, were thriving. A programme of The Messiah performed at Smedley's in 1927 listed a summary of the Choir's awards so far: 42 firsts, 24 seconds, 11 thirds, 32 shields, 5 cups and over £500 in cash prizes. In 1933 they performed for the radio. In August 1938 the "whole town" tuned in to hear the Band broadcast from Manchester, one of several such concerts.

In 1933 the Venetian Fete itself had suffered three wet events which had reduced their reserve balance from £400 to £10. They asked to share some money from the gas works sale, but were told they had to support themselves. Other events seemed to occur at irregular intervals. In 1930 a gala day included swimming, decorated boats, a river gymkhana, country dancing and a fell race to Riber. In 1937 Matlock Bath's floral fete was revived with hundreds of blooms woven into patterns and a river gymkhana. The Jubilee Bridge and the bandstand were described as a solid mass of flowers.

The annual big event in Matlock was the carnival, said to be the biggest in the county. The revelry lasted for three days each September. The profits were given to the Whitworth Hospital and Derby Royal Infirmary – vital income for them before the National Health Service.

On the first day the Carnival King and Queen gave speeches at the Town Hall, followed by a procession round the town. Visiting carnival queens were later introduced, who processed through Rockside and Smedley's Hydros collecting money. In 1934 Smedley's was floodlit for the first time with coloured lights: it was described as looking like a German castle. On the second day was a baby show and children's fancy dress competitions, followed by a ball. On the final day, girls sold flowers, the decorated shops were awarded prizes and a treasure hunt was held. Over the years, other events were added: a [6]Dunmow Flitch competition, mock trials, balloon races, and wrestling and crooning championships. In 1933 the Motor Cycle Club held a gymkhana which included a rider jumping through fire with a lady riding pillion.

That same year, the Whitsuntide holiday had been very hot. The tar on the roads melted and, "visitors in shorts or beach pyjamas – in some cases even in bathing suits – look comfortably cool".

In 1934 Bertram Mills circus came direct from London to the cricket pitch for three days. (Did that not ruin the grass?) The show included cricketing elephants and

6. Named after a village in Essex, couples had to convince a jury that they had not regretted being married any time in the previous year. Successful couples won a flitch or side of bacon.

Ross Robot Mechanical Man. (He was actually a real man pretending to be a robot, controlled by a Miss Sophie Ross.) The big top was lit by 2000 electric lights and seated 3000 people, who could also visit the menagerie and stables.

In July 1937 the UDC and the "attraction committee" held their first tennis week during a spell of good weather: they awarded 36 prizes. The first bowls week attracted 217 entries. In November, a table tennis week was held in the Town Hall. The following year, four County table tennis titles were awarded during the competition.

In 1936 the publicans in Matlock Bath asked for a bar extension to 10.30pm from June to September, as permitted in Bakewell and Buxton. They argued that evening excursion trains arrived at 6.00pm and did not leave until 11.00pm. They were actually granted the extension from April to October on probation. The Reverend Alfred Phibbs said the town had "rather an evil reputation" but the police reported they had had only six convictions for drunkenness, all local men. The UDC criticised the vicar for exaggerating; but he had hardly started – see below!

At the end of each busy Bank Holiday, the police gathered by the school on Derby Road. Then they "swept" the visitors through Matlock Bath, until they could be sure they were all safely back on their trains and buses.

NEVER ON A SUNDAY – BUT IT DEPENDS WHO YOU ARE!

Sunday visitors, who had hoped the departure of the Arkwright family would change the regime on the river, were still disappointed. Even the ferry remained fastened up. The councillors were afraid that allowing Sunday boating would encourage all the sports to make demands. However, in 1930 Sunday boating was allowed from Hall Leys, even though one councillor objected it would attract the "scum of outlying towns". In 1937 the question of Sunday boating came up again, because the UDC had promised that once they actually owned the Lovers' Walk it might become possible. At their May meeting, the Council took an inexplicable decision. Not only did they not allow Matlock Bath any Sunday boating, they forbade it in Matlock!

Matlock Bath traders called a public meeting and forced the decision to be reversed. The step was so popular that two more rowing boats had to be purchased and the hours increased to 9pm in mid-summer. One resident, who spent her childhood in one of the shops backing onto the river, can remember summer evenings lying in bed and watching the light from the river reflected on her bedroom ceiling as she listened to the calls of the rowers and the splash of the oars.

In August 1936, everyone seemed taken aback by an attack in the form of a resolution from the Matlock Bath Parochial Church Council to the UDC, deploring "Continental Sunday" behaviour. The management at the Pavilion seemed to be their main target, but their complaints managed to sound vague and vitriolic at the same time. The amusements at the Pavilion were of "a questionable nature" and a "gambling den" which led parents to worry about "demoralising influences". In the Derwent Gardens (not actually named) was an "indecent peep-show machine" and their loudspeakers gave out a racket which disturbed church services. Female cyclists were indecently dressed. They demanded a purge of the "unprofitable tripper element". The Council did have some sympathy and resolved to meet with Matlock Cinema Company. They certainly wanted rid of the chair-o-planes which had appeared in the car park. Unfortunately, of course, the trippers were not unprofitable. One could not encourage excursion trains and then veto the passengers.

The affair became a farce because the *High Peak News* headline, "One of most wicked spots in England" was taken up by the national dailies. The public flocked in to see what they were missing! The UDC could only hope the issue would quietly go away. Judism, a columnist in the *News*, had some fun:

> With bated breath tis said,
> (With many a leerin' grin),
> That Matlock Bath alas in troth
> Is a city full of sin.
>
> And in surprisingly short time,
> Chicago read the news,
> And her racketeers and gangsters
> Were depressed and got the blues.
>
> "Sawed-off Shotgun Riley",
> A noted racketeer,
> Said, "Say, Boys, Matlock Bath's gone bad –
> Let's emigrate to there".
>
> In New York too, Red Killer,
> The G Men's deadly foe,
> Packed up his grip and took a trip
> And to Matlock Bath did go.
>
> And in Hollywood, those bad, bold vamps
> Read the news with consternation
> And solemnly concluded
> That they'd lost their reputation.

Whenever Sunday restrictions were in danger of becoming relaxed, the wicked Spanish were always invoked. As Councillor Petts remarked, "If we keep drifting on in this country, we should be as bad as Spain". What did they imagine went on there? The vicar of Matlock said that the UDC should make no changes to games in Hall Leys without a clear mandate from the ratepayers.

Those who saw no problem with Sunday sports pointed out that the amusements in Derwent Gardens made the town noisier than Skegness or Blackpool, but they could not have a quiet game of tennis. In Hall Leys visitors could use the boating lake, the swings and the paddling pool, but not play tennis or bowls. The new Lido did open on Sundays.

The fact was not lost on the general public that the visitors in the hydros could play any game they wished anytime. Furthermore, the sanctimonious councillors, who forbade Sunday games, enjoyed their golf on a Sunday afternoon, well-hidden up on Matlock Moor, while the frustrated park visitors could only gaze wistfully at the locked tennis and bowls huts. The Council were sent a poem:

Matlock Golf Clubhouse.

Of all the days that's in the week,
I much dislike but one day
And that's the day that comes between
A Saturday and Monday.

All games taboo – there's nought to do
But sit and smoke; and view and view
Of empty courts and greens and stands,
Where should be young and old, and bands.

In desperate mood the bus one takes
And seeks the moor so breezy:
Finds lucky toff can play his golf.
Naught said makes him uneasy.

But don't despair and tear your hair:
One favour now they've granted:
If you should wish the boats are there,
To hire "cash down" if wanted.

THE OPEN ROAD

In the 1920s there had been a helpful regular feature in the *High Peak News* entitled "Is skidding dangerous?" There were also weekly columns on "The state of the roads", listing bad surfaces, road works and other hazards. For motorists in trouble, or needing a map, patrolmen from the AA (founded 1905) and RAC (founded 1897) were a common sight, whizzing around on their motor cycles. The Automobile Association had been founded partly to aid motorists to avoid speed traps, but after a test case, when this was deemed to be obstructing the police, they concentrated more on helping with advice and repairs. However, failing to salute a member displaying the AA badge was still a signal that there was some hazard (or policeman) ahead.

The hydros provided garages, but at an extra cost.
[Glynn Waite]

Henry Douglas, the last manager of Smedley's, and his
brother (Alfred) George, were keen motor cyclists.
[Jean Douglas]

The 1930s saw a huge increase in the use of motor cars and cycles. It is no exaggeration to say that two or three people were killed in road accidents in the Peak District every week. The reports of these accidents and subsequent court proceedings were a major feature of the *High Peak News*. It is not possible to state if this area was particularly hazardous, but the steep hills must have played a part. The Via Gellia and Cromford Hill were blackspots, but a surprising number of people came to grief in the towns, especially on Dale Road, where lamp posts and walls were frequently damaged. There were several fatal motor cycle accidents at Artists' Corner where the road was very narrow and had a bad camber until widened in 1935.

In June 1935 additional 30mph signs went up in the town. Several were on pavements and pedestrians walked into them. The Council called them "daft things" and agreed with the public that they should be removed. There was confusion locally because initially the restriction sign at the Derby end of Matlock Bath was not repeated all through Matlock and Darley Dale until being de-restricted at the far side of Rowsley. Visitors to Smedley's had to be careful because drivers racing along Smedley Street, to avoid being seen speeding in the valley, tended to shoot past the front door with merely a warning hoot.

Many motor cycles and some cars did not actually have speedometers. Strangers could not believe they should be going at 30mph through the rural parts of Darley Dale; in the first months, two thirds of all visitors were caught speeding. The first successful prosecutions – all for transgressions in Darley Dale – resulted in fines of 10 shillings.

The Magistrates had some sympathy with the motorists and contacted the Police. In October 1935 the 30mph restriction disappeared, for the time being, between Matlock gas works and Rowsley. When the road in the Dale had been widened and improved, the Magistrates immediately asked for the 30mph speed limit to be removed between Greatorex's quarry and Holme Road and this was granted. For those who wanted to speed legally, the first local grass track race meeting was held in 1928. The Motor Cycle and Light Car Club began meeting on High Tor, but soon moved to Cromford Meadows.

The AA had made itself responsible for putting up many village signs and warnings of hazards such as sharp corners. But in 1937, the County Council began to do the work systematically with "halt at major road ahead" signs etc. Again, the magistrates were often lenient as motorists were taken by surprise. One visitor, prosecuted for driving down the wrong side of the new dual carriageway at Picory Corner, said he had never seen such a thing. How was he supposed to know what to do?

Pedestrian crossings appeared with Belisha beacons. All this was too much for a correspondent in the *High Peak News*. He was going to Europe on holiday to get away from all the legislation. With an "au revoir Belisha", he wanted to go where no town was disfigured by a cross between a "pawnbroker's dream of paradise and an artificial orange grove"; where the only speed limit would be common sense; he could drink at any time; and he did not need headlights where there were street lights.

However, many casualties were unwary pedestrians, especially children. A local motor engineer gave a demonstration on how to get run over without injury. The secret, apparently, was to keep the bonnet away from one's head and to use one's legs to lever the car over one's body!

Until the late 1920s, there was no ambulance service in the Matlocks. Any casualty, including anyone injured in a quarry or mill, was bundled into a passing car, or, if they were lucky, the doctor's car. In 1928 a local St John's Ambulance brigade was formed, with a drill room on Imperial Road. The UDC bought them a new ambulance in 1935, an ex-demonstration Ford which cost £465. However, in 1936 there occurred a bitter row between the Red Cross and the St John's Ambulance. It seemed to be about whether certain people were qualified enough in first aid to be trusted with the vehicle. Neither side would back down, so the Council solved the matter by keeping the vehicle behind the Town Hall with the fire engine. A driver would respond to a telephone call to Matlock 1. The minimum charge was five shillings, but a trip to a Derby hospital cost £1, and to Sheffield £1 5s. The Whitworth Hospital had to bear the cost of minor accidents to visitors: these numbered 115 per year in 1929, a rise from 11 in 1900.

FURTHER AFIELD

Access to the countryside, and its preservation, was a major concern in the 1930s. Several organisations became involved as the working and middle class masses were being granted whole weeks of paid leave and were no longer satisfied with one annual outing on a Bank Holiday.

Visitors to the hydros still ventured out on short local walks. The "Come to Derbyshire" guide extolled that the town is "a paradise for the walker. Go in any direction from Matlock and new delights will be found".

One sunny day Miss Round and Mrs Allen walked the five miles from Smedley's to Rowsley:

> As you get into Rowsley you might easily imagine you were coming to a huge town for the railway tracks, sidings and the noise of engines and the smoke are enough to herald a fine town approach, but lo and behold the place is just a pretty country village with a river running through and about two or three shops and a bridge and a station but so dear and old fashioned. The Station Hotel [now the Grouse & Claret] where we thought we would have to stay for tea didn't look inviting at all, more like a barrack room, so we went on in the hope of finding a clean little cottage as one reads

about in books. We did not find the cottage, we did not even look for it, for as we turned the corner there stood The Peacock. It does not sound as pretty as it looked with its tiny old fashioned windows, its open doors, its gleaming old oak panelling and chests, all of which invite us in and in we went, expecting to pay through the hat for all the old things and not for the tea. By the funny little fireplace were several motorists and I should imagine in the summer especially it is a favourite resort for travellers.

Our tea was served up beautifully on a tray which had a real linen cover on and all the blue and white china was painted with the Peacock design and everything was so dainty and sweet. We had hot buttered scones, bread and butter and jam, sugar and cake, quite a nice tea and what is more we paid the same as tea at any old house.

Another day the pair went on the bus to Cromford, but were not impressed:

Did I say bus? Think of a Ford engine with two sides and the roof stuck together by stamp paper and a seat or two stuck in anyhow, a horn held on with dirty tape, then you have the "bus".

They decided to walk back to Matlock over the hills; they had already lost their way on previous rambles round the towns, even admitting to knocking down walls in frustration. Up on Matlock Moor they had asked a local man if they could go a particular way, and he had replied, "Oh yes, I've bin me sel, you will find a road somewhere up there"!

The instructions we had for reaching Matlock by the hill way were very typical. "You turn to the right up a steep hill (as if all the hills were not steep) and when you think you have come to the last house enquire again." We passed three cottages at the foot of the hill then climbed up and climbed up again, but we never came to the last house for the simple reason there were no houses at all. All we could see to the left of us were walls, walls, walls and Nestle's[7] milk sheds. It seems they collect the milk from miles around here. Dotted about here, there and everywhere are these stone cattle sheds, hence of course the title Nestle's Swiss Milk! The sheds are there, the cans are there, but where were the cows?

On arriving down to the bottom of the hill, we found ourselves in a village called Bonsall, certainly the queerest thing we struck for a long time. Just a few poor little straggling cottages and there is a notice up saying that if the people neglect to pay the poor rate they will be fined. Why the poor things look as if they ought to have the poor rate paid to them.

The lady we enquired the way told us to go through two stiles over two fields, then ask the man with the muck rake, in other words the man spreading manure. We came to the manure, but alas the man had vanished. Round and Allen

Motorised charabancs allowed longer day trips than previously. Chatsworth was still the favourite nearby destination, but Haddon Hall was closed for much of the decade, as the family made more use of the house. A fire in 1925 had destroyed the

---

7. The Nestlé factory in Ashbourne, opened in 1912, collected milk direct from the farmers.

A motor charabanc in Matlock Bath.
[Glynn Waite]

" Silver Service Coaches "
Luxury Motor Coaches For Hire to Private Parties.
Day Excursions to the Seaside a Speciality.
J. H. WOOLLISCROFT & SON LTD.,
SILVER SERVICE GARAGE, MATLOCK.
Phone : Darley Dale 25.

stable tearoom, along with many tapestries which were being stored upstairs during restoration of the banqueting hall. In 1931 Mrs Sarah Eads died, the chatelaine who had welcomed thousands of visitors. Notices warned hikers not to trespass and trees were growing to hide the view. However, visitors could now easily reach Bolsover and Peveril Castles. Chatsworth Hydro ran outings to Welbeck, Rufford and Clumber. Rockside organised a visit to watch the polo at Osmaston Manor.

There were coach tours for visitors who did not mind mixing with the hoi polloi from the town. Mr J H Woolliscroft ran a bus service between Matlock and Bakewell, but branched out with his Silver Service motor garage. He advertised "sun saloon" coaches which ran "Over Hill and Dale" to Lathkill and Bradford Dales or set out on "mystery tours" and days at the seaside.

In 1932 East Midland Motor Services began an express motor coach between Matlock and Sheffield for 4/6d return. The North Western Road Car Company ran excursions daily from Crown Square. Trent Motor Traction provided buses and coaches to destinations all over the county. Even James Smith's nurseries washed their lorry out at weekends and called it the "Primrose Bus".

Aeroplanes were being sighted. In 1922 the first 'plane to arrive in Matlock Bath landed in a field up at Hearthstone near Riber. The pilot from Doncaster had become lost, but spotted Chatsworth and flew down the river valley. Friends of his had climbed the Heights of Abraham to await his arrival, knowing that he needed quite a large field to land safely. In 1928 an RAF 'plane famously crash-landed in a field near Matlock Golf Club on a flight from Chester to Woodford in Nottinghamshire. The machine was fairly undamaged until willing volunteers tried to turn it round. In thick grass, they hit a wall and turned the plane over in the lane. In 1930 free flights from Riber were offered by Wolverhampton Aviation Company

Cyclists and ramblers could stay in a new type of accommodation. The Youth Hostel movement was begun by a German schoolmaster called Richard Schirrmann, who had opened his first hostel in Altena Castle in 1912. The movement spread after the First World War and Schirrmann became President of the International YHA in 1933-36, before the Nazis removed him from office.

Richard Schirrmann, founder of Youth Hostels, at Overton Hall.

In 1934 the International YHA's third annual conference was held at Willersley Castle, with German as the official language. *The Derbyshire Countryside* emphasised the importance of German youth travelling to Britain as an "obvious important contribution to world peace". Herr Schirrmann visited Overton Hall and Hartington Hall Youth Hostels. At the latter, he planted a copper beech tree, which is still there with its plaque. He praised the friendly atmosphere in our hostels, which he attributed to the fact that they had previously been real homes. They included at this time Errwood Farm in the Goyt valley, Pool Hall Farm in Hartington, Flaxdale House in Parwich and Melbourne House on Temple Road in Matlock Bath. As *The Derbyshire*

Countryside commented, "a delightful and somewhat strenuous six days can be spent in a Derbyshire tour". The YHA's own advertisement called Derbyshire the "Finest Tramping Area".

The Prince of Wales had already opened Derwent Hall Hostel on a visit to Derbyshire in 1932 to inspect the work of Rural Community Councils; he also laid the foundation stone of the Florence Nightingale village hall in Lea. (Derwent Hall was demolished in 1944 when the reservoir was built.)

William Twigg bought Ilam Hall in Dovedale for £1,000 in 1933, probably intending to demolish the building for recycling, as he had done in the case of Wingerworth Hall. But he sold it on to Sir Robert McDougall, who gave it to the Youth Hostel Association, along with large tracts of land to the National Trust. In 1935 Ilam Hall became an International Youth Hostel and one of England's largest, thanks to funding from McDougall, the Cadbury family and the Carnegie Trust.

Tor Cottage in the Dale had become empty, when no longer needed as an annex to Matlock Modern School. In 1933 it opened as a 40-bed ramblers' hostel, with a Mr and Mrs W Barton as wardens. However, they left in 1937 and the property became High Tor Guest House. The vicarage in Matlock Bath became a hostel in the 1950s.

Rambling groups of predominately working-class men came in their hundreds to Derbyshire and Staffordshire from Greater Manchester and Sheffield. Some were bent on gaining open access to the private moorland grouse-shooting areas: their most famous action was the Mass Trespass on Kinder Scout in April 1932. This was followed by a gathering of 10,000 people at Winnats Pass. The Ramblers' Association was founded in 1935, which led to coordinated efforts to support the Access to Mountains Bill of 1938 and the establishment of National Parks.

In the *"Come to Derbyshire"* Guide of 1934, Mr du Garde Peach predicted, "A day

The National Trust did not want litter in Dovedale.

will come when the whole of the High Peak will be taken over by the nation and turned into a great National Park". There were already proposals to make Dovedale the first part of this scheme. Mid-decade large areas of the Dove and Manifold valleys were bequeathed or handed over to the National Trust. In 1937 the disused Manifold Railway track became a footpath. The *High Peak News* reported at regular intervals as other large tracts of land near the Matlocks became protected by the National Trust: Alport Heights, Shining Cliff Woods and some of Stanton Moor. In 1933 a fire in Alderwasley Woods lasted for several days, which revealed fresh views of Shining Cliff.

Not everyone was thrilled by the actions of the ramblers and other newly enthusiastic visitors to the wild places. Motor bikes became a nuisance on rural lanes. Landowners, whether they were justified or not in keeping walkers off grouse moors, could see the dangers to natural habitats when groups camped in large numbers in the fields. Damage was done to bird nesting sites and wild flowers were uprooted. In 1933 a letter from a resident of Bradwell said walkers had "destroyed the haunts of the nightjar and nightingale". The ramblers were accused of lighting fires; they did certainly leave far too much litter, especially in Dovedale, where the countryside wardens collected it by the sack-load.

Many walkers were satisfied with the existing paths, deploring the actions of the more aggressive agitators. Peaceful ramblers and cyclists arrived on weekend trains and passed through the Matlocks, patronising the cafes and shops. However, the local clergy did worry about the morals of mixed groups: in August 1932 there came a report of 300 couples sleeping in one field at Hathersage.

The Hikers' Debacle (with apologies to Longfellow)

Came the hikers from the city
With their packs upon their shoulders,
With their wigwams and their stew-pots,
With their squaws in summer garments,
Out to camp midst fields and heather,
In the sunshine and the summer.
It was August, glorious weather,
When they left the smoky city,
Hiking for the fields and woodlands,
Laughing, singing, full of pleasure,
Bending, singing, kissing, laughing,
Full of life and joie-de-vivre;
Set the wigwams on the hilltops,
Lit the fires and cooked the victuals,
Lay down on their folded blankets,
Sleeping, dreaming of the morrow,
Of the sunshine and the [8]Lido,
Where they bathe down by the river.
Hundreds slept there under canvas
As the moon lit up the heather.
Dark clouds gathered on the sky-line,
Like an army swift invading,
Casting gloom o'er all the landscape,
Hollow winds broke o'er the heather,
Thunder muttered in the distance,
Lightning flashed down in the valley,
And the squaws, they muttered trembling,
"Will the lightning strike our wigwams,
Will the canvas stay the raindrops?"
But the young bucks from the city
Smiled quite bravely on the women,
Trembling, cowering in the wigwams,
"We're none feared for we are hikers,"
Bragged the young bucks from the city,
Smoking Woodbines in the wigwams.

Broke the storm in violent fury,
Beat the wigwams to the heather,
Blew the stew-pots down the gully,
Strewed the blankets o'er the meadow,
Then the hikers fled their wigwams,

8. Hathersage swimming pool was opened in 1936.

Chased their blankets o'er the meadows,
Waiting for the storm to subside –
But the lightning gained in fury,
And the thunder roared a horror
To the squaws now weeping, crying
For their mothers in the city.
Then they gathered up their blankets,
Bending, cringing, with their burdens,
Fast stampeded for the village,
Begged for shelter till the morning,
From the people in the village.
They for profit, shillings, florins,
Let them shelter in their houses,
Gave them tea and gave them coffee,
Eggs and bacon, bread and butter,
For the money from the city.

In the grey of early morning,
Soaked and stooping went the hikers,
Back home to the smoky city,
To the light and to the comfort
Of their homes within the city.
"Go back, go back," screamed the red grouse,
"Hope that you have learnt a lesson
From the storm upon the moorland:
Life, O hikers, is not sunshine,
Moonshine, kissing, laughing, joking.
There are storms and there are troubles,
And our life is but a medley;
When the sun shines out tomorrow
Then forget the rain and thunder,
All the misery and discomforts
Of the night up on the moorlands.
Life is full of great surprises –
Love it as it comes upon you."

VISITORS

Mrs Allen and Miss Round delighted in describing their fellow guests in their diary:

On the hydro bus from the station were: "Fur and Oranges" The gentleman was really a furry man, furry hair, furry moustache and a furry coat, with a swarthy skin and a huge broad nose, and he was NOT an Englishman, whilst the lady, she had Orange with a capital O hair, an orange coat and seemed to suggest marmalade everywhere.

Harry Douglas greeting the Duke of Devonshire at Smedley's.
[Jean Douglas]

The same list of famous visitors is often reproduced in the literature. But what is the evidence? Celebrities were rarely mentioned in the *Visiting List*: perhaps they avoided having their names recorded. One bathman recollected that many patients were drying-out alcoholics, often from the families of large department stores such as Brown, Muff's and Busbys'.

Henry Douglas wrote that there was a map in his office where crosses were placed for each visitor and the overwhelming number came from London and Lancashire. Many others came from Ireland and Scotland. His short list of the famous did include Thomas Beecham, Harry Lauder (who had lunch in 1932) and George Robey. The mothers of Ivor Novello and John Wyndham were residents, but presumably under their real names of Davies and Harris. A frequent guest until his death in 1936 was Shapurji Saklatvala, the Indian-born Labour MP for Battersea North. He had married Sarah Marsh from Tansley in 1907, after meeting her as a waitress at Smedley's. They visited with their three sons and two daughters. In October 1931 the Prime Minister Ramsay MacDonald came to Rockside Hydro for a rest.

Football teams continued their training at the hydros. In 1934 Queens Park Rangers came to use the whirlpool bath at Rockside. In 1937 Tottenham Hotspurs also visited Rockside before a cup tie against Chesterfield. They practised on the football pitch, held a golf tournament, and went to the cinema. Several fellow guests travelled to see them win the match.

The hydros were used by local people for Rotary club dinners and the like, but occasionally they hosted conferences. At Chatsworth Hydro in 1933 came the annual conference of Young Launderers – ninety of them. They listened to papers

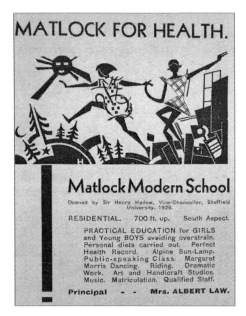

MATLOCK FOR HEALTH.

Matlock Modern School

Opened by Sir Henry Hadow, Vice-Chancellor, Sheffield University, 1926.

RESIDENTIAL.   700 ft. up.   South Aspect.

PRACTICAL EDUCATION for GIRLS and Young BOYS avoiding overstrain. Personal diets carried out.   Perfect Health Record.   Alpine Sun-Lamp. Public-speaking Class.   Margaret Morris Dancing.   Riding.   Dramatic Work.   Art and Handicraft Studios. Music. Matriculation. Qualified Staff.

Principal - - Mrs. ALBERT LAW.

with titles like *The washing of coloured goods* and *The value of sodium aluminate in water treatment*. Smedley's rarely seems to have filled their rooms with large groups, but in 1937 sixty members of Middlesex County Automobile Club stayed. In 1938 they held the Derbyshire Teachers' Association conference; 120 stayed in the Hydro, but nearly three hundred others were lodged in the town.

Mr Law, of Matlock Health Centre and the Modern School, liked to host summer schools. In 1933 he welcomed the National Credit Association of Great Britain. Guests included the Dean of Canterbury and the Marquis of Tavistock.

POSTSCRIPT

Sadly the last pre-war Christmas Day fell on a Sunday, which was never quite as enjoyable because the celebrations were pushed forward one day. On New Year's Eve 1938 the guests in the hydros stopped dancing as midnight approached and gathered in one huge circle to sing *Auld Lang Syne*.

> *Then from the radio comes the first stroke of Big Ben. It gives us a shudder of apprehension. How many times during the last few years have we heard those solemn strokes as we listened to hear how one crisis after another is going to turn out. Outside it is snowing heavily and the wind whistles round the building. Nineteen thirty eight is going – we never wish to experience another year like it. We stand in our circle here at Smedley's, and we hope and we pray with all the force of which we are capable that nineteen hundred and thirty nine will not bring what looks inevitable.*

The Gala Dinner menu on 2 January 1939 quoted Samuel Pepys, writing in 1666: "Thus ends this year of publick wonder and mischief to this nation and, therefore, generally wished by all people to have an end". It was not to be.

The year 1939 had actually begun on several high notes, which many would have seen as a just reward for the UDC and tradespeople finally working together. The Publicity Association reported 1,412 accommodation queries in May, a record number. (In 1938 they had received nearly four thousand overall.)

Also in May, Lord John Sanger's Royal Command Circus had filled the football pitch and the first round of the Derbyshire Amateur Ballroom Dancing Championship had been held in the Town Hall. In June the Derbyshire County Show was held with great success on Cromford Meadows and the floral fete had been a triumph for Matlock Bath – for once they had had a fine day. The English Counties tennis final between Yorkshire and Warwickshire had been staged on Hall Leys Park. At the third UDC tennis week in July, a Rumanian international player called Tanasescu had, not surprisingly, won every competition he entered. The bowls week had also been well supported.

A diving demonstration at the Lido.

The Lido was attracting acrobatic high divers such as Vera Tells and the American Tony Zucas. The "fittest woman in Northern England", Madame Hazeldene of Sheffield, had brought her juveniles to demonstrate speed and fancy swimming. (Aged over fifty, she had already trained 6000 girls to achieve life-saving awards.)

Everyone was trying to look forward to the usual autumn highlights of Matlock Carnival and the Venetian Fete, followed by Christmas at the Hydros. But as the decade closed, the Matlocks could feel themselves sliding towards war. The Smedley's Hydro correspondent had observed many times that horrible events were unfolding elsewhere, while the visitors seemed bent on enjoying themselves in a safe, cushioned world. In spring 1939, Captain Douglas had tried to joke at the

Matlock Lido and Cafe, Derbyshire   PN1259

*A 1960s view of the Lido. Plate glass windows are being installed
in the furniture store, now Haydn Stanley's.*
[Peak District Lead Mining Museum]

Publicity Association AGM, "I hope our friend Hitler is not going to step in and stop some of these parties".

In 1936 members of the UDC and St John's Ambulance had travelled to London for an air raid precautions meeting. In 1937 a searchlight trial was due to be staged with an aeroplane, but the night was too foggy; however, a good crowd had turned up to the air raid depot at Darley Dale, where gas masks were demonstrated. The UDC advised providing a sealed room in every house against gas attacks; the masks were distributed in October 1938.

Air raid sirens had been positioned on the taller buildings between Masson Mill and Mill Close Mine. They were tested in March 1939 – the church bells were stopped for the occasion – but very few could actually hear them. The hydros had been warned to be ready for evacuees from city hospitals, as they in turn took war casualties. Volunteers were asked to take 3000 children from Dr Barnado's homes in Manchester: many had already arrived. Holiday crowds at Easter and Whitsuntide had included many men in blue and khaki uniforms.

Mill Close Mine was on its last legs. The smelting works had been moved from Lea to Darley Dale in 1934. Lorry loads of lead seen leaving the station were said to be for making German bullets. A bad shot-firing in 1938 had resulted in the mine flooding, putting three hundred men immediately out of work. A year later, the remaining lead was becoming too expensive to extract without a new shaft and closure came in June 1940. H J Enthoven re-opened the smelter site in 1941.

There was an "end of era" feeling as Dr Harbinson died; he had been the consultant at Smedley's since 1899. His long-time partner Dr McLelland retired.

They were replaced by Drs Rhys-Davies and Geoffrey Holmes, a rheumatism specialist from Harrogate Royal Baths Hospital. There were other deaths. William (Bill) Furniss had carried thousands of visitors down the years in his "four in hand" coach, charabancs and motor buses. He wore his long jacket, riding breeches and red waistcoat up to the end, but sadly had never really recovered from being charged by a bull at Bakewell Show some years before. He was missed at the clubs as a famous billiard player. One week saw the deaths of Mrs Donegani, the well-known landlady at Belle Vue House in Matlock Bath, and Mr Potter, the hosier on The Dimple, who died after 53 years in the business. In 1938 William Smith, one of the last spar and Blue John workers, had died. He had once employed seven ornament makers and his family still owned the Royal Museum and petrifying wells.

Lubin Wildgoose of Oldham House Hydro retired after twenty seven years on the UDC; he had also been a County Councillor. He was still a governor of Ernest Bailey School and a director of the Publicity Association and the Operatic Society.

When war was actually declared, several quick decisions were made. Matlock Carnival (except for the baby show) and the Venetian Fete were cancelled. They still sold the Carnival programmes for charity. The Operatic Society stopped rehearsing the aptly named *Goodnight Vienna*. The Lido closed at the end of the month to save fuel, but Matlock Cinemas were asked to resume films at the Pavilion so that residents of Matlock Bath did not have far to travel. Ironically, Hitler achieved what many people had been demanding for years – the Lovers' Walk and Promenade were thrown open free of charge.

But the happenings on the Bank heralded the real doom for the Matlocks as a centre of hydropathy. During the last week in August 1939, the *Visiting List* described as usual the tennis tournaments and concerts at Smedley's and Rockside; the following week only a few brief reports came from Chatsworth, Lilybank and

Chatsworth Hydro, Matlock.

Sycamore House Hydros. There was no explanation. It was as if Shangri La and Brigadoon had faded into the mist.

Within 45 minutes of the outbreak of war, Harry Douglas was told he had four weeks to clear Smedley's before the War Office would move in, although it was actually six months before the Army Military School of Intelligence had made the necessary changes. There were over a hundred people for whom the Hydro had become their home. They were moved out to the Memorial Hospital, Lilybank, local homes and even the houses of bathmen.

That first September night of the war, an air raid warning rang out. Smedley's staff had been trained for black-out duties and fire watches. Temporary shelters had been organised in the basement. The store manager, Bob Walters, had spent the day rounding up and listing all the silver and crockery, while the housekeeper and chambermaids did the same for the bed linen and towels as the bedrooms emptied. These lists can still be seen, as described in an earlier chapter. All these moveable items were packed away, although later scarcities meant the army eventually used some of them. Unused food was returned to the shops for credit. Jackson House was taken over as an extra billet.

Orderlies also arrived at Rockside on the morning war was declared to transform the building into an RAF psychiatric hospital. Answering a query about re-opening in August 1945, Jennie Goodwin wrote, "It was taken over as it stood and I know there is hardly any carpets left at all, no crockery and hardly any linen". She regretted it would be too difficult to start again.

Gloria Hollingworth, the granddaughter of Lubin Wildgoose, remembered that the family was away when war was declared. They returned to find that a deputation from the Air Ministry had walked into Oldham House Hydro on 3 September and commandeered the property as living quarters for the nurses arriving at Rockside. The family were given ten days to move out. Again, some residents were moved to Lilybank. Lubin became the local fuel control officer, "his duties in connection with Oldham House Hydro having ceased for war reasons". One source suggests that Chatsworth Hydro was eventually used as the wartime offices of C & A Modes, but the firm have no record of this in their archives.

The only mention of Smedley's fate in the *High Peak News* was when Harry Douglas raised at a UDC meeting the question of whether the Hydro or the Army should pay the next rate instalment. For dozens of families, Christmas 1939 was the first one spent away from their friends in Smedley's, Rockside and Oldham House Hydros.

Smedley's was derequisitioned in 1946 and the Hydro re-opened. In the 1950s Harry's son Henry took over as manager. After taking a commerce degree, he had trained in hotels in Park Lane and on the French Riviera. But the life had gone out of hydropathy. Harry Douglas senior, as Managing Director, had his health ruined by falling profits and the unsuccessful attempt at compulsory purchase by Derbyshire County Council. He died after an operation on the last day of 1954, with the future still uncertain. The Hydro closed in September 1955, after the shareholders finally decided to sell to the Council. On 6 December the struggle ended. Henry waited for a telephone call from London to say that contracts had been exchanged. Alderman Charles White was outside with the Press but Henry could not face the fuss. He placed all the keys on the hall counter and slipped out of the

The daffodil yellow jug is part of a washtable set
from a servant's room at Smedley's.
The Matlock Bath pin tray was probably made in Germany.

'Mr Henry' was last manager of at Smedley's Hydro

back door. The Douglas and Challand family had kept John Smedley's dream alive for over seventy years – he could not bear to see Mr White's triumph.

The contents of the Hydro were sold by auction over several days and the people of Matlock flocked to buy a souvenir of the building which had dominated the town for so long. Many houses still contain a small piece of furniture or pottery with the Smedley's crest. The building sold for £120,000 and other properties made £8,210. The sale of the contents raised £24,000. Henry was very concerned that employees, who had spent all their working lives in the hydro, should receive pensions, because there had been no formal scheme.

Henry moved to run the Buckingham Hotel in Buxton until he retired. He took with him several members of Smedley's staff and long-term guests, some of whom invested in his new business. Later in life he enjoyed giving talks about Smedley's, one of which the author remembers attending at Tawney House. He eventually wrote a booklet of his memories which is in the Local Studies Library. He died in 1994.

Rockside and Chatsworth Hydros became Matlock Training College; several large houses on Cavendish Road, such as Mr Challand's Rockwood, were used as student accommodation. After the College closed, Rockside was left derelict, but is now converted into apartments. Chatsworth Hydro is part of the County Council's offices. Some of the gardens remain and the gateposts facing Chesterfield Road still

bear the inscription "Hydropathic Establishment".

Oldham House Hydro became Woodlands School after the War, which moved from Bakewell Road. It was run by two sisters of Charles White until 1965. The main block has since been demolished and the buildings are private property.

Lilybank Hydro remained as a hotel until 1962, although the baths had been removed. It was taken as a Nagle Preparatory School and boarding house by the nuns at the Convent, but is now a retirement home.

Did hydropathy work? In 1926 *Truth* magazine was still advocating its ability to "restore each flagging function (of the body) to efficiency by gentle repetition of such measures as are the most simple and natural". Many people still believed in its methods. The speeches every year on festive occasions were given by men who spoke of being given up for dead by their doctors. Yet here they were on their umpteenth visit, hale and hearty.

It could not cure chronic disease. It was noticeable that when Dr Hunter fell ill doctors were called in from Manchester. Dr Marie Orme, the doyen of Rockside, was under a heart specialist in Derby when she died in 1929. But even the critically ill, like my own grandfather, probably benefitted from the ample rest, simple diet and good company at the close of their lives.

Why did hydropathy die out? Richard Metcalfe in *The Rise and Progress of Hydropathy in England and Scotland* (1912) could already see the writing on the wall.

> With the hydros generally becoming more pleasure resorts for social entertainment and the like, there is extreme danger of what we may call the better and more desirable objects of the system being lost.

Metcalfe thought progress in hydropathy had really ceased when the original protagonists such as Archibald Hunter and John Smedley had retired or died. He was very sceptical of the electric treatments: some of the more way-out ones may even have brought the business into disrepute. He did not blame the hydros for filling their rooms for profit with people who sought an enjoyable holiday, with only a little mild treatment thrown in. He did blame the genuine patients for not sufficiently spreading the word about their cures.

However, the real problem was that orthodox medical training made no mention of hydropathy. Metcalf wanted doctors to be aware of it as a complementary treatment and he probably had a point; but the public were finding conventional medicine more effective and safer than in Victorian times. Once we had a National Health Service, it would be many years before patients and the medical profession began to wonder if alternative medicine had a role to play.

ECHOES

What of my grandfather, the inspiration for this book? I had always thought he came alone in 1936. Now I know, from the *Visiting List*, that my grandmother came too. They stayed from Whitsuntide to the August Bank Holiday. To my great surprise, they were preceded in 1934 by my great aunt and uncle, who perhaps recommended the experience. They were farmers in Essex and must have endured quite a complicated journey.

The summer of 1936 was warm enough to sit on the terraces, but there were several torrential showers. There was an eclipse, but those who got up especially early found an overcast sky. I suspect my grandfather was too ill to enjoy very much, but I hope he was able to sit in the Winter Garden and listen to Miss Hampson's quartet playing selections of Mendelssohn, Tchaikovsky and Schubert. The Matlock Prize Band played in the grounds on several afternoons. My grandmother may have watched a conjuror called Presto Cooper and enjoyed a short play called *The Black Sheep* performed by the Rowsley Players. One afternoon, a Dr Stewart Empey gave a well-received slide show on "The Abyssinian as I knew him". He had recently returned from Africa where his Red Cross Hospital had been bombed by the Italians, a much-criticised incident that summer.

A time-travelling visitor from the past would recognise our towns. If he looked above the parked cars, he would see the same variety of colourful shop fronts in Matlock Bath, mostly still catering for tourists. Although some have become rather shabby, a few have kept the pretty balcony railings and the mechanism to lower their window blinds. At Matlock Bridge, apart from the unfortunate Firs Parade, the shops remain the solid Victorian and Edwardian stone edifices and Dale Road is admired as a cohesive set of historic buildings – from the front at least.

The visitor might think the Pavilion looks a little care-worn, but hopefully that problem will soon be addressed. By the roadside, the fish still swim in the gently steaming pond. One can still have a drink in the Temple Hotel, the Fishpond, Hodgkinson's, the Midland or the Boat House. However, the visitor would be horrified by the sight of the New Bath Hotel, abandoned one morning (in 2013) like the Mary Celeste: its ghostly basement swimming pool no longer even lit by electric light, its underground stream sounding as eerie as if it ran through a deep Derbyshire cavern.

The visitor could still arrive by train, but the stations would seem strangely quiet without the stationmaster and his staff politely opening the doors and stacking luggage on their trolleys. The bustling, clanking goods sidings are now covered in car parks and a bus station. There is a footbridge over the tracks at Matlock which is possibly even more unsightly than the original; but there might be the reassuring smell and hiss of an approaching steam locomotive on the heritage line.

The visitor could look up the hillside and see Smedley's vast dark bulk still looming over the town, although he would be well-advised not to look inside. Any remaining grandeur in the public rooms is ruined by the out-of-place modern light fittings and office furniture. However, he might find his old bedroom in the warren of offices, where most of the original numbers remain on the doors.

Rockside still hovers near the hillside summit and is thankfully once again a blaze of homely lights at night. Other hydros have found modern uses and most survive in various states of repair. The least loved is the crumbling Chatsworth Hydro, owned by the County Council like Smedley's, and surrounded by the ugliest buildings in the town. In contrast, Bank House Hydro, later Ernest Bailey School, is now gleaming with new paint and clever stained-glass windows, restored as the new Record Office and Local Studies Library. And, perhaps most remarkably, there is once more the glow of lamps behind the new windows of Riber Castle.

The time-traveller would be surprised to see office buildings and a supermarket standing in silent quarries. He might wonder where the Lido has gone, the switch-back railway, Victoria Hall, or the gas holders. He would be pleased to see the tidy Twigg's works and only one advertisement hoarding. The air might seem very clear without the dust from the quarries and roads – but the potholes would be familiar!

A visitor can still sit in the sunshine in Derwent Gardens. He can hire a boat, play

bowls or tennis, and listen to a band in Hall Leys Park. He can still climb to the top of the cliff in the Lovers' Walk through drifts of wood anemones and walk on over High Tor. On the opposite hillside, he can still climb the Heights of Abraham and explore a cavern. He can even join the dreaded day tripper to marvel at the fireworks after the Venetian Fete. Taken as a whole, more remains than has been destroyed.

The saddest moment for a visitor from the past would be coming upon the vast empty car park where once the Royal Hotel stood and looking up to see the old Pavilion replaced by Gulliver's Kingdom. For ten brief years the Royal must have been the most wonderful place to visit – a hotel de luxe, with its glass palace and beautiful gardens – all the richness and glamour of a German spa, set in a

Derbyshire valley.

If we shut our eyes, perhaps we too can imagine sweeping up the drive in our open motor, and entering a haven of perfectly-managed comfort. We might glimpse the colourful swirl of dresses and parasols on the sunlit terrace, or hear an echo of music from the drawing room, where the beautiful voice of Mrs Buttgen once more soars over the buzz of conversation and the tinkle of teacups....

The long goodbye at Smedley's – a lonely lady in a sparsely furnished lounge corridor.
[Picture the Past]

BIBLIOGRAPHY

A window on John Smedley's World J Margaret Oakes, Country Books, 2009
Highways and Byways in Derbyshire J B Firth, Macmillan & Co, 1905
The Matlock Cable Tramway Glynn Waite, Pynot Publishing, 2012
Darleys in the Dale Lewis R Jackson, Country Books, 2002
Bulmers' History and Directory of Derbyshire 1895
Gem of the Peak William Adam, Moorland Reprints, 1973
John Smedley of Matlock and his Hydro L du Garde Peach, Bemrose
The Bath at War Charles Beresford, Country Books, 2007
Tuppence Up, Penny Down M J Arkle, 1983
The Smedleys of Matlock Bank Henry Steer, Elliot Stock, 1897
The Matlocks and Bakewell Famous Derbyshire Health Resorts J S Rochard, 1893
Matlock and the Great War 1914-1919 Keith Taylor, Country Books, 2010
Matlock and District in the Second World War Keith Taylor, Country Books, 2012
Recollections of the late John Smedley of Matlock Joseph Buckley, John Heywood, 1888
Matlock Bank as it was and is Joseph Buckley, 1866
The Rise and Progress of Hydropathy in England and Scotland Richard Metcalfe,
    Marshall etc.,1912
Hydropathy: its Principles and Practice for home use Archibald Hunter,
    John Menzies, 1883
Derbyshire A R Hope Moncrieff, A & C Black, 1927
The Peak Country A R Hope Moncrieff, A & C Black, 1908
Practical Hydropathy John Smedley, 1862
Listen to the Country S P B Mais, 1939
A Brief Jolly Change: the diaries of Henry Peerless 1891-1920 E Fenton, 2003

The Derbyhsire Local Studies Library and Record Office's collection of guide
    books, brochures, almanacs and directories etc.
Periodicals and newspapers:
Buxton and Matlock Times and List of Visitors
The Derbyshire Advertiser
The Derbyshire Countryside
Derbyshire Times

High Peak News
Matlock and Matlock Bath Advertiser and Visitors' Guide
Matlock Register
Matlock Weekly
Matlock Visitor
Matlock Visiting List
Matlock Fashionable Visitors' List
Matlock, Buxton, Bakewell and Tideswell Advertiser
Matlock Bath Telegraph

Most of the photographs used have passed through many hands and it is no longer possible to trace the copyright owners, although efforts have been made to do so. Items not in the author's collection are attributed to their current owners.